'This new textbook takes into account the reverberations that have affected the marketing of financial services following the global financial crisis. The international coverage reflects the increasingly global nature of financial services, whilst the up-to-date cases draw the readers' attention to the challenges that both existing players and new entrants face in marketing these products, to the increasingly demanding financial services customer.' – **Professor Steve Worthington**, *Department of Marketing, Monash University, Australia* .

'The global financial crisis of 2008–09 has highlighted the pivotal role played by the financial services sector, these events have clearly demonstrated that the way in which the sector designs and markets products to a retail market can have major implications for economic and social wellbeing. And, in turn, this underscores the importance of understanding the principles and practice of marketing financial services. This revised edition of one of the classic texts in the area is timely and topical; key elements of marketing as they apply to financial services are clearly articulated and supported with practical illustrations. Building on extensive accumulated experience of the sector, Meidan and Dawes Farquhar provide students with a thoughtful and insightful treatment of the many challenges associated with fair and effective marketing for retail financial services.' – **Professor Christine Ennew**, *Pro-Vice-Chancellor and Professor of Marketing, University of Nottingham, UK.*

'An excellent book combining the closely related activities of financial services, services marketing and strategic marketing in a well presented, logically strong and scientifically correct method with plenty of advice, case studies, easy to follow charts, and graphs. This book can be used by anybody who wishes to learn the intricacies of customer relationships and relationship management in the financial services. I strongly recommend this clever book to all in the financial services markets and students of marketing.' – **Professor Tevfik Dalgic**, *School of Management, University of Texas at Dallas, USA.*

'The authors provide a comprehensive review of the theory and take it in to a contemporary setting. The book provides a framework for decision making and better marketing practice in the financial services industry.' – **Professor Sandra Vandermerwe**, *Chair of International Marketing and Services, Tanaka Business School, Imperial College London, UK.*

'An invaluable resource for all those interested in learning more about the marketing of financial services. The coverage of the book is extremely comprehensive, incorporating discussion of all main elements of marketing financial services. The main text is complemented very effectively with the use of examples, leading to an excellent blend of theory and practice. I would strongly recommend this book to both students and practitioners.' – **James Devlin**, *Professor of Marketing, Director of Undergraduate Programmes, Business School, University of Nottingham, UK.*

'Jillian Dawes Farquhar and Arthur Meidan have succeeded in capturing the complexities and nuances of financial services and have presented a most understandable interpretation of how marketing should be practised in this sector. Their second edition is impressively up to date, presenting an

analysis of recent developments in the international financial sector and their implications for marketing. Students and practitioners alike will welcome the strategic approach of this successful textbook.' – **James G. Barnes**, *Faculty of Business Administration, Memorial University of Newfoundland, Canada*.

'I particularly like the "strategic" treatment of the topics and the highlights for me are the chapter dealing with creating value, and the strategic overview. The case studies and vignettes are truly international which is so important for teachers of financial services who reside outside Europe or North America. The turbulent financial times of 2008–09 have been captured adroitly as have the recent advances in mobile telephony, social media communication, etc.' – **Ron Garland**, *Associate Professor, Department of Marketing, Waikato Management School, University of Waikato, New Zealand*.

'The authors have brought a new dimension to what was already an academic marker in this field. The text follows a structured thinking process and has a challenging up-to-date context, lively content with real relevance to industry, as well as a good monological approach.' – **Professor Luiz Moutinho**, *Foundation Chair in Marketing, University of Glasgow, UK*.

'Written by two outstanding scholars in the field, this book is a must read for the students of financial services marketing and practitioners alike. Comprehensive coverage of well-structured topics combined with thought-provoking case studies and excellent examples make *Marketing Financial Services* indispensable as a one-stop source on financial services marketing.' – **Ugur Yavas**, *Department of Management and Marketing, East Tennessee State University, USA*.

'Prof. Dawes Farquhar and Prof. Meidan have managed to give a European flavour to this book, especially through examples and end-of-chapter cases, which makes it suitable as core material in financial services marketing courses in different countries. They have included an interesting and original chapter that covers the issue of building the financial services brand, a challenging task for every services marketer. This adds to the originality of this textbook, which is a must-have for academics, students, practitioners and marketing managers.' – **Shpëtim Çerri**, *Lecturer, Department of Marketing, Faculty of Economics, University A. Xhuvani, Elbasan, Albania, UK*.

'This second edition has been significantly improved, with the following new features:

* Content has been thoroughly reviewed, revised and updated.
* The structure has been modified with several new chapters very relevant to the financial services market – reflecting changes in the sector and the availability of new technologies.
* The text is more student friendly, and includes many case studies and vignettes plus many useful pedagogical features.' – **Dr Essam B. Ibrahim**, *Director of the Doctoral Programme, Senior Lecturer in Marketing, University of Edinburgh Business School, UK*.

JILLIAN DAWES FARQUHAR
& ARTHUR MEIDAN

MARKETING FINANCIAL SERVICES

SECOND EDITION

palgrave
macmillan

First edition 1996
Reprinted five times
Second edition 2010

Published by
PALGRAVE MACMILLAN

Palgrave Macmillan in the UK is an imprint of Macmillan Publishers Limited,
registered in England, company number 785998, of Houndmills, Basingstoke,
Hampshire RG21 6XS.

Palgrave Macmillan in the US is a division of St Martin's Press LLC,
175 Fifth Avenue, New York, NY 10010.

Palgrave Macmillan is the global academic imprint of the above companies
and has companies and representatives throughout the world.

Palgrave® and Macmillan® are registered trademarks in the United States,
the United Kingdom, Europe and other countries.

ISBN 978-0-230-20118-7

This book is printed on paper suitable for recycling and made from fully
managed and sustained forest sources. Logging, pulping and manufacturing
processes are expected to conform to the environmental regulations of the
country of origin.

A catalogue record for this book is available from the British Library.

A catalog record for this book is available from the Library of Congress.

10   9   8   7   6   5   4   3   2   1
19   18   17   16   15   14   13   12   11   10

Printed and bound in China

Contents overview

This book is dedicated to Gail and Faith Dawes, both of whom make me an exceedingly proud mother

Contents

List of figures

List of tables

List of exhibits

Acknowledgements

Books are rarely if ever written in isolation and so many people have assisted in bringing it to completion.

Jillian would like to thank Barbara Lewis, formerly of Manchester Business School, and Professor Christine Ennew, of Nottingham University, who started her off on the financial services marketing path. Professor Jenny Rowley gave direction and incentive in the early days. Senior management at Leek United and Britannia Building Society have provided invaluable support and material, with particular thanks to David Crawshaw of Britannia Building Society. Dr Julie Robson, Sally McKechnie and Professor Steve Worthington, as well as colleagues and students at Oxford Brookes Business School, encouraged efforts at writing and publishing.

She also needs to convey a discrete thank you to all informants in the world of financial services whose anonymity she carefully preserves. The case study contributors have given freely and willingly of their time and are: Dr Rita Faullant of Johannes Kepler University and Professor Kurt Matzler, University of Innsbruck, Austria; Brigitte Fünfgeld, Senior Financial Consultant, and Mei Wang, Assistant Professor in Finance and Financial Markets at the Swiss Finance Institute (ISB) University of Zurich, and project leader of the University Priority Research Program: Behavioural Finance and Wealth Management at the University of Zurich, Switzerland; Professor Rita Martenson, Professor of Marketing at the School of Business, Economics and Law, University of Gothenburg, Sweden; Dr Deirdre O'Loughlin of Limerick University, Ireland; Dr Loic Plé of IESEG School of Management, Lille, France; Clive Woolger of Woolger Associates, London; Professor Steve Worthington, Professor of Marketing at Monash University, Australia, formerly Britannia Building Society Professor of Marketing at Staffordshire University Business School; Conrad Klopotek, formerly of Oxford Brookes Business School.

Both authors would like to thank the anonymous reviewers whose insight and constructive feedback has strengthened the book.

The authors and publishers thank the following for permission to reproduce copyright material: Experian for permission to use Table 4.1; Alan Leach of Finaccord for permission to utilize Figure 7.3.

Introduction

Contents

Background to the book

Both writers have a deep and long-held interest in marketing and, in particular, the marketing of financial services. We have both, taught, researched, written and conducted consultancy for financial services institutions for a number of years. Financial services are endlessly fascinating, diverse, dynamic, complex and, at times, unfathomable – and there is always something happening in this industry that impacts on marketing. Equally, marketing is such a vibrant discipline that there are events in marketing that impact on financial services. This book attempts to capture and convey the inherent intricacy involved in the marketing of these services, which we all need, one way or another.

Core themes

- Excitement of marketing financial services: diversity, dynamism and complexity
- Inertia of customers – or is it resignation?
- Financial services in themselves are rather uninteresting and do not engage customers' interest easily; how can they be 'sold'?
- Financial institutions tend to have a short-term outlook and are disinclined to adopt strategies for the longer term
- The fall-out from the credit crunch; how can financial institutions respond to the current environment in Europe and globally?
- The latest thinking in services marketing and marketing in general, with a focus on customer value and stakeholder perspectives
- How can financial institutions appreciate current marketing theory and respond more effectively to the changes in the marketplace?

Who is the book intended for?

Undergraduates will find this book invaluable for any financial service modules on their programmes. They will also find the book provides them with both the theory and examples that they need for writing projects, reports and dissertations on financial services marketing. The book is equally directed at postgraduates studying on taught masters' programmes with a financial services element. They will find that the book provides a valuable framework for their studies. Again, the book is essential background reading for dissertations and projects on the marketing of financial services. The book is also suitable for banking and insurance practitioners studying or updating marketing, for institute examinations or as a reference book. The language in the book is suitable for non-native speakers.

Distinctive features

The book has been written to capture the marketing of financial services within a European context and the cases have been written by researchers and consultants working in European countries. Each chapter contains a number of highly topical exhibits for information and interest. The book uses up-to-date examples, with recent contributions to theoretical debates in marketing. Furthermore, the book has been written during a time of massive global upheaval in financial services – the credit crunch. The long-term impact of the credit crunch on the marketing of financial services is hard to predict, but, as argued in the book, it has further weakened customers' and stakeholders' perceptions of financial institutions. Financial institutions should develop strategies to address these poor perceptions but at the time of writing seem slow to respond.

Pedagogy

Each chapter concludes with a contemporary European case study and questions, written by specialists in the marketing of financial services using material from their research or consultancy activities. There are also further questions about the material in the chapter to support the understanding of the text. There is, additionally, suggested further reading, as well as on-line references, for each chapter to enable students to deepen their understanding of financial services marketing. Lectures and tutor notes are available on the website: www.palgrave.com/business/farquhar

Contributors

We are deeply appreciative of the contributions of our colleagues as follows:

Dr Rita Faullant of Johannes Kepler University and Professor Kurt Matzler, University of Innsbruck, Austria.

Brigitte Fünfgeld, Senior Financial Consultant, and Mei Wang, Assistant Professor in Finance and Financial Markets at the Swiss Finance Institute (ISB) University of Zurich, and project leader of the

University Priority Research Programme: Behavioural Finance and Wealth Management at the University of Zurich, Switzerland.

Professor Rita Martenson, Professor of Marketing at the School of Business, Economics and Law, University of Gothenburg, Sweden.

Dr Deirdre O'Loughlin of Limerick University, Ireland.

Dr Loic Plé of IÉSEG School of Management, Lille, France.

Clive Woolger of Woolger Associates, London.

Professor Steve Worthington, Professor of Marketing at Monash University, Australia, formerly Britannia Building Society Professor of Marketing at Staffordshire University Business School.

Conrad Klopotek, formerly Oxford Brookes Business School.

About the authors

Dr Jillian Dawes Farquhar is Professor of Marketing Strategy at the University of Bedfordshire, where she teaches strategic marketing and research methods, supervises research students and continues her research into the marketing of financial services. She is editor-in-chief of the *International Journal of Bank Marketing*, a journal that publishes refereed work on the marketing of financial services across the world. Her research interests range from customer loyalty to branding.

Dr Arthur Meidan is Emeritus Professor at Sheffield University Management School, where he has taught, published and consulted for some 25 years. Professor Meidan has published some ten books, including the first edition of *Marketing Financial Services* (Macmillan 1996), which has been translated into Chinese, and some 70 refereed papers and articles.

1

Marketing and financial services: an overview

Contents

Learning outcomes

By the end of this chapter, the reader will be able to:

- Understand how marketing theory underpins the marketing of financial services

- Appreciate how recent thinking in marketing and services marketing applies to financial services

- Be able to identify key issues for marketers of financial services

Introduction

services: an offering in which the dominant part is intangible, which is the case in most financial services

value: the aim of marketing is to create/deliver an offering that allows the consumer/stakeholder to derive benefits particular to their needs/wants

Services are products that we purchase and consume in ever-growing quantities; they range from restaurant meals to university education. In business markets, services include such things as cleaning and IT. The businesses that provide these services understand that delivering **value** and customer satisfaction are key to ensuring their businesses survive and flourish. Such is the importance and pervasiveness of services provision that it is argued that services now dominate marketing (see Vargo and Lusch 2004), whereas goods used to have the upper hand.

What are financial services?

Financial services are any service or product of a financial nature that is traded in financial markets; specifically, they are financial instruments – for example, treasury bills and government bonds. There are a number of ways that financial instruments can be classified. Do they have a fixed or variable interest rate? How long to they take to mature? Are they offered by a deposit-taking or non-deposit taking intermediary? Financial services cover an extensive range of instruments and in the United Kingdom the Financial Services Authority (FSA) provides information to the consumer marketplace on bank accounts, equity release schemes and long-term care (moneymade-clear.fsa.gov.uk/products/products_explained.html). The marketplace for financial services is extensive, as banks, insurers and investment banks operate in a global marketplace and have a wide range of customers, including retail consumers, business customers of all sizes and other financial institutions. Other examples of financial services can be seen in Figure 1.1, which also shows services offered to businesses, domestic and global, for profit and not for profit.

From a marketing perspective, there are some important points to remember about financial services. Looking at Figure 1.1, it is clear that none of the products is very desirable, especially when compared with other things that money can be spent on, such as cars, designer handbags or holidays. In fact, several of the examples are downright unattractive, such as pensions and funeral plans. This lack of intrinsic desirability is key in the marketing of financial services. Marketers of these products have to be aware that customers, whether retail consumers or business customers, do not purchase these items because they are in themselves desirable or 'must have' products. What financial services generally do allow customers to do is to purchase or acquire those products and other services that *are* desired, such as holidays, or indeed the 'must have' handbag; or, for business customers, these products offer the possibility

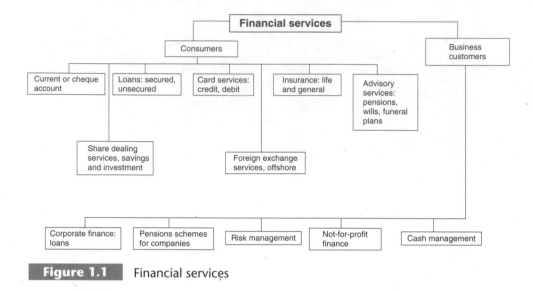

Figure 1.1 Financial services

of avoiding the 'hassle' of managing complex financial arrangements. Financial services are also acquired to avoid an undesirable state or outcome, for example, health insurance. Exhibit 1.1 illustrates some of the options for ensuring that you have beautiful teeth.

EXHIBIT 1.1

Dental insurance

Finding a dentist in the UK National Health Service (NHS) has become increasingly difficult. Dental insurance allows the customer to choose a dentist and claim the cost of the treatment, whether they use a NHS dentist or go private. The scheme usually requires the customer to pay the dentist for the treatment and then claim the money back from the insurer, but dental policies often will not pay for the full cost of the treatment. Most policies set maximum amounts that they will pay out in any 12-month period. Some insurers will only pay 75 per cent of the treatment with an annual maximum cap. Customers normally have to enrol three to six months prior to using the plan. Insurance premiums, that is, the amount that the customer pays for the insurance, are based on the age of the customer and can vary widely. Two types of dental insurance scheme exist: capitation schemes allow customers to pay on a monthly basis instead of settling a bill each time. Cash plans can include health cover and providers offer part-cover for dental treatment, typically between 50 per cent and 75 per cent, as well as other benefits, such as help with optical treatment and health screening. Although dental plans cover all major and minor treatments, they do not cover dental implants, treatment of injuries sustained during sports, cosmetic and orthodontic treatment, oral cancer treatment, salivary gland treatments and treatment of severe dental abscesses. Most insurers will insist that that the customer has no dental work pending, and has reasonably good dental health. Some may even ask the customer to declare in writing that they visit a dentist regularly for a check-up.

Denplan is the United Kingdom's leading dental payment plan specialist, with 6,500 member dentists across the United Kingdom (approximately a third of practising dentists) treating over 1.8 million Denplan patients. The Denplan premium depends on several factors, including the customer's dental health. These plans are best suited for those who need regular treatment, and are therefore looking to spread treatment costs. The concept behind Denplan allows dentists to charge their patients a fixed monthly fee, based on the condition of their teeth and gums, which provides them with regular examinations and treatment. The stable income that this system provides means that dentists can focus on quality of care rather than the quantity of patients they see. Dentists can practise at the highest standards, whilst retaining independence and control of their business. In addition to personal dental payment plans, Denplan also provides corporate dental cover for companies and their employees and Denplan for schools, an insurance plan for pupils at independent schools. Denplan has grown substantially since its inception in 1986 and is now part of a worldwide insurance company dealing with life, health and other forms of insurance, as well as investment management.

Compiled by the authors from: www.moneysavingexpert.com/insurance/dental-insurance, www.moneysupermarket.com/dentalinsurance, www.cosmeticdentistry guide.co.uk/dental-insurance.html.

In general terms, insurance is something that consumers and businesses purchase to avoid a worse outcome than not having it. Insurance is often compulsory – for example, for car ownership or mortgages. Businesses have insurance also to meet with legal requirements such as health and safety legislation. Financial services, therefore, are enabling products; that is, they enable the ownership of a house, the booking of tickets on-line for entertainment, the availability of cash for holidays or the ability of businesses to import goods from other currency areas. They also allow both consumers and businesses to have things before they can actually pay for them, or 'credit'.

We use the term 'financial institutions' (FIs) throughout the book as it embraces the diversity of players in the business of financial services. The key activity of FIs is intermediation, which means that 'they create assets for savers and liabilities for borrowers, which are more attractive to each than would be the case if the parties had to deal with each other directly' (Howells and Bain 2007: 6).

An example of intermediation is the building society, which takes in investments from savers, which the society then uses to lend on to people seeking to buy their own home. Building societies have been doing this since the eighteenth century and, until legislation in 1986, could only lend on what they actually had in terms of investments. Financial institutions that actually create products rather than merely distribute them are then considered to have created liquidity (Howells and Bain 2007). FIs can be divided into deposit-taking and non-deposit-taking intermediaries. A bank, for example, takes deposits, whereas an insurance company does not. Although not all FIs are intermediaries in this sense, marketing financial services is an activity that is shared by the following types of institution (Cheverton *et al.* 2005):

- Retail, corporate, investment and private banks
- Mutual funds, investment trusts
- Personal and group pensions
- Life and general insurance and reinsurance companies
- Credit card issuers
- Specialist lending companies
- Stock exchanges
- Leasing companies
- Government saving institutions
- Brokers and agents

As this list of organizations indicates, there are a great many different types of provider. Indeed, supermarkets and retailers, such as Marks & Spencer and Asda, can be added to this list. Debenhams, the department store, for example, offers a range of insurance products, including insurance for weddings and honeymoons (www.debenhams.co.uk). Some FIs have specific customers in mind – for example, the private banking sector as shown in Exhibit 1.2; for some customers, the idea of having an exclusive bank providing for their financial needs is attractive.

EXHIBIT 1.2

Private banking

Private banking is becoming close to losing the cachet that was once attached to the intensely secret dealings between a Swiss banker in Zurich and his wealthy clients. Almost every bank aspiring to the global market provides special rates of interest to wealthier private depositors as part of private banking. The larger banks offer premium services to individuals with savings or investments of at least £50,000, with an annual income of £75,000. Clients receive premium credit cards, advice and additional services. This category or segment of client has been labelled the 'mass affluent'; the word 'mass' is significant, as these clients do not really receive a gold-plated service. They are still routed via a call centre rather than a dedicated adviser. Interest rates are not that attractive either, with some accounts attracting just 1 per cent. However, if larger amounts of money are deposited, say over £1 million, with an income of over £250,000, then the service level increases. Clients with this amount of money are known as 'high net worth' (HNW) customers; there are over 3.5 million in Europe. There is even a group known as 'ultra HNW'! Banks compete fiercely to capture the growing number of clients (until recently) with money to invest. They look to the future, aiming to increase client wealth with a view to increasing the value of that client to the bank. Banks of any description like to lend money, especially when the probability of being repaid is high. Depositing money is reward enough for the bank, whether directly into an account or through the purchase of one of its financial products. Private banking may also charge fees for its services, although banking charges and fees are often complicated and not readily apparent. Provided the sum involved is large enough to justify the fee costs, developing a relationship with a private bank or division may be worthwhile. The bank will get the benefit from time to time of being able to offer bridging finance, or of holding large amounts in transit.

Compiled by the authors from www.investorsoffshore.com, www.arbuthnot.co.uk and with assistance from Conrad Klopotek.

Building societies, mutually owned insurers, credit unions and friendly societies (see case below) do not have shareholders; ownership rests with its members, who are usually its customers. The notion of an FI being owned by a group of individuals is firmly rooted in many countries, such as in those dealing in savings and loans in the United States. There is a further distinction between these organizations, as mutual institutions aim to make a profit whereas credit unions do not. Although credit unions are non-profit organizations, it would be wrong to think that marketing is not relevant to them. Credit unions and any other not-for-profit organizations have customer/member bases whom they serve and with whom they have relationships. Credit unions have a wider range of stakeholders with whom they maintain relationships such as their voluntary staff and municipal authorities. Their marketing activities will recognize, perhaps in an informal way, that they have a range of interested parties or stakeholders to serve (Arnett et al. 2003).

The financial services industry

As far as the mainstream financial services sector is concerned, the British Banking Association (BBA) of the United Kingdom states that banking employs close to half a million people, with the wider financial industry employing over 1.1 million and, together with related activities (accountancy, business, computer and legal services, etc.), some 3 million people rely on the financial industry for their jobs. Additionally, banks and financial services contribute £70 billion to the United Kingdom's national output, which is equivalent to 6.8 per cent of GDP. Banks and financial services provide 25 per cent of total corporation tax (£8 billion) to the UK government. The main retail banks provide over 125 million accounts, clear 7 billion transactions a year and facilitate 2.3 billion cash withdrawals per year from its network of over 30,000 free ATMs. Banks provide cost-effective banking services to 95 per cent of the United Kingdom's population. In 2005, 24 million personal customers registered to access their bank accounts on-line, while 42 million are registered to access their accounts by telephone. The value of foreign exchange business passing through London every day is £560 billion (www.bba.org.uk).

Similarly, the UK insurance industry is the largest in Europe and now the second largest in the world, accounting for 11 per cent of total worldwide premium income. The industry employs 309,000 people, which is almost a third of all financial services jobs, and twice as many as employed in both motor vehicle manufacturing and in the electricity, gas and water supply sectors combined. The industry controlled 15 per cent of investment in the London stock market in 2006. This compares to 13 per cent held by company pension funds, 3 per cent by banks, 2 per cent by unit trusts and 10 per cent by other financial institutions. Therefore, it is a major contributor to the United Kingdom's tax take. In the 2006/7 tax year, the industry contributed £9.7 billion in taxes. The industry is a major exporter, with a fifth of its net premium income coming from overseas business. Premium income from overseas is £48 billion, of which long-term business accounts for £34 billion and general business £14 billion. In 2007, the UK insurance industry paid out £211 million per day in pension and life insurance benefits, as follows (www.abi.org.uk):

- £193 million to pensioners and long-term savers
- £18 million in death and disability benefits
- £59 million per day in general insurance claims.

A further £59 million per day is paid out in general insurance claims that include:

- £17.1 million in private motor car claims (more than one in six private car drivers make a claim each year)

- £12.4 million to householders for property damage or the loss of possessions
- £5.9 million to businesses for property damage
- £6.2 million in liability claims, such as for accidents at work, professional liability and injuries to the public on commercial premises.

The number of financial services that any consumer has tends to increase with age, so the older you are generally the more financial products you have. Therefore, in Europe, especially those countries that have formed the core of the European Union, practically everyone over the age of 14 will 'consume' some form of financial service.

Marketing

Marketing is the discipline and practice that allows both practitioners and theorists to learn more about markets and the customers in those markets and to provide companies with the knowledge that equips them to strive for competitive advantage. Approaches and interpretations to marketing vary quite dramatically, but there is agreement that marketing is not concerned with selling but with the identification and fulfilling of customer needs. The focus of any marketing activity, therefore, has long been acknowledged as the consumer or customer. It has equally been understood that the consumer/customer has to gain benefit from what is offered for satisfaction to occur. However, the notion that customer satisfaction is central to successful marketing has not proved sufficient to gain the levels of customer loyalty or retention to which many companies aspire. Marketing is an evolving discipline and views about what marketing may involve develop all the time. Accordingly, definitions of what marketing is change; the current definition provided by the American Marketing Association (in 2007) is:

> Marketing is the activity, set of institutions, and processes for creating, communicating, delivering, and exchanging offerings that have value for customers, clients, partners, and society at large. (www. marketingpower.com)

The first thing to notice about this revised definition of marketing in comparison to earlier definitions and much received understanding is the absence of any mention of customer satisfaction. The concept of value has been important in marketing for some time but it now takes centre stage, with profound implications for organizations in interpreting and understanding how their customers perceive value. Satisfaction is measurable; it is often measured by organizations through the use of some form of rating scale (very satisfied…very dissatisfied). The value of these ratings may be questionable in terms of organizational outcomes but value itself is more elusive. The second thing to note is that the focus extends beyond the customer to society at large. Finally, the emphasis is on the exchange of offerings that have value for that extended marketplace. In spite of the advantages of formulating robust marketing strategies in terms of revenue generation, there continue to be companies that have not adopted the **customer-centric** marketing processes and capabilities that will allow them to compete effectively (Shah *et al.* 2006). The argument for being customer-centric is irrefutable according to these authors, who cite five trends that reinforce the need for companies to undergo transformation from product- to customer-centricity, and which are as follows:

- Intensifying pressures to improve marketing productivity
- Increasing market diversity
- Intensifying competition
- Demanding and well-informed customers and consumers
- Accelerating advances in **technology**.

customer-centric: FIs' actions are centred on the meeting and satisfaction of the customer

technology: in the context of financial services, technology embraces the systems that underpin the delivery of the services, the information systems and the digital revolution driving fundamental changes in marketing, e.g., marketing communications

Financial institutions are just as exposed to these pressures as other companies and the need for them to reinvigorate their marketing and understand their customer needs more precisely is more acute than ever. Table 1.1 provides a valuable comparison between an emphasis on products and one on customers.

Comparing the two approaches is an important reminder that selling products in itself is not the objective of successful marketing, although it usually forms part of it. Notice particularly, the performance metrics for the two approaches, where the desired metric for the customer-centric view is not market share but the how much the consumer spends with one organization on a particular category. FIs have this particular metric high on their list of aims, as do other retailers. It is not a question of what you can sell to a customer but what proportion of that customer's spend on that particular category (groceries or financial services) is spent with you. The implications for this metric on a product-centric company are significant: the company will continue to gauge its success on sales, without gaining insight into how the product is used and with what other products it is used. The company will not know how many products a particular customer has and, importantly, how brand loyal they are. In a rising market, sales may well increase, but lack of knowledge means that the company is very vulnerable to competitors who have better customer knowledge and understand the interaction between the customer and the product. FIs probably know more about their customers in terms of their financial position than any other company, especially if the institution holds a customer's current account, so should be in a strong position to understand which financial products a customer may be seeking. However,

Table 1.1   Comparison of product-centric and customer-centric approaches in financial services

	Product-centric approach	**Customer-centric approach**
Basic philosophy	Sell products: we'll sell to whoever will buy	Serve customers: all decisions start with the customer and opportunities for advantage
Business orientation	Transaction-oriented	Relationship-oriented
Product positioning	Highlight product features and advantages, promoting headline rates	Highlight product benefits in terms of meeting individual customer needs
Organizational structure	Product profit centres, product managers, product sales teams, e.g. mortgages	Customer segment centres, customer relationship managers, customer segment sales team, e.g. high net worth
Organizational focus	Product profit centres, product development, new account development, market share growth, customer relations are issues for the marketing department	Externally focused, customer relationship development, profitability through customer loyalty, employees are customer advocates
Performance metrics	Number of new products, profitability per product, market share by products/sub-brands	Share of customer wallet, customer satisfaction, customer lifetime value, customer equity
Management criteria	Portfolio of products	Portfolio of customers
Selling approach	How many customers can we sell this product to?	How many products can we sell to this customer? How do we co-create value?
Customer knowledge	Customer data are a control mechanism	Customer knowledge creates a valuable asset

Sources: Adapted from Shah *et al.* 2006, and Vargo and Lusch, 2008.

there may be a rather negative response to direct mailing of information about funeral planning!

The selling approach is also highly topical, as it is this strategy that has, in part, contributed to the credit crunch where mortgages were sold to customers who did not have the means to keep up the payments. These customers are now defaulting on their mortgage payments and banks and other lenders have run out of funds. The way in which an FI is structured (see organizational structure) in many cases is representative of their 'centricity'. One of the authors conducted research with high-street financial providers and was told by an informant that the product 'silos' in her company meant that it was very difficult to build relationships with customers. The informant was referring to the way in which the company was structured around products such as mortgages, credit cards, current accounts, which made it difficult for them to have a view of the customer across a number of product categories, thus hampering the gathering of information about an individual customer. The focus of an organization is closely linked to its structure and changing one involves re-aligning the other, hence structural changes are an indicator of a shift in focus. Customer information, the way in which it is managed and analysed and then used as part of strategic planning, is a source of competitive advantage, as demonstrated by retailers. As Table 1.1 shows, a customer-centric approach enables information to be used much more creatively in strategic planning. Very few companies would consider themselves product-centric, but an analysis of the various characteristics in Table 1.1 might tell another story.

Marketing services

In recent marketing discussions, much of the established understanding about services and the impact that the nature of services has on their marketing has been overturned and a new perspective on services is emerging. The Nordic school of services also argues that value is central to marketing, although it substitutes interactions for exchanges (Gronroos 2006), which emphasizes the consumer role in the service experience. Because the focus of this school is services, the customer is deemed to have a role in the service itself; this role has been labelled as the 'co-creator of value'. In other words, in using the service (this can also be applied to goods) the customer creates his/her own value based on the way that the service is used. The view, therefore, that emerges from the Nordic school is that marketing has to design and manage the experience to achieve 'value-in-use'; in other words, the value of the offering arises from the way in which the user/consumer uses it. Internet-only current accounts seem to meet some of the requirements of value-in-use, such as 24/7 access, easy bill payment, straightforward transactions and generally acceptable levels of security.

This new perspective argues that service has become the dominant component of any offering through the application of specialized skills and knowledge, where the customer is always the co-producer (Vargo and

Lusch 2004). Vargo and Lusch also suggest that customers be considered as resources (in terms of co-production) rather than targets for products and sales (see Table 1.1). There are major implications for marketing from these two propositions. First, the role of the customer is not that of a passive customer but that of a participant in the process. How might this actually work in financial services? To a certain extent, it already does –consider the example of the current account given in the previous paragraph. Mortgages, savings and insurance are already available on-line, where the consumer inputs all the information and requirements. If provider and consumers are satisfied with the 'deal' then the transaction is accomplished. In this situation, the customer has acted as a resource in providing and entering the information and subsequently making a choice from the options available. Financial services do not sit in neat lines on shelves waiting for a consumer to come along to choose the preferred offering. They only exist, in any sensible interpretation of the word, when they form part of an interaction between the FI and the consumer, such as the registering and subsequent use of a credit card.

Figure 1.2 demonstrates how the firm can co-create value. The outer circle represents the marketing environment over which companies have little or limited control; the middle circle represents marketing decision variables derived loosely from the four 'Ps'; and the innermost circle is the

Figure 1.2   Service-dominant marketing
Source: Adapted from Lusch and Vargo (2006).

service-dominant logic: an evolving term that argues that services are now dominant in the marketing exchange

customer. The theme in the **service-dominant logic** view of marketing is that customers are resources and that marketing is achieved with the customer through co-creation of value. How might this concept translate into financial services? One enduring issue with financial services is the complexity of the offering. Consider, for example, all that fine print that accompanies the purchase of most financial services. This complexity means that the FI usually has better information or understanding about the product than the customer; this is referred to as asymmetric information. This asymmetry may have contributed to product-centric perspectives or, at worst, opportunistic behaviour on the part of FIs in the past (see Table 1.1). The service-dominant logic view of marketing would be to maximize the knowledge that the FI has, both about the customer and the product, to create a product that generates value to both parties; for example, a mortgage that meant that particular borrower would be able to keep up the repayments. Selling mortgages to consumers who will, in all likelihood, be unable to keep up repayments results in everyone losing.

The contributions of the service-dominant logic model, which continues to evolve, and the Nordic school of services management have yet to impact fully on the way that FIs understand, interpret and operationalize their marketing.

Components of services marketing

Although the view of marketing as co-creating value is considered to be a very pertinent one, this perspective is very new and may take sometime to be absorbed into the mainstream of the financial services sector. It is, therefore, practical to consider some of the more conventional approaches to services marketing. Services have been viewed as sharing a number of characteristics but customers and consumers, we would argue, are familiar enough with these characteristics for them to have been subsumed into many current marketing strategies. However, there are some considerations that still apply to the marketing of services; just as conventional marketing has been underpinned by the four 'Ps', services marketing too has a marketing mix which consists of eight 'Ps' (Lovelock 2001). The 'Ps' are listed below, with examples of financial services provided:

Product element: the features of the core offering and the bundle of supplementary service elements that surround it. The benefits of the service must be of value to the customer. It is a legal requirement that car owners have car insurance in the United Kingdom, but the core offering is extended through a number of additional benefits which the consumer can choose, depending upon his/her circumstances or particular risk perceptions. Many car insurance packages feature a hire car in case the car is undriveable, legal cover in case of a dispute and/or breakdown cover.

Place and time: these elements represent the way in which the service is delivered to the customer. Many of the basic financial services are available 24/7 or during a working day (via automated telling machines). Other services are available through personal interaction with FIs or their representatives or intermediaries, depending upon the service.

Process: this refers to means through which the service is created and consumed (or even co-produced). The consumer plays a significant role in the process or creation of the service. In on-line mortgage brokering, the consumer, who has to be fairly confident about their financial services competence, is taken through the process of choosing a mortgage. Insurance comparison websites are a similar idea; the sums of money involved here, however, are considerably smaller. The way in which the process is designed can generate competitive advantage through transparency, ease of use and control (see www.charcolonline.co.uk).

Productivity and quality: are, it is argued, inseparable. Productivity refers to the way in which the inputs of the service are translated into outputs that are valued by the customers. In financial services where economies of scale are considered to be critical in driving down costs (not necessarily prices), efficient production has to be central. It is also essential to maintaining quality, without which customers will switch to competitors who offer better quality. However, what constitutes quality and how consumers perceive quality is complex and varied.

People: the days of the local bank manager have passed, but branch staff, call centre staff and back office staff are vital for the creation of new services, developing systems, selling the services, building and maintaining relationships; investments in training and career development, remuneration and appropriate incentives all form part of a lean but effective workforce. First Direct, the first virtual bank, has excellent front-line staff who are alert to individual customer's expectations of interaction and customization of the service.

Promotion and education: refers to marketing communications, of which retail financial services make great use of. Education informs how the service can benefit customers and ways in which they can derive additional benefits. Promotion in financial services may spell out the advantages of a particular service provider over its rivals, as the sector is highly competitive and differentiation between products and providers is difficult to establish. Regulation also influences the way in which marketing communications are developed.

Physical evidence: a traditional means of overcoming the intangibility of most services by providing some element of tangible evidence.

Bank branches have often been used to endow the providers with a sense of permanence and security, although many of them now resemble contemporary retail spaces with strong merchandising. Elsewhere branding and the use of symbols or 'spokescharacters', such as the Churchill dog, are used to create similar images.

Price and user costs: customers pay for their financial services either directly or indirectly, although pricing is highly competitive. Banks are regulated as to the way in which they can advertise the rates or charges that they make, but bank charging has become a highly contentious issue in financial services.

As the service-dominant logic (S-DL) view of marketing gathers momentum, the 'Ps' of services marketing will be less of a consideration but they still have relevance for the time being and are discussed at greater length in the ensuing chapters.

Financial services

Much of the services marketing literature attempts to classify services using such criteria as how a service may be customized for the customer or how the service is differentiated (e.g., Kasper *et al.* 2006). The value of classifying services is to enable strategies to be developed for marketing the service. When attempting to classify services, it becomes clear that financial services vary enormously, as mentioned above. For example, investment services to wealthy and financially literate customers are high in customization and differentiation, whereas automated telling machines are low in both but offer value creation for the consumer. Doyle (2002) classifies financial services as competitive but other aspects of his classification, such as customer contact, goals, ownership and type of market, vary, depending upon the nature of the service and to whom it is being supplied. What unifies financial services is that they are often hard to evaluate, they are offered through a range of delivery systems, there is opportunity for co-production and they are generally acquired as a means of achieving an end.

Of equally great interest and importance to marketers are the markets that they operate in; for example, business-to-consumer (B2C) or business-to-business (B2B). Bank websites indicate that they initially divide their markets into several categories; for example, HSBC offers premier banking, personal banking, business and corporate banking, global banking and markets and private banking (www.hsbc.com). Private banking involves the offering of special levels of financial relationships to customers who have been identified as core affluents, high net worth, ultra high net worth and also whether they are 'old' or 'new' money (Foehn

2004). AXA insurance cites three possible markets: personal, business and intermediaries (www.axa.co.uk). Insurance companies have not fared as badly as banks in the credit crunch, apart from the US company AIG.

EXHIBIT 1.3

Giant brought down

AIG (sponsor of Manchester United Football Club) has been bailed out by the US government to the sum of $150 billion. Their chief executive explained that they had strayed from their core business of general insurance, adding policies that covered financial products and transactions. AIG provides insurance to large companies and, most importantly, to banks. If an investment bank undertook a major, complex trade, for example, AIG would insure them against the deal going wrong, through instruments called 'credit default swaps'. AIG has been under financial pressure for some time after posting three quarterly losses in a row totalling $18.5 billion. The losses were related to the problems afflicting housing and credit markets, with AIG playing a key role in insuring risk for financial institutions around the world. AIG is a rich company, but its money is tied up in deals and investments that are either not easy to sell or difficult to value. To survive, the company urgently needed cash, and the US Federal Reserve was the only organization prepared to supply it. The Fed will also take over AIG's troubled credit default swaps and the mortgage-backed assets in the company's securities lending unit, which are the two divisions that caused the insurer's near-collapse in September 2008. The continued fall in the value of those assets has drained billions of dollars from AIG's balance sheet by forcing it to put up extra capital to its counter-parties.

Compiled by the authors from www.bbc.co.uk, www.ft.com.

The S-DL view emphasizes the value that the consumer/customer co-creates or produces, which has implications regarding the way products are currently grouped. The S-DL view requires organizations and FIs to review their product ranges from the perspective of value creation for the customer and to consider services as interactions and processes. What do financial services allow customers to do: they are not ends in themselves? What are the benefits of financial services? Loans, for example, involve payment of the loaned sum plus interest; credit cards have different rates of interest; the range of mortgages (whether repayment, interest-only, fixed rate, capped rate, standard variable rate, discounted etc.) is designed to meet the needs of different consumers. Although classification of financial services is an important activity for marketers, these classifications vary according to the product, which then runs counter to S-DL and customer-centricity views.

Technology

The impact of technology on financial services has been remarkable and ranges from automated telling machines (ATMs) to Internet-only banks and the information systems that track transactions and store customer information. Technology has also lowered barriers to entry (Howells and Bain, 2007), enabling supermarkets and other retailers to enter the marketplace thus, raising levels of competition. Significant changes that have occurred in financial services in the last few years include the growing use of technology in the delivery and consumption of services, the growth in customer confidence in the consumption of financial services, the globalization of financial services (though perhaps less noticeable at retail level), the increase in regulation and the profitability of the providers.

Corporate social responsibility

corporate social responsibility: a term indicating a company's approach to behaving in accordance with social, ethical and business norms through self-regulation

Momentum in concern about the way in which companies conduct themselves in a range of activities is gathering. High-profile events such as the events surrounding Enron and, of course, the credit crunch have shown that companies have not behaved in accordance with accepted business practices, industry guidelines or, indeed, what people in general consider to be ethical or sustainable. **Corporate social responsibility** (CSR) is a broad term with a number of different interpretations that can be concerned with ethical business practices, green and environmentally aware policies and social causes. Financial services have embraced the notion of CSR (see, for example, barclays.com/sustainabilityreport07), but the issue facing banks (mortgage banks in particular) is how to move on from the credit crunch with marketing strategies that demonstrate responsible and sustainable practices.

After the credit crunch

The actions that contributed to the credit crunch are endlessly debated but seem to entail both poor decision-making and weak regulation. It would appear that some of the decisions that were taken in some of the more troubled institutions were about targeting certain customer groups – generally a marketing strategy. The difference in these cases is that loans were made to consumers who would not normally have been considered owing to a high probability of defaulting on the loan. These customer groups are known as the sub-prime market. The financial and emotional hardship that these consumers are currently experiencing, such as arrears in mortgage repayments, repossession of their homes and shattered dreams, is a severe indictment of the lending practices of some banks, which have been taken over since by the UK government and other banks. In the worsening economy in the United Kingdom, the number of households in arrears in the first half of 2009 stood at 24,100, compared with a forecast for the whole year of 65,000. The half-year total of 205,600 mortgages in arrears by 2.5% or more of the outstanding mortgage balance compares with a forecast of a total of 360,000 by the end of 2009. In June, the Council of Mortgage Lenders revised downwards its expectations for arrears and possessions for the year as a whole. (cml.org.uk). Repossessing a property is a lose/lose situation for everyone concerned; the borrower loses a roof over their head, the lender loses the repayments and, as in recent instances, acquires an even worse reputation.

Has the banking scene changed forever? Certainly, there has been consolidation among the high-street banks, with the take over of HBOS by Lloyds TSB going ahead. Foreign banks, such as Santander, have been able to grow quickly with some bargain acquisitions such as Alliance & Leicester. The UK government currently owns Northern Rock and part of Bradford & Bingley and probably, in due course, will return these banks to private hands. In the short term, banks are concerned with achieving some form of equilibrium, meeting the requirements of their customers and regaining some kind of standing in the eyes of their stakeholders. From a marketing perspective, this will involve thinking about how they can rebuild confidence, which should really involve a thorough reappraisal of the way that they do business. It may also provide opportunities for other non-bank companies to increase their presence in the financial services market. The current debates, with an emphasis on the co-creation of value, could provide some guidance on how financial institutions could look on marketing in future.

Summary

- Marketing is not concerned with products but with creating value. How can value be created in financial services?
- There is a vast range of institutions engaged in offering financial services and a very wide range of offerings.
- There is still a tendency to 'sell' financial services. The increasing momentum of the S-DL view has profound implications for the way in which services are viewed by financial institutions (FIs). The concept of co-creation of value will bring about changes in the way that services are classified, produced and consumed.
- Corporate social responsibility (CSR) and related activities have been taken up by FIs, but, in spite of the outward manifestations of CSR, it

is not clear how it really influences the way in which FIs conduct their business.
- The credit crunch may encourage FIs to move towards a customer-centric perspective of marketing or S-DL view of value co-creation.

References

Arnett, D., German, S. and Hunt, S. D. (2003) 'The Identity Salience Model of Relationship Marketing Success: The Case of Nonprofit Marketing', *Journal of Marketing*, Vol. 69, No. 2, pp. 89–105.

Cheverton, P., Hughes, T., Foss, B. and Stone, M. (2005) *Key Account Management in Financial Services*, London and Philadelphia, Kogan Page.

Doyle, P. (2002) *Marketing Management and Strategy*, Harlow, FT Prentice Hall.

Foehn, P. (2004), 'Client Valuation in Private Banking: Results of a Case Study in Switzerland', *Managing Service Quality*, Vol. 14, No. 2/3, pp. 195–204.

Gronroos, C. (2006) 'Adapting a Service Logic for Marketing', *Marketing Theory*, Vol. 6, No. 3, pp. 317–33.

Howells, P. and Bain, K. (2007), *Financial Markets and Institutions*, 5th edn, Harlow, FT Prentice Hall.

Kasper, H., van Helsdingen, P. and Gabbott, M. (2006) *Services Marketing Management: A Strategic Perspective*, 2nd edn, Chichester, John Wiley & Co.

Lovelock, C. (2001) *Services Marketing: People, Technology, Strategy*, 4th edn, Upper Saddle River, Prentice Hall.

Lusch, R. and Vargo, S. (2006) 'Service-Dominant Logic and a Foundation for General Theory', in R. Lusch and S. Vargo (eds), *The Service-Dominant Logic of Marketing: Dialog, Debate and Directions*, New York, ME Sharpe.

Shah, D., Rust, R., Parasuraman, A., Staelin, R. and Day, G. (2006) 'The Path to Customer Centricity', *Journal of Service Research*, Vol. 9, No. 2, pp. 113–24.

Vargo, S. and Lusch. R. (2008) 'From Goods to Service(s): Divergences and Convergences of Logics', *Industrial Marketing Management*, Vol. 37, pp. 254–9.

Further reading

www.bba.org.uk
www.abi.org.uk
www.cml.org.uk
www.fsa.gov.uk

Exercises

1. Turn to the 'best-buy' tables of common financial services in a Sunday newspaper. Select one of the products – for example, savings. Imagine that you are saving up for a car; you already have £1,000 ready to deposit and you are going to add to that over the next nine months, after which time you will want to withdraw the money the moment you find the right car. Looking at the accounts listed, draw up a table of those which are most suitable in terms of interest rates, minimum deposit, access, penalties, how often the interest is paid, withdrawal notice and, of course, the lender. Was the decision easy? How many choices did you have?
2. How might FIs address the question of confidence from customers?
3. How does the idea of co-creating value fit into your lifestyle? What value might be obtained for you and your FI if you could co-create a financial service? Which financial service would lend itself most easily to this reinterpretation?

CASE STUDY

Long live mutuality! The friendly society

Mutually owned FIs and friendly societies are experiencing a surge of interest in their products. There is a feeling that the public is seeking alternatives to commercial profit-making institutions for financial products. Mutual FIs are organizations that are owned by their members, that is, their customers; they do not have shareholders like most banks and larger insurance companies. These organizations argue that they are in a position to offer better returns, lower charges and better service than FIs with shareholders. In spite of the de-mutualization of many FIs (e.g., Northern Rock, Abbey), it has been argued that mutuals should seek to build on their heritage and strengthen their role in economic and social life (Carbo *et al.* 2000). Their customers are usually older individuals who are financially knowledgeable and who understand what mutuality represents in financial terms. These customers also tend to be confident in choosing a product to match their lifestyle and, importantly for these FIs, ethos. Members or customers feel more comfortable that there are no shareholders to satisfy and no bonus-inflated salaries to support. The Association of Mutual Insurers has also found that younger savers are now joining the mutual societies, which is a welcome surprise. The upturn in business for mutuals may also be fuelled by a growing interest in socially responsible organizations that do not reward ill-judged behaviour by managers. Despite this renewed enthusiasm for the mutual model, the question remains whether these organizations are intrinsically safer or offer better value than other FIs or whether they just appeal when other options seem risky.

An example of mutuality in financial services is the friendly society. These societies were established to encourage self-help and personal responsibility and to enable people with limited financial resources to improve their economic status. Friendly societies have been around for hundreds of years and may even have their origins dating back to Roman times. They grew from the simple premise that if a group of people contributed to a mutual fund, then members of the group could receive benefits at a time of need. Early meetings of these societies were often held as a social gathering, when the subscriptions would be paid. The friendly societies movement grew as new towns and industries developed in the nineteenth century and people found it difficult to rely on village communities. State provision for the poor included the threat of the workhouse. The government in the United Kingdom encouraged membership and passed the Friendly Societies Act 1875 that created a system of auditing and registration. People joined friendly societies in large numbers and, by the late 1800s, there were about 27,000 registered friendly societies. Friendly societies, as a reflection of their heritage, often have names that fall into a number of categories: for example, a place name, such as Liverpool; a product type, such as healthcare. The founders of the Shepherds Friendly Society, known originally as the Loyal Order of the Ancients Shepherds and established in 1826, chose the name because of the 'Good Shepherd' looking after his flock. The society is based in Cheshire in the United Kingdom and offers a range of tax-exempt savings, as well as an innovative mortgage-payment protection plan.

Prior to the creation of the Welfare State just after the Second World War, friendly societies were often the only source of help for a working person in times of ill health or old age. In the days when having no income normally meant a life of begging or living in the poorhouse, the importance of friendly societies to their members and the invaluable social service they provided cannot be overstated. When the Welfare State was introduced, during the last century, the staff of the friendly societies already had the expertise to run the new scheme and they were instrumental in administering it, but its creation led to a reduction in the number of members of friendly societies. However, current government policies seek to reduce their own responsibility to provide; it is likely that organizations such as friendly societies will have an opportunity to re-establish themselves as providers of essential financial products such as pensions.

There were approximately 200 friendly societies in the United Kingdom in 2008. Many have remained locally based, while others have grown into national organizations, offering sophisticated financial services products to their members. Driven by both economic and social concerns, cooperative and mutual insurers are member-owned organizations that care not only about the bottom lines of their businesses, but also about the quality of life of their members in their communities. On 13 September 2004, 13 of the United Kingdom's largest mutual insurers formed the Association of Mutual Insurers (AMI), which became the first national trade association to represent mutual insurers in the country; it represents the mutual business model.

Table C1.1	Typical friendly society products
Savings/investment	Tax exempt savings, endowments, unit trusts, ISAs, bonds, child savings, funeral expenses and the new child trust funds
Health insurances	Medical cash, sickness, permanent health/income protection, private medical, critical illness
Life insurances	Term assurance, whole of life assurance
Pensions	Personal pensions
Annuities	Compulsory purchase annuities, impaired life annuities, purchased life annuities
Other	Discretionary benefits, social and benevolent activities, general insurance and other services via subsidiary companies

Source: www.shepherdsfriendly.co.uk

Friendly societies continue to encourage savings and provide financial products, notably pensions, healthcare, insurance and banking, within an ethos of mutuality and friendliness. These products enable people to make their own decisions and to take responsibility for their own lives and those of their families. They also include tax-efficient savings plans designed to provide a head start for a child or grandchild. Many products take advantage of tax concessions available only to friendly societies and, of course, the profits go to friendly society members rather than shareholders. The Friendly Societies Act 1992 enabled friendly societies to incorporate, take on new powers and provide a larger variety of financial services through subsidiaries.

Although the history of the mutual society is not entirely without incident (the collapse of Equitable Life), the Association of Mutual Insurers believes that the collapse led to better governance within the mutual sector, ensuring better safeguards for investors. Another performance measure by which mutuals can be assessed is their ability to provide long-term value to customers. AMI figures show that investors who put aside £6,000 over the past ten years would receive an average return 14 per cent higher with a mutual than with a public company. The story is much the same with policies over 15, 20 and 25 years, with mutuals returning more money to policy-holders, therefore providing higher returns than profit-making FIs.

Questions

1. What is the significance of not having shareholders to an FI?
2. Is being friendly and having a strong mutual ethos important when purchasing financial services?

3. Looking at the products that friendly societies offer; how can value be co-created? How might friendly societies promote the value of their products? What other marketing suggestions could be made regarding the products?
4. What are the opportunities offered by the credit crunch to friendly societies? How could friendly societies make the most of these opportunities?

References

Carbo, S., Gardener, E., Molyneux, P. and Williams, J. (2000) 'Adaptive Strategies by European Savings Banks: A Case Study of Spain', in E. Gardener and J. Falzon (eds), *Strategic Challenges in European Banking*, Basingstoke, Macmillan Press.
Compiled by the Jillian Dawes Farquhar from: www.afs.org.uk, www.mutualinsurers. org.uk, www.open.ac.uk/socialsciences, www.times online.co.uk/tol/money, www. shepherdsfriendly.co.uk

With grateful thanks to Wendy Beckett of Shepherds Friendly Society and her colleagues.

2

The financial services environment

Contents

Learning outcomes

By the end of this chapter, the reader will be able to:

- Comprehend the key external influences in the marketing of financial services

- Appreciate the importance of environmental scanning in the marketing of financial services

- Integrate a stakeholder perspective into environmental scanning

---

Introduction

The financial industry employs over 1.1 million people and, together with related activities (accountancy, business, computer and legal services, etc.), some 3 million people rely on the financial industry for their jobs in the United Kingdom alone. Banks and financial services contribute £70 billion to the country's national output (6.8 per cent of GDP). Banks and financial services provide 25 per cent of total corporation tax (£8 billion) to the UK government. The main retail banks provide over 125 million accounts, clear 7 billion transactions a year and facilitate £2.3 billion cash withdrawals per year from its network of over 30,000 free ATMs. Banks provide cost-effective banking services to 95 per cent of the United Kingdom's population. In 2005, 24 million personal customers registered to access their bank accounts on-line, while 42 million are registered to access their accounts by telephone. Since April 2003, banks have opened a net total of 1.8 million Post Office-accessible basic bank accounts. The value of foreign exchange business passed through London every day is £560 billions ($1 trillion), with the United Kingdom the largest single centre for international banking. The United Kingdom, according to the British Banking Association, enjoys one of the most competitive, efficient and secure banking systems in the world and it is one of the cheapest countries in the world to bank – with 'free if in credit' banking (www.bba.org.uk). During 2008, there was enormous turmoil within financial services, considered to be a global financial crisis, which was largely attributed to 'toxic mortgage-backed assets' that originated in the United States but spread rapidly to the United Kingdom and some other European countries.

The crisis arose principally from a desire for growth amongst certain banks. The identification of a potentially new segment of customers who sought loans to buy homes both in the United States and the United Kingdom spurred investigation of how the high levels of risk associated with these segments might be covered. This market was known as the sub-prime market, as it represented a market that was less attractive than the prime or less risky market. Lenders thought that they would be able to manage this market by 'rolling up' the debts from this market with less risky debts from other activities, through a process known as **securitization**. These rolled-up packages or instruments were then sold quite normally around the world to other financial institutions. This plan seemed to work quite well until rates of lending in the United States began to rise in 2005, which resulted in the sub-prime borrowers defaulting on their loans. The size of this market and the amounts of money that had been lent were virtually impossible to calculate, as 'good' and 'bad' (toxic) debt had all been packaged up together. The first UK institution to get into trouble was Northern

securitization: a means of distributing risk in financial services through aggregating debt vehicles in a pool and then issuing new instruments

Rock, a former building society, which had converted into a bank and achieved meteoric growth by lending mortgages that exceeded the value of the property and lending to higher risk segments. Unable to meet its obligations, the bank was nationalized by the UK government in 2008. Until that moment, the bank had been viewed by the City, as being a 'wunderkind' and its business model praised. Since the nationalization of Northern Rock, a number of well-established mortgage banks have been either nationalized or acquired by other banks with less exposure to the sub-prime market or, more recently, to the failure of all the Icelandic banks.

Building societies have not been immune from the securitization crisis. Nationwide, the largest building society, acquired both the Cheshire and Derbyshire building societies, two smaller regional societies, in the latter half of 2008. The number of banks and building societies has been shrinking for some time, but in 2008 consolidation amongst institutions accelerated sharply as banks and lenders who had been exposed to the sub-prime market were unable to borrow money on the wholesale markets to meet their obligations.

The financial services environment

PEST analysis: one of the various analytic tools used to organize a scan of the macro environment (political, economic, social and technological)

An important part of developing marketing strategies is understanding the environment in which the company operates. This understanding is usually achieved through a process known as environmental scanning. A number of frameworks exist that allow organizations and financial services institutions to scan in a systematic way the environment in which they operate, such as **PEST** (Kotler *et al.* 2008) or STEP (Brassington and Pettitt 2006) which are acronyms covering similar elements: political/regulatory, economic, social/cultural and technological (see Figure 2.1). Financial services operate in a global marketplace; this may not always be obvious in day-to-day activities, but transactions take place across continents all the time, banks provide funds to each other to lend on and large companies operate across the world and need the financial infrastructure to support their activities. The interdependence of financial institutions (FIs) was made abundantly clear in the 2008 crisis, as the sub-prime debts passed from institution to institution across the world. In such a large industry with so much power and influence, bankers might be tempted to think that financial services can drive their own destiny. The events of 2008 have demonstrated that the sector is subject, just as any other industry, to changes in the environment and that a continuous appraisal of this forms a fundamental part of marketing. A systematic framework is needed that serves to remind FIs of

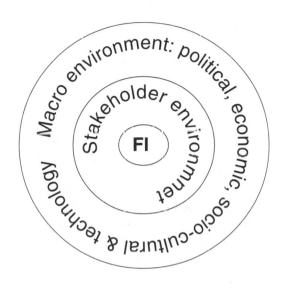

Figure 2.1   Framework for environmental scanning in financial services

macro environment:
the wider business environment, including global economic and social trends

stakeholder environment:
stakeholder theory states that shareholders at customers are not the only groups that an organization needs to serve and that there are a number of parties to whom it has responsibilities, such as employees

the world in which they operate, encouraging them to look outside their immediate environment, which might prompt a more objective evaluation of their business situation.

Figure 2.1 suggests that there are two key environments that financial services need to consider. The first is the **macro environment**, which consists of the four main factors suggested above: political, economic (which includes the natural environment here), socio-cultural and technology. The **stakeholder environment**, which is discussed later in the chapter, has a greater number of 'actors' who operate more closely with the institution and is more in keeping with the definition of marketing provided in Chapter 1. We will now consider the macro environment.

Political/regulatory environment

As a result of its size and central role in the supply of money, the financial services industry has a unique role with government and yet is subject, at least in theory, to tight control. The reasons for regulating financial markets are as follows:

- To protect the investor: the quality of many financial instruments is not easily assessed; it is, therefore, important for the investor to be made aware of the risks, although the investor is expected to assume some degree of responsibility.
- To encourage competition in the marketplace by opening it up to new entrants, which can avoid concentration through the domination of a few large financial institutions (FIs). However, the credit crisis of 2008 has resulted, due to mergers, in a significant reduction in the number of retail financial institutions in the United Kingdom and the rest of Europe. The most significant takeover has been the absorption of HBOS by Lloyds TSB, which in less turbulent times would, in all likelihood, not have been countenanced by the regulatory bodies such as the Competition Commission, the Department of Business, Enterprise and Regulatory Reform (BERR).
- To reduce the amount of illegal activity on the part of criminals who might use the system to 'launder' money (see, for example, www.hm-treasury.gov.uk/2643.htm).
- To attempt to address externalities – actions that could undermine the stability of the financial services system. An example of an externality would be the creation and distribution of mortgage-backed assets (MBAs) (Heffernan 2005).

In order for these various objectives to be managed, a wide range of authorities, bodies, organizations exist at national and international level that oversee financial service activities. Some of the key players are introduced and described in the following section.

Regulatory bodies

In the United Kingdom, the Financial Services Authority (FSA) is responsible for regulating financial services:

> 'Supervision' is the term we use to describe our day-to-day regulatory relationship with authorised firms. It is our process of monitoring and regulating firms to ensure they are complying with the regulatory requirements.
>
> www.fsa.gov.uk

The FSA has, for example, responded to the need to protect the investor (see above), particularly through the recognition of unfairness, as the following exhibit shows.

EXHIBIT 2.1

Unfairness and the FSA

Some products and information are difficult for consumers to understand

Some products lack transparency, are virtually impossible for most consumers to understand and are structured in a way that is liable to give rise to consumer detriment (including high up-front charges, hidden penalties and taking unfair advantage of one-sided discretion).

Customers are not kept appropriately informed after the point of sale

Customers are not always kept informed of how a product or service is performing or of other products/services now available that might be more suitable for them.

Products and firms don't always deliver what consumers are led to expect

Financial promotion and the sales process can create expectations among consumers, which are unlikely to be met, often with unpleasant surprises further down the track.

Customers are discouraged from changing products and product providers

In some areas there are financial penalties unrelated to the costs of changing product or provider; in others the 'hassle factor' can deter people from changing to better-value services and products.

Customers cannot always get their complaints dealt with fairly

Practice varies but many firms don't give adequate priority to the effective handling of their customers' queries and complaints and this is reflected in systems, resources, cultures and outcomes.

Financial Services Authority, 'Treating Customers Fairly After the Point of Sale', June 2001

The Bank of England has a wider responsibility of promoting and maintaining monetary and financial stability as its contribution to a healthy economy. Every month the Monetary Policy Committee of the Bank of England meet to consider the current bank rate, which governs the rate at which banks and other financial institutions lend and borrow money.

Europe

Looking beyond the United Kingdom, the EU is working to create a single financial services marketplace. In macro-economic terms, retail banking, which is over half of the total banking activity, generates 2 per cent of EU GDP annually in gross income. An ageing population puts added pressure on public finances, increasing the potential need for more private and work-based retirement provisioning and health cover. It also helps to explain the growing economic importance of the pension, insurance and investment fund sectors. Significant progress has been made in delivering a single market for retail financial services, with a framework in place to ensure the financial soundness and integrity of Europe's providers in the areas of banking, insurance and securities. This framework is designed to achieve multiple policy goals, including prudential stability, competition and a high level of consumer and investor protection. In some areas, such as investment services and life assurance, comprehensive rules have been put in place to protect the interests of retail customers and investors. The introduction of the euro, combined with the effects of the Financial Services Action Plan, has spurred greater competition in Europe's financial services markets, particularly wholesale markets (Commission of the European Communities 2007).

Regulatory bodies also exist at national level. The Commisão do Mercado de Valores Mobiliários in Portugal (CMVM) has taken measures against the crisis in financial services by strengthening its powers. In Poland, the Polish Financial Supervision Authority was set up in 2008, based on the evolution of the Polish financial market and the growing significance of multinational financial groups and cross-sector financial products. In Poland the authority is known as the KNF (Komisja Nadzoru Finansowego). The Bank of Spain, as regulator of the banking industry, has won plaudits over its handling of bank solvency and liquidity, with the result that Spanish banks have been less affected by losses in the mortgage-backed industry than other European banks and those in the United States. Nonetheless, in 2008, the government created a regulatory body – the National Commission for Financial Services. The new body replaced the stock market watchdog, the Comisión Nacional del Mercado de Valores, and has a wider remit, taking in the entire financial services industry and its relationships with users. The current insurance industry watchdog will be absorbed by the Bank of Spain, which will remain the regulator of solvency in financial markets.

However, regulation is only as robust as the regulators. In the FSA's audit of its own actions before the collapse of the Northern Rock bank in the United Kingdom, it was noted that, in spite of the bank being subject to 'close and continuous' supervision, records of meetings between the bank and the FSA were not kept. Furthermore, the FSA incorrectly assumed that the Bank of England would automatically step in should Northern Rock run out of money (www.fsa.org). In fact, the government was obliged to nationalize the failed bank other bodies such as Ofcom monitor marketing activities of financial service institutions in the United Kingdom; for example, it has recently fined Barclaycard (see Exhibit 2.2).

EXHIBIT 2.2

Silent calls fine for Barclaycard

Barclaycard has received the maximum possible fine for the 'most serious and persistent' case of silent calls ever seen by regulator Ofcom. The credit provider was hit with a £50,000 fine after an Ofcom investigation uncovered an extremely high number of silent calls. Silent calls occur when call centres with automated systems dial more numbers than staff can deal with, so when a connection is made, there is no staff member available to talk to the consumer, leaving them bewildered and frustrated. Ofcom investigated Barclaycard from October 2006 to May 2007 and found that people receiving calls had no idea where they were coming from. Rules on silent calls in 2006 stipulated that abandoned calls must carry a short message identifying where they came from and must account for no more than 3 per cent of all live calls made in the space of 24 hours. Ofcom declined to say what Barclaycard's silent call rate was, but said the number of silent, abandoned calls made by Barclaycard was 'substantially more' than the 16,000 calls for which Abbey National was fined in a previous case. The regulator also found that some of Barclaycard's call centres had no procedures in place to prevent people receiving repeated abandoned calls over a short period of time. Ofcom consider it 'the most serious case of persistent misuse by making silent and abandoned calls that Ofcom has ever investigated'. A higher fine would have been imposed owing to the severity of the offence but there is a statutory maximum. Barclaycard have offered a full apology for any inconvenience and distress to customers caused by the calls, with assurances that 'robust and lasting changes' have been made to their processes, operations and reporting.

Compiled from www.bbc.co.uk and www.ofcom.gov.uk.

The Treasury in the United Kingdom has the objective to secure an innovative, fair dealing, competitive and efficient market in financial services, while striking the right balance with regulation in the public interest (www.hm-treasury.gov.uk). The ownership of the failed bank, Northern Rock, passed to the Treasury in February 2008 and in September partial ownership of the mortgage bank Bradford & Bingley followed suit. Both of these organizations had been building societies and converted from their mutual status to banks. However, their core expertise was to finance home purchases and in the expansion of the house market from 2000 onwards, they had seen the opportunity to grow. Their strategy appears to have been based on lending to customers who may have fallen into high-risk groups such as those who provided self-certification of their income, an area where fraud is rife; they derived their funds for lending from the wholesale market. When borrowers defaulted on their loans and the wholesale funds dried up, these organizations were left high and dry.

The Office of Fair Trading (OFT) is responsible for making markets work well for consumers, by promoting and protecting consumer interests throughout the United Kingdom, while ensuring that businesses are fair and competitive. In 2004, HSBC acquired Marks & Spencer's Money after the OFT made the decision not to refer the case to the Competition Commission. The rescue of HBOS in 2008 by Lloyds TSB would normally contravene competition limits, as both these banks figure in the top five banks in the United Kingdom, but it was thought by government that in such grave circumstances consumers were sufficiently well protected by UK regulations on market abuse (www.oft.gov.uk/news/press).

There are also a number of professional bodies or associations in the financial services sector. In the United Kingdom, for example, there is the British Banking Association (BBA) (www.bba.org.uk), the Council of Mortgage Lenders (CML) (www.cml.org.uk) and the Association of British Insurers (ABI) (www.abi.org.uk). The ABI is the trade association for Britain's insurance industry, with nearly 400 member companies who provide over 94 per cent of the insurance business in the United Kingdom. Similarly, across Europe, there are organizations, such as the Swiss Bankers' Association (www.swissbanking.org). The emphasis in this association, as in the BBA, is on self-regulation. The Swiss association has been meeting with the BBA to discuss the credit crunch, in an effort to bring back confidence to the markets. This is such a pressing matter that every stakeholder – financial institutions, central banks, policy-makers, supervisors, credit rating agencies, even investors – is playing a part in their respective field of expertise.

Basel Accord

The Basel Accord is an attempt by the Group of Ten (Belgium, the Netherlands, Canada, Japan, France, Switzerland, the United Kingdom, Germany,

Italy and the United States, plus Spain and Luxembourg) to establish common global regulatory standards for international banks. After the first agreement in 1998, revisions have been made and, in 2004, Basel II was agreed. This agreement covers three mutually reinforcing pillars that cover risk, supervision and market discipline. The implications of the Basel Accord cover aspects such as: assessing risks for loans and mortgages; supervision at national level that ensures that banks hold capital above minimum requirements; and provision of information that is timely and transparent.

Economic environment

The interaction between FIs and the economic environment is arguably closer than with companies in other fields. At times, it can be difficult to separate the economy of countries, regions and sometimes even the globe from the massive institutions that both operate within it and influence it. This section illustrates some of the ways in which economic factors influence and are influenced by FIs.

Eurozone

For the European community, specifically the Eurozone, the European Central Bank (ECB) plays a major role in attempting to bring together financial systems. Retail financial services are important in macro-economic terms; for example, retail banking (over half of total banking activity) generates 2 per cent of EU GDP annually in gross income. An ageing population, in addition to increasing pressure on public finances, helps to explain the growing economic importance of the pension, insurance and investment fund sectors. At the end of 2004, for example, investments by insurers reached €6 trillion and EU private pension funds managed €2.5 trillion in assets, with life insurance premiums alone representing 5 per cent of EU GDP (www. hm-treasury.gov.uk).

In the past, the financial systems in the euro area were organized with a national focus, each for its own currency. As a result of the single market and the euro, the European financial system is becoming more and more interlinked. This means that national boundaries are becoming less relevant. Such links are being established for financial markets, their related financial infrastructure and also for financial institutions: for example, banks merge across borders, such as Grupo Santander, or establish branches in other countries, for example, Kaupthing Bank. Ultimately, financial integration increases the potential for higher economic growth, which means that the GDP of the euro area is higher the more its financial system integrates. Looking at the individual economic agents, that is, FIs, a bigger and more integrated financial system enables them to better exploit economies of scale and scope. In return, households can benefit from access to a larger variety of financial products – like mortgage loans for house purchases – at relatively lower costs. Financial integration also has implications for the task of safeguarding financial stability in the euro area and the EU; for example, the pursuit of financial integration can have beneficial effects on financial stability as more integrated financial markets could provide the necessary conditions for the smoother absorption of financial shocks, such as those experienced in the UK and US markets. Although this statement seems a little ironic post credit crunch, the cooperation of European governments and banks has gone some way to alleviate some of the most severe consequences.

The Bank of Spain is especially prudent on risk after a Spanish banking crisis in the 1970s and as a consequence has not allowed bankers to take huge amounts of high-risk mortgages off their books by repackaging them as investment vehicles, which then plummeted in value. Although it is tempting to see Spanish banks as the champions of the best forms of risk assessment, it is still unclear whether the regulation will help the Spanish banks to cope better with the current financial storm than other banks in Europe and the rest of the world. Santander is the Eurozone's largest bank; it continues to strengthen its position in the United Kingdom with the acquisition of two struggling banks, formerly building societies. The bank already has a significant presence in South America. There are concerns that smaller banks are vulnerable as liquidity tightens globally, unable to match Santander's access to wholesale funding markets at premiums which few banks are able to pay. While many of Spain's *cajas* (smaller savings banks) have, like UK building societies, thrived for the last decade by supplying enthusiastic homebuyers with competitive mortgages, they are now vulnerable. The Spanish housing bubble, fuelled also by UK purchasers, has burst, with few customers able to afford mortgages. Businesses that took out loans with banks are also facing tougher times, particularly in the construction sector where they are laying off thousands of workers, after years of building new properties (www.guardian.co.uk).

To foster the integration of the euro area financial system, the ECB and the national central banks provide a Europe-wide payment system, known as TARGET. The ECB, at times, helps market participants to make progress in certain initiatives, where it acts as catalyst, enabling them to overcome potential coordination problems. This occurs, for example, in the area of retail payments, where the banks, with the help of the ECB, are preparing a euro area-wide framework so that in the future citizens and enterprises can make payments throughout the euro area from a single bank account using a single set of payment instruments, as easily, cheaply and safely as today in their national systems. Commentators have observed that free market approaches favoured by governments in the United Kingdom and United States may have contributed to the financial crisis.

Although the crisis of 2008 was brought about largely as a result of activities on the part of US and UK FIs, rises in energy and food prices are contributing to the global turmoil. FIs raise funds principally from two main sources: first, from the deposits and investments that customers make to the banks; and, second, from borrowing from other sources such as other banks, international deposits and brokers, often referred to as wholesale funding. These funds are then used to lend to customers to buy homes, finance businesses, purchase goods and services. In 2008, however, the money markets shut; that is, banks stopped lending to each other and sources of funding dried up. Funds for expanding businesses, mortgages and loans were therefore not available and, with higher energy prices and anxieties about even higher bills for the approaching winter, people were generally unwilling or unable to spend money, impacting heavily on the construction and retailing sectors.

From a period when the supply of money was readily available, fuelling high spending – particularly in the UK housing sector – funds have dried up dramatically. Unemployment in the financial services sector has increased and layoffs of staff continue into 2009. Levels of debt in the United Kingdom are increasing – in particular, levels of 'extreme debt'. The Consumer Credit Counselling Service (CCCS) states that the number of its clients owing more than £100,000 has nearly doubled from 1.4 per cent to 2.7 per cent in a year. Statistics for the 280,000 customers of this service for 2005 showed people aged between 40 and 59 had the highest level of debt and owed an average of £34,456. The CCCS said the amount of money owed by people over 60 who contacted the group had soared by 25 per cent to an average of £33,658. The number of young people aged between 18 and 24 struggling with debt has also increased and those who contacted the charity owed an average of £15,079 in 2005, compared with £11,935 two years earlier (www.cccs.co.uk). The turmoil in the mortgage market has led the Council of Mortgage Lenders to estimate that 170,000 mortgages would be over three months in arrears by the end of 2008 but the council was able to revise the figures downwards for 2009 www.cml.org.uk. Not only do individuals get into difficulties with repaying money that they have borrowed, but also the crisis that started in 2008 has brought countries to the edge.

EXHIBIT 2.3

Icelandic edge

A terrifying example of the seriousness of the financial situation in 2008 is Iceland, where, for years, higher interest rates were available than in many parts of the world. The country's financial institutions, therefore, borrowed substantial funds from abroad, especially Japan, where interest rates were effectively zero, for lending to institutions in high-interest-paying economies, such as the United Kingdom. Investors in the United Kingdom noticed the attractive rates offered by a new bank on the scene called Kaupthing Edge, which bought a small but well-established British bank Singer & Friedlander. The Icelandic economy expanded rapidly, making Icelanders among the richest people in Europe, but critics argue it was built on too much debt, which backfired in the current credit crunch. The whole country has been likened to a 'toxic hedge fund'. The GDP in Iceland is about $20 billion; but its big banks borrowed some $120 billion in foreign currencies and the country could not service this kind of debt. Even if the Icelandic government had underwritten all these liabilities, its national debt-to-GDP ratio would have been at a level that would leave little for even the most basic of spending. Kaupthing Edge and Icesave had been offering attractive rates to investors in the United Kingdom, so Iceland's problems had a direct impact on the British economy, with levels of exposure extending to charities and local authorities as well as private investors. In the autumn of 2008, the Icelandic government nationalized their largest banks. Inflation reached 14 per cent and the Icelandic krona fell 32 per cent against the euro in a month; credit became very hard to obtain in Iceland. Over the past decade, Iceland's banking sector had grown to dwarf the rest of the economy, with assets at nine times annual GDP of £6.8 billion. The effects of the behaviour of Icelandic banks rippled out across Europe and the rest of the world. For example, the retailer Baugur, an Icelandic company, owns stakes in several British retailers; talks of its rescue involve Philip Green, the UK high-street retailer. Amid reports of panic buying in foodstores in Iceland, the governor of Iceland's central bank maintained that the bank had enough reserves to cover the cost of all imports for eight to nine months.

Compiled by the authors from www.fool.co.uk, www.bbc.co.uk, www.telegraph.co.uk, www.guardian.co.uk and www.ft.com.

Ukraine is also facing very severe economic difficulties with other EU states taking action to bail the country out. The global crisis that unfurled in 2008 resulted from a lack of funds or liquidity; banks were unable to assure the market that they could honour their promises to pay back the money that they owed. Since planning and forecasting went so catastrophically wrong, how did the modelling that banks conduct fail to foresee these events? Banks are vulnerable to problems with liquidity because they borrow money that has to be repaid in the short term, which they also use to back up more lucrative long-term investments. If depositors withdraw their money and other lenders refuse to lend the bank the funds they need to meet their obligations, the bank then cannot easily turn its long-term assets into cash to make up any shortfall. Liquidity crises are extremely rare, and standard modelling will generally not include very rare events (Jameson 2008). Liquidity crises also vary – one crisis will have different characteristics from others in the past. Banks generally run two models:

- Day-to-day models that assume that market prices will continue to behave much as they have in the past. Unfortunately, this kind of model does not take into account the development of new instruments, such as the repackaging of high risk lending.
- Other models estimate the risk from borrowers but overlook how bad news can affect the sector. Word gets out that some asset has dramatically lost value, which means that other banks are reluctant to lend money, reducing liquidity even further.

Recommendations for addressing shortcomings in risk models include looking beyond individual risks to a wider appraisal; this would cover the exposure of the industry as a whole, rather than just a particular company. This recent crisis has emphasized the close links between financial institutions; although the 'outliers', such as Northern Rock, were the first to go under, there are very few organizations that have not been affected by the problems of liquidity in the sector.

The natural environment

Changes in the climate also have implications for financial services. For example, heavy flooding in 2007 and 2008 in the United Kingdom resulted in major claims from insurance companies for flood damage, exceeding £1.5 billion in 2007 and tens of thousands of pounds again in 2008. The Department of Environment, Food and Rural Affairs (DEFRA) and the ABI arrived at a set of actions that both the government and the industry will take over the long term and which include:

- Improving understanding of flood risk
- Government to put in place a long-term investment strategy, which will set out strategic flood prevention aims and assess future policy options and funding needs
- Ensuring that the planning system prevents inappropriate development in flood-risk areas
- Raising awareness in areas where flood risks are significant, encouraging property owners to take sensible precautions and providing more information about how to obtain flood insurance
- Promoting access to home insurance for low-income households.

www.defra.org.uk

This is an interesting example of industry and government working together to address changing circumstances. The final bullet point is consistent with government policy of improving access to financial services for marginalized groups.

Recycling and green behaviours

There has been a significant shift away from using paper in financial services; for example, the use of cheques has roughly halved over the past decade. In 1990, approximately 11 million cheques were written every day, but in 2008, the figure was just under 5 million per day. Consumers increasingly avail themselves of non-paper systems for consuming financial services, using direct debit or the Internet to pay bills. Although HSBC states that the decline of the cheque as a method of payment has been exaggerated, citing the example of its own customers amongst whom there has been little or no fall in cheque usage. The bank finds that there is a strong core of people using cheques as their preferred means of buying high-value items. Overall, it is predicted that the decline in the use of cheques will slow but with no prospect of the payment method, which has being in use since the eighteenth century, becoming extinct. Small business people also continue to use cheques, finding them convenient and easy. Recycling documents in financial services can be problematic owing to their confidential nature. Even if financial service companies operate a secure disposal scheme, materials for recycling can be left in bins for several days awaiting collection, during which time the information in these documents can be accessed with criminal intent.

Sustainability

Many companies prefer to use the word 'sustainable' to describe their activities in supporting communities, the natural environment and charitable works, as these extend beyond behaviours that are environmentally friendly or 'green'. Standard Chartered Bank, for example, lists under the heading of **sustainability** the following practices:

sustainability: strategies and practices that focus on the long-term future of the organization and its stakeholders

- Sustainable finance – that is, lending only to projects that are run in a socially responsible way
- Tackling financial crime. Money laundering activities run at over $500 billion and the bank has stringent procedures in place to fight this crime
- Providing financial services to the 'unbanked'
- Responsible selling and marketing, where customers are treated with openness and transparency

- Community investment across the globe
- Being a good place to work, attracting an inclusive and diverse work environment.

www.standardchartered.com

'Sustainability' and 'corporate social responsibility' are phrases and concepts that are attracting a great deal of attention. Any business that does not promote a sustainable or socially responsible position runs the risk of acquiring a poor image. However, the challenge is for financial institutions to be consistently sustainable or socially responsible in all their practices, whether that be responsible lending, the creation of products that benefit stakeholders or promotional activities that are not hedged around with restrictions in tiny print. Securitization or at least the way in which it was implemented by FIs was an example of unsustainable behaviour where the focus was on short-term gain and it would appear boosting bonus payments to bankers.

There are numerous definitions of sustainability (see, for example, www.nps.gov/sustain), but the following seem to have some application to financial services:

> A sustainable society is one which satisfies its needs without diminishing the prospects of future generations.
> Lester R. Brown, Founder and President, Worldwatch Institute

> Sustainability is equity over time. As a value, it refers to giving equal weight in your decisions to the future as well as the present. You might think of it as extending the Golden Rule through time, so that you do unto future generations as you would have them do unto you.
> Robert Gilman, Director, Context Institute

Actions are sustainable if:

> There is a balance between resources used and resources regenerated.
> Resources are as clean or cleaner at end use as at beginning.
> The viability, integrity, and diversity of natural systems are restored and maintained.
> They lead to enhanced local and regional self-reliance.
> They help create and maintain community and a culture of place.
> Each generation preserves the legacies of future generations.
> David McCloskey, Professor of Sociology, Seattle University

All these definitions feature the notion of looking to future generations and communities, equity and maintaining balance.

Socio-cultural environment

People's attitudes to money and what to do with it vary hugely, influenced by personal factors, family and reference groups. Increasing social diversity, accompanied by growth in global banking, has led to new types of banking, including Islamic banking. Islamic banks appeared on the world scene as active players over two decades ago, but many of the principles upon which Islamic banking is based have been commonly accepted all over the world, for centuries rather than decades. The basic principle of Islamic banking is the prohibition of Riba (that is, usury or interest) and, although this principle has seldom been recognized as applicable beyond the Islamic world, many of its guiding principles have. The majority of these are based on simple morality and common sense, which form the bases of many religions, including Islam (www.islamic-banking.com). With ever-stronger foundations in the Middle East and Asia, Islamic finance is now starting to take hold in London. The United Kingdom's first standalone Shari'a-compliant bank opened its doors in 2004. If Islamic finance is to move deeper into mainstream global finance, the industry needs to improve transparency and foster credibility by harmonizing standards and practices, not least as Shari'a interpretation varies between regions and even institutions. Regulatory oversight needs to be sharpened as well, which could be critical in broadening the appeal of Islamic finance and bridging the gap between Islamic and conventional financial systems. Shari'a-compliant products can be more complex than conventional ones because every transaction is backed by a non-financial trade. Many instruments are still lacking, including corporate treasury and derivatives products, but innovation is hampered by the limited number of Islamic scholars able to vet financial products for Shari'a compliance (adapted by the authors from the economist.com).

Attitudes to debt vary within Europe, with prudence appearing to be a national characteristic in France. The country as a whole takes far fewer financial risks than the United Kingdom; household debt is 47 per cent of GDP, compared with a figure over twice that in United Kingdom. French shoppers are constrained in their desire to purchase goods and services by strict credit limits, as French credit cards are little more than debit cards. If there are insufficient funds in a purchaser's account to cover the cost of the purchase, the bank will just block the transaction (www.bbc.co.uk). French banks have very strict criteria about lending; they also endeavour to limit risks by spreading their investments much more widely than those in the United States or the United Kingdom. Only about a quarter of banking activity is related to investment banking and dealer-broker activity, with the rest in retail banking. Nonetheless, French banking has suffered significantly from the credit crunch. Caisse d'Epargne, a mutual savings bank, lost €600 million in October 2008 in what was called a derivatives trading incident. Caisse d'Epargne, which, in 2008, was in the middle of a merger with its rival Groupe Banque Populaire, dismissed the team involved in the incident.

Technology

Technological developments continue to accelerate in financial services, as in other industries. This impacts on the marketing of financial services in the way that customers consume financial services, such as using mobile phones to pay for services – from paying at a parking meter to accessing an account. Credit and debit cards are not new, but there is scope for technology to develop cards to cope with contemporary lifestyles, as well as generating advantages for businesses.

EXHIBIT 2.4

The contactless card

Barclaycard has introduced a new system of payment for goods valued at less than £10 by touching their card to a reader without entering a PIN number or signing for the transaction. A trial conducted in selected outlets of Coffee Republic in the first quarter of 2008 showed an increase of 50 per cent in contactless payments during the trial period. The One Touch system will be introduced in company-owned outlets, with a possibility of extending it to the franchises. Advantages are that during peak time transaction times are significantly shortened, enabling a higher volume of customers to be served, reducing queuing times for customers and avoiding loss of customers. Barclaycard has developed the OnePulse card, which is a three-in-one card that combines an Oyster card from Transport for London, a credit card and cashless OneTouch payments. Commuters therefore use the same card to get on a bus or the Underground and to buy breakfast.

Adapted by the authors from www.silicon.com and www.Barclaycard.co.uk.

A further advantage for the provider is the added revenue generated by retailers' purchase and use of the new technology.

Another aspect of technology in financial services is the way in which providers have adopted it to support selling, delivery, strategy and lower costs. Fraud is a major problem in financial services and technology has gone some way to assist in its reduction; as Exhibit 2.5 indicates, however, there is still some way to go.

EXHIBIT 2.5

Technology lowering some losses through fraud

In 2006, total card fraud losses fell by 3 per cent to £428 million, a decrease of nearly £80 million over the previous two years. The figure for the period between January and June 2008 was £47.4 million. The success of chip and PIN has meant that face-to-face fraud has continued to drop, falling a further 47 per cent on 2005. Lost and stolen card fraud showed an overall decrease of 23 per cent from 2005. In 2006, counterfeit card fraud increased by just 3 per cent to £99.6 million, showing a further fall in growth rate from 2005. The main area of card fraud to rise in 2006 was card-not-present (CNP) fraud. This increased by 16 per cent compared with 2005, and, although it is increasing at reducing rates, at £212.6 million, it now accounts for half of all losses. However, criminals in some European countries, where the technology has yet to be rolled out, are stealing millions of pounds from UK consumers' cards. In 2005–6, £121 million was lost to foreign card fraud, up 11 per cent on the previous year and nearly 190 per cent on three years previously; this occurred mainly in European countries where chip and PIN cards are not yet in use and where criminals will typically use stolen UK card details at retailers and ATMs. By 2010, chip and PIN cards are expected to replace older cards in Europe. Criminals are also targeting other channels where they can make transactions without chip and PIN, including phone, Internet and mail order, where fraud increased to £161.9 million, up 18 per cent on the previous year.

Adapted by the authors from www.ukpayments.org.uk and www.silicon.com.

Many customers remain wary of using the Internet for shopping and banking owing to these levels of fraud, even though banks will generally ensure that customers are not out of pocket. It is this wariness that still encourages the 'hard core' of cheque users to continue using this means of paying for more expensive items in spite of the inconvenience of carrying a cheque book around plus the card that guarantees the cheque. Technology has had a profound effect on banking and financial services and will no doubt continue to do so. Equally, customers and other stakeholders need assurance that the technology is secure.

E-banking, mobile banking and telephone banking have created completely new ways of managing finances for consumers and businesses. The emergence of companies such as PayPal, which offers payment services for other services – principally eBay – allows money transmission for individuals and companies alike. However, perceptions of risk remain one of they key issues in the adoption of electronic or remote forms of banking.

The stakeholder environment

micro environment:
the FI's own operating
environment, its
competitors, customers
and stakeholders

For financial services, the **micro environment** traditionally includes a number of players, such as customers, but developments in relationship marketing (RM) have pointed to a possible wider circle of people who interact with financial service providers. This model for perceiving the micro environment is derived from stakeholder theory. Stakeholder theory argues that managers should make decisions to take account of the interests of all stakeholders in a firm, including not only financial claimants, but also employees, customers, communities and governmental officials (Jensen 2001). Increasingly, stakeholder theory extends beyond the firm to take account of others who fall within the orbit of the company. Stakeholder theory has value in the marketing of financial services because it encourages companies to think outside an immediate loop of customers, competitors and shareholders, to think about marketing as – illustrated in Figure 2.2.

This model demonstrates the number and variety of stakeholders in the micro environment of a financial institution. The dominant player in many of the financial institutions in the world often, according to the financial institutions themselves, has been the shareholder, but as this model shows the shareholder is one amongst many.

Competitors

It might be surprising to see competitors cited as stakeholders in another financial institution, but there are close relationships between FIs

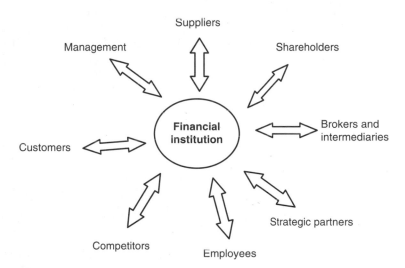

Figure 2.2 Stakeholder model for financial services
Sources: Adapted from Buttle (1996) and Kumar and Reinartz (2006).

even though they are all operate within a highly competitive sector. In fact, they all lend funds to each other, their strategies are often based on what their competitors are doing and they are chasing similar customer segments. A lack of differentiation between who they are and what they sell has plagued FIs for years. In particular, the inability of most FIs to gain any distinctive competitive advantage reinforces their closeness and their interdependence. The crisis of 2008, though, has significantly reduced the number of players in the marketplace, at the same time perhaps clearing the way for untainted companies to expand their presence, which has implications for competition and fair trade.

Brokers and intermediaries

Many financial services are delivered or distributed to customers through the services of brokers or intermediaries – for example, insurance products. The Automobile Association (AA) in the UK is an intermediary, although owned by HBOS and, therefore, now by Lloyds TSB. This organization, originally set up to serve the interests of car drivers, now supplies a range of financial services, including life insurance (see www.theaa.com); it trades on a strong brand as a provider of service to motorists, both private and business. Although many intermediaries are independent, there are a number who are owned, often discreetly, by major financial institutions. John Charcol, the mortgage broker, started off independently, was then acquired by Bradford & Bingley bank and is now independent again. Whether an intermediary is independent or not, the relationship between the provider of the product and the intermediary (often referred to an 'introducer' in the business) is potentially full of tensions. Some of the larger FIs believe that intermediaries undermine any loyalty between the customer and the provider of the product, as the intermediary may recommend a product based on commission alone. On the other hand, the intermediary is a cost-effective channel through which the FIs can sell its products.

Suppliers

FIs are dependent upon their suppliers, as is any other business, to enable them to make the value propositions that contemporary interpretations of marketing suggest. As shown above, technology plays a critical role in financial services and, although it does not usually generate competitive advantage, keeping up with technological development and integrating these developments into the strategies and practices of the banks is necessary for survival. Britannia Building Society, not a particularly large institution, has always been able to punch above its weight owing to extensive and informed investment in marketing information systems that have allowed it to 'know' its customers better than many of its competitors. FIs also use the services of consultants to advise them on their strategies. One large bank spoke to one of the authors about their relationship with Fred Reichheld, Fellow of Bain and Company and author of many influential articles on customer retention.

Employees

All organizations are dependent upon their employees; indeed, service organizations are traditionally more reliant on their staff than non-service companies. As described in Chapter 1, FIs essentially supply a service and the importance of conveying satisfaction and, more recently, delivering value frequently falls on the employee. FIs provide development opportunities for their employees (whether in a customer-facing role or in a support function) to try to ensure that they are in a position to be able to act as proponents for the strategy of the institution. Internal marketing is a concept that recognizes the importance of employees in services marketing.

Management

It may be rather surprising to see the inclusion of management in the stakeholder model. Evidently, managers do have a stake in the business, but surely they are so close to the core of the business that they cannot be regarded in quite the same way as other stakeholder groups. Managers, though, form a diverse group of people with differing interests, training, backgrounds and, most significantly, objectives. For example, the chief executives of Northern Rock and HBOS had very different backgrounds, the former having worked in Northern Rock for many years, the latter being a recent appointment with a background in retailing. Many marketing strategies presume a long-term horizon—for example, relationship marketing. The demands of providing returns for investors often seeking a quick return on their investment can impact negatively on marketing strategies which require a long-term investment. For marketing directors and managers, involving managers from other functions in strategic planning is essential to ensure that the activities of one function do not undermine those of another.

Strategic partners

Strategic partnerships have enabled the entry of new institutions into the financial services sector. When Tesco saw the opportunities of offering financial services as part of its product range, it was limited by its lack of experience, the necessary infrastructure and regulatory approval. The retail company therefore 'partnered' RBS to enter the marketplace. Carrefour, the French-based retailing giant, has BNP Paribas as its financial services partner.

Customers

Financial institutions supply financial services to a range of customers, from governments to sole traders, as well as retail customers. Customers change their behaviour according to changes in the macro-environment, as indicated in Figure 2.3, which illustrates how consumers might respond to a recession or, indeed, the current global credit crunch. As the figure shows, there are two axes that relate to a consumer's relationship to products/brands and the consumer response to the economic climate. The top left-hand quadrant illustrates possible responses to a consumer who

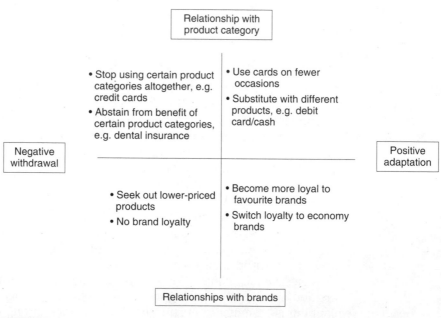

Figure 2.3   Changes in consumption patterns during a recession
Source: Adapted from Kotabe and Helsen (2008).

retreats from spending within a product category – for example, a credit card or dental insurance. The bottom right-hand quadrant demonstrates the response of a consumer who relates strongly to brands and adapts to lower levels of spending. Although branding of financial services is uneven in terms of success, there may be a reluctance to switch to untried brands.

New house lending depends on the availability, usually of wholesale funds, which has been significantly reduced. Borrowers who can put down a 25 per cent deposit on a home benefit from lower borrowing rates. Rising energy and food prices mean that less money is spent on discretionary items. Although financial services may not necessarily fall into that category, the sector is affected by a downturn in spending. Different customers, in terms of age and financial status, respond differently to changes in the economy, with economic changes being their most important consideration. If the economy is not 'favourable', the marketing departments of FIs need to be very selective about targeting their products because only certain groups are likely to be purchasing. If unemployment starts to rise, as it did in the latter half of 2008, those whose purchasing drops off least are the rich and the over 55s. If the stock market falls, the over 55s will cut back on their financial service purchases. If consumer prices start to rise, then the oldest are least affected and the youngest are most affected, while interest rates rises affect the under 20s hardly at all (Tang *et al.* 2007).

Shareholders

Most of the larger FIs are companies that are owned by their shareholders, some of them in themselves large companies. Shareholders invest in these companies and expect a return on that investment either in terms of dividends on the shares that they hold or a profit on the buying and selling of their shares in the bank. In the failed banks of 2008 and 2009, the UK and US governments have been obliged to take large shares to stop the banks going under entirely and failing to meet their obligations. Building societies do not have shareholders, thus enabling profits to be channelled back into the organization.

The analysis of the environment provides an essential first step in developing marketing strategies and plans. FIs have to be attuned to changes in the environment through continuous scanning. Analyses of the data enables them to develop appropriate strategies and to revise existing plans that take account of these changes. It could be argued that the turmoil of 2008 arose because of a tendency to

Table 2.1 Variables and examples in the financial services environment

Type of environment	Environmental variables	Examples
Macro environment	Political/regulatory	Financial service regulators, international agreements
	Economic	Currency zones, international trading, sustainability
	Socio-cultural	Cultural and religious banking, e.g. Islamic banking
	Technology	Cashless cards, IT-based systems
	Competitors	Interbank lending, undifferentiated marketplace
Stakeholder environment	Brokers	Independent advisors
	Suppliers	IT consultants
	Employees	Branch, call-centre staff
	Managers	Non-marketing managers, senior executives
	Strategic partners	Supermarkets
	Customers	New/existing, potential

look only inside the industry, developing means of generating short-term growth without considering sufficiently the wider environment within which these companies operate. Table 2.1 summarizes the macro and stakeholder environments with the variables in each, providing examples.

The notion of a stakeholder environment is probably fairly new to banks and insurance companies and in the current environment may take some time to 'catch on'. Times of difficulty are also times to seize opportunities and, whilst FIs grapple with funding, risk and competition, there is a strong argument for looking afresh at the way they do business, seeking innovative and creative ideas by scanning the environment and looking to other non-financial companies to benchmark against.

Summary

- A method of analysing the macro environment is essential for financial institutions, including such factors as political, economic and socio-cultural environments and technology.
- Regulation by governments, central banks, financial authorities and other agencies has not been successful in bringing about responsible and sustainable behaviour in financial institutions.

- The micro environment can be analysed using a model developed from stakeholder theory that includes shareholders but also other stakeholders, such as managers and suppliers.
- Financial institutions are closely linked, lending and borrowing from each other. By adopting sustainable behaviours, consistently applied and practised, there is an improved chance of a longer-term view being taken.
- Marketing is generally concerned with developing strategies that have a medium- to long-term horizon; environmental scanning is central to this.

References

Brassington, F. and Pettitt, S. (2006) *Principles of Marketing*, Chelmsford, FT Prentice Hall.

Buttle, F. (1996), *Relationship Marketing: Theory and Practice*, London, Paul Chapman.

Commission of the European Communities (2007) 'Retail Financial Services in the Single Market' (Green Paper), Brussels, Commission of the European Communities.

Heffernan, S. (2005) *Modern Banking*, Chichester, John Wiley & Sons.

IBM (2008) 'No Bank is an Island', *IBM Global Business Services*, New York, Somers.

Jameson, R. (2008) 'The Blunders that Led to the Banking Crisis', *New Scientist*, 25 September, downloaded from www.newscientist.com on 2 October 2008.

Jensen, M. (2001) 'Value Maximization, Stakeholder Theory, and the Corporate Objective Function', *Journal of Applied Corporate Finance*, Vol. 14, No. 3, pp. 8–21.

Kotabe, M. and Helsen, K. (2008) *Global Marketing Management*, 4th edn, Chichester, John Wiley & Sons.

Kotler, P., Armstrong, G., Wong, V. and Saunders, J. (2008) *Principles of Marketing*, 5th European edn, Harlow, FT Prentice Hall.

Kumar, V. amd Reinartz, W. (2006), *Customer Relationsip Management: A Databased Approach*, Hoboken, NJ, John Wiley & Sons.

Tang, L. Thomas, L., Thomas, S. and Bozzetto, J.-F. (2007) 'It's the Economy, Stupid: Modelling Financial Product Purchases', *International Journal of Bank Marketing*, Vol. 25, No. 1, pp. 22–8.

Further reading

www.ukpayments.org.uk
www.guardian.co.uk
www.telegraph.co.uk/finance

www.oft.gov.uk/news/press
www.defra.org.uk
www.money.co.uk
www.nps.gov/sustain
www.hm-treasury.gov.uk/media/D/D/ec_retailfinservices_greenpaper.
   pdf
www.barclaycard-onepulse.co.uk
http://news.bbc.co.uk/player/nol/newsid_7130000/newsid_7138300/
   7138341.stm?bw=bb&mp=wm&asb=1&news=1&ms3=22&ms_java
   script=true&bbcws=2.
www.competition-commission.gov.uk
www.berr.gov.uk

Exercises

1. Consider the way that you use financial services and the way in which you embrace technology. Have you any preferences for continuing to use paper-based systems? If so, why?
2. How are the ways that you conduct your financial services influenced by your social and cultural heritage? In what way does your financial institution recognize this?
3. Prepare a brief outline of sustainable banking behaviours, as advertised on any of the banking websites, in the light of the definitions given above. How closely do the practices of the banks appear to follow the definitions?
4. What benefits are there to a financial service provider in building a relationship with a supplier? Surely, selecting by price is the best way of being competitive?

CASE STUDY

Financial services in China – a case study of the credit card

The centre of the world

China is the world's most populous country; its 1.3 billion people make up one-fifth of the world's population and it has a continuous culture stretching back nearly 4,000 years. The Han Chinese make up over 92 per cent of the population of China and, whilst there are also 55 other official ethnic groups, the dominance of the Han Chinese is reflected in their strong sense of identity about what it is to be Chinese. This is also felt by the Chinese diaspora, the 30 million Chinese who live outside mainland China. Indonesia and Thailand have the largest numbers, estimated to be between 7 and 9 million per country, whilst Singapore has the highest concentration,

3 million, or 75 per cent of its population. The Chinese people believe that China has always been a world power and, now that its economic strength is growing so fast, it wants to regain its rightful place in the world – that is, at the centre.

Prior to the so-called Opium Wars of the mid-nineteenth century, China saw itself as not just a great civilization, but also as a great power. Historians estimate that China may have accounted for almost one-third of world GDP in 1820. In fact, this figure may have been even higher during the preceding Tang, Sung and Ming dynasties. In China's view, all of this began to fall apart with the Opium Wars, when waves of foreign (i.e., western) invasions brought about China's internal political collapse and consequent economic disintegration. It began what China regards today as its century of national humiliation, from the first Opium Wars in the 1840s, through to the final expulsion of the Japanese in the 1940s, culminating in the proclamation of the People's Republic in 1949. The ambition of the Chinese since then has been to achieve wealth and power, so that China can resist 'foreign' influence and assume what they believe to be their rightful place as a leader in the international community of nations.

The reform process

It is now 30 years since China started to reform its economy and open up itself to the rest of the world. During that time it has been transformed from a poor and introspective communist backwater, to one of the world's most important economies. Thus, in April 2005, the World Trade Organization (WTO) was able to report that China had overtaken Japan, as the world's third largest exporter, following a surge in demand for Chinese-made electronic goods. With its annual economic growth rate close to 10 per cent, China has already become an economic giant.

In many respects China's development has been shaped by its geography, with most of the economic development taking place in the eastern coastal provinces, leaving the western provinces and the rural interior relatively underdeveloped. This has encouraged a great movement of population from the rural interior to the cities in the east. In 1950 the urban population represented less than 13 per cent of the total; it is now about 45 per cent and expected to reach 60 per cent by 2030. A similar shift has taken place in wealth, with the richest 20 per cent of the population now accounting for 50 per cent of consumption, while the poorest 20 per cent do not even reach 5 per cent.

To drive and channel its economic growth, China adopted the East Asian model of export-led growth. Overseas Chinese provided the expertise and connections in outsourcing manufacturing to China; the mainland Chinese people provided the savings which the state directed as investment in infrastructure to keep the export sector competitive; this virtuous circle delivered annual rises of around 10 per cent in per capita income over the last 25 years. China has relied on administrative power rather than market forces to guide the allocation of capital and as a consequence this is inefficient and prone to corruption, as demonstrated by the level of non-performing loans that reside in the banking system. The Chinese government realizes that reform is required, but China is still many years away from an independent and market-driven financial system.

When China initiated its early reforms in the late 1970s, it focused on manufacturing as the key growth driver for the economy. This has resulted in manufacturing currently having a 52 per cent share of GDP in China, compared with 15 per cent for agriculture and 33 per cent for services. Much of the investment in manufacturing was financed by the savings of the increasingly employed Chinese population. China's savings rate has increased from about 25 per cent in the mid-1960s, to 34 per cent in 1980 and around 45 per cent in 2006. Whilst the export-led drive continues fuel the growth of the manufacturing sector, the Chinese government is now attempting to also encourage domestic consumption to achieve further development of the economy. Thus, in February 2005, the Washington-based Earth Policy Institute claimed that China had overtaken the United States in the consumption of basic agricultural and industrial goods. As a country, China is now the biggest consumer of grain, meat, coal and steel; oil is the only commodity that the United States consumes more. Moreover, China is well ahead of the United States in the consumption of goods such as television sets, refrigerators and mobile phones. The official Chinese National Bureau of Statistics confirmed, in March 2008, that retail sales in China grew by 20 per cent, year on year, in January and February of that year, driven by strong consumer spending. This is the fastest growth in retail sales, since monthly data started being gathered in 1999.

Cash at the centre

How do Chinese consumers pay for their purchases? The answer at the moment is overwhelmingly with cash. China is very cash-centric and figures released by the central bank, the People's Bank of China (PBOC), in February 2005 revealed that spending in 2004 on all types of plastic payment cards (generically called bankcards) accounted for RMB 5.26 trillion, or around only 5 per cent of total retail consumer goods sales – up, however, by 2.9 per cent on the figure three years earlier. Bankcard spending in the major Chinese cities such as Beijing, Shanghai, Guangzhou and Shenzhen, was as high as 20 per cent, giving some indication of the potential for payment by plastic card in China.

One product area where foreign banks are already active in China, and where much activity is forecasted once the Chinese market is fully open, is in the plastic payment card market, particularly the credit card. China is already ranked second only to the United States in the number of plastic cards in issue, with figures from ChinaUnionPay (CUP) for the end of 2005 revealing that there were 960 million payment cards issued, 920 million of which were debit cards and the remaining 40 million credit cards, of which only 12 million were revolving credit cards. The remaining 28 million credit cards were what are known in China as 'quasi' credit cards, in that they require a secure deposit from the cardholder to be held by the card issuer. These would elsewhere be called 'secured' credit cards.

The PBOC is pushing for a much wider use of plastic payment cards to meet the needs of the mainland's developing economy. In China the relative scarcity of electronic payments is thought to have limited growth in consumer spending; this is a key concern for the Chinese economic planners as they try to shift the country away from its previous reliance on export-driven growth.

The savings culture

Savings are central to the culture of the Chinese people, as reflected by popular phrases such as 'hardworking and thrifty' and 'save first, consume later'. This culture of saving is in direct contrast to the culture of borrowing, which in China is seen as a sign that an individual is incapable of making ends meet. Spending according to your means is a prevalent ideology in China and people also tend to pay in cash, even for 'big-ticket' items, such as cars. Furthermore, with fee-paying education replacing free education in China and state-subsidized housing and health care no longer available, more Chinese will be saving, to climb the 'three mountains' that dominate Chinese culture: education of children, accommodation and medical care.

Chinese consumers prefer to borrow through 'informal' channels, such as family members, relatives and friends, either at very low or even no interest rate. Much of this type of borrowing relies on the Chinese view of relationships, often called *Guanxi*. This can be described as 'personal relationships' or 'connections' with other people and its fundamental base is created through pre-existing relationships with people from the same birth place, relatives, superiors, subordinates in the workplace and so on. Hence, in China everyone has *Guanxi* with a certain number of people and, once they belong to this social network, they perceive each other as 'insiders' and other people as 'outsiders'. This distinction between insider and outsider is very important, because insiders are seen as trustworthy and reliable and they can approach each other for favours, resources and further contacts. Also, because of a long history of mistrust between individuals, business organizations and the legal system, the Chinese prefer to use *Guanxi*, both to exchange benefits and to expand their social network. Thus, if an outsider wants to establish *Guanxi* with another network, the most effective way is to get a third-party intermediary involved to effect an introduction and thus construct a new *Guanxi* relationship.

For new entrants into the Chinese market for financial services, in this case credit card issuers, the concept of *Guanxi* presents both opportunity and challenge. The opportunity is that although relationship development with Chinese customers is complicated, it is the only way forward to obtain trust and hence repeat business – and hopefully eventually cross-sell opportunities and good referrals to other potential customers. This is because not only does such trust help retain existing customers and broaden the relationship with them, but it can also extend the relationship to that customer's own network under the concept of *Guanxi*.

The challenge for new-entrant credit card issuers, however, is how to achieve a 'critical mass' of cardholders, with whom they have no existing

Guanxi relationships. The favoured approach to date has been to form part-nerships/alliances with existing Chinese financial institutions, who already have *Guanxi* relationships with their customers, and to then use these as the third-party intermediary, to introduce their payment card products to an existing customer base. At the time of writing, however, there is an underdeveloped market for credit in China, with banks seen mainly as a place for savings, consequently lacking personal credit information, as very little borrowing takes place through the more 'formal' financial institution channels.

China has one of the (if not the) highest per capita savings rates in the world, with most families choosing a bank deposit account as a means of preserving their wealth. Other investment options are limited and most bank accounts offer very limited benefits. Bank deposits interest rates are lower than the rate of inflation and investing in the stock market is not for the risk-averse. The Chinese save for their child's education, for housing and care for elderly parents.

The average savings rate in China between the years of 1997 and 2004 was 40.3 per cent, compared to 13.6 per cent for the United States during the same time period. Partly based on this, investment in China as a per-centage of GDP was an average of 40 per cent between 1997 and 2004, largely funded by the savings of the Chinese people. PBOC statistics show that savings amounted to RMB 11.4 trillion (US$1.37 trillion) at the end of August 2004, an increase of 15.3 per cent on the previous year. According to a PBOC survey, the reasons for savings were, in order of importance: educa-tion, pension, accommodation and emergencies. These priorities stem from the culture of 'deposit first, consume later', which is very much part of life in China, and in more recent times from the fact that the state has with-drawn from providing many of the services it originally took on after the communist revolution. For example, fee-paying education has replaced free education in China and state-subsidized housing and health are no longer available in urban centres. Thus, more and more Chinese are either saving or borrowing to climb the 'three mountains'.

Target population groups

Clint Laurent, the Chief Executive of Asian Demographics, was reported in *The Australian* newspaper in October 2004 as saying that, 'even among the richest top 10 percent of Chinese households in urban areas – the emerging middle class – the average household income is still low by Western stan-dards'. His research, a major study of all China broken down into all its 31 provinces, showed that the average annual income of an urban household in China is US$3,294, while the average of the top 10 per cent of house-holds is US$10,000 a year. This top 10 per cent numbers around 17 million households and, even with a conservative economic growth rate for China of 5 per cent for the next ten years, that number will grow to 55 million households by 2013.

Such figures give some comfort to prospective credit card issuers in China, for it is from this emerging middle class that many commentators expect consumption to occur, some of which will be financed from borrowing via credit cards. Laurent also claims that consumerism is becoming increasingly accepted in China, but that the propensity to spend varies considerably by region; the average urban household still 'spends' 25 per cent of its income (RMB 7,052) on savings, as opposed to 20 per cent (RMB 5,779) on food and 15 per cent (RMB 4,230) on rent/mortgage/utilities, etc.

There are, however, some fundamental changes taking place in Chinese society which will substantially affect these spending patterns. These include the age profile of the population, with China having an ageing population as the effects of the country's one-child policy start to impact. Over the next 20 years, Laurent expects the number of Chinese under 20 to halve in absolute terms to 173 million in 2023, compared to 367 million in 2003, whilst the population overall will peak in 2014 at 1.3 billion. Indeed, some observers argue that China is facing a labour shortage, with Professor Peter McDonald, the head of demography and sociology at the Australian National University, claiming at a conference in March 2005 that fertility in Shanghai, Beijing and Tianjin had sunk to the 'extraordinary low' rate of 0.8 births per woman, probably the lowest in the world. The labour force in China is currently being augmented by a huge population movement from the rural to the urban areas. The three cities above are thought to collectively have a 'floating population' of 120 million, comprising of both men and women who are separated from their families and who live largely in dormitories. Their families mostly still live in the rural areas, as the cities lack the infrastructure to house them, even if the workers were allowed to take them there.

Professor McDonald also raised the issue of the sex rates disparity, with Chinese males outnumbering females at a rate of 120 men to 100 females, compared with a global average of 105 males. He also pointed out that, during the past 20 years, China had by contrast had a 'demographic dividend', with a large youthful labour force readily available. Now, he claims, development is being held up by a lack of workers and that the decline in fertility rates in China (and indeed in Asia generally) had been faster and further than demographers had previously believed possible.

The impact of the one-child policy over the next ten years will, according to Laurent's research, be a decline of the child sector (0–14) by 35 per cent; a decline of 17 per cent in young adults (15–24); a decline of 9 per cent in young households (25–39); but an increase of 33 per cent in older households (40–59); and a 49 per cent increase in the aged (60+). He therefore contends that the 'sweet spot' for business (and this includes credit card issuers) will be the growing number of working 'empty-nesters'. These are parents, aged 40–59, whose children, or more likely child, has left home, leaving them suddenly with larger than expected disposable incomes. The number of these 'empty-nesters' is expected to more than triple from 103 million now, to 343 million by 2025. Also, increasing numbers of young Chinese are either staying single longer and hence delaying marriage or choosing not to have children, but instead to build their careers and enjoy their dual incomes.

Certainly the growth sector in the labour force is the white-collar segment, which creates a lifestyle which can call upon the use of credit to finance consumption, particularly as these people are often better educated and have higher earnings. Laurent argues that households earning less than RMB 40,000 per annum, will still devote as much of any additional income to basic spending categories (e.g., food), as to discretionary categories (e.g., entertainment). He calculates that over the next eight years the proportion of Chinese households earning over RMB 40,000 will grow from 18.4 per cent to 35.7 per cent. In actual numbers this will mean an increase from the current 32.5 million households to 81 million households by 2012. These households spend three times as much as other lower-income households on eating out, recreation, health care and communications. Furthermore, this Chinese 'consumption class' is heavily concentrated in 11 of the 31 provinces of China, mostly along the eastern seaboard.

China is rapidly transforming itself from an exporter to a voracious consumer nation, to further fuel its rapid growth. As the new 'superpower' in Asia, China is set to join the United States as one of the main drivers of world economic growth. China's manufacturing prowess, its supply of relatively cheap labour and its currency still at what many feel is an artificially low rate result in complaints that its competitors are all handicapped in the global export market.

However, it is the Chinese consumer that will be the driving factor behind China's continuing growth, as the government is now encouraging consumption, in an attempt to give a broader base to the country's economic development. A growing middle class and increasing urbanization have sparked a change in attitudes and there is now more of a propensity to spend, rather than to save. Rapidly increasing incomes in China's coastal cities have fuelled demand for cars, homes and mobile phones and investment in property has made cities such as Shanghai expensive places to buy. The biggest spenders are in the 20–40-year-old age groups, living in the so-called 'showcase' cities.

Thus, there are opportunities for credit card issuers in China, but success will partly depend on a good understanding of who consumes in China, what they consume and how they pay for it.

Questions

1. What aspects of Chinese history, cultural and contemporary demographics would a western financial services organization need to be aware of before contemplating entry into the Chinese market for financial services?
2. If you were a western credit card issuing bank, what aspects of these Chinese attitudes towards consumption and savings would you need to consider if you were thinking of entering the Chinese market with this product?
3. How would an understanding of the concept of *Guanxi* help western financial services organizations better understand their prospects in the Chinese market?

Case further reading

'The Adoption and Usage of Credit Cards by Urban-Affluent Consumers in China', *International Journal of Bank Marketing*, Vol. 25, No. 4, 2007, pp. 238–52.

'Entering the Market for Financial Services in Transitional Economies: A Case Study of Credit Cards in China', *International Journal of Bank Marketing*, Vol. 23, No. 5, 2005, pp. 381–96.

'The Chinese Payment Card Market. An Exploratory Study', *International Journal of Bank Marketing*, Vol. 21, No. 6–7, 2003, pp. 324–34.

Professor Steve Worthington, Monash University, Australia.

3

The financial services customer

Contents

Learning outcomes

By the end of this chapter, the reader will be able to:

- Understand the importance of integration of consumer behaviour into marketing strategies

- Evaluate customer behaviour theories, both business to customer (B2C) and business to business (B2B), with reference to financial services

- Appreciate how important theories of customer satisfaction, dissatisfaction, inertia, loyalty, switching, word of mouth, risk and trust affect financial services marketing

- Develop arguments for strategies built around customer behaviour (demand-side) in the marketing of financial services

Introduction

The subject of customer behaviour is extensive and full of conflicting views and findings; nonetheless for the marketer it is a body of knowledge that must underpin every action, whether strategic or operational. The body of knowledge relating to customers considers both business to consumers (B2C) and business to business (B2B) and both are discussed in this chapter. The first part of the chapter concentrates on B2C marketing and the second part considers behaviour in B2B financial services.

It is difficult to do justice to such an extensive subject in a chapter, so we will concentrate on those aspects of customer behaviour that financial institutions (FIs) need to understand to enable them to develop appropriate strategies. Exhibit 3.1 is an example of how understanding can be achieved.

EXHIBIT 3.1

Money for nothing

The 18–34-year-old age group is the most likely (60 per cent) to have unsecured debt. The impact of the relatively new exposure to high-level student debt can be seen when comparing 22–5-year-old recent graduates with their age equivalents who did not go on to higher education. The former student group have a 10 per cent greater likelihood of being debt-averse than do their less highly educated (and possibly less debt-burdened) peers. Today, the average 18–34-year-old is carrying more than £3,200 in unsecured debt, 40 per cent more than the average adult and four times that of the over 55-year-old group. But the particularly worrying aspect of this is that amongst those in their late teens and early 20s the main reason for borrowing money is frivolous spending, with 25 per cent of 18–24-year-olds admitting that they borrowed money to buy things that they didn't really need. Both 'fledglings' (15–34s living at home with their own parents, without children of their own) and 'flown the nest' (15–34s who are unmarried but do not live with anyone defined as being their own relations) show the same comparatively strong disregard for the problems of debt, but they do so from two very different perspectives. While both are likely to be of the view that they can live now and pay later, those who have moved away from the parental home are far more likely to be faced with the commitment of paying rent or a mortgage. The consequences of debt are that much greater, as well as having become almost a way of life. Amongst the older 25–34-year-olds, buying a house is the number one reason for borrowing money. But not only are these young adults running up very high levels of unsecured debt, rising house prices have meant also that their mortgages are now some £20,000 higher than the national average. The average mortgage for 18–34-year-olds is almost £111,500, compared to the national figure of around £92,000. Many young adults have clearly adopted an easy-debt lifestyle, fuelled by cheap borrowing costs and willing lenders. But they have not necessarily ever been through the rough part of an economic cycle and have not been required to learn that a little bit of financial prudence can pay dividends. If the economy does start to turn any time soon, they really will feel the sharp end of being in debt.

Compiled by the authors from *Consumer Attitudes towards Debt*, Mintel, 2008; *Attitudes to Debt*, BMRB, 2008.

Consuming financial services

loyalty: a state in which a customer displays both a positive attitude and repeat purchase behaviour to a provider

Understanding your customers is axiomatic in marketing and there are some key aspects of customer behaviour that really impact on the financial services sector – for example, trust and **loyalty**. In order to have an overview of consumer behaviour, we will look at how consumers make decisions about the purchase of financial services and the influences on those purchases. Against the common interpretations of consumer behaviour that we shall be reviewing, there is also the notion of the 'new' consumer accompanied by or embedded in postmodernism; although the purpose of this book is not to become embroiled in philosophical debate, the postmodernist contribution to marketing has been significant.

Consumers are far more able to decode messages and, perhaps through their own experience and that of others, approach consumption situations with a higher degree of cynicism than may have been the case before. A failed instance of service recovery or indifference on the part of a provider engenders a feeling that they matter little. Asymmetry of information (where the financial service provider understands the offering, including its terms and conditions, better than the customer, but does not attempt to redress that imbalance) undermines trust in any relationship. Transparency in the contract, exchange or relationship is something that the contemporary consumer expects and experiences cynicism where it is lacking. Generally, consumers today are more knowledgeable about financial services than they have been in the past, although the complexity of many of the products – such as pensions, annuities and other investment offerings – serve as a examples of financial service providers making little attempt to simplify matters for their customers.

Taking decisions

Traditional models of consumer behaviour assume a rational and logical approach to decision-making and usually consist of five stages in the process (see Table 3.1), depicting the consumer as an information processor and problem-solver.

The first stage of the process is recognizing that there is a problem. The problem may range from the legal requirement to insure a motor car, the need to obtain foreign currency or a lack of cash to pay for a can of baked beans. Once the problem has been recognized, then a means of addressing that problem needs to identified, which means that consumers undertake some form of information search. Many of us now resort to the Internet at this point, to access the extensive choice of money advice websites (see www.fool.co.uk for an example). It would seem an obvious move for financial service companies to ensure that they are represented on these websites so that they become part of the

Table 3.1   Stages in consumer decision-making for a personal loan

Stage in decision-making	Situation
Need recognition	Car fails MOT so badly that repair bills exceed what the car is worth. You have no money to replace it.
Search	Check your bank loan rates, ask parents, note supermarket loan rates while shopping, check with friends, classmates for loan opportunities
Pre-purchase evaluation	Three choices: existing bank loan – not particularly good rate supermarket loan attractive rate but borrowing money from supermarket a bit weird loan from parents but has 'strings', also want to demonstrate independence
Purchase/consumption	Choose supermarket loan, best rate and why not? Sign agreement and repayment arrangements
Post-purchase evaluation	Seem to have got a good rate when chatting to colleagues and seeing adverts from competing loan suppliers. As to the car, well that's a different story. How bound up are these two 'purchases'?

evoked set: a set of products already in the memory of the customer which are under active consideration in the choice process

evoked set or set of alternatives that consumers arrive at at the end of this stage; but this is not always the case (see the Exhibit 3.2 below). Research conducted by the Financial Services Authority (Financial Services Consumer Panel 2006) also shows that consumers take advice from an extensive range of sources, such as newspaper articles, specialist publications, information picked up in a branch, broker recommendations or direct mail.

EXHIBIT 3.2

Direct Line

Direct Line has attacked price comparison websites and does not promote itself via these sites. The core of the argument is that these websites are not comprehensive and do not survey the whole market. They often feature just a select set of providers. The information that the sites offer is biased by commercial considerations; for example, some sites prioritize the results of the providers who pay them the highest commission rates and others refuse to list providers who do not pay them commission. The choice that a consumer is presented with may have little to do with the best product for them but instead represents the nature of the relationship between the price comparison site and the financial services company. These sites also focus on a single attribute – that of price; do they compare like with like. Consider the complexities of comparing packages across the details – for example, excess, replacement vehicle, breakdown cover and legal/administrative support. Is price the most important element in choosing a financial service? The consumer is really looking for a product that offers them the benefits that they seek and this will vary. Also, they may require advice in making the decision, which, as yet, is not available on these sites.

Compiled by the authors from *Marketing Week*, 28 June 2007.

After the information search, the consumer will form a set of possibilities, at which point he/she will weigh them up. These possibilities are known as an 'evoked set', and in financial services could consist of about three possible choices, as these services are quite hard to evaluate owing to their intangibility and complexity. The evaluation will be affected by previous experience, such as satisfaction, word of mouth and family patterns. Financial service providers would very much like consumers to be influenced by the brand, but financial service brands are not as strong in decision-making as FIs would like (O'Loughlin and Szmigin 2007).

Family patterns of financial behaviour are quite strong and banks are aware that parents have an influence on the choice of bank for their children. Having evaluated the information, the consumer makes a decision and purchases/chooses the product. The final stage is after the purchase, when the consumer then considers whether the purchase provides the benefit that they sought. In financial services this is not always easy, as the benefits of the service may be far from immediate. Consider, for example, a pension, when the benefits of a pension – that is, the income – are not experienced for decades and often when it is too late for any changes to be made. The benefits of insurance policies are often only experienced when the accident/mishap/disaster occurs, at which time help, support or money that the consumer requires can be held up by inefficient systems in the insurance companies themselves. It is at this stage that satisfaction and word-of-mouth play an important role in the choice of other customers.

The model that has been discussed above is often referred to as the cognitive model but there are other models of consumer choice that have been summarized by East *et al.* (2008). The reinforcement model, for example, postulates that purchases are made as a result of learned behaviour – when a consumer has a positive experience, they will repeat that experience. A negative experience tends to result in that behaviour not being repeated. A reinforcing experience will increase the frequency of a consumer's responses, which, in the case of financial services, could mean that the consumer purchases more from that FI. A punishing experience has the opposite effect and reduces the rate of response. The message for FIs is unequivocal – to ensure that customers have positive experiences with their purchase and consumption! Building societies were and, in many cases, are still proud of the way that their staff interact with their customers in branches, often providing a personalized service over a period of years and ensuring continuous positive experiences. However, as these societies expand to reach new markets out of their former 'heartland', this level of personalized service is less easy to maintain, so these reinforcing stimuli are lost. In the absence of reinforcing stimuli, the consumer will eventually lose any preference for the provider and look afresh at the marketplace, seeking competitive rates. The society will therefore have to compete on price, as do its competitors.

Consumers will often rely on habit for purchases in that they buy the same brands or visit the same outlet (physical or virtual). A habit is recurring behaviour on encountering a particular stimulus (East *et al.* 2008) – for example, visiting a particular ATM when running out of cash. Banks have been quick to realize the potential for using ATMs to market messages that build on consumer habit. Existing providers want to discourage consumers from the lengthy decision-making process, as they might find competitor offers more enticing, and will try to instil habitual behaviour. From the consumer's perspective, of course, the time and effort dedicated to a thorough evaluation of the alternatives is not always regarded with delight, so the consumer is equally happy to take advantage of any shortcuts that might be offered by providers. FIs may do this through making it easy to renew insurance, direct mailings and, of course, branding. Consumers do review their habitual behaviour, especially when the outcome is particularly good or bad, but habit restricts consumers' openness to trying new experiences; some consumers will remain unaware of the advantages or better deals that competitors may offer.

Decision-making units

Individuals often refer to friends, colleagues or family when deliberating about financial services; decisions are rarely arrived at without an element of consultation. FIs are aware of this, particularly the power of the family. A typical decision-making unit might consist of five different roles. Each role can be performed by a group of people or an individual; two or more roles can be shared by one individual or a group, as follows:

- The initiator recognizes that there is a problem or a need to be addressed
- The influencer is someone (or more than one person), perhaps with relevant experience or expertise, to whom the decision-maker refers whilst arriving at the decision
- The user is the person who will be using the service, who is not necessarily the decision-maker – for example, when purchasing insurance for a new driver
- The gatekeeper may be someone who limits access to a number of possible providers
- The decision-maker is the person or group who makes the final choice.

It is important for financial service providers to recognize that they can play more than one role in the choosing process; they can then structure buying situations and marketing messages accordingly. The role of the influencer in services is particularly important; positive word-of-mouth can be pivotal in gaining custom. Decision-making units (DMUs) are common in B2B situations as well; a model of decision-making in business behaviour is given later in the chapter.

Alternative perspectives on consumption

Although the models of consumer decision-making discussed above frequently appear in textbooks and academic publications, it is important to note that there are alternative views about the way that consumers behave which may shed light on the way that financial services are consumed. The particular danger for marketers is an interpretation of the models that promote the view that consumers can be managed or manipulated with an appropriate 'mix' of marketing activities. A view of consumers that is embedded in a postmodernist view has influenced a number of writers in marketing, balancing, to some extent, the rational explanations of contemporary consumption. Postmodernism promotes the primacy of the individual, accompanied by ephemerality and plurality in society – in particular, growing multiculturalism and multi-ethnicity (Dawes and Brown 2000). The dynamism inherent in postmodern thought has led to fragmentation of markets, at the creation of volatile tribes as apposed to stable segments. (Aubert-Gamet and Cova 1999).

Tribes, rather than segments, are key in understanding alternative perspectives in consumer behaviour or consumption, as tribal members interact socially and form communities (Cova and Cova 2001). The heterogeneity of the marketplace has brought about a proliferation of products (Brown 1995) and heightened the power of the consumer in the exchange process; a significant characteristic of the postmodern individual is that he or she avoids commitment. In commercial terms, for example, where the modernist customer may have been assumed to be loyal to a firm or a product, the postmodernist consumer exercises freedom to move where choice or whim indicates. Not only do consumers possess multiple lifestyles and often highly incompatible value systems, these lifestyles are often at odds with existing business and marketing strategies, founded on the modernist values of orderliness and consistency (Brown 1995). Postmodernism places the consumer at the heart of the production process, and points to the 'mercurial' consumer (Firat and Venkatesh 1993). The following table provides some idea of how a consumer's characteristics or attributes drive the kind of experience that they might seek from a financial service experience and shows how the attributes or qualities of the postmodern consumer, such as being time-poor, influence what they seek from their customer experience. The time-poor consumer seeks an experience that is relevant to them and does not want to spend a scarce resource, that is their time, in an experience, which they see as being irrelevant. For FIs, it is important to recognize the time-poor consumer and to offer relevant products which are easy to understand and which can be readily customized to meet a range of needs.

As the table suggests, the 'new' consumer might be seeking something quite different from their financial services experience than other models of consumer behaviour might suggest. For example, do we recognize the cynical consumer? How can FIs address the consumer's desired experience for integrity/honesty? There are some suggestions in the final column as FIs move from a mass-market orientation to acknowledging the power of the consumer

Table 3.2   Consumers and the experience that they seek

Consumer attributes	Desired consumer experience	Financial service implication
Cynical	Integrity, honesty, transparency	Corporate image, sustainable and ethical practices
Knowledgeable	Meaningfulness, appropriateness	Fitting their lifestyle, needs, fit-for-purpose
Time-poor	Relevance, convenience	Customer-driven product development, customization
Tribal	Tribal validation, i.e. in tune with affiliation groups	Awareness and some understanding of tribes or segments
Individual	Customization	Individualizing the experience, not just selling
Demanding-ness	Excellence in expectation	Recognizing that one size does not fit all
Experience-seeking	Participation, co-creation of value	Acknowledging and harnessing the consumer in the service experience, value co-creation

Source: Adapted from Stuart-Menteth *et al.* (2006).

as an individual. The implications of a postmodern view of the consumer are profound for FIs, which tend to be large, structured and not always consumer-oriented organizations. How quickly can they respond to the dynamism of the postmodern society; do they even view it as important or of significance?

Risk

risk: refers to a perception that a product or the non-purchase of a product may have negative outcomes

The intangibility of financial services debated earlier creates problems for consumers in making evaluations prior to consumption. The way consumers perceive **risk** in the consumption of financial services and whether they trust FIs are therefore important considerations in their marketing. One particular problem that occurs with services is that, unlike goods, consumers are unable to find out how the product performs in advance. For example, consumers can try on clothes or test drive a car and, in the worst cases, the customer can return a good. Most goods consist of attributes or characteristics that can be evaluated in advance of the purchase, such as colour, fit and performance; these are known as *search* qualities. Services generally do not have these characteristics, so providers of services offer cues that give some indication of the performance/quality/fitness for purpose of the service, which can be tied to the price or the promises of the brand. Consumers have to use other indicators to try to decide on whether this service is going to be satisfactory – one of these is experiencing the service. *Experience* qualities are those aspects of a service that are assessed during the actual consumption of a service – for example, going to the theatre, eating out or going to a theme park. Marketers can also respond to a customer's desire to have some prior experience of the service by offering a trial period. Health clubs are particularly good at this. Some FIs have also offered a trial, such Alliance & Leicester's offer to new businesses of two years' free banking. This trial may also encourage customers to switch, so it is also about gaining new customers!

FIs also need to ensure that the customer experience is such that the customer is willing to repurchase or purchase more. There are some services that do not lend themselves to trial or experience, where a decision to purchase a service is based on a belief that the purchase meets the needs of the customer and/or in the ability of the provider to perform the service for the customer. This is known as a *credence* service. Examples of credence services are the more complex offerings that may have a long-term element in terms of benefits, such as investment services and, particularly, pensions. Belief in an FI's ability to deliver the benefits may be derived from the brand, a relationship or some faith in the expertise on the part of the seller. Independent financial advisers (IFAs) are frequently viewed as repositories of such expertise. IFAs set out to build good levels of communication with the client so that he/she understands his/her role in the consumption process. With this rapport established, both IFA and client can contribute to the co-creation of the service (Auh *et al.* 2007), with an increased likelihood, therefore, of that service meeting expectations.

By understanding the levels of risk that customers perceive in the consumption of financial services, FIs can develop measures that can lower these perceived levels. Palmer (2008) suggests a number of measures that any service provider can use to achieve this. Tangible cues or evidence reassure customers about the reliability and trustworthiness of the provider; for FIs this could consist of welcoming branches, staff uniforms, a user-friendly website and informative advertisements without small print. The level of risk will depend upon the level of **involvement** in the offering, with long-term investment and pensions carrying higher levels of risk than car insurance. First-time buyers will perceive higher levels of risk than experienced consumers; by identifying these purchasers, providers can address risk perceptions. Customers

involvement: a process in which a consumer will process information regarding a product/provider

vary significantly in their willingness to take risks. Some customers are risk-averse; they want a safe investment product and are prepared to receive a lower rate of return accordingly. Other consumers are at the other end of the spectrum and are comfortable with risk. These customers will go for higher rewards, knowing that this choice may mean a loss. Safeguards, provided either by the institution or by an independent body such as the UK FSA, can lower levels of perceived risk.

An interesting outcome of the credit crunch is the rise in the number of high-denomination notes in circulation. European banks issued €30 billion of cash in the autumn of 2008, which is the largest jump since 2004. In the United Kingdom, security firms observed that they processed higher volumes of cash, as consumers use cash for purchases and payments in spite of an overall drop in retail turnover. The number of £50 notes in circulation rose 20 per cent during 2008 (*The Observer*, 2 November 2008).

Customers' perception of risk has also been lowered by government ownership of failed FIs. In the case of Northern Rock, customers initially were desperate to get their money out of the bank and formed long queues at branches to do this. After the intervention of UK government in Northern Rock, money flowed in, as the FI was now seen as being very low risk.

Involvement

In deciding about financial services, a customer's level of involvement in the purchase is a major consideration as it reflects the amount of effort that he/she will put into the purchase; it will, of course, vary from one individual to another – for example, a cognitive miser is someone who is disinclined to expend effort on processing information. Involvement can, therefore, be interpreted as the motivation to process the information required to satisfy needs, including such dimensions as interest, pleasure, situation and risk. Although risk and situation apply in financial services, interest and pleasure are less obvious (Howcroft *et al.* 2007), suggesting that involvement research may need to consider financial services as a distinct category. There are two principal issues about involvement that impact on financial services marketing. First, from a product perspective, it is important to understand that the offerings probably follow an involvement continuum, ranging from high to low in the mind of the customer. A study tested two involvement scales with eight financial services: but the scales indicated different levels of involvement in the eight financial services, although mortgages and investments were found to be high-involvement services with both scales (Aldlaigan and Buttle 2001).

The second consideration is the effort that consumers and buyers will expend in ensuring that they are well informed about their choice. A UK study identified six clusters of customers across four financial product categories of varying complexity (Howcroft *et al.* 2007). The largest cluster of 'repeat passive customers' was characterized by an unwillingness to switch, a low level of confidence and relatively low levels of knowledge and understanding, as well as uncertainty when selecting financial products. These studies tend to confirm the view that involvement is important in the consumption of financial services, but that as a construct it is hard to measure and challenging for FIs to address in their marketing.

Satisfaction and dissatisfaction

Achieving customer satisfaction is a prime goal of marketing and of all organizations, whether commercial or non-profit making, supplying goods or services. Without customer satisfaction, it is widely argued, customers will eventually seek alternative offers from other providers. Although, definitions of satisfaction vary, the consensus is that the concept of satisfaction implies the presence of a goal that the consumer wants to achieve; that is, they seek to be satisfied by the service or product that they are consuming. Consequently, most organizations undertake significant research to discover how satisfied their customers are on a continuous basis; this includes FIs. Research into satisfaction with bank, credit card and investment websites in the United States (Forbes 2008) leads to positive results linking it to future activity in the following ways:

switching: occurs when customers change from one provider to another, often to obtain better prices or services

- Loyalty: bank customers are significantly more likely to continue to use the bank's services, rather than **switching** to the competition, when compared to customers of credit card and investment companies. 'Likelihood to continue to use company's services' quantifies the role of the Web in fostering overall loyalty to the institution. The role of satisfaction in customer loyalty is stronger than any costs incurred in switching, reinforcing the need for banks to achieve high levels of satisfaction (Beerli *et al.* 2004)
- Share of wallet: customers of banks and investment firms are much more likely than credit card customers to purchase additional services.
- Word of mouth: bank customers have the highest likelihood to tell friends, family and colleagues about both the bank and the website. Word of mouth is an important and low-cost means of customer acquisition for financial services organizations.

- Cost efficiencies: as financial institutions strive to encourage use of the cost-efficient and convenient Web channel, banks are doing slightly better than investment firms, which slightly outperform credit card websites in this area.

These are compelling arguments that drive FIs to gain a better understanding of how to obtain high levels of customer satisfaction; this involves an academic conceptualization of satisfaction. In Figure 3.1, a model or conceptualization of customer satisfaction is offered that fits the situation in financial services.

This model more usually applies to routine situations such as consumption of an insurance product, as suggested. Low levels of discontent may be experienced when negative expectations are met, such as long queues in branches or on the phone, errors with changes of address or other routine information. The customer is unlikely to complain about the problem, being more likely to exhibit **inertia**. It is only when questioned that consumers reveal their discontent (East *et al.* 2008).

inertia: a consumer state in which choices are made from habit and a lack of motivation to find an alternative product/provider

The range of financial services and the extent of the situations that a consumer may encounter suggest that a more elaborate version of customer satisfaction could also be considered within the financial services literature. Where contact between the provider and the customer may be higher and customized solutions required, a more complex understanding of customer satisfaction may emerge. The most common component of evaluation for the customer is previous experience. Customers are satisfied when their purchase results exceed their expectations; each experience leads to an evaluation and an accompanying emotional reaction by the customer (Molina *et al.* 2007).

Satisfaction may also be attributed to different dimensions, such as satisfaction with front-line employees, the core service or the organization in general (Lewis and Soureli 2006). Customer satisfaction is not only based on the judgement of customers regarding the reliability of the delivered

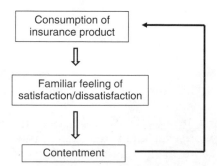

Figure 3.1 Confirmation model of customer satisfaction: meeting expectations
Source: Adapted from East *et al.* (2008).

service, but also on the customers' experiences with the service delivery process, which may be affected by demographic differences (Jamal and Naser 2002). This type of situation is unlikely to result in the customer leaving the provider, but will probably mean that this customer is not profitable for the FI and, indeed, may be a cost. Disconfirmation is an important concept in marketing theory as it refers to the psychological interpretation of an expectation–performance discrepancy (Oliver 1997).

This model is more elaborate than the previous one but draws attention to the perception/expectation approach to service quality. In this model, FIs manage the expectations of their customers particularly with reference to the products that they sell. For example, it is essential that banks communicate clearly regarding the features of their products so that customers can have realistic expectations of what the performance of the product might be. Before going abroad, whether on business or for a holiday, customers usually take out holiday insurance, which might consist of a number of features – such as cover for personal goods, personal liability and missed departure. The customer expects that if baggage is lost in transit the insurance company will cover the cost of the lost baggage. What often happens is that the airline and the insurance company argue about who should pay for the lost baggage; the customer, in the meantime, remains out of pocket. As the insurance company did not pay out or delayed paying out, the consumer has had a poor experience and *attributes* (see Figure 3.2) this poor experience to neglect on the part of the insurance company. It is likely that the customer will avoid this company

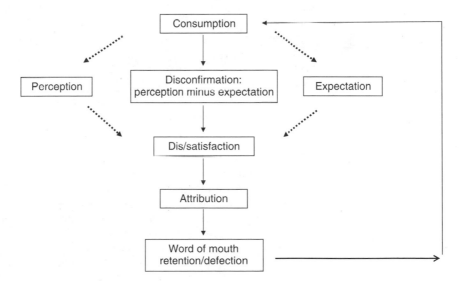

Figure 3.2 Disconfirmation model: exceeding or falling short of expectations
Source: Adapted from East *et al.* (2008).

in the future and any word-of-mouth (WOM) will be negative. The link portrayed in Figure 3.2 between customer satisfaction, WOM and retention or defection is not necessarily as straightforward as one might think. Probably the most sensible way of looking at this link is to consider satisfaction as a necessary but not sufficient condition for customer retention. Dissatisfaction does not necessarily lead to defection, but dissatisfaction is a powerful state, which can lead to highly negative actions on the part of the consumer.

How can FIs satisfy their customers? To achieve this, they must first discover how satisfied their customers are currently, which can be done by survey or by continuous measurement systems. The prompts in Table 3.3 seek to find out the major causes of dissatisfaction with a financial services call centre.

satisfaction: an outcome in which customer expectations of a product/experience are met

The second step is to analyse the causes of customer **satisfaction** and dissatisfaction – for example, why are customers being kept on hold for too long? The answer may be that the call centre, at certain times, is short-staffed; one response might be to take on more staff so that customer dissatisfaction levels for that particular complaint are reduced. Staff may also appreciate that customers are less grumpy when they do finally get through and so are able to process the matter more efficiently and pleasantly, thus leading to higher levels of employee satisfaction, which, in turn, leads to more satisfying service encounters. A more common response from FI call centres appears to be to ask customers to phone at less busy times, which is not going to lead to customer satisfaction.

Table 3.3   Questions to uncover levels of dissatisfaction with a call centre

- Being kept on hold too long
- Having to repeat information to multiple representatives
- Representatives' lack of the answers I need
- Representatives' trying to sell me other products and services
- Representatives' inflexibility
- Representatives' slowness in responding
- Representatives are not personable
- Representatives do not offer customized solutions
- Customer service computers are often down
- Representatives ask for too much personal information
- Representatives ask too many questions
- Representatives create too much paperwork
- Representatives have poor command of English/heavy accents

Source: Adapted from Accenture 2008.

From a theoretical perspective, it is important to note that satisfaction and dissatisfaction are not directly related; that is, what satisfies customers is not the same thing poorly done that dissatisfies them. For example, if a customer has to queue for a service – either on the phone, in a branch or for an ATM – they often feel dissatisfied, whereas not having to queue does not necessarily lead to satisfaction. Queuing for too long is considered to be a 'dissatisfier'. Satisfiers are those elements of a service that have the ability to bring about satisfaction, such as a well-performing savings account or a speedily handled insurance claim. An FI must identify both satisfiers and dissatisfiers in their institution and develop strategic plans to promote the former and eliminate the latter. To bring about meaningful customer satisfaction, action has to be taken at the highest level in the organization and plans for monitoring and looking for ways of increasing satisfaction have to be in place. The key is to engender a climate in which staff and systems are enabled to satisfy customers; changes in reporting structures, behaviour and priorities of senior staff, reward systems, key performance indicators (KPIs) and staff development may be called for, to cite but a few. Customer satisfaction, however, is not static; customers' expectations increase – what they might have tolerated last year, this year they may find unacceptable. Customer satisfaction can contribute to customer loyalty and, although the connection between these two concepts is not clear cut (see Oliver 1999), customers are unlikely to be loyal, as distinct from inert, without feelings of satisfaction.

Customer loyalty

The precise nature of the interaction between customer satisfaction and loyalty is notoriously elusive, but satisfaction appears to have a positive effect on service loyalty (Bloemer *et al.* 1999). Satisfaction can be transformed into loyalty given appropriate cultivation (Oliver 1999). As part of developing long-term relationships with customers, organizations are increasingly concerned with loyal customers who, it has been asserted, contribute to increased revenues, make further purchases and generate positive word-of-mouth. Loyalty emerges from studies as being the dominant, significant and direct determinant of repurchase intentions (e.g., Bell and Eisingerich 2007). Advocacy, or positive word-of-mouth, has been positively associated with loyalty (and a powerful influence on the behaviour of others (Gremler and Brown 1999).

In a seminal contribution to the loyalty literature, Dick and Basu (1994) conceptualize four different types of loyalty that depend upon the interaction between two components of relative attitude and intention to

		Intention to repurchase	
		High	Low
Relative attitude	High	Loyalty - long-term relationship with multiple products, an advocate of the provider	Latent loyalty - occasional contact with existing provider to enquire about a product
	Low	Spurious loyalty - inertia and/or propensity to switch. Susceptible to price changes and competitor offerings	No loyalty - could switch, may only be restricted by high switching costs. Inert

Figure 3.3 Loyalty states and financial services customers
Source: Adapted from Dick and Basu (1994).

repurchase (see Figure 3.3). In this model, the loyalty of a consumer is determined by the strength of the relationship between attitude and behaviour; true loyalty only ensues when levels of both relative attitude and intention to purchase are high. The remaining loyalty types are *no loyalty*, where both relative attitude and intention to repurchase are low; *latent loyalty*, where attitude is high but intention to purchase is low; and *spurious loyalty*, which is based on behaviour only. Spurious loyalty is similar to customer inertia, which is discussed below. Behavioural measures are usually used to gauge consumer loyalty, as they are easily collected – for example, the number of purchases made, frequency of visits or access. Behavioural loyalty does not provide a complete picture of loyalty nor is behaviour necessarily a predictor of profitability (Kumar and Shah 2004). The other dimension of loyalty is attitude, but its measurement within a customer base is challenging. As a pragmatic solution to this problem, customer recommendation plays a useful role in loyalty research and recommendation or positive word-of-mouth has been linked to repurchase decisions as an indicator of strengthened relative attitude (Reinartz and Kumar 2000). Figure 3.3 maps financial services loyalty descriptors onto the model proposed by Dick and Basu (1994).

To build true loyalty, cultivating attitudinal loyalty is therefore an organizational imperative. Looking at Figure 3.3, the obvious target for that cultivation is the spuriously loyal customer, with whom the institution should seek to build a relationship over time (Kumar and Shah 2004). Overall, loyalty can be sustained by leveraging information from the FI information systems with the use of cutting-edge analytics so that individual customer differences can be identified. Reward schemes that are relevant and of value to customers can be subsequently developed, possibly in partnership with other companies (see www.nectar.com for an example).

Customer switching and inertia

If customers are persistently or deeply dissatisfied, where there is a repeated gap between expectations and perceptions, they may switch or defect from one FI to another. Switching occurs when a customer changes the provider of the service that they currently consume – for example, changing car insurer at the time of renewal because an Internet search has indicated that the current insurer is too expensive or has provided poor service. Switching providers in financial services is a relatively new phenomenon; the sector has traditionally experienced high levels of customer inertia – customers who have not switched providers but who may not be satisfied customers. However, switching is increasing and FIs are continually trying to 'poach' customers who appear to have the potential to be profitable from their business rivals. Given the levels of dissatisfaction that customers seem to experience with their FIs, it seems a little odd that customers do not switch more often. This may be because they perceive barriers to switching, including cognitive and emotional costs. If the customer switched to a competitor, those social or special benefits would be lost, which might even offset sources of dissatisfaction. There may be uncertainty about the consequences of switching and whether it could prove to be adverse. These risks might be related to financial issues (for example, loss of investment in a collapsed bank or pension fund) or related to loss of time or convenience (for example, access to service outlet has become easy and tied into other habitual behaviours).

It is important to note that just because a customer does not defect, it may not indicate that they are satisfied or even loyal; they may perceive that the switching costs as too high. A dissatisfied customer, who does not defect or switch, is not necessarily beneficial for a bank or financial service provider, as these customers may generate high costs in terms of frequent complaints and high levels of 'maintenance', with relatively low levels of revenue. Alliance & Leicester's offer of free banking (www.alliance-leicestercommercialbank.co.uk) not only begins to address experience qualities of services, but, perhaps less altruistically, also relies on the inertia of bank customers. Inertia is most prevalent in the case of current accounts, both with business and personal customers. What the FI will seek to create is a 'stickiness', or exit barrier, between it and its customers. These barriers do not generate loyalty in the same way customer satisfaction does (Beerli *et al.* 2004).

Inertia has been described as passive service patronage, without true loyalty, but at the same time not exhibiting a readiness to make the effort to switch (Huang and Yu 1999). Although the behaviour between brand loyalty and inertia may be similar, that is, continued repurchase, the difference between the two states is captured in Figure 3.3, where the missing component is a favourable attitude. Inertia can result in repeat purchasing being susceptible to marketing activities, such as marketing communications and pricing adjustments. Inertia is unstable in that it can change at any time with little forewarning; marketers cannot rely on inert customers continuing to repurchase. Complaining behaviour was not a significant indicator of inertia, with cheque-holder customers complaining less than other account types in an Australian study (White and Yanamandram 2004), but the closure of bank branches was. The study also identified a group who they labelled 'dwellers', who were customers who opened new accounts but did not close old ones; the underlying suggestion is that this group did not have a good relationship with FIs in general and that they felt that they were all the same. Older respondents in this study were less likely to have changed their account in the last five years, but people that earnt more were more likely to change. The implications of these findings is that the highly desirable, wealthier segments (or high net worth) may be difficult for FIs to retain, or they may be multibanked (i.e. have a number of different financial service providers). It would be a mistake to assume that the inert are a homogeneous customer group. Three groups of inert customers were identified in the study: customers who are happily inert; those unwittingly inert; and a final group of concerned inert (White and Yanamandram 2004), who might be considered 'at risk', that is likely to switch or defect.

Persistency

An area of particular concern to governments is why customers stop paying into long-term investment instruments such as pensions and annuities. Both of these instruments are part of planning for after-work provision, which could be retirement or choosing a different lifestyle. Paradoxically, financial service consumers are showing a lack of inclination to continue to pay into this type of product, which means that they may have insufficient funds to support them post-work life, even when this period is lengthening considerably. This lack of provision has considerable implications for government, which may in due course have to make provision for poor older citizens. The exhibit below presents some of the key findings regarding the phenomenon of persistency that policy-makers will have to overcome if poverty in later life is to be alleviated.

EXHIBIT 3.3

Personal characteristics in persistency

The FSA (2004) analysed persistency and regular premium personal pensions and found that individuals in the lowest earnings band have the lowest persistency. Worsening financial circumstances have a significant and positive effect on the likelihood of lapsing. In around 40 per cent of cases, income and affordability issues were the single most important reason for lapsing. These reasons break down as follows:

- For 15 per cent of lapsers, a change in work/employment/income circumstances
- For 14 per cent, they could not afford to continue
- 7 per cent wanted to free up money to spend on other things.

Changes in personal circumstances – which had implications for income – were the single most important reason for lapsing, issues such as change in marital status, family circumstances, or moving home affecting around 10 per cent of cases. Unemployment significantly increases the probability of surrendering, as does the arrival of a new baby or changing to a job with an employer pension. People who are not saving regularly elsewhere are more likely to lapse their pension savings. Low persistency for low-income people may be because they are more likely to experience negative life events and are less likely to be able to cope with them. There is a profile of the 'lapsing consumer', with women having lower persistency than men, as they earn less and are more vulnerable to income changes. In addition, taking a career break to have children has a significant impact on income.

Adapted by the authors from material supplied by 'Understanding Switching: A Consumer Survey-based Approach to Switching and Persistency for Pensions and Investments'.

Consumer behaviour not only has significance for marketing in financial institutions, it is also relevant for government. It would appear from this particular example that if consumers do not understand a complex and expensive product with long-term benefits, there may be problems in keeping up payments. Although the problem is far from being solved, this study into the behaviour of consumers has drawn attention to particular reasons why payments into these vehicles are not continued.

Business behaviour

In the United Kingdom, four large banks – Barclays, HSBC, Lloyds TSB and Royal Bank of Scotland – controlled 85 per cent of small business accounts (news.bbc.co.uk, 2007). These accounts share similar levels of inertia to consumers in financial services. There are other similarities between consumer and business behaviour in financial services, such as loyalty and risk, as shown in Exhibit 3.4.

EXHIBIT 3.4

Findings from a survey on small businesses and their banks

The six most frequently used banks by small businesses are, in order: NatWest, HSBC, Lloyds TSB, Barclays, Co-operative Bank and the Royal Bank of Scotland. The relatively high market share of the Co-operative Bank among Federation of Small Businesses (FSB) members may be due to the availability of preferential banking services for FSB members.

Number of banks used

Seventy-nine per cent of respondents used only one bank to run their business, and fewer than 3 per cent of respondents used more than two banks. This replicates the findings of the Competition Commission that small businesses do not spread their banking services, preferring instead to use only one bank.

Bank loyalty

The majority of small businesses have no wish to switch banks, preferring to stay with the one they know, but this very much depends on the personal relationship built up between the business and the bank. When things go wrong, a business will normally try to find an alternative bank. However, given the difficulties encountered when changing banks, and the timescales involved, small businesses often do not have the time or the resources to seek alternatives. Better levels of service and a greater understanding of the individual needs of a business by the bank are needed. The better the relationship with the local bank, the more likely it is that problems are solved satisfactorily at the local level.

Small businesses' experience of their banks

Key findings from a FSB survey show that small businesses:

- tend to bank with one of the four main clearing banks
- are unlikely to use a smaller bank
- tend to do all their banking with one institution that is near their main place of business
- require regular contact with their bank, frequently contacting and visiting their local bank branch for their banking needs
- prefer to be able to have one point of contact at their bank that has knowledge of their account and the banking needs of their business
- are generally satisfied with the overall quality of their banking services
- find that where problems are encountered, they can often affect the overall performance of the business.

Small businesses are, on the whole, reasonably happy with the quality of their business banking services and experience relatively few problems with the service in general. Encountering problems with the bank can be very detrimental to a business. Small businesses find it difficult to bring problems to the attention of the bank or challenge the bank, which deters some from mentioning the problems in the first place. Many respondents felt that they were not taken seriously by bank staff and were not given access to an appropriate level of authority. The time taken by this and its impact on the day-to day running of the business often discourage small business owners from pursuing complaints. Many small businesses feel that their bank charges are too high and are on the increase, an issue that causes resentment, particularly when personal customers receive their banking free. Although FSB members do have access to free banking, this can often be accessed only under certain conditions, such as having to keep a minimum amount in their current account in order to be given this option. Few small businesses are keen to switch banks, as they often hold an account with a bank based on their ability to access banking services at their own convenience. If they do decide to switch and attempt to do so, they often encounter excessive delays and problems so severe that they can be dissuaded from completing the switch. Additionally, the perceived difficulties in switching accounts can discourage small businesses from even attempting to do it in the first place, even if they are dissatisfied with their current provider.

Adapted by the authors from Federation of Small Businesses: Report on Small Business Banking, 2007.

Similarities between consumers and businesses, at least small ones, also exist with the decision-making unit, as shown in Figure 3.4.

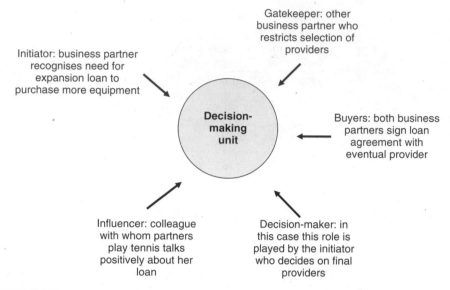

Figure 3.4 Decision-making unit in a small business for an expansion loan
Source: Adapted from Brassington and Pettitt (2006).

Decision-making units occur in consumer marketing, as stated earlier in the chapter. Figure 3.4 shows how a DMU may work in a small business for an expansion of business loan, with similar roles as in the B2C situation. This figure shows how the two partners in the small business arrive at a decision about which institution to borrow money from to allow them to expand. From the side of the financial services provider, it is important to understand the differing roles in a DMU; they can then develop strategies accordingly. The influencer, for example, was able to speak positively about her loan experience. If the loan and the experience of the loan is a satisfactory one, then the provider could be in a strong position to provide further financial services.

Larger businesses display a different set of behaviours, where increased resourcing may result in a more informed approach to the purchase and consumption of financial services. Brassington and Pettitt (2006) suggest that there are a number of criteria that might influence the choice of a supplier, which may also fit for financial institutions. Businesses as consumers are advised to 'shop around' for the best prices for the services, although bundling of services does not make it easy for customers to be able to make comparisons. Businesses will want to know if the products that the FI offers are the most suitable for the needs of the business, which will in all likelihood change over a period of time. Since time is money, it is important for the business to know that any problems will be speedily rectified by the FI, so customer service and service quality need to meet any promises made. There are non-economic factors that might influence the choice of provider, such as prestige – for example, banking with one of private banks, such as Coutts (part of the RBS group). A relationship or friendship between purchaser and supplier may also be an influence in the choice, although there may be ethical issues arising if friendship dominates the final choice.

The study of customer behaviour, both in B2C and B2B markets, is even more important post-credit crunch, as customers have lost trust in FIs and have become even more cynical about the sector as a whole. A good understanding of customer behaviour is indispensable for FI marketers in developing strategies.

Summary

- This chapter discusses customer in financial services, whether B2C or B2B.
- Customers can use rational models of decision-making in selecting financial services, with decision-making units often playing a role. Non-rational models have been suggested by postmodern contributions to marketing.
- Customers perceive risk in the consumption of financial services owing to lack of service qualities, and may lack involvement.
- Satisfaction with financial services can exist at various levels according to the different types of services consumed.
- Customer loyalty operates at attitudinal and behavioural levels, with many customers being inert.

Business and consumer behaviour in financial services, unlike other areas of marketing, shares some common characteristics.

References

Accenture (2008) *Experiencing the Brand; Branding the Experience*, downloaded 15 August 2008.

Aldlaigan, A. and Buttle, F. (2001) 'Consumer Involvement in Financial Services: An Empirical Test of Two Measures', *International Journal of Bank Marketing*, Vol. 19, No. 6, pp. 232–45.

Aubert-Gamet, V. and Cova, B. (1999) 'Servicescapes: From Modern Non-Places to Postmodern Common Places', *Journal of Business Research*, Vol. 44, pp. 37–45.

Auh, S., Bell, S., McLeod, C. and Shih, E. (2007) 'Co-production and Customer Loyalty in Financial Services', *Journal of Retailing*, Vol. 83, No. 3,
pp. 359–70.

Beerli, A. Martin, J. and Quintana, A. (2004) 'A model of customer loyalty
in the retail banking market', *European Journal of Marketing*, Vol. 38,
No. 1/2, pp. 253–75.

Bell, S. and Eisingerich, A. (2007) 'The Paradox of Customer Education:
Customer Expertise and Loyalty in the Financial Services Industry',
European Journal of Marketing, Vol. 41, No. 5/6, pp. 466–86.

Black, N., Lockett, A., Ennew, C., Winkelhofer, H. and McKechnie, S. (2002)
'Modelling Consumer Choice of Distribution Channels: An Illustration
from Financial Services', *International Journal of Bank Marketing*, Vol. 20,
No. 4, pp. 161–73.

Bloemer, J., de Ruyter, K. and Wetzels, M. (1999) 'Linking Perceived
Service Quality and Service Loyalty: A Multi-dimensional Perspective',
European Journal of Marketing, Vol. 33, No. 11/12, pp. 1082–106

BMRB, 'Attitudes Towards Debt', www.bmrb.co.uk/news/article/attitudes-
to-debt/, downloaded 20 January 2009.

Brassington, F. and Pettitt, S. (2006) *Principles of Marketing*, Chelmsford,
FT Prentice Hall.

Brown, S. (1995) *Postmodern Marketing*, London, Routledge.

Cova, B. and Cova. V. (2001) 'Tribal Aspects of Postmodern Consumption Research: The Case of French In-line Roller Skaters', *Journal of
Consumer Behaviour*, Vol. 1, No. 1, pp. 67–76.

Dawes, J. and Brown, R. (2000) 'Postmodern Marketing: Research Issues
for Retail Financial Services', *Qualitative Marketing Research: An International Journal*, Vol. 3, No. 2, pp. 90–8.

Dick, A. and Basu, K. (1994) 'Customer Loyalty: Towards an Integrated
Customer Framework', *Journal of the Academy of Marketing Science*,
Vol. 22, No. 2, pp. 99–113.

East, R., Wright, M. and Vanhuele, M. (2008) *Consumer Behaviour: Applications in Marketing*, London, Sage.

Federation of Small Businesses (2007) *Report on Small Business Banking*,
www.fsb.org.uk/news, downloaded 15 January 2008.

Financial Services Authority (2004) *Stopping Short: Why Do So Many Consumers Stop Contributing to Long-term Savings Policies?*, London, FSA
Occasional Papers in Financial Regulation.

Financial Services Consumer Panel (2006), *Survey of Consumer Attitudes to Financial Services and their Experience in Buying Them*,
www.fs-cp.org.uk.

Firat, A. and Venkatesh, A. (1993) 'Postmodernity: The Age of Marketing',
International Journal of Research in Marketing, Vol. 10, pp. 227–49.

Forbes (2008), *How Financial Services Institutions Can Build Share of
Wallet and Loyalty Online*, ForeSee Online Financial Services Study,
Forbes.com.

Fornell, C. (1992) 'A National Customer Satisfaction Barometer:
The Swedish Experience', *Journal of Marketing*, Vol. 56, January,
pp. 6–21.

Gremler, D. and Brown, S. (1999) 'The Loyalty Ripple Effect: Appreciating the Full Value of Customers', *International Journal of Service Industries Management*, Vol. 10, No. 3, pp. 271–91.

Gwinner, K., Gremler, D. and Bitner, M.-J. (1998) 'Relational Benefits in Services Industries: The Customer's Perspective', *Journal of the Academy of Marketing Science*, Vol. 26, No. 2, pp. 101–14.

Howcroft, B., Hamilton, R. and Hewer, P. (2007) 'Customer Involvement and Interaction in Retail Banking: An Examination of Risk and Confidence in the Purchase of Financial Products', *Journal of Services Marketing*, Vol. 21, No. 7, pp. 481–91.

Huang, M. and Yu, S. (1999) 'Are Consumers Inherently or Situationally Brand Loyal? A Set Intercorrelation Account for Conscious Brand Loyalty and Non-conscious Inertia', *Psychology & Marketing*, Vol. 16, No. 6, pp. 523–44.

Jamal, A. and Naser, K. (2002) 'Customer Satisfaction and Retail Banking: An Assessment of Some of the Key Antecedents of Customer Satisfaction in Retail Banking', *International Journal of Bank Marketing*, Vol. 20, No. 4, pp. 146–60.

Jones, H. and Farquhar, J. D. (2007) 'Putting It Right: Service Failure and Customer Loyalty in UK Banks', *International Journal of Bank Marketing*, Vol. 25, No. 3, pp. 161–72.

Kumar, V. and Shah, D. (2004) 'Building and Sustaining *Profitable* Customer Loyalty for the 21st Century', *Journal of Retailing*, Vol. 80, pp. 317–30.

Lewis, B. and Soureli, M. (2006) 'The Antecedents of Consumer Loyalty in Retail Banking', *Journal of Consumer Behaviour*, Vol. 5, pp. 15–31.

Mintel (2008), *Consumer Attitudes towards Debt*, June, London.

Molina, A., Martin-Consuegra, D. and Esteban, A. (2007) 'Relational Benefits and Customer Satisfaction in Retail Banking', *International Journal of Bank Marketing*, Vol. 25, No. 4, pp. 253–71.

news.bbc.co.uk/1/hi/business/6959833.stm, accessed 23 July 2008.

O'Loughlin, D. and Szmigin, I. (2007) 'Services Branding: Revealing the Rhetoric within Retail Branding', *Service Industries Journal*, Vol. 27, No. 4, pp. 435–52.

Oliver, R. (1997) *Satisfaction: A Behavioral Perspective on the Consumer*, New York, McGraw Hill.

Oliver, R. (1999) 'Whence Consumer Loyalty?', *Journal of Marketing*, Vol. 63 (Special issue), pp. 33–44.

Palmer, A. (2008) *Principles of Services Marketing*, 5th edn, Maidenhead, McGraw-Hill Education.

Reinartz, W. and Kumar, V. (2000) 'On the Profitability of Long-Life Customers in a Noncontractual Setting: An Empirical Investigation and Implications for Marketing', *Journal of Marketing*, Vol. 64, No. 4, pp. 17–35.

Stuart-Menteth, H., Wilson, H. and Baker, S. (2006) 'Escaping the Channel Silo: Researching the New Consumer', *International Journal of Market Research*, Vol. 48, No. 4, pp. 415–37.

The Observer, 'Slump Sets Circulation of £50 Notes Soaring', 2 November 2008.

White, L. and Yanamandram, V. (2004) 'Why Customers Stay: Reasons and Consequences of Inertia in Financial Services', *Managing Service Quality*, Vol. 14, No. 2/3, pp. 183–94.

Exercises

1. Make a short list of 'reinforcers' and 'punishers' that you have experienced from your main financial service provider. How have these stimuli impacted on your behaviour?
2. Compare the two models of customer satisfaction with your own experiences. Find examples of where you have experienced each one and note how the two situations have differed. What are the implications of your own experiences for financial service providers?
3. Study Table 3.3. Using the questions that have been designed to uncover dissatisfaction, draw up a list of items that might uncover customer satisfaction. Provide arguments in favour of using both sets of questions in learning about customers.
4. Ask your relatives and/or friends how long they have been with their current bank? Ask them if they are happy with the service provided. If they are not happy, ask them why they have not switched. Are you able to group any of these responses under the headings of switching barriers and inertia? What are the implications of these responses for FIs?
5. Draw up a list of potential satisfiers in financial services and then a list of dissatisfiers. What would be the benefits to the financial service provider of eliminating or reducing the dissatisfiers?

Further reading

Financial Services Consumer Panel (2006), *Survey of Consumer Attitudes to Financial Services and their Experience in Buying Them*, www.fs-cp.org.uk.

CASE STUDY

Consumer attitudes to finance and pensions – a Swedish case study

Almost everyone will live long enough to retire and live on his or her pension or funds that they have saved for their post-work life. Most people, however, have not fully appreciated that they will have to adapt to a lower standard of living when they stop working. Although there is some understanding about what stopping work means, most people fail to take measures to ensure that their post-work life is sufficiently funded. The majority of Swedish consumers interviewed in a recent study thought that their pensions would be inadequate.[1] Indeed, this problem is endemic and many pensioners worldwide run a very real risk of becoming poverty-stricken pensioners.

A study of 600 Swedes showed that only every sixth person understands how s/he will get her or his pension.[2] The study revealed that the majority of respondents had a limited knowledge of the pension system, as well as a low level of involvement in questions related to the system. One-third of the respondents could not name any single company or authority they could contact regarding their pensions. There are, of course, several reasons why the situation is as it is. Most significantly, the majority of consumers are just not interested in financial matters in general and, particularly, those related to retirement. It does not matter where these questions are asked – the United Kingdom, Sweden, the United States or Australia – the conclusion is the same. In the Swedish case, the second factor is the way in which information about pensions is presented. There is no organization with overall responsibility for pension information that consumers can turn to to give them information about how much they will get when they retire. Instead, they need to access three different sources to obtain this sort of information. Consequently, it comes as no surprise that they find such fragmented information incoherent, biased and impersonal.[3] This lack of information contributes to the low involvement and poor knowledge that Swedes have about their future pensions, which probably contributes to Swedes not saving or investing adequately for their post-work life.

A British sociologist, Alan Aldridge, is surprised that sociological work on consumption and consumerism does not contain any discussion of personal financial services.[4] Surely the impact of personal finance on people's life chances makes it worthy of academic attention, he contends. He argues that, in Bourdieu's terms, marketization requires consumers to possess high levels of cultural capital.[5] As already mentioned, that is not the case for financial services. In 1995, Virgin launched a mutual fund (index fund) under the Virgin brand, which lowered the threshold of economic and, more importantly, cultural capital needed. The company simplified a sophisticated product to fit the mass market, but it is not clear whether consumers are ready for a development where complex products are sold as if they were groceries.

The Swedish government has invested a lot of money in informing Swedes about their pensions.[6] The most important piece of information is called the 'Orange Envelope'; it has been sent out annually since 1999. The envelope is orange to attract people's attention and contains information about the guaranteed old-age pension. Despite all the efforts to make that information accessible and interesting for people to read, only one in five considers the information appropriate for them. This is because the envelope contains information that is not always relevant for consumer decisions – for example, different age groups have different needs; the information should really be targeted at various groups. A vital part of pension information is an estimate of the amount that a consumer will receive when they retire. Unfortunately, such estimates differ depending on who the provider of the information is – for example, the estimates in the Orange Envelope can be up to 25 per cent lower than other estimates. That sort of discrepancy only causes confusion and deters many from reading the information and from the pension itself. About 20 per cent of those who receive the Orange Envelope do not even bother to open it.[7] Just over a quarter of those who opened it and looked at the information found it difficult or rather difficult to understand. In spite of the expenditure of a considerable amount of money to improve the quality of the information since 1999, there has been no decrease in the number of consumers who think that the information is difficult or rather difficult to understand. As a consequence, about two-thirds of Swedes think that they have low or no knowledge of the pension system.

The key problem is that it is hard to inform financially uneducated and, perhaps, uninterested consumers about complex financial issues. In the Swedish case, follow-up studies revealed that consumers do not understand what 'normal' growth of the economy is, nor do they understand how growth is related to the size of their own pension. In the Orange Envelope, consumers can read that their pension will be €X if the economy grows, for example, 2 per cent annually, and €Y if it does not grow at the same rate. This sort of information pre-supposes an understanding of how growth in the economy affects pensions. Communication in these terms is not getting the message across. Would face-to-face or personalized communication be more successful? In Sweden, around 50 per cent of the households use a financial adviser, but, at the same time, 40 per cent of those very households do not actually trust this adviser.[8] Half of those who have used a financial adviser think that they can handle financial questions better themselves and 29 per cent do not trust the advice they get.[9] One of the problems with financial advice is where to draw the line between advice and selling. Financial advisers receive commission on the sales of the products that they sell, not for the advice that they give to consumers.

The European Union has published studies on consumer attitudes to finances and financial services.[10] When responding to: 'I find thinking about my finances and financial services...', consumers in the 25 EU countries gave a negative picture of how they look at it. A quarter of respondents thought that financial services were complicated, 21 per cent thought that they were intimidating, 21 per cent that they were depressing, 17 per cent dull, 14 per cent comforting and 8 per cent enjoyable.

The conclusion arising from these studies is that new and innovative methods must be developed in order to bring about significant change in the way that financial services are perceived. This Swedish example demonstrates that it is hard to increase consumer knowledge and involvement about financial services merely by sending out information, however brightly coloured the envelope. It is even harder to prepare relevant information for different groups. Other studies have shown that financial advisers may have a vested interest in the sales of financial services, causing a conflict with the best interest of the consumer. With an ageing population across Europe, finding a solution to the problem of lack of engagement with preparing for post-work finances is overdue, but as yet there is little consensus on how to solve the problem.

Case study notes

1. Hushållens ekonomiska förmåga. Report 2007–0627, Finansinspektionen, Stockholm, p. 2. A study based on interviews with 1,019 households.
2. www.unionen.se, Report 'Pensionen – långt borta och nära', Stockholm, summer 2008. 'Bara ar sjätte förstår hur man skall få pension'. Dagens Nyheters nätupplaga, www.dn.se (2 July 2008).
3. *Ibid.*
4. Aldridge, Alan (1998) 'Habitus and Cultural Capital in the Field of Personal Finance', *The Sociological Review*, pp. 1–23.
5. *Ibid.*
6. Riksrevisionen (2008) Staten och pensionsinformationen. RiR 2008: 3, Stockholm.
7. *Ibid.*
8. Financial Services Authority (2004) 'Consumer Understanding of Financial Risk', prepared for the Financial Services Authority by Conquest Research Ltd, Consumer Research 33, November, p. 3.
9. Hushållens ekonomiska förmåga. Report 2007–0627.
10. 'Public Opinion in Europe on Financial Services, Special Eurobarometer 230', European Commission (2005). Approximately 1,000 consumers interviewed in each of the 25 countries (EU25).

Professor Rita Martenson

Questions

1. What is the role of an independent party in the provision of pension information; how might this improve knowledge and involvement with pensions?
2. What is cultural capital and how does it impact on financial services. What is the relevance of commoditization in financial services?
3. What provision have you made for your later years? What sort of messages might prompt you to start saving or to purchase the appropriate product. Where would you go for advice?

4

Segmenting and targeting the financial services marketplace

Contents

Learning outcomes

Readers, at the end of this chapter, will be able to:

- Distinguish between different approaches to segmentation in consumer and business markets

- Appreciate the contributions of multisegment marketing to targeting strategies

- Develop rationales for outline segmentation strategies and subsequent targeting

- Understand and articulate the key aspects of the positioning of financial services

Introduction

In the previous chapter, we looked at customer behaviour in the marketing of financial services and argued that an understanding of this is essential to success for financial institutions (FIs). Given the size of markets – not only in Europe but across the world, in which FIs increasingly operate – developing strategies around individual consumers and companies, except for huge global operators, is not practicable, so some kind of approach that breaks up diverse marketplaces into smaller units of customers is needed. Although, financial services marketers may talk about mass or volume markets, it would be a mistake to think that segmentation is not a key strategy in financial services. The days of looking at the consumer market as a whole are over as investments in information systems and analytic capabilities have increased. These developments have allowed financial service marketers to understand their customers better and to uncover characteristics that enable them to group customers better to target them with specific offerings and services. In business markets too, the marketplace is as diverse as the consumer marketplace in terms of customer needs, particularly when FIs operate globally. In this chapter, the vital strategy of market segmentation in financial services will be reviewed and discussed, and then the way segmentation leads onto decisions about which segments to target and how an FI might position itself in the marketplace to attract these segments.

What is segmentation?

Segmentation is an essential marketing planning activity that involves identifying groups of customers displaying a similar responsiveness to a particular strategy; value propositions can then be developed to elicit that response from these groups. From a strategic perspective, segmentation allows the company to maximize its resources in identifying and targeting groups of customers, both consumers and businesses, demonstrating a probability that they are likely to respond to the company's offerings. To segment customers, markets are split into homogeneous groups, but, of course, the tricky thing is to identify the shared characteristics that will make a viable and profitable segment. Consumer segmentation and business segmentation, like customer behaviour, differs and we will look at them separately, beginning with consumers. For marketers, terms such as 'average', 'the majority', 'a large proportion' and stereotypes are not only unhelpful but, in fact, positively dangerous, as they may be based on vague measurements, assumptions and prejudice or unfounded beliefs.

What marketers need is accurate and up-to-date information about customers.

Changes in the marketplace mean that segmentation is always developing and defining ever-smaller segments as customers become more empowered in the marketing exchange. The financial services marketplace is subject to continuous complexity and turbulence and segmentation has to keep up with that. The advent of IT, fierce competition and the oversupply of financial services has contributed to an intense interest in segmentation, accompanied by spending of significant amounts of money on the information required for its execution.

Consumer segments

a priori: a term originally referring to deductive reasoning, therefore in segmentation referring to predetermined segments

post hoc: a means of segmenting customers on an analysis of their behaviour, usually using data based on behaviour

geographic segmentation: a means of grouping customers according to where they live or work. Increasingly based on postcodes

In this section, we will consider some of the issues related to segmenting consumer markets. There are essentially two broad approaches to segmentation: one where segments are developed in advance, based on established criteria (***a priori***), such as geography; or, second, an increasingly widely used method using data based on customer behaviour (***post hoc***). We will consider *a priori* segmentation approaches first.

Predetermining segments

Geographic segmentation groups customers according to where they are located. This is a common means of segmenting with smaller building societies, who have traditionally served a local community; this is still clearly visible in their names – for example, Scarborough Building Society or Kent Reliance Building Society in the United Kingdom. These institutions now aim to serve a wider geographic market by post, phone or the Internet, thereby increasing the number of customers. In so doing, though, they have found that they are undermining both the long-standing relationships with their existing customers and the local knowledge that have been built up over years. Looking at customers on the basis of where they live may provide some insight into their profile; differentiating between the north and the south in the United Kingdom, for example, has always provided some broad generalizations, notably life expectancy. Broad generalizations about consumers, however, do not provide financial institutions with the information that they need to be able to compete effectively in the saturated financial services marketplace.

demographics:
characteristics of human
population, e.g. age,
educational achievement

Marketers have also relied on consumer **demographics** for segmentation, which consist of such information as age, sex, race, income and occupation. There is some clear benefit to financial institutions here, as customers are likely to wish for certain financial services at certain times in their lives – for example, graduate loans, mortgages or health care. Exhibit 4.1 shows how the sex of a consumer may also drive the identification of a market segment.

EXHIBIT 4.1

Sheilas' Wheels: car insurance for women

A car insurance brand for women named Sheilas' Wheels was launched in the United Kingdom in 2005 to provide much-needed competition in the rapidly growing market of female insurance consumers. Promotion of the brand uses Australian role-reversal themes, where power – in the shape of lower premiums – shifts to the sassy Sheilas, sparking insurance-envy in a range of 'Bruces', who are left wishing, ruefully, that they were women – so inverting the derogatory tone of the Australian expression. A Sheilas' Wheels singing trio – who front the adverts – were the stars of a multimillion pound advertising campaign launched nationwide. Based on an independent survey, over half of women who insure with Sheilas' Wheels save an average of £203; customers are also offered breakdown cover at the lowest price in the direct insurance market. Sheilas' Wheels' insurance includes a number of unique benefits designed for the female driver, such as £300 handbag and contents cover if your bag is stolen from your car, a 24-hour counselling line for drivers suffering trauma on the road and a network of repairers trained to follow a female-friendly code of practice. By focusing on women, the brand reflects the relative safety of female drivers (when compared with their male counterparts) through attractive premiums.

The 'Sheilas' that the product appeals to are smart, sassy and feel they deserve a better deal. Women account for 45 per cent of all UK drivers, which represents around 14.4 million, and the female insurance market is growing. In the last decade alone, the percentage of motor insurance policies bought by women has increased by a third. Women are a good insurance risk. Men are responsible for 97 per cent of all dangerous driving convictions, 94 per cent of all car accidents involving death or bodily harm, 89 per cent of all drink- and drug-driving convictions, 85 per cent of all careless driving convictions and 83 per cent of all speeding convictions. Consequently women's claims are, on average, less costly than those for men. The TV advertising campaign comprises three executions which feature a trio of singing 'Sheilas' (glamorous and empowered because they get a better deal on their car insurance for being women) and typical 'Aussie blokes' aspiring to be more like women to benefit from these better deals. Sheilas' Wheels is a division of esure.com. Its chairman Peter

> Wood is also esure's chairman (and founder of Direct Line). The female senior management team put together to launch the product is led by Jacky Brown.
>
> Compiled by the authors from material on www.rbs.co.uk.

As the Sheilas' Wheels exhibit also demonstrates, customers are increasingly 'smart and sassy' and, rather than conveniently falling into the pre-determined segments discussed above, they tend to group themselves. As McDonald and Dunbar argue (2004) customers choose between offerings based on their assessments of superior value, that is, they choose the proposition that offers them the bundle of benefits that they seek. Demographics are now more usually used to describe segments after they have been formed, but the popularity of this method of segmentation rests on the availability of the data and its ability to relate to other data, thereby increasing precision and effectiveness.

Given the limitations of a single method of segmenting customers, techniques were developed that combined two bases – for example, combining location and demographic data is known as *geodemographics*. In geodemographics, the primary unit of analysis is the postcode, data for which (precise details of addresses) can be used to segment people into homogeneous groups (see www.caci.co.uk), and compile a map of classification groups, especially for financial services, ranging from wealthy investors to impoverished pensioners. Combining data sources, Experian has produced 13 financial classifications, which are then further broken down into 82 groups of people. To give an illustration, one of the classifications is called Credit-hungry families as shown in Table 4.1.

Table 4.1 An example of a financial services segment

Group	Household description	UK household proportion	Type	Description	Person type, description and name
			F18	Overspending optimists	Darren and Claire
	Credit-hungry families	9.18%	F19	Savvy big spenders	Shaun and Tracy
F			F20	Downscale mortgages	Dale and Lyndsey
			F21	Hocked to the hilt	Wayne and Anne-Marie

Source: Table compiled with information from Experian UK (2005).

From even this brief description, this sub-classification of Credit-hungry families provides valuable information for decisions about what sort of products these consumers may already use and which services they may require. Mapmechanics of Switzerland offer to provide businesses with data for their segmentation strategies. One issue that emerges immediately relates to the number of languages spoken in Switzerland and the implications for segmentation. Would you segment by language, for example? Marketing would have to recognize the languages in developing communication strategies, as demonstrated in Exhibit 4.2.

EXHIBIT 4.2

Multilingual segments

According to census data, the languages spoken in Switzerland are as follows: German/dialect only, French only, English only, Italian only, Rumantsch only. There are speakers who speak a combination of English and French, or German and Italian. The total number of speakers of each language fall into the following socio-professional categories: managerial, liberal professions, farmers, other independents, knowledge workers and middle management, intermediate professions, qualified employees (white collar), qualified workers (blue collar) and not qualified. Education levels, occupation type by gender (full time, part time), unemployment, apprentices, voluntary activity, home tenders, retired people, inactive and hours worked per week (less than 6, 6–19 hours, 20–39, 20–45, over 45 hours) are further categories in which the population of Switzerland can be grouped.

Adapted by the authors from www.mapmechanics.com.

---

psychographic: segmentation where grouping is based according to lifestyle data or assumptions

But what does this information tell us about how these consumers think or believe? For example, it is important for financial institutions to know about consumers' attitudes to borrowing; if they are unwilling to borrow then they are unlikely to take out a loan or use a credit card. Do these consumers consider themselves financially astute or do they prefer to have advice about their financial purchases? Building on the combination of two types of data for segmentation, **psychographic** segmentation goes further and includes information relating to consumer lifestyle, such as attitudes, beliefs and opinions, often abbreviated to AIO. When psychographics are segmented, the need to oversimplify or use averages evaporates and communicators can select the most effective strategy for each segment – for example, a targeted message will aim to change a mindset about a financial offering. According to Morgan and Levy (2002), return on investment can be further enhanced by examining a psychographic segment's demographics; for example, although receptive to an offering, those in a particular segment may avoid mass media to such an extent that few messages, no matter how relevant, will reach them. Looking at all the facets of a psychographic segment establishes whether or not it is a worthwhile target, allowing efforts to be focused on the most profitable segments, as well as those with the highest potential (Morgan and Levy 2002). By understanding what people believe and what they aspire to, for example, marketers can develop offerings which then enable consumers to engage with these beliefs and aspirations, via credit cards that are affiliated to charities or personal loans to buy a classic car or an environmentally friendly means of transport.

However, determining consumer groupings according to *a priori* methods may not be enough. Study of consumers' behaviour has led to the development of a group of techniques which can be described as *post hoc* or **behavioural segmentation**.

behavioural segmentation: groups customers according to some extent of the way in which they have behaved, e.g. frequency of purchase, amount purchases

Behavioural segmentation

Competitive pressures and the complexity of consumer lifestyles, however, have shown that, in segmenting, it is inadvisable to rely on the traditional predetermined approaches (McDonald and Dunbar 2004) based on age or location. A powerful means of grouping consumers and customers together is by considering their behaviour. A useful example of behavioural segmentation relates to the benefits that consumers seek from a product. This is especially apt in financial services, where the product itself does not have an end use, but rather is acquired to enable the acquisition of something else. In the case of a credit card, for example, those whose attitude to money is relaxed can avoid the need to save up for purchases, thus allowing immediate gratification. Even for those who are more concerned about debt, a credit card offers the benefit of detailed monthly records of transactions, using different cards for different types of purchases. Indeed, the advice in the press is for customers to use their credit cards for the purchase of holidays as they provide a level of protection in the case of holiday companies going under. Credit cards initially segment the market by offering benefits according to the 'value' of the card – see, for example, Mastercard Platinum (www.mastercard.com). What might be the aspirations of a customer that chooses a platinum card? Institutions' capacity to make use of whatever information they can get has proved a very valuable way of segmenting their consumers and, indeed, their business customers as well. One of the reasons that banks want customers to open current accounts with them is to provide information about a customer's incoming money and outgoing spend. Customer relationship management (CRM) systems have been developed especially to track the 'lifetime' of a customer with a particular institution, by logging all the interactions between the company and the customer.

Methodologies for segmenting customers are based on advanced statistical techniques that usually attempt to 'cluster' consumers into groups; the following study gives some detailed insight into the particular problem of the relationship between loyalty and profitability for retail banks. Garland (2005) provides a framework for segmenting customers by their longevity, their share of wallet and their short-term value to the bank. He was able to gain access to a bank database in New Zealand to study the profitability (or 'contribution') of the customers; he then combined these data with data which he collected by means of a survey from the same customers (1,700) and so was able to converge data sets and gain an in-depth view of this customer base. The analysis of the data sets yielded eight segments (see Tables 4.2 and 4.3). The important issue here is that the data that this author has collected from

Table 4.2 Financial service segments, according to profitability and length of time as a customer

Category	per cent of respondents	FI share of wallet	Individual Profitability	tenure of banking at main bank
True strangers	11	Low	Low	Low
Worrying strangers	8	High	Low	Low
Costly barnacles	6	Low	Low	High
Hopeless barnacles	7	High	Low	High
Interesting butterflies	16	High	High	Low
True butterflies	16	Low	High	Low
Acquaintances	17	Low	High	High
True friends	19	High	High	High

Source: Adapted from Garland (2005).

Table 4.3 Financial service segments, according to probable behaviour

| | Mean satisfaction | Probabilities in the next 12 months | | | | |
| | Scale 1–7 | Recommending | Increasing business | Decreasing business | Open account at competitor | Close all accounts |
	mean	per cent	per cent	per cent	per cent	per cent
True strangers	5.2	61	40	25	27	17
Worrying strangers	6.2	73	50	14	14	10
Costly barnacles	6.2	80	53	17	16	6
Hopeless barnacles	6.5	88	51	17	9	7
Interesting butterflies	6.2	79	52	15	13	10
True butterflies	5.8	71	48	19	18	11
Acquaintances	6	71	43	22	12	10
True friends	6.4	83	43	16	7	7

Source: Adapted from Garland (2005).

the bank consists of information about individual customer behaviour, which lends itself to *post hoc* analysis, where groups are based on past behavioural patterns. The relevance of this history is that it can act as a means of predicting future behaviour, specifically likelihood of purchasing particular financial services or responding to particular marketing messages. In the absence of more accurate predictors, past behaviour is often used.

These tables summarize the analyses from Garland's paper and show eight bank segments with significant implications for the loyalty/profitability problem for the bank. Four categories of customers had been identified in previous work by Reinartz and Kumar (2000) as follows: strangers, barnacles, butterflies and acquaintances/friends. Garland subdivides these four categories into eight groups. The second column in Table 4.3 reports the mean level of customer satisfaction with the bank on a scale of 1–7, where 7 is highly satisfied. Customer satisfaction is a measure collected by all FIs; it is important here as it is often used as an antecedent of customer loyalty. The data indicate that only two customer groupings report less than a mean value of 6 on a scale of 1–7, which can be interpreted as meaning that the levels of customer satisfaction are generally high with this bank. The first category or grouping of customers, true strangers, have the lowest levels of customer satisfaction with the bank, have a low proportion of their money at the bank and share their custom across two or three other banks. The bank would like to remove them as they probably cost the bank money.

This type of customer has been recognized elsewhere. One solution to the problem they create is not to send them any direct mail or contact them in any way, hoping that through neglect they may choose to take their business elsewhere (Farquhar and Panther 2008). Worrying strangers are even more of a concern as they are also loss makers but have all their banking and products with the bank in the study and stand a chance of becoming hopeless barnacles. Barnacles is the name given to a category or segment of customers, initially developed by Reinartz and Kumar (2000), who are loyal but loss-making customers but who might be converted into profit, or from lead to gold (Zeithaml *et al.* 2001). The hopeless barnacles only represent 7 per cent of the customer base, as the Table 4.2 shows, have all their banking business with the bank, but their profitability is low. Costly barnacles have a low share of wallet with the bank, meaning that most of their money is lodged in other, probably competing, institutions but they have a high probability of recommending in the next 12 months and a 53 per cent chance of increasing business (the highest). Not all of these groups may be desirable as segments for the bank, but this analysis provides a valuable tool for decision-making.

dynamic segments:
segments are not fixed
and will change in
nature, size and
desirability

Dynamic segments

Not only is segmentation challenging in the number of variables that companies have to use to arrive at a level of accuracy in a competitive marketplace, but, additionally, they must grasp the dynamic nature of segments. Segments are not fixed and they will evolve – some segments may 'die' (i.e., they may no longer exist as customers no longer need or require the offering or their tastes and needs have changed). This may come about as people move house, lose their job, experience some incapacity or go 'green'. It may also be that FIs change their strategies and choose to serve new segments that are more likely to enable them to meet their organizational objectives. Segmentation is a continuous process and financial services marketers need to engage in those tasks outlined in Chapter 2 to identify and respond to changing conditions. For example, the choice of channel is increasingly important in financial services, not only for the purchase but also for an information search. The number of decision-makers is important and the family unit is recognized by financial services as important in decision-making, raising the question of how to manage decision-making units that do not resemble the classic nuclear family but are the modern proxy. The value of the customer and their financial strength is quite a complex dynamic, which can be revealed in a credit check (see www.experian.co.uk). The notion of 'share of wallet' is dear to many businesses and the larger share, generally, the more profitable the customer. However, consumers are increasingly disposed to be multibanked and therefore providers are keen to measure value in a range of ways, from size of mortgage or size of loan to amount borrowed on credit card and not repaid at the end of the month. A consumer's understanding of the offering is rather a contentious point in financial services, as an asymmetry of information has long existed.

Exhibit 4.3 shows how political and economic transformations have created the opportunity for a bank to serve the particular needs of customers grouped geographically.

EXHIBIT 4.3

European arrivals

Lloyds TSB has opened the doors to a new superstore bank in Manchester, offering customers who have only just moved to the United Kingdom from Poland the opportunity to enjoy tailored banking services. The new store has been set up at St Mary's Gate, central Manchester, and is specifically designed to cater for the city's Polish community, which is said to be growing 'rapidly'. Fluent Polish speakers will man the desks at the new bank and Lloyds TSB literature will be provided in the language as well, to ensure an easier transition to British banking for the immigrants. Gerrard Schmid, Lloyds TSB transaction banking director, explained: 'Our new international superstore will really help to take the fear factor out of opening a bank account for customers new to the United Kingdom. There is a clear demand for a tailored banking service and to meet this demand we have been adapting our procedures; in particular we have focused on making the account-opening process as straightforward as possible for all our customers.' The move by Lloyds TSB, which plans to convert a number of UK branches into international superstores, is intended to address the fact that over 400,000 people from the EU have entered Britain in the past two years, including almost 265,000 Poles.

Compiled by authors from www.moneynews.co.uk.

Once an account is opened, the bank will log all the data onto their CRM system and collect data from this point onwards – about salary payments in, address and the way that the money is used – to group these new customers into sub-groups sharing similar characteristics.

A significant group of customers has appeared in Europe and the United Kingdom – a group of super rich customers. Although Britain's super-rich have lost money since the credit crunch, Indian steel tycoon Lakshmi Mittal remains No. 1 but has seen his wealth decline in the last year by £16,900m to a mere £10,800m (business.timesonline.co.uk/tol/business). The super-rich may present opportunities for financial services but this group is not homogeneous and in many cases its members are rich because they are very well informed and advised about their personal and business finances. Another group that are of great interest to financial institutions is known as the 'mass affluent'. Banks will offer premium services to individuals with, say, savings or investments of at least £50,000 or earnings of £100,000 (although precise figures will vary from bank to bank). The service levels that banks offer this group of mass affluent (not a particularly flattering term) are considerably less personalized than for the high net worth (HNW) clients; for example, customers will be served by a call centre rather than a named individual and rates on balances in accounts are unattractive – as low as 1 per cent.

At the other end of the wealth spectrum lies a group of customers who may fall at the edges of any segmentation approach – people living on

financial inclusion: a strategy to ensure that segments or groups of people not normally targeted by FIs are accorded basic financial services

low incomes, or what have become know as the 'financially excluded' (www.financialinclusion-taskforce.org.uk) who do not have a current account with a bank. This group of people does not present to any company, let alone a bank, the conventional criterion of revenue generation or profit. There is accumulating evidence is that de-regulation in financial sectors improves **financial inclusion** for some societal groups (more products become available to a bigger customer base), but may at the same time exacerbate it for others (for example, by emphasizing greater customer segmentation, with more focus on risk-based pricing and 'value added'). Concern with financial exclusion is emerging in many European countries and a variety of different policy approaches are being developed. The issue of financial inclusion has also long been an issue throughout the developing world particularly in strongly market-oriented financial systems such as the United Kingdom and the United States (Carbó *et al.*, 2005). The government in the United Kingdom is taking action to ensure that this group has access to banking, affordable credit and face-to-face money advice.

The United Kingdom had until recently one of the largest, most sophisticated and competitive financial services sectors in the world, which appears to have responded quickly to the demands of a rapidly changing economy. New technologies have been developed and new products have come to the market that meet the way that people live and conduct their businesses. Yet there is growing evidence that the market is not able to meet everyone's needs. A small but significant minority are unable to access even the simplest financial services, meaning that they pay more to manage their money, find it harder to plan for the future and cope with financial pressures, and are more vulnerable to financial distress and over-indebtedness. Within the United Kingdom and the EU, governments support the policy that everyone should be able to: manage their money effectively and securely; plan for the future with a reasonable degree of security; and have the information, capability and confidence they need to prevent avoidable financial difficulty, and know where to turn if they do find themselves in financial distress (www.financialinclusion-taskforce.org.uk).

Internet users

One of the most important issues that FIs have been addressing is the need to uncover the characteristics of customers, who use the internet for banking and financial services. For FIs, the Internet offers significant cost reductions in serving customers – perhaps as much as 1000 per cent – providing a strong incentive to understand and identify those who are or could be prepared to use the Internet for their banking and financial services requirements. Internet users not only cost FIs less to serve, but it also seems that they are potentially more valuable/profitable customers, making them even more desirable. A recent survey carried out by the UK Payments Association indicates that over half of Britons currently use Internet banking, with over half of them aged between 25 and 34, compared to just 15 per cent of people aged 65 and over (www.moneynews.co.uk). Indeed, during the 12 months from October 2006, the share of the UK Internet population made up by under-25s dropped from 29 per cent to 25 per cent (Neilsen 2008). What's more, those aged 55 and over increased their share from 16 per cent to 19 per cent and those aged 55+ are soon set to overtake 35–44-year-olds as the age group with the largest representation on-line. As a consequence, this is a group of customers that banks would like to grow but there really is not any support for the proposition that there is a segment of consumers who are Internet users across the product range – the picture is a great deal more complex.

Although customers seeking convenience tend to prefer Internet or self-service technologies (SSTs) and attitudinally are favourably disposed to change and technology (Thornton and White 2001), they also use personal interaction, dependent upon the type of transaction required (Howcroft *et al*. 2003). Although, there is a group of customers in the financial services marketplace who have a preference for SSTs, it cannot be assumed by FIs that this is a segment that can be served entirely by these channels. The adoption and use of SSTs provides some insight into the challenges that segmenting the marketplace pose for financial services – in particular, the use of a range of variables for segmentation – and, once more, points to customer perceptions of the diversity of products in the financial services range.

Segmenting the non-adopters of technology has values as the category can be further segmented into those who will soon adopt and those who are likely to remain non-adopters (i.e., persistent non-adopters) (Lee *et al*. 2005). Behavioural measures such as current use of the phone, ATM usage and use of computers at work were found to increase the chances that a non-adopter would use Internet banking within 12 months. Therefore, the authors conclude that if banks want to migrate customers to Internet banking, they need to appreciate that consumers will need to be proficient in the use of computers, as a lack of experience will inhibit adoption in spite of any attitudinal characteristics. They identify three segments – current adopter, prospective adopter and persistent non-adopter – based on behavioural variables and by grouping them into clusters the institution can offer services that meet a particular cluster more effectively, create higher levels of satisfaction and increase the chances of retaining these customers. In a study into the adoption of Internet banking the respondents stated, overall, that the most important attributes in the selection

| Table 4.4 | Segments of Internet users |

Segment	Selection criteria
Speed seekers	Download speed User-friendly website Transaction speed Privacy Innovativeness
Cautious users	Reliability of the bank Security of the website Service quality Loyalty
Exposed users	Advertising Suggestions of colleagues

Source: Adapted from Akinci *et al.* (2004).

process were related to security, reliability and privacy (Akinci *et al.* 2004).

The findings also identified the segments shown in Table 4.4 amongst those who already used the Internet for their banking, based on their selection criteria. Speed seekers and cautious users are readily identified by their criteria; it is the third group that is of interest, as they are susceptible to the influence of others in their use of Internet banking. For banks, the implications of isolating this group are that these users can be persuaded to take up further offerings by actions on the part of the provider through good service and persuasive advertising.

Segmentation practice

We have provided several examples of segments that may be of interest to financial services providers, giving some indication of the level of precision that can be achieved. In order to achieve this sort of accuracy, *a priori* consumer segmentation studies usually involve the following steps.

1. A consumer survey, collecting product/brand usage data, perhaps media usage and a range of rating scales or items form the basis for analysing the data.

2. A statistical procedure known as 'factor analysis' works out which are the most useful items in the rating scales to develop a relatively small group of underlying dimensions in the data. This requires some creativity on the part of the analyst to arrive at a 'best' solution.

3. Respondents to the questionnaire are clustered, using cluster analysis, on the basis of their scores.

4. The clusters are profiled, using the rest of the survey data, such as classification questions. This procedure is common, but highly suspect technically, and a number of researchers have proposed ways to improve it. Apart from technical failings, a common criticism is that clusters are unusable or uninformative. Part of the fault appears to lie in the way scales operate, especially on international studies, and improvements and refinements are always being offered.

5. Once the clusters have been identified, it is common practice to give them distinctive names; although this is often criticized, it can be seen as an aid to understanding, and helpful to creative people who have to target communications to specific groups. Systems like Claritas's PRIZM (a set of geodemographic clusters) divide whole populations into groups with names like 'Affluentials' (more flattering than 'hopeless barnacles'). The practical reason for doing this is to render the segments both recognizable throughout the company, and hence more usable – and used. Nothing is more useless than an expensive segmentation study gathering dust in a cupboard. Segmentation is at the heart of marketing. It seems sure to remain there, even if the technicalities are less than perfect (www.warc 2006).

Consumer segmentation continues to provide challenges to financial institutions and the levels of data mining and analysis are considerable. Institutions use a range of techniques to segment their markets, to develop and revise strategies where information and the power of information processing allows them to track customers and assess their value to the organization.

Business segments

Just as in consumer markets, business markets are heterogeneous and the marketer faces a choice of what criteria he/she is going use to group similar customer together. There are two levels of segmentation to consider. First, macro segmentation, which is evident on the websites of financial institutions, where the market is divided up into three customer macro segments: personal, commercial and corporate. As we have seen in the first half of the chapter, the personal banking market is subject to considerable further segmentation and it is the same for the commercial market as well. For an efficient strategy, the company needs make a clear choice about the relevant segmentation criteria; we discuss below key questions and common methods for identifying groups within the client base.

The descriptive category is based on classifying businesses by specific descriptors, such as business revenue, number of employees, number of product lines, number of key competitors, market share and similar items (Richarme 2004). A disadvantage of this method is that many of these descriptors are not publicly available and add little information to the segmentation goal of describing the unique groups of decision-makers. A more up-to-date approach to the descriptive category uses a commercial version of the established Mosaic system to classify all UK businesses into 13 groups and 50 types, based on key variables that influence business behaviour, with descriptions such as 'Local solid rocks' and 'Small-scale suppliers'. A second technique attempts to divide firms into segments according to the type of business, with a standardized classification scheme such as the Standard Industrial Classification (SIC) code. Though generally available from public sources (www.statistics.gov.uk), this method also provides challenges when attempting to classify businesses that have many different lines of business – for example, Virgin. A third technique examines the physical addresses of businesses and uses geography as the major clustering factor. While this approach may produce differentiated groups among organizations with one physical location, it becomes unwieldy when applied to geographically dispersed divisions, branches, or retail locations but has implications for selling, for product delivery, for billing, for customer service and for almost every other facet of a firm. Experian and its partners (Experian, 2008) also identify a category is known as *Propensities*, which again provides a broad description based on statistical modelling that indicates a business's likely behaviour, such as purchasing intentions or profitability. They have identified 24 sector-specific models, ranging from beer and soft drinks to chemicals, hotel services and telecoms. Barclays Commercial offer specialist teams for the following businesses with turnover in excess of £20 million: charitable organizations, education, financial services, government, health care, hospitality and leisure, manufacturing, oil and gas, professional services, property finance, recruitment and consultancy, retail and wholesale, social housing, support services, technology and telecoms and transport and logistics (www.barclays.com).

The above examples again suggest that financial institutions can approach segmentation from a number of different angles.

Organizing segmentation

We have provided some insight into the range of segments and variables that financial institutions consider. There are, additionally, some critical questions that have to be debated by marketers when developing segmentation strategies. It is all too easy to get overwhelmed by the detail and overlook the fundamental considerations that underpin what segmentation is trying to achieve.

Organizational structure

McDonald and Dunbar (2004) identify two dimensions to classifying market segmentation in organizations (see Figure 4.1) and argue that high levels of organizational integration and being customer-driven unequivocally provide the best way to develop strategies and operations that achieve organizational goals. Sales-based segmentation looks at the marketplace from the perspective of how the sales function is organized – for example, around life insurance rather than customer characteristics. Structural segmentation is defined by the way that the organization is constructed – for example, bank branches were competing against on-line

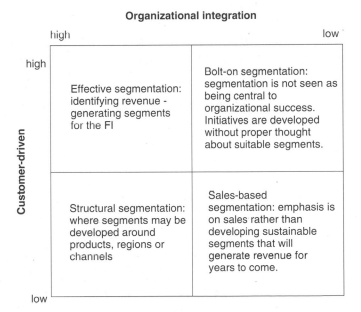

Figure 4.1   Market segmentation in financial institutions
Source: Adapted from Jenkins and McDonald, 1997.

channels and telephone banking rather than ensuring a positive customer experience (Farquhar and Panther 2008). Although bolt-on segmentation combines some of the attributes of sound segmentation practice, such as use of customer data from within the organization combined with external classification systems, Jenkins and McDonald (1997) contend that this type of segmentation is closer to sales-based segmentation as the overall intent is to sell rather than develop appropriate and sustainable strategies. The optimum approach is where customer orientation and organizational integration are at the highest levels. The company can supply information and levels of analysis that generate defined customer segments.

This particular figure is deceptively simple but the two axes are critical in deriving the benefits to the organization that segmentation can offer. This is particularly the case in financial services, which have not always had the level of integration that is the most supportive of effective marketing strategies. The range of financial services that many financial institutions offer can be extensive; often these have been structured around administration by departments for mortgages or for businesses foreign exchange management. Yet many consumers and businesses may choose to use more than one offering, therefore operating across the bank or company, whose horizontal integration can still be weak (Farquhar and Panther 2008).

Double-checking

There are some intuitive questions which need to be asked about the results that these procedures suggest (WARC 2006), in addition to rigorous statistical procedures. *Does the segmentation generate clusters that fit what we think we understand about our market?* If the clusters do not seem to have this fit, then the commitment and vigour required to target the segments may be lacking. *Does the clustering process provide me with new or valuable insights into the category and/or my brand?* Having gone through all the efforts and expenditure that rigorous segmentation involves, some benefits must be seen in terms of new information that can be implemented. *Are the clusters 'usable' in terms of either creative approaches or media planning (preferably both)?* Segmentation provides a critical, informed basis for a number of activities within the company so that resources can be used more effectively, starting with marketing communications, branding and marketing planning. *Are the clusters likely to be reasonably stable over time?* As we have discussed before, segments are not everlasting but they do need to have some durability so that a company can make the plans mentioned above. *Can I apply the clusters internationally or, at least, on a broad regional basis?* Financial service organizations are increasingly global in their scope – for example, HSBC, AXA and Grupo Santander – and these companies look for segments that cross national boundaries. Equally, smaller companies will be looking to extend their markets beyond their traditional 'heartlands' and so looking regionally and nationally. *Can I apply the clusters to my existing customer database?* The mining of an existing customer database is one of the most significant changes in segmentation practice; identifying clusters either using predetermined means or emerging clusters from an analysis of in-house data has to be one of the most cost-effective ways of arriving at targetable segments (WARC 2006). Ultimately, segmentation provides the means for the financial services institution to manage its resources as effectively as possible by identifying groups of new or existing customers who are *most likely* to generate revenue for the company.

Targeting

Targeting is a widely used term in marketing and, indeed, in business, but it is absolutely central to successful marketing. Classically, having identified segments that provide compatibility to the company's offering, marketers swing into action to serve these segments through a strategy of differentiation. Differentiation is concerned with developing strategies that serve different segments in the marketplace and, most importantly, track and monitor these segments, noting their developments and shifts. HNW customers have had financial institutions pretty excited in the past, but identification of this 'segment' did not generate the business that the institutions perhaps initially believed it would. HNW customers are not just defined by their wealth, but also by a number of other characteristics; they often demonstrate higher levels of financial sophistication than many other financial services consumers – for example, they will use independent financial advisers and may share the characteristics of some companies in terms of abilities to manage money. Nevertheless, for private banking and asset management in the United Kingdom there is considerable potential here. A major bank with a private banking division, for example, offers services to its private customers as illustrated in Exhibit 4.4.

EXHIBIT 4.4

Offerings in private banking, according to segments

- Individual advice and tailored solutions – private banking and wealth management are all about personal service and a relationship built around you. It is about seeing your affairs in totality and offering individual advice and sophisticated tailored solutions to meet complex financial problems.

- A personalized investment plan – a relationship manager will work with you and our Investment Strategy Group to create a customized strategic asset allocation model specific to your risk and return objectives, time horizon and liquidity requirements. Using our private bank's proprietary portfolio implementation programme, we help you construct a bespoke portfolio, using one or more absolute or relative return strategies.
- Discretionary and advisory services – the bank does not make assumptions about the level of control and involvement you want in the investment decision-making process.

The emphasis is on the individuality of the service, using such terms as 'tailoring', 'relationship' and 'bespoke', the bank's message is that the service is developed around the customer's needs and requirements, using relatively sophisticated terminology to match the expectations of this group. The message also conveys explicitly that the bank has significant expertise in the area with the use of such terms as 'Strategy Group' and 'asset allocation model'. Considerable effort may be expended on acquiring these customers; the goal is to retain them by developing a relationship that may involve the bespoke services mentioned in the snippet. This approach could be likened to concentrated or niche marketing.

However, the larger banks also have much larger markets that they deal with and, although they have developed highly detailed segments, they target a number of segments through advertising and other marketing communications. For example, a large building society in the United Kingdom has been encouraging customers of other banks to switch to them by highlighting the hidden charges that some of their competitors have been making. In this case, the target market has been customers dissatisfied with hidden bank charges and introductory rates. The development of insurance companies such as Sheilas' Wheels and Churchill are also examples of targeting specific segments with specific offerings.

Positioning

The aim of positioning is to locate a unique spot in the marketplace which sets the institution apart from its competitors; when that is established, the rest of the marketing activities – such as marketing communications and pricing – follow. Positioning activities involve defining the dimensions of a particular space that adequately represents the target audience's perceptions of the company/product/brand. An assessment then needs to be made about where the company/product/brand exists within that space, leading to modifications of the actual characteristics of company/product/brand, as well as to the perceptions of the target audience. These modifications are usually achieved by means of marketing communications and branding strategy, thus drawing strong connections between branding and positioning. Positioning, however, ensures that branding is developed to engage with perceptions of the target market – that is, it is customer-based. To develop robust positioning strategies, some good questions that financial service companies should ask themselves are as follows (adapted from Lovelock 2001):

- Which customers do we serve now and which do we want to target in the future?
- What are the characteristics of our current offerings and at which segments are they targeted?
- How do our service offerings differ from our competitors'?
- How well do the customers in the chosen segments perceive our offerings as meeting their needs?
- What changes can we make to our offerings to strengthen our competitive position within those segments?
- What does the company/brand stand for in the minds of our stakeholders?

Product differentiation is particularly challenging for financial service companies, as one insurance offering looks remarkably like another. Furthermore, they offer products that are not purchased for themselves but to enable or to avoid a particular outcome, and so are usually purchased on the basis of price or convenience rather than particular attributes of the company/brand. Positioning for financial services can be achieved by means of occupying a 'space' along dimensions that are not directly related to products – for example, branding.

Many FIs have a corporate brand; Barclays, for example, have recently repositioned their commercial division to make it a forward-thinking bank well placed to help businesses succeed today and in the future. There is also scope for positioning products. In a study into credit and charge card positioning, Blankson and Kalafatis (2007) develop a typology of positioning strategies for credit cards, although they claim that it has a wider application in services (see Table 4.5). The rankings of the positioning statements were arrived at in consultation with card executives and experts.

Their investigation, which included consumer data, showed that there was ambiguity in the positioning of credit and charge cards.

Table 4.5   Typology of positioning strategies

Dimensions	Items/statements
1. Top of the range	Upper class, top of the range, status, prestigious, posh
2. Service	Impressive service, personal attention, consider people as important, friendly
3. Value for money	Reasonable price, value for money
4. Reliability	Durability, warranty, safety, reliability
5. Attractiveness	Good aesthetics, attractive, cool, elegant
6. Country of origin	Patriotism, country of origin
7. Brand name	The name of the offering, leaders in the market, extra features, choice, wide range
8. Selectivity	Discriminatory, selective, high principles

As Table 4.6 shows, there is some overlap between the typologies suggested in Table 4.5, which suggests that no single positioning strategy was significant across the four card brands in the study. Country of origin was not used in any of the positioning strategies but all the other typologies, to a greater or lesser degree, were found. Top of the range is a position that was found to be significant in the charge card market (for which there is usually an annual fee). Brand name was common to three of the positioning strategies used by the cards in the study, with other dimensions being reliability, top of the range and service.

The current economic volatility could provide FIs with opportunities through repositioning. Many better-off consumers are looking for new

Table 4.6   An example of positioning in the credit card market

Card brand	Overall positioning strategy
Visa	Reliability and brand name
Mastercard	Brand name
Amex	Top of the range and brand name
Diners Club	Top of the range and service

providers as their faith and confidence in existing providers has been undermined. If FIs move quickly to reposition themselves along dimensions that consumers are seeking, then they may be well placed to gain new and profitable customers. Using the brand to communicate the values and the position in the marketplace that the FI occupies, the company could size some territory. Consumers are now saving rather than spending; hence, they are looking for suitable investments in companies that are transparent, behave in a sustainable way (no massive bonuses) and treat their stakeholders fairly.

Summary

- Segmentation, targeting and positioning are key strategic activities, driving much of the marketing that financial institutions carry out.
- There is some tension as the larger banks have to adapt to targeting those segments that fit with their strategic objectives – for example, growth – while maintaining their connection with the segments that generate their profits.
- Indications show that serving the segments chosen by the financial service providers can be incompatible with the desired efficiencies of standardized offerings. Furthermore, many of us expect bank services as a matter of course; yet quite clearly bank shareholders expect a return from their investment, which raises the question of serving customers who do not fall into the desired segments.
- Positioning for financial service companies, brand and products is not easy to achieve, with overlaps and ambiguities arising.

References

Akinci, S. Aksoy, S. and Atilgan, E. (2004) 'Adoption of Internet Banking Among Sophisticated Consumer Segments in an Advanced Developing Country', *International Journal of Bank Marketing*, Vol. 22, No. 3, pp. 212–32.

Black, N., Lockett, A., Ennew, C., Winkelhofer, H. and McKechnie, S. (2002) 'Modelling Consumer Choice of Distribution Channels: An Illustration from Financial Services', *International Journal of Bank Marketing*, Vol. 20, No. 4, pp. 161–73.

Blankson, C. and Kalafatis, S. (2007) 'Positioning Strategies of International and Multi-cultural-oriented Service Brands', *Journal of Services Marketing*, Vol. 21, No. 6, pp. 435–50.

Business.timesonline.co.uk/tol/business, accessed 12 May 2008.

Carbó, S., Gardner, E. and Molyneux, P. (2005), *Financial Exclusion*, Basingstoke, Palgrave Macmillan.

Farquhar, J. and Panther, T. (2008), 'Acquiring and Retaining Customers in UK Banks: An Exploratory Study', *Journal of Retailing and Consumer Services*, Vol. 15, No. 1, pp. 9–21.

Garland, R. (2004) 'Share of Wallet's Role in Customer Profitability', *Journal of Financial Services Marketing*, Vol. 8, No. 3, pp. 259–68.

Garland, R. (2005) 'Segmenting Retail Bank Customers', *Journal of Financial Services Marketing*, Vol. 10, No. 2, pp. 179–91.

HM Treasury (2007) *Mapping the Demand for, and Supply of, Third Sector Affordable Credit*, London.

Howcroft, B., Hewer, P. and Durkin, M. (2003) 'Banker-Customer Interactions in Financial Services', *Journal of Marketing Management*, Vol. 19, pp. 1001–20.

Jenkins, M. and McDonald, M. (1997) 'Market Segmentation: Organizational Archetypes and Research Agendas', *European Journal of Marketing*, Vol. 31, No. 1, pp. 17–32.

Kumar, V. and Reinartz, W. (2006) *Customer Relationship Management*, Hoboken, NJ, J. Wiley & Son.

Lee, E.-J., Kwon, K.-N. and Schumann, D. (2005) 'Segmenting the Non-adopter Category in the Diffusion of Internet Banking', *International Journal of Bank Marketing*, Vol. 23, No. 5, pp. 414–37.

Lovelock, C. (2001), *Services Marketing: People, Technology, Strategy*, 4th edn, Upper Saddle River, Prentice Hall.

McDonald, M. and Dunbar, I. (2004) *Market Segmentation*, Oxford, Elsevier Butterworth Heinemann.

Michel, D., Naudé, P., Salle, R. and Valla, J.-P. (2003) *Business-to-Business Marketing*, Basingstoke, Palgrave Macmillan.

Moneynews.co.uk, accessed 27 April 2008.

Morgan, C. and Levy, D. (2002) 'Psychographic Segmentation: How to Increase Communication ROI by Examining Values, Beliefs and Motivations', Communication World, December.

Neilsen, A. C. (2008) www.uk.nielsen.com/site/index.shtml, accessed 17 August 2008.

Reinartz, W. and Kumar, V. (2000) 'On the Profitability of Long-life Customers in a Non-contractual Setting: An Empirical Investigation and Implications for Marketing', *Journal of Marketing*, Vol. 64, No. 4, pp. 17–35.

Richarme, M. (2004) *Business Segmentation: Emerging Approaches to More Meaningful Clusters*, www.decisionanalyst.com/publ_art/b2bsegmentation.dai

Rugimbana, R. (2007) 'Youth-based Segmentation in the Malaysian Banking Sector', *International Journal of Bank Marketing*, Vol. 25, No. 1, pp. 6–21.

Thornton, J. and White, L. (2001) 'Customer Orientation and Usage of Financial Distribution Channels', *Journal of Services Marketing*, Vol. 15, No. 3, pp. 168–85.

uk.biz.yahoo.com/25042008/404/granny-online.html, accessed 27 April 2008.

www.financialinclusion-taskforce.org.uk, accessed 10 May 2008.

WARC (2006) *Segmentation*, Henley, World Advertising Research Center.

Zeithaml, V., Rust, R. and Lemon, K. (2001) 'The Customer Pyramid: Creating and Serving Profitable Customers', *California Management Review*, Vol. 43, No. 4, pp. 118–42.

Exercises

1. Consider a group of friends (for example, in your class or on Facebook) and try to identify various characteristics that they share and how they differ. Once you have identified four or five characteristics, try to group your friends into segments that might be of relevance to financial institutions. To get you going, where is their principal place of residence?

2. Get out two recent bank statements and credit card bills. Look at what you have spent and what you have purchased. What lifestyle details do these documents provide your financial services providers with?

3. Study Table 4.3 and decide, on the basis of the information presented in the table, which groups of customers might make suitable segments to target in the next 12 months. When you have identified the segment(s), outline marketing messages built around these data to encourage these groups to increase their business with the bank. What would you do with the groups that present little scope for developing business?

4. Write down three the names of three companies with which you are fairly familiar; try to ensure that they are a little different in terms of size, location and the nature of their business. From a banking services perspective, would they all fall into a homogeneous segment? If so, what are the segmentation criteria? If they appear not to fall into a homogeneous segment, how do they differ from a bank's perspective?

Further reading

Brassington, F. and Pettitt, S. (2006) *Principles of Marketing*, 4th edn, Chelmsford, Pearson Education.

McDonald, M. and Dunbar, I. (2004) *Market Segmentation*, Oxford, Elsevier Butterworth Heinemann.

Michel, D., Naudé, P., Salle, R. and Valla, J.-P. (2003) *Business-to-Business Marketing*, Basingstoke, Palgrave Macmillan.

www.dinersclub.co.uk

CASE STUDY

Customer segmentation in Swiss retail banking

Switzerland is a major international financial centre where many assets are managed. The financial services sector is well developed, highly diversified and firmly established. Nevertheless, banks are facing strong competition, as well as increasing customer requirements, and customer satisfaction depends on the extent to which the professional expertise of the banks matches the customers' need for advice. Therefore, future success will be determined by the stringent implementation of customer segmentation towards adequate products and services in order to fulfil individual needs.

The Swiss banking market

Switzerland, a small country with 7.6 million people and one of the most prosperous and economically advanced nations, is an international financial centre that includes a number of the world's major financial institutions. The country has a lengthy tradition of political, economic, legal and social stability and a long history of private banking, which began before the French Revolution, one example being the private bank Wegelin & Co. established in 1741. The Swiss franc (CHF) is one of the world's most stable currencies (Roth 2005) and the Swiss financial sector performs a significant international intermediation function within the global financial system (IMF 2002). The financial industry comprises a large part of the Swiss economy: at the end of 2007, the banking sector's total assets exceeded CHF 4,700 billion or over nine times Swiss annual GDP, by far the biggest ratio among the G10 countries (Germany 2.9 times, the United Kingdom 3.6, the United States 0.9 [SNB 2008b]) and staff employed in the banking sector numbered over 130,000 (full-time equivalents [SNB 2008a]). It is estimated that approximately 30 per cent of all internationally invested private wealth is managed in Switzerland, making it the world leader of market share in private banking services (Roth 2005).

The Swiss banking system is, in contrast to those in English-speaking countries and Japan, based on the concept of universal banking, where every bank can provide all banking services (SBA 2006). The advantages of universal banking include the ability to spread risk over a greater number of banking sectors and customers from all areas of the economy. Nonetheless, banking in Switzerland is extremely diverse and, in 2007, there were 330 banks (excluding institutions with a special field of business [SNB 2008a]). They consist of major banks (Crédit Suisse, UBS), cantonal banks, regional banks and savings banks, the Raiffeisen Bank, other banks (including commercial, stock exchange and foreign-controlled banks), branches of foreign banks and private banks. The activities and products of the institutions in these sub-sectors vary widely, from basic mortgage lending funded by local deposits to the offering of highly sophisticated products to foreign investors (IMF 2002).

Customer segmentation within financial services

The Swiss financial sector is well developed and diversified, with a high standard of risk management, supervision and regulation and near-consistent profitability (IMF 2002). Yet recently, the banking sector has been faced with increasing competition at home and abroad and the demands made by customers on their banks have risen considerably, accompanied by declining customer loyalty and multiple relationships with different banks. In this increasingly competitive marketplace, some further consolidation is likely and financial institutions need to emphasize customer relationships and the retention of existing customers, which require an in-depth understanding of their attitudes and behaviours. The decisive factor for customer satisfaction will be the extent to which a bank can effectively coordinate its professional expertise with the customer's personal need for advice (Hambrecht *et al.* 2004). Increasingly stringent implementation of customer segmentation and innovation in products and services, tailored to satisfy customer needs, will prove decisive for success.

Customer segmentation aims to recognize patterns of financial behaviour, identified by segment predictors that group individuals according to their product needs. Previous research has shown that there are various benefits from taking a segmented approach to the marketplace: a better serving of customer requirements, a tailoring of offerings and higher customer satisfaction. It can increase customer retention and create loyalty and long-term relationships, which positively affect performance. In the financial services industry, market segmentation is a common method to understand better and serve the diverse customer base with its wide ranging needs and various behaviours. Yet, marketing in the financial services industry today is still predominantly based on the income and assets of the customer, and sociodemographic features such as gender and age, which are easy to identify and easy to apply in the composition of groups. A prediction of needs from these characteristics cannot be assumed; therefore these widely used *a priori* segmentations are under review. In contrast, *post hoc* methods entail the grouping of respondents according to their responses to particular variables, focusing on customer motivations (i.e., needs/behaviour), which are more likely to result in a service based on individual needs. The refinement of existing customer segmentation and consequential implementation in specific products and services becomes increasingly important for the bank because of the need to meet clients' requirements.

A behavioural and psychographic approach to segmentation

Against the background of this competitive situation in Switzerland, a financial company in Zurich developed a new segmentation approach based on attitudes and behaviour and interviewed more than 1,200 clients and non-clients to ascertain their daily financial behaviour through a wide range of questions. An exploratory factor analysis (Principal Component Analysis) was used to determine underlying dimensions of the financial attitudes and behavioural tendencies. Five underlying dimensions – anxiety, interest in financial issues, decision styles, need for precautionary savings and spending tendency – emerged from the analysis and are described in Figure C4.1.

Subsequently, the individuals were classified into groups, based on the five factors, by applying the methodology of cluster analysis. The aim is to obtain clusters whose members are as similar in the cluster and, at the same time, as distinct to the other clusters as possible. Cluster analysis has become a common tool in marketing and is an adapted method for market segmentation as well as applied factor analysis. In the first step, a hierarchical cluster procedure (Ward) was used to identify the number of clusters,

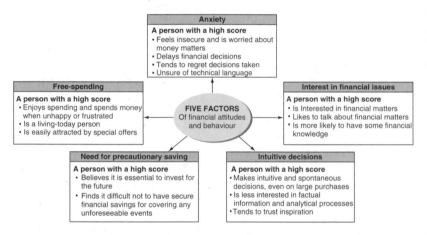

Figure C4.1   Five segments of financial attitudes and behaviour

as it provides a good criterion for the total number of possible clusters. The main disadvantage, however, is that the allocation of subjects is final, with no possibility of reassignment to another (more appropriate) group during the procedure. The necessary flexibility can be provided by adding a non-hierarchical cluster analysis in order to profit from the possibility of 're-sorting'. In the second step, therefore, the non-hierarchical cluster analysis K-means method was used to improve the results of Ward's method. It checks for each case, as to whether the previous assignment from the hierarchical analysis is best or, whether, with another assignment, the homogeneity of the new target cluster is less affected than with the previous one. These cluster procedures resulted in five clearly defined groups. The data is based on the customers' attitudes and self-stated behavioural tendencies, which allows for psychographic and behavioural segmentation of the customer base to be drawn. The following clients of the Swiss company are typical examples of the members of each cluster:

A financially attuned individual, say Ms Müller, reads the business section of the newspaper every morning attentively and likes to join conversations about financial matters. She feels quite assured and comfortable in the 'financial world' and takes her decisions in an analytical way, compares risks and likes to read about results of product comparisons. She sees a need for precautionary saving and therefore makes extra contributions to old-age provision. For her, money does not have a value of its own but is a tool to be wisely handled. [Rational consumers]

A confident person, perhaps a 29-year-old Mr Schmidt, who is in the early stages of a focused career, belongs to the secure, and not anxious, type of people. Technical language cannot unsettle him, and he states a medium interest in financial matters. He is neither a big shopper nor a big spender. Altogether, he appears to be in control of his financial matters, although he sees no need for precautionary saving at all. [Myopic consumers]

In contrast an older and more cautious person, here a Ms Wyss, considers future financial security to be essential. She needs some money away for bad times. She enjoys saving more than spending and does not like spontaneous purchasing. She prefers an analytical approach to decision-making, product and risk comparison. However, she tends to feel anxious about financial issues, is uncertain about financial terminology and postpones financial decisions. Moreover, she shows little interest in financial issues in general. [Anxious savers]

An intuitive person, given the name Ms Schwarz, has a spontaneous and intuitive way of taking decisions and spends money spontaneously. She does not think that money is just a means of becoming happier, but she does not recognize any need for precautionary saving. She does not care about 'boring' financial matters at all, but this does not make her feel insecure or anxious. [Gut-feeling followers]

A person who likes spending, perhaps a Mr Metzger, feels absolutely insecure about financial matters and financial language, and declares virtually no interest in financial topics. Furthermore, he states a need for precautionary saving, but at the same time enjoys spending and views spending as a remedy against frustration. He decides intuitively and spontaneously, even on large purchases. His self-stated spending behaviour is in conflict with a self-stated need for precautionary saving. [Anxious spenders]

The financial company segments the individuals based on the five factors and can identify five clearly interpretable profiles where from cluster I to

V, the need increases for a better handling of financial matters. Table C4.1 gives an overview.

Tailored products and services based on segmentation

Customers' financial profiles are helpful in defining the specific parameters of professional financial advice. To illustrate how financial behaviour can be modified to improve personal finance specifically for each group, examples from the area of retirement savings are chosen, as it is an important aspect of personal financial management.

Table C4.1 Five clusters related to five factors of segmentation

Cluster Factor	I. Rational consumers	II. Myopic consumers	III. Anxious savers	IV. Gut-feeling followers	V. Anxious spenders
1. Anxiety	low	low	high	medium	high
2. Interest in financial issues	high	medium	low	low	low
3. Intuitive decisions	low	medium	low	high	high
4. Need for precautionary saving	high	low	high	low	high
5. Free-spending	medium	medium	low	medium	high

The 'Rational consumers' manage their financial matters in a rational way, are involved in economic and financial matters and feel comfortable in the 'financial world'. They take their decisions in an analytical way and therefore it is important to provide them with facts and figures through clear and transparent reporting. It is important for them to understand the products before they consider their purchase.

The 'Myopic consumers' also manage their financial affairs in a rational way, except that they deny the need for precautionary saving, a kind of over-confidence in their future finance. 'Myopic consumers' are neither uninterested in financial affairs nor emotional decision-takers. In order to help them to realize the importance of retirement savings, the bank can advise them with systematic information, such as expected consumption after retirement.

The 'Anxious savers' are cautious, make their decisions in an analytical way and share a need to diminish their insecurity and their level of anxiety.

Their insecurity can be alleviated by a clear decision-making process. Greater knowledge diminishes anxiety and a higher level of information can lead to less cognitive dissonance. An authoritative base may encourage people who otherwise feel insecure in taking financial decisions: this could, for example, be a recommendation from an employer. Likewise, tax incentives can encourage them to invest in retirement plans, as a kind of approval from governmental authorities. These measures can be automated, such as with regular annual payments, which is beneficial given their disinterest in financial affairs.

The situation is more severe for the remaining two clusters. The 'Gut-feeling followers' show a spontaneous and intuitive way of decision-taking, disinterest in financial subjects and a lack of awareness for the need of provision. A critical issue is how to reach these people, as they are not interested in financial matters. This implies that conducting a campaign highlighting the importance of retirement arrangements in the business section of a newspaper will not reach them. In order to avoid people using their savings because they have a spontaneous way of decision-making, and do not have a deeper understanding of the need for making provisions, features to limit imprudent spending are possible, such as short-term or long-term restricted access to financial resources.

And, finally, the 'Anxious spenders' are those in most need of expert financial advice. These people have a strong desire for precautionary saving, but feel insecure in financial matters. As the 'Anxious spenders' enjoy spending, even use spending as a remedy against frustration, and decide spontaneously, this makes precautionary saving difficult. Features to curb spontaneous spending must be taken into consideration. Short-term restricted access can include the use of cancellation periods. Mechanisms to avoid modifying actions could be implemented, such as commitments with scheduled penalties for premature access and mid-term cancellation costs to avoid opting out of contracts. Long-term features include access to a pension only upon arriving at pensionable age. The detachment from financial issues makes it difficult to argue for or to initiate remedial action. Mechanisms to draw members of this group into financial issues can include mandatory pension funds, compulsory insurances and the offer of employer matching. High anxiety demands a clear decision process, with information to rationalize actions in order to feel assured (see Table C4.2).

Table C4.2	Plausible tailored products and services for the clusters

Cluster	Examples for services per cluster
I. Rational consumers	– clear and transparent reporting, with benchmark comparison – transparency about financial products – facts and figures more important than personal chemistry between client/advisor

Table C4.2	continued
Cluster	**Examples for services per cluster**
II. Myopic consumers	– clarification of facts about income after retirement – mandatory pension funds – risk disclosures
III. Anxious savers	– clear decision-making process, step by step procedure – recommendations (e.g., offer of employer matching) – tax incentives like IRAs (individual retirement accounts), 401k plans in the United States or Third Pillar in Switzerland – regular automated payments (e.g., in pension system)
IV. Gut-feeling followers	– choice of advisor important to promote ease – regular automated payments (e.g., in pension system) – short-term restricted access to resources (e.g., a 30-day notice period) – long-term restricted access (e.g., a feature of a long-term savings instrument)
V. Anxious spenders	– choice of advisor important to inspire confidence – restrict access to resources (e.g., cancellation periods) – mechanisms to avoid modifying actions (e.g., scheduled penalties for premature access, access to a pension only upon arriving at pensionable age) – mandatory pension funds, compulsory insurances – less frequent transaction dates (e.g., last day of the month)

Each cluster raises key issues in meeting needs, and cluster membership allows for guidance to design and adapt instruments to assist in specific financial needs.

Questions

1. This study demonstrates that by segmenting private individuals on the basis of their self-stated financial attitudes and behaviour, a yield of clearly interpretable profiles can be realised. Characterize the five customer groups on the basis of the five identified dimensions of behaviour and attitudes.

2. Different steps were needed to identify the five clusters. Can you outline the process used to achieve the five customer groups?
3. Each cluster raises key issues as to how its needs can be met and how adequate financial instruments can be used. What specific services and products would you recommend for each cluster?

References

Fünfgeld, B. and Wang, M. (2008) 'Attitudes and Behaviour in Everyday Finance: Evidence from Switzerland', NCCR working paper No. 466, University of Zurich, Zurich, June.

International Monetary Fund (IMF) (2002) 'Switzerland: Financial System Stability Assessment, including Reports on the Observance of Standards and Codes on the following topics: Banking Supervision, Securities Regulation, Insurance Regulation, payment Systems, and Monetary and Financial Policy Transparency', IMF Country Report No. 02/108, June, Washington DC.

Hambrecht, M., Grünebaum, B., Neugebauer, N. and Bernet, B. (2004) 'The Swiss Banking Industry in the Year 2010', Accenture and University of St Gallen, available at: http://www.accenture.com/NR/rdonlyres/42D43E61-3E43-4B82-A0AA-B7BF6B6F4AFB/0/SwissBanking2010_e.pdf (accessed 20 October 2008).

Roth, U. P. (2005) 'A Center of Excellence in Global Banking', Swiss Bankers Association (SBA), 14 June 2005 at the Swiss-American Chamber of Commerce, New York NYC, available at: http://www.amcham.ch/events/content/downloads05/Roth_NYC_June_2005-A4.pdf (accessed 20 October 2008).

Swiss Bankers Association (SBA) (2006) 'The Swiss Banking Sector', Compendium Edition 2006, Basel, available at: http://shop.sba.ch/11116_e.pdf (accessed 26 October 2008).

Swiss National Bank (SNB) (2008a) 'Banks in Switzerland 2007', Vol. 92, June, available at: http://www.snb.ch/en/iabout/stat/statpub/bchpub/stats/bankench (accessed 26 October 2008).

Swiss National Bank (SNB) (2008b) 'Financial Stability Report', June, available at: http://www.snb.ch/en/iabout/finstab/id/finstab_report (accessed 26 October 2008).

This case study was written by Brigitte Fünfgeld, a Senior Financial Consultant in Switzerland, and affiliated to the Swiss Banking Institute at the University of Zurich, Switzerland, and Mei Wang, Assistant Professor in Finance and Financial Markets at the Swiss Finance Institute (ISB) University of Zurich, and project leader of the 'University Priority Research Program: Behavioural Finance and Wealth Management' at the University of Zurich, Switzerland.

The material in the case has been drawn from a variety of interviews, published sources and research reports. For more details see Fünfgeld and Wang 2008.

5

Information regarding marketing financial services

Contents

Learning outcomes

At the end of this chapter, the reader will be able to:

- Appreciate different types and sources of data that underpin decision-making in the marketing of financial services

- Describe the processes in customer relationship management

- Provide an outline of the main considerations of managing customer information for marketing decisions

Introduction

Without information about the markets in which they operate and about the customers whom they serve, financial institutions (FIs) would be at an enormous competitive disadvantage. In this chapter, we will be providing an overview of the ways in which FIs use information to achieve their marketing objectives. Significant resources are allocated to maintaining state-of-the-art information systems that support the advanced statistical analyses underpinning segmentation. IT has changed the face of marketing information in the amounts of data that can be stored and manipulated, giving rise to the term data warehouse – which refers to the repository of data in an organization, often incorporating the means of retrieval, loading, extracting and analysing. FIs are also required to provide information for external agencies, as described in Exhibit 5.1.

EXHIBIT 5.1

Treating customers fairly

The Financial Services Authority's (FSA's) supervisory objectives are under-pinned by an initiative known as Treating Customers Fairly (TCF), meaning that FIs must be able to prove that fair customer outcomes are central to everything they do. By the end of March 2008, FIs were expected to have appropriate management information in place to demonstrate whether they treat their customers fairly. By the end of December, they needed to be able to demonstrate, to themselves and to others, how they consistently treat their customers fairly through embedded business practices. The FSA has called for firms to accelerate their progress towards TCF outcomes. Any evidence of significant potential or actual customer detriment will meet with more intense FSA supervisory and enforcement action.

Compiled from KPMG, Working to Rules: Regulatory Bulletin, 2008.

As discussed in Chapter 2, the financial services industry is subject to a number of regulatory bodies, one of which is the FSA. As Exhibit 5.1 shows, information needs to be collected, compiled and provided to the FSA that shows that FIs are complying with the TCF initiative. FIs therefore need to resource both staff and systems to set up and maintain the collection of this information to meet the deadline and to satisfy the FSA in future that these systems are in place.

Researching the marketplace

Although, philosophically and practically, there is a difference between knowledge and information, we would subscribe to the view that information can be transformed into knowledge, which contributes to an organization's competitive advantage (Vargo and Lusch 2004). The challenge for companies and individuals in the twenty-first century is to be able to manage the information that they receive in order to be able to make decisions, which ultimately lead to that competitive advantage. Conventional models of systems that provide information for marketing decision-making (e.g., Brassington and Pettitt, 2006) show that information generally flows from two principal sources: external sources and internal sources. External sources can consist of both secondary data such as published reports – for example, government reports, British Banking Association [BBA] and FSA publications, commissioned research via commercial companies such as Ipsos MORI [www.ipsos-mori.com], purchased reports such as Mintel) and, of course, the press and sources available via the Internet. It has been suggested that market research could be a key advantage of *social networking* for businesses. MySpace and Facebook aim to educate, enlighten and share experiences, expertise and knowledge, but there is also scope for firms to conduct valuable market research and get to know their customer base. The following exhibit provides an example of the business opportunities for FIs and other businesses that arise from social networking.

EXHIBIT 5.2

LinkedIn: Professionals networking

The biggest on-line social network intended for professional use has been valued at more than $1 billion. LinkedIn was launched in 2003 by Reid Hoffman, a veteran of on-line payment company PayPal. The network has 23 million members, with more than a million new ones joining each month. Members of LinkedIn use the site to make professional contacts, recruit staff or find new jobs. Although it has its headquarters in Silicon Valley, it claims to operate the largest on-line professional network in Europe. The company's record in finding ways to make money sets it apart from other social networks that have struggled to meet high expectations for advertising revenue. Besides carrying job advertising, LinkedIn charges members a subscription for 'premium' services that let them do things like make professional introductions through the network. It also has a 'software as a service' business, charging a subscription to corporate recruiters to help them manage their hiring on the site. The site generated revenues of approximately $85 million in 2008, more than double those of 2007. With over 1 million professionals in the United Kingdom, LinkedIn has become one of the United Kingdom's fastest-growing on-line brands, according to Nielsen Online. In the United Kingdom, 75 per cent of the group's users are graduates, with a particularly strong presence in the IT, new media and finance sectors – the latter of which is one of the fastest-growing sectors on the site. The average salary across the website's UK members is around £60,000. To earn its $1 billion price tag, LinkedIn has a diverse revenue stream – with four sources of income: premier subscriptions, job sales, on-line advertising and company recruitment. Although the vast majority of its members take up the free service, a small number pay £10 a month to make contact with people outside their own network. Despite concerns for the advertising market in the United Kingdom, the personal information LinkedIn collects on its members can prove invaluable to advertisers, who can target their adverts at specific groups of people. LinkedIn's decision to open an office in London earlier this year follows that of Facebook, who reshuffled its European operations.

Compiled by the authors from material in the *Financial Times*, www.LinkedIn.com and the *Daily Telegraph*.

There are also physical networking opportunities such as the British Banking Association once again, the Council for Mortgage Lenders, the Association of British Insurers and the Chartered Institute of Marketing where FI marketers can interact.

Organizational learning

All the information in the world will not necessarily result in competitive advantage; it is the way that the information is used, interpreted and transformed into knowledge that generates competitive advantage. Learning about markets can contribute to knowledge about how these markets function and how the company can work most effectively within them. Organizations learn if they continuously acquire, process and disseminate knowledge about markets, products, processes and technologies from a wide range of sources, including competitors. If the FI is market-oriented, then managers know the importance of market sensing and interpretation of market intelligence (Cravens and Piercy 2006). Market sensing can be envisaged as a structure where managers identify the most significant events that affect their business and its markets over a three- to five-year horizon (see Figure 5.1). The bottom left box shows that there is a very high probability of imminent danger to the business that is likely to have a severe impact. Managers need to take immediate action to minimize the impact of this event.

Managers use this framework to identify the most significant events that are likely to occur in their environment by positioning each one in

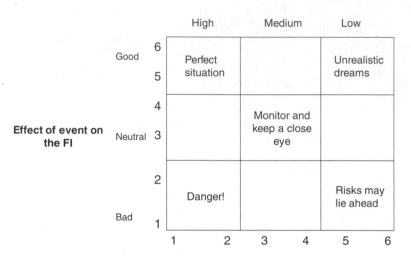

Figure 5.1 Framework for market sensing
Source: Adapted from Cravens and Piercy 2006.

the matrix according to the estimated probability and the effect that the event would have on the business. For example, banks might have used this framework to estimate the impact of purchasing collateralized debt instruments. The effect would have been severe if the instruments were to fail and the probability of this happening should have been detected as being relatively high, but the aim was to pass on the debt around the world. The probability of the borrowers of the home loans in the United States not being able to repay was high and, if buying into the instruments was going to have a damaging effect on the company, it is mystifying how so many FIs bought so extensively into this area. Cravens and Piercy (2006) propose a number of dimensions that underpin market sensing as follows:

Objective enquiry: where it is important to be open to new ideas and new ways of looking at the marketplace. This activity seems to be something that FIs find particularly difficult, which contributes to the lack of differentiation in the sector.
Information distribution: where information is disseminated throughout the FI, sharing information on customers and competitors. Previous ways of directing information to organizational functions can

result in an unwillingness to share information across departments. The speed of information systems also helps to unlock and spread information formerly restricted. Obtaining a 'customer view' means that staff have to have access to update customer information, but access to strategic information may vary from company to company.

Mutually informed interpretations: the full power of information will only be released if the FI shares a vision about the direction of the company and the marketplace with its stakeholders.

Accessible memory: what happened previously has an important role to play in an FI moving forward. How can the experiences and learning of staff be captured when they move on? These experiences need to be integrated into the information systems of the FI.

Organizational learning does consist of a set of practices and activities, but it is also concerned with a state of mind within the organization where an FI learns from its mistakes and embeds that learning in its collective memory, demonstrating an open-mindedness about new initiatives. The sustainability and ethics of the creation of financial instruments that contain both 'good' and toxic debt, which are then sold on, are indefensible, but the action of governments in taking a stake in the businesses has moderated the severity of the outcomes.

Customer relationship management (CRM)

customer relationship management (CRM): usually refers now to the systems that support relationship marketing

loyalty programmes: schemes that a FI develops to foster customer loyalty, often consisting of rewards to customers

Customer relationship management (CRM) is related to relationship marketing, as it is concerned with improving customer service through delivering value, coordination and selling efficiency supported through information systems (Cooper *et al.* 2008). CRM initiatives focus on important goals for marketing such as **loyalty programmes**, call centre management and sales force automation, requiring involvement of IT and senior management. CRM has often been used to describe technology-based customer solutions for sales of an information-enabled relationship marketing strategy, but it has a number of interpretations in practice, such as direct mail, loyalty card schemes or databases. CRM, and the systems that underpin it, allow FIs to identify customers and access their records, including personal information as well as products purchased, payment histories and an extensive array of information that summarizes the relationship that that customer has with the FI. However, companies have different interpretations of what CRM is and how it can be implemented, as shown in Figure 5.2. CRM has not always been successful and has, in some cases, been merely the means of selling products without using

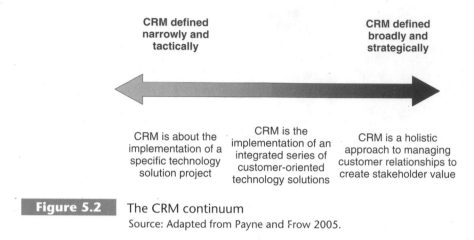

CRM defined narrowly and tactically

CRM defined broadly and strategically

CRM is about the implementation of a specific technology solution project

CRM is the implementation of an integrated series of customer-oriented technology solutions

CRM is a holistic approach to managing customer relationships to create stakeholder value

Figure 5.2 The CRM continuum
Source: Adapted from Payne and Frow 2005.

appropriate information to target the products to customers who show a high probability of purchase.

A further reason that has been put forward for the failure of CRM initiatives has been an over-emphasis on its technology component. The paler end of the arrow denotes the use of CRM as a technological solution purely to facilitate a particular activity – for example, a database that supports direct mailing for sales, that it works at a functional level (Kumar and Reinartz 2006). The middle of the arrow probably represents how CRM is implemented commonly in most banks and larger building societies, where it supports multichannels, call centres and direct mailings by focusing on the customer experience, building a 'single customer view' across all channels. The implementation of CRM at the darker end of the arrow focuses on its strategic contribution to an FI and its network of stakeholders such as suppliers, customers and employees.

The key to CRM and marketing as a whole is the value creation process (Kumar and Reinartz 2006, Payne and Frow 2005), specifically: the value that the customer receives and the value the FI receives from the customer, including **lifetime value**. Value creation is the fulcrum of contemporary marketing, therefore needs to be incorporated at every level of marketing. One of the current challenges that CRM has to address is multichannel marketing, especially being able to integrate channels to meet customer needs, using information collected from one channel to provide service in another. Payne and Frow (2005) propose that the integration of channels rests on an **information management** process that collects, collates and uses customer data and information from all customer contact points ('touches') to generate customer insights and appropriate marketing responses. According to these writers, the key elements of an information management process are:

lifetime value: a metric that attempts to calculate the value of a customer to an FI during the time that the customer remains with the FI

information management: the activities that support the collection and supply of information to stakeholders, sometimes referred to as knowledge management

Data repository – provides a corporate memory (possibly a data warehouse) that is capable of the appropriate analyses (e.g., identifying clusters of customers suitable for a direct mailing for car insurance). An enterprise data model manages data to minimize duplications and inconsistencies.

IT systems – integration of databases is often required (see Exhibit 5.2) where a new company has been acquired. Technology integration is required before user access can be provided and data integrated. Marketing and IT do not have a record of successful cooperation.

Analytical tools – the vast amount of data that FIs have is worthless unless it can be made to work and to do this a range of analytical techniques is applied, some of which will be discussed later in the chapter.

Front- and back-office applications – this phrase refers to the difference between the customer interface and all the activities that support that interface. For example, when a customer calls the call centre, the FI employee needs to be able to access that file quickly and have the information needed there to respond to the customer's need and to update the file with the outcome of the conversation. This kind of interaction, therefore, involves the design of an IT system that supports this interface and the network of suppliers, staff, finance and logistics.

CRM technology participants – the planning of the system that provides this kind of service cannot usually be bought off-the-shelf and requires a partnership with the relevant IT systems provider, as shown in Exhibit 5.3.

EXHIBIT 5.3

Maintaining the edge?

Bradford & Bingley (B&B) considered how it could unite its new businesses culturally and technologically to optimize the strength of its combined assets. The aim of the new web infrastructure was to integrate newly acquired businesses rapidly into the group to deliver new services. B&B saw clear benefits for installing one future-proof, flexible solution. For one thing, it would cost less than separate upgrades with each change. A flexible infrastructure would be able to adopt new IT applications and businesses as needed. It would also help the business to market new products and services faster, providing customers with a speedier, more informed service. Sharing the cost of a single IT management service across the group would work out cheaper than maintaining independent networks. This fitted in with the group's vision to drive down costs and encourage strategic planning. While B&B was adding new acquisitions, its infrastructure simply evolved, resulting in a number of network agreements. In 1998, when B&B decided to ratio-nalize its approach, it appointed BT as a strategic partner to streamline all its networks over a five-year period. BT now delivers managed voice and data services, collaborative tools, security services, disaster recovery and hosts the group's e-infrastructure. It also provides management and maintenance of wide and local area networking, which connects more than 550 branches in the United Kingdom. Staff now have remote access to calendar, diary, e-mail and the intranet – a huge benefit to a mobile salesforce that depends on remaining in touch with market developments. Having outsourced its IT, B&B can concentrate on its core business and dedicate its resources to enhancing customer service.

Compiled by the authors from material formerly available on www.bradfordand bingley.co.uk before its takeover by Santander.

CRM should operate at strategic level in the organization; Figure 5.3 shows the key dimensions that contribute to its strategic imple-mentation.

By adopting a customer value orientation, the FI develops the vision that can drive the CRM strategy at the most senior levels within the company. In order to deliver the customer value, all processes, whether IT-driven or people-based, need to be structured and supported to that end.

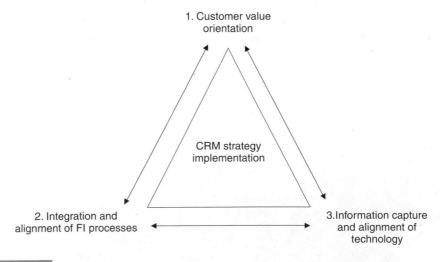

Figure 5.3 Strategic CRM
Source: Adapted from Kumar and Reinartz 2006.

Customer value

Customer value in marketing has two interpretations as follows:

- Value emerges for the customer during a value creation process (Grönroos 2000)
- The economic value of the customer relationship to the firm (Kumar and Reinartz 2006).

The first interpretation refers to a core dimension of contemporary marketing thought about what marketing is actually about and the second, which we will be discussing in this section, is concerned with the profitability of a customer to the company. A customer, of course, will only engage in a relationship with the company if they can realize value from the relationship, from which in turn, the company should be able to generate some revenue.

How does a company measure its performance? Traditional measures include sales volume/value, profits and market share (volume/value), total number of customers and awareness. However, metrics need to reflect the strategic priorities of the company and the implementation of CRM systems allows FIs to look at customers individually, thus generating additional metrics that can measure individual customer value to the FI. Kumar and Reinartz (2006) provide examples and evaluations of a number of customer value metrics that companies use.

Size of wallet

This metric is the amount of a buyer's total spending in a category or with a particular FI and is measured in monetary terms. A customer may spend a total of £1,750 a month on financial services, which is made up of spending on a mortgage, house and car insurance, regular savings into a savings account, credit card bill and overdraft fee, spread over as many as six different providers in this instance. Each FI knows how much that customer spends with them but they do not know, without gathering extra information from market research, the exact proportion of the customer's wallet that that 'spend' represents. Size of wallet is a critical piece of information to an FI as it tells them the customer's buying potential. Generally, the larger the wallet, the more attractive the customer, which explains the interest in high net worth individuals (HNW) displayed by FIs.

Share of wallet (SW)

Share of wallet is the proportion of category value accounted for by the FI within its base of buyers. This metric can be measured at individual customer level or at an aggregate level – for example, a segment. Individual share of wallet is the proportion of category value accounted for by the FI from the buyer's total purchases (from other FIs) of financial services. Using the size of wallet example above, if the consumer spends £350 per month on credit card purchases then the credit card company has 20 per cent of that customer's financial services expenditure. The information for that figure comes from the internal records of the credit card company and from surveys. As Kumar and Reinartz (2006) observe, these data are expensive to collect, but can be extrapolated to the entire customer base, thus justifying the high costs. SW is an important indicator of customer loyalty, from a behavioural perspective, but is not useful for predicting future revenues from a customer.

Share and size of wallet are important metrics for FIs and Figure 5.4 shows how segmenting customers along these two dimensions provides information for allocating resources to customers.

This particular figure demonstrates a very straightforward way of analysing the options that an FI may consider when a customer's size and share of wallet have been calculated. When the size of the wallet is small and the share of wallet is low, then the FI should not pay this customer a great deal of attention as the chances of generating a reasonable income from this customer are small. When the size of wallet is known or calculated to be large, but the existing share small, then it is

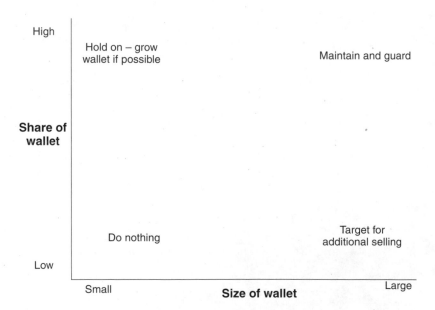

Figure 5.4 Size and share of wallet
Source: Adapted from Kumar and Reinartz 2006.

worth the FI expending resources on this customer to try and enlarge their share of this customer's sizeable wallet. The ideal situation is when share of wallet and size of wallet are large, in which case the FI needs to guard this customer from any attentions from competitors, as this is a customer of whose business other FIs would like to have a share.

These metrics are concerned with individual customers or buyers. Market share, on the other hand, is calculated across buyers and non-buyers. Some FIs have a small market share but have a high share of wallet with a relatively low number of wealthy people; a number of smaller building societies in the United Kingdom would fall into this category – for example, National Counties (www.ncbs.co.uk).

Cross-selling and up-selling

An aim of CRM is to identify opportunities for cross-selling and up-selling financial services to customers of an FI. 'Cross-selling' means increasing the number of services or products which a customer acquires from the FI – for example, selling a customer insurance as well as providing a mortgage. The best prospects for cross-selling are those customers who have a high propensity to use the service within the bank, but do not yet use it. These customers may already use this service from another bank and must be persuaded to switch (Kamakura *et al*. 2003). 'Up-selling' focuses on improving the conditions of previously acquired products to keep customers consuming – for example, migrating a customer from an ordinary current account to one where there are extra benefits and a fee (Salazar *et al*. 2007). Although different, both these activities aim to reinforce the attachment between the FI and the customer through continued consumption (possibly using recency/frequency/monetary value [RFM] analysis). It is important not to offer customers products that they show little indication of needing; this creates alienation and a resistance to responding in future to more relevant offerings, owing to negative feelings about the FI. An analytic basis for cross-selling and up-selling in three stages has been proposed using data from an FI database (Salazar *et al*. 2007) consisting of:

Segmentation – customers do not buy financial services frequently and purchases tend to be centred on life stages (e.g., marriage and home loan). A statistical analysis of Experian types available on the FI database was performed to refine customer groupings.

Repurchase behaviour – to analyse the pattern of acquisitions, the 'Purchase tree' method displayed the patterns from the root upwards with the most popular first purchase by each segment, showing whether successive purchases were examples of up- or cross-selling. Analysis of customer characteristics available on the database, such as demographic and behavioural variables, should then facilitate an understanding of factors driving the repurchase.

Time sequence – not only is offering the right product desirable, but also it should be offered at the right time according to an appropriate point in the lifecycle. Therefore, the final stage of the analysis tries to identify the moment when a customer is most likely to respond positively to an offer. A survival curve plots the influence of time against the probability of the repurchase.

Among the findings of this study, the researchers note that analysis of acquisitions pattern shows how products interrelate, with age and previous experience (channel, value) with the FI being important. It was found also to be advisable to contact customers shortly after their purchases as a means of increasing repurchase ratios, perhaps as a result of satisfaction or familiarity. The key problem for FIs is being able to estimate the probability of customer propensity to use the service within and outside the FI concerned; therefore, there is a need to develop statistical models that can provide these probabilities. Having a database and using CRM techniques is not in itself a means of achieving strong relationships. Indeed, as Kamakura *et al.* (2003) argue, injudicious mailings have created resistance. The mass of data that FIs have accumulated about their customers can, if analysed appropriately, provide a firm basis for cross- and up-selling. Often data available in-house needs to be supplemented by external information supplied through market research. Usage indicators used by Kamakura *et al.* (2003) were grouped as follows:

- Conveniences – ATM, channel usage, automatic bill payment
- Investments – special cheques, savings, mutual funds and gold
- Risk management – life insurance, car insurance
- Credit – mortgage, loans, credit card.

Customer attrition

As stated above, the aim of CRM is to facilitate customer relationships to minimize the chances of a customer leaving the relationship. In order to understand how to retain customers, FIs also need to understand how and why customers leave or defect. Customer turnover is often referred to as customer attrition or, more often, churn. If an FI is successful in reducing customer churn then profits are increased owing to improved revenue from these customers and a reduction in the costs of seeking new customers, such as advertising. The challenge for FIs is to be able to model attrition, not just over a year but over a number of years, which will show how, by increasing the retention rate by just 1 per cent, revenue will improve significantly. Customer churn has been calculated on the basis of a number of variables, such as product ownership, phone banking, card ownership, age and gender (Van den Poel and Larivière 2004). The findings of this study suggest that there are two critical periods during the relationship when attrition or churn is likely to occur – during the first few years of the relationship (with the relationship stabilizing after about seven years) and at 20 years. The variables that were likely to influence retention were demographic characteristics and environmental change (e.g., during a period of prosperity). Behavioural measures of how many products were owned and how recent interactions have been were also important (Van den Poel and Larivière 2004). For FIs, knowledge about these critical periods allows them to plan appropriate interventions, such as carefully targeted offers, personal contact and loyalty rewards.

Customer persistence

Persistence regards the extent to which currently profitable or unprofitable customers are likely to remain in that state. It is common practice in the financial services industry to estimate future customer profitability on existing profitability, even though there is little to suggest that this is a good predictor (Campbell and Frei 2004); indeed, it is a metric that looks back rather than forward. Assumptions about loyalty suggest that current profitability may not be a good indicator of future profitability because customers become less price-sensitive, less costly to serve and purchase higher quantities of services the longer that they stay with an FI. If tiers of service levels are based around current profitability, then there is a danger that low current profitability customers may be placed in a tier that masks their future profitability. For example, an FI might note from its information system that a particular customer is a relatively low spender and so decide to place this customer in a tier where service levels are basic. Although this customer has the potential to be profitable, they are not going to be encouraged to up their spending with this particular FI when they receive basic service levels. There may be any number of reasons for a period of relatively low spend during a given period, such as a period of ill-health or embarking on a new career. In estimating the profitability of a customer, Campbell and Frei (2004) used the following variables:

- interest revenue – the interest that the bank earns from customer deposit balances
- fee revenue – all the fees that relate to monthly service charges, overdrafts, minimum balances, etc.
- total revenue – represents the revenue less the transaction cost
- transaction cost – these costs are determined by an FI's costing system and would include staff, supplies, equipment, etc.

FIs may use other criteria for calculating customer profitability, but these researchers found that interest revenue appeared to predict future profitability better than fee revenue.

Given that, for FIs, a relationship with a customer can be lengthy, it is important for them to know how much a particular customer is worth to them over the period of the relationship. Have they managed to cross-sell or up-sell? How much has it cost them to do that? How much has it cost to generate the levels of satisfaction for the customer to enlarge their share of wallet with the FI? A metric that has gained a great deal of interest is customer lifetime value (CLV), although ways of estimating CLV are varied and highly contentious. One perspective is that CLV is a function of a customer's future gross profits (revenue after deducting costs of services sold and other marginal and variable costs), the propensity for a customer to continue in a relationship (customer retention) and the marketing resource allocated to the customer (Berger *et al.* 2006). Unlike using existing profitability as a measure, CLV is a forward-looking metric. Another question that arises is whether CLV is calculated on an individual basis or whether, as with most FIs, on an aggregate basis across segments. A strong argument against this latter practice is presented by Berger *et al.* (2006), who reckon that individually calculated CLV metrics will enhance overall shareholder value in spite of the higher cost.

Linked to the notion of customer profitability is the idea of balancing resources involved in the acquisition and retention of customers. Since there is inevitably some churn or attrition in the customer base, there is a need to replace customers that are lost – a process referred to as customer acquisition. But there remains the question of how much to spend, in terms of both acquiring new customers and retaining existing ones. The overall aim is to achieve profitability from the customer and this model pulls together the activities that contribute to that profitability.

In Figure 5.5, the process from prospect to profitability stage is shown. Prospects are potential customers – that is, consumers, whose overall profile suggests that they may be appropriate targets for the FI, perhaps according to their size of wallet. Not all of the prospects are acquired, whether this be through a direct mail campaign or the development and promotion of a savings account. It is important to avoid under-spending in the acquisition and retention of customers, as it is detrimental to return on investment. Retention, in particular, must be resourced, as it has been argued extensively (Farquhar 2005, Reichheld 1996) that retention contributes significantly to long-term customer profitability.

Satisfaction and share of wallet

Loyalty to brands is thought to be declining, with customers increasingly being polygamous (Bennett and Rundle-Thiele 2005), therefore it is of

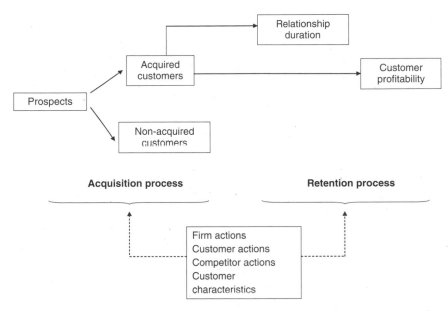

Figure 5.5 Linking customer acquisition, relationship duration and customer profitability
Source: Adapted from Reinartz et al. (2005).

interest to understand what share of a customer's expenditure an FI actually has and what influences that share. It has long been thought that customer satisfaction has an important influence on customer behaviour and links between satisfaction and retention have been proposed. Retention and share of wallet are related, as the relationships that customers have with companies implies a link, therefore an association with share of wallet and satisfaction can be expected. Research has shown that changes in satisfaction are positively related to the share of wallet a customer allocates to a particular FI over time. This relationship is moderated by demographic and situational customer characteristics, particularly income and length of relationship (Cooil et al. 2007). The implications of this study are that satisfaction needs to be considered in relation to customer share of wallet, so that customers reach the levels of satisfaction that correspond to higher share of wallet levels. The authors also emphasize the importance of a longitudinal as opposed to a cross-sectional evaluation of customer satisfaction and behavioural data.

Loyalty programmes

An important feature of business in the last 20 years or so has been the introduction of loyalty programmes, where companies seek to retain

Table 5.1	Opportunities and risks of a loyalty programme

Benefits	Risks
Customer loyalty	Dissatisfaction with rewards
Steer customer behaviour	Dissatisfaction with reward process
Up-sell and cross-sell opportunities	Improper cost/benefit analysis
Reduction in churn	
Promotion of new or poorly performing products	

Source: Adapted from www.mahadiscounts.com.

customers, to encourage them to spend more and to increase the frequency of their purchasing. One of the most celebrated loyalty schemes has been that of Tesco, which will probably be developed further as the company penetrates the retail financial services market. Although customer retention does not necessarily generate profitability, especially in financial services, so loyalty programmes within financial services tend to be patchy. Reward schemes tend to operate with credit cards offering cash back, points or air miles. As Table 5.1 indicates, there are opportunities and risks for the company in designing and maintaining a loyalty programme.

A debate rages whether loyalty programmes are effective – that is, whether the benefits outlined in Table 5.1 exceed the risks. Underpinning loyalty programmes is the notion of repurchase and/or continued patronage; FIs will use their CRM systems to quantify the influence of the programme on customers' future purchase behaviour. Research into the effectiveness of loyalty programmes is limited, but a recent study into convenience stores has drawn distinctions between the behaviour of heavy, moderate and light users. Heavy users claimed the rewards but did not increase their spending levels or loyalty. The programme did have a positive effect on light and moderate buyers, who increased their purchases and became more loyal. However, the customers' response to the loyalty programme was varied, reinforcing the notion that a relationship is with an individual customer (Liu 2007).

EXHIBIT 5.4

Reward scheme

Britannia is the only building society to share its profits directly with its customers. The society's unique membership reward is an example of how they are promoting their message of building a fairer society. Each year they reward their members for their loyalty with a share of the profits. As a building society, they do not have shareholders but instead customers are members of the society. Over the last 12 years, the society has shared more than £500 million with its members, with individual members enjoying a reward of up to £500 a year. When a customer takes out a mortgage or opens a qualifying savings account with the society – as with any building society – they become a member, and therefore eligible to earn the society's unique Membership Reward. Once an individual has been a member for two years, they can start to earn reward points on every qualifying Britannia product they have.

Compiled by the authors from www.britannia.co.uk, before it merged with the Co-operative Bank.

Not only does this membership scheme reward members for staying with the society (two years), but also for the number of products that a customer has with the society. Britannia Building Society have invested substantial amounts over the years in their information systems, recognizing over a decade ago that information would be part of gaining competitive advantage (Dawes and Worthington 1995). In spite of the attractiveness of the rewards, it is likely that the society's customers share only part of their wallet with the society, having other products with other FIs or buy more than one brand in any category (Uncles *et al.* 2003). The challenge for any loyalty programme is therefore to address the underlying reasons for polygamy (for FIs this means being multibanked) and to convince customers to buy enough of their brand to cover the costs of any loyalty programme. Managers, therefore, need to understand how to encourage customers to increase usage and to discourage engagement with competing brands; as Uncles *et al.* comment, it is only an exceptional programme that will change purchasing behaviour.

There appear to be three possible strategies open to loyalty managers based on loyalty programmes (Uncles *et al.* 2003) for FIs. The first strategy is to grow the size of the brand by making the brand acceptable to a large number of potential customers. This is a strategy that appears to have been adopted by some of the larger high-street banks, through advertising, offering attractive rates and trying to offer greater value. The second strategy is to create a niche brand by keeping the number of customers perhaps relatively low but trying to increase the average spend of these customers. Medium-sized and smaller building societies are in a strong position to be able to pursue this strategy (see Exhibit 5.4). A third strategy is for a big brand to become a super-loyalty brand, where customers demonstrate strong commitment and have higher levels of repeat purchase. It is hard to think of an FI that is in this position, although Tesco may well be in a position to pursue this strategy in the future.

The scarcity of loyalty schemes in the financial services sector may be self-explanatory in that there is little evidence to suggest that they work. A fairly damning statement from Kumar and Reinartz (2006) is that loyalty programmes do not change behaviour as much as reinforcing existing behaviour and at a much higher cost to the company!

Organizing information

The aim of this chapter so far has been to give some insight into how FIs mine the information that they amass about customers to develop coherent marketing strategies. Internal information has emerged very clearly from this overview as playing a major role in providing detailed information about customers, both personal and business. Valuable though this information undoubtedly is, it does not tell FIs much about prospective customers and for that they need to rely on traditional marketing research practices. Exhibit 5.5 provides an example of a business-to-business project conducted by an agency for a client.

EXHIBIT 5.5

B2B and business banking: a client example

The client, a current niche provider of corporate benefits, wanted to refocus its efforts on the UK market and introduce new product packages. The target markets were both direct (employers themselves) and indirect (through independent financial advisers [IFAs] and employee benefits consultants [EBCs]) in the United Kingdom. The agency conducted research among a) medium to large employers; and b) IFAs and EBCs to understand attitudes towards providers, including the client, and the likely new products. The employers were structured by size, in terms of number of employees. The research was conducted in two stages: a qualitative exploration of the market and issues around provider branding and product enhancements; followed by a quantitative measurement of attitudes towards different providers and products and an assessment of the barriers facing our client in their aim of making a more serious entry into the UK market.

Adapted by the authors from www.gfknop.com/customresearch-uk/sectors/financial/casestudies.

However, many FIs operate across the globe and require information about markets in different economies, continents and cultures. Research companies, such as ACNeilsen, TNS and Euromonitor, prepare reports for sale to companies – for example, a report on credit card spending in

Venezuela (see www.euromonitor.com/Financial_Cards_in_Venezuela). The globalization of financial services requires global marketing information systems. FIs garner vast amounts of information, which presents a challenge to managers in organizing that information so that it is available in appropriate formats to those who need the information for decision-making. Consequently, creation and management of information systems so that decisions can be reached that are based on good information and analyses are essential. To meet this need, specialist suppliers develop and supply integrated suites of software, but the problem lies not in the technical systems but in integration within the company – for example, between marketing and advertising, marketing and sales. Therefore, FIs need to be able to have integrated systems that allow them to meet their marketing objectives. In Figure 5.6, a model of information systems (IS) support is proposed based on research conducted by Daniel *et al.* (2003). In this model, marketing is envisaged as four major stages as follows:

Define markets and understand value – this stage is concerned with identifying which markets the FI is in and any which it might seek to enter, including the segments that it wishes to target. How will the customers in those segments understand value and how well does the competition deliver that value?

Create value proposition – to achieve this aim, it is necessary to understand customer needs and the relative attractiveness of customer segments – for example, high net worth. What value does the FI seek in terms of volume or revenue? What value will be offered to the customers?

Communicate and deliver value – communications are integrated and consist of channels such as direct mail, telephone, Internet, personal selling and mass media. FIs are heavy users of advertising where images and scenarios can vigorously convey the value proposition of the intangible offerings. The delivery of financial services can take place through a similar range of channels, offering opportunity for positive interaction between customer and institution.

Monitor value – this stage consists of evaluating the value that the FI receives from the selected customers; for example, are those high net worth customers really generating value for the company or just tying up a lot of resources? Are the objectives that were set for marketing communications and marketing strategies being met?

The advances of IT offer enormous benefits to marketing but may, in some cases, leave marketing behind or expose weaknesses in marketing sophistication in some FIs. It has been proposed that five factors of strategic perspective, marketing 'not just in name', proactive use of IT, marketing orientation and monitoring competition underlie the sophistication of retail financial services information systems (Colgate 2000). It

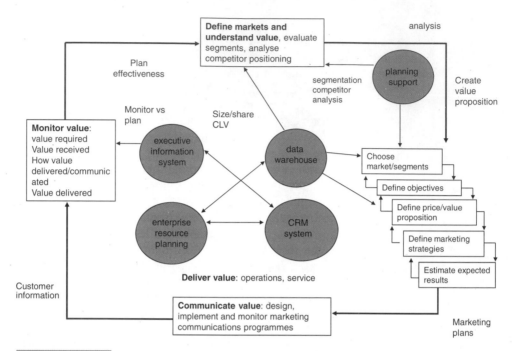

Figure 5.6 IS support for financial services marketing
Source: Adapted from Daniel *et al.* (2003).

cannot be assumed that FIs have highly developed marketing orientation and levels of skills and knowledge; like many industries and sectors, there is considerable variation in the capacity of these organizations to conduct the stages of marketing cited above.

Ethics in research and information management

ethical codes: codes that an FI follows in order to practise marketing or business according to moral values

Research and information is governed by **ethical codes** and conduct promoted by the Market Research Society (www.marketresearch.org.uk/code.htm) that inform privacy, data protection and human rights. However, the ease with which information can be stored and transported has resulted in a number of breaches when laptops and data storage devices have been either mislaid or stolen. FI customers are naturally concerned that their personal and commercial activities can become available to thieves and that their accounts can be accessed. FIs have to respond to these incidents by ensuring that customer data is fully protected and that they respond quickly to customer concerns. In these instances, trust has to be rebuilt. Security breaches have occurred and crime on the Internet is ever present, specifically phishing and spyware. Customers are naturally concerned with what happens to their data, especially the possibility that information about them could end up in the hands of identity thieves. Strategies to build trust are important in the face of sophisticated Internet scams that threaten to erode consumers' confidence in the ability of their FIs to keep information secure (www.guardian.co.uk/money/2008/aug/26/consumeraffairs.banks).

Summary

In this chapter, we have explored the role of information in the marketing of financial services. FIs have to meet the requirements of regulatory bodies, as well analysing customer and market data to develop strategies. In order for FIs to make the most of the information that they collect, the organization itself has to have a learning culture so that it can move forward, learning through experience. FIs use the information that they have collected on their customers to develop strategies for a number of marketing activities as follows:

- Develop relationship marketing strategies.
- Cross- and up-sell financial services to customers that they have selected through analysis of their data.
- Through analysis, understand how to manage customer attrition or defection, customer satisfaction, customer persistence.
- To gain insight into managing customer share and size of wallet.
- To develop and maintain information systems that deliver value to selected segments and customers.

The chapter has also discussed loyalty schemes and their contribution to customer loyalty in the financial services sector. Information and research is increasingly subject to ethical scrutiny and all organizations have legal, social and ethical obligations to collect and manage customer information.

References

Bennett, R. and Rundle-Thiele, S. (2005) 'The Brand Loyalty Life Cycle: Implications for Marketers', *Journal of Brand Management*, Vol. 12, No. 4, pp. 250–63.

Berger, P., Eechambadi, N., George, M., Lehmann, D., Rizley, R. and Venkatesan, R. (2006) 'From Lifetime Value to Shareholder Value', *Journal of Service Research*, Vol. 9, No. 2, pp. 156–67.

Bolton, R., Lemon, K. and Verhoef, P. (2004) 'The Theoretical Underpinning of Customer Asset Management: A Framework and Propositions for Future Research', *Journal of the Academy of Marketing Science*, Vol. 32, No. 3, pp. 271–92.

Brassington, F. and Pettitt, S. (2006), *Principles of Marketing*, Chelmsford, FT PrenticeHall.

Campbell, D. and Frei, F. (2004) 'The Persistence of Customer Profitability: Empirical Evidence and Implications From a Financial Services Firm', *Journal of Service Research*, Vol. 7, No. 2, pp. 107–23.

Colgate, M, (2000) 'Marketing and Marketing Information System Sophistication in Retail Banking', *Service Industries Journal*, Vol. 20, No. 1, pp. 139–52.

Cooil, B. Keiningham, T., Aksoy, L. and Hsu, M. (2007) 'A Longitudinal Analysis of Customer Satisfaction and Share of Wallet: Investigating the Moderating Effect of Customer Characteristics', *Journal of Marketing*, Vol. 71, January, pp. 67–83.

Cooper, M., Gwin, C. and Wakefield, K. (2008) 'Cross-functional Interface and Disruption in CRM Projects: Is Marketing from Venus and Information Systems from Mars?', *Journal of Business Research*, Vol. 61, pp. 292–9.

Cravens, D. and Piercy, N. (2006) *Strategic Marketing*, 8th edn, New York, McGraw Hill.

Daniel, E., Wilson, H. and McDonald, M. (2003) 'Towards a Map of Marketing Information Systems: An Inductive Study', *European Journal of Marketing*, Vol. 37, No. 5/6, pp. 821–47.

Dawes, J. and Worthington, S. (1995) 'Customer Information Systems and Competitive Advantage: A Case Study of a Top Ten Building Society', *International Journal of Bank Marketing*, Vol. 14, No. 4, pp. 36–44.

Farquhar, J. D. (2005) 'Retaining Customers in UK Financial Services: The Retailers' Tale', *Service Industries Journal*, Vol. 25, No. 8, pp. 1029–44.

Foehn, P. (2004) 'Client Valuation in Private Banking: Results of a Case Study in Switzerland', *Managing Service Quality*, Vol. 14, No. 2/3, pp. 194–204.

Grönroos, C. (2000), *Service Management and Marketing: A Customer Relationship Management Approach*, Wiley & Sons, Chichester.

Kamakura, W., Wedel, M., de Rosa, F. and Mazzon, J. A. (2003) 'Cross-selling Through Database Marketing: A Mixed Factor Analyzer for Data Augmentation and Prediction', *International Journal for Research in Marketing*, Vol. 20, pp. 45–65.

Kumar, V. and Reinartz, W. (2006) *Customer Relationship Management*, Hoboken, NJ, J. Wiley & Son.

KPMG (2008) *Working to Rules*, Regulatory Bulletin, February.

Liu, Y. (2007) 'The Long-Term Impact of Loyalty Programs on Consumer Purchase Behavior and Loyalty', *Journal of Marketing*, Vol. 71, October, pp. 19–35.

Payne, A. and Frow, P. (2005) 'A Strategic Framework for Customer Relationship Management', *Journal of Marketing*, Vol. 69, October, pp. 167–76.

Reichheld, F. (1996), 'Learning from Customer Defections', *Harvard Business Review*, March/April, pp. 56–69.

Reinartz, W., Thomas, J. and Kumar, V. (2005) 'Balancing Acquisition and Retention Resources to Maximize Customer Profitability', *Journal of Marketing*, Vol. 69, January, pp. 63–79.

Salazar, M. T., Harrison, T. and Ansell, J. (2007) 'An Approach for the Identification of Cross-sell and Up-sell Opportunities using a Financial Services Customer Database', *Journal of Financial Services Marketing*, Vol. 12, No. 2, pp. 115–31.

Uncles, M., Dowling, G. and Hammond, K. (2003) 'Customer Loyalty and Customer Loyalty Programmes', *Journal of Consumer Marketing*, Vol. 20, No. 4, pp. 294–316.

Van den Poel, D. and Larivière, B. (2004) 'Customer Attrition Analysis for Financial Services using Proportional Hazard Models', *European Journal of Operational Research*, Vol. 157, pp. 196–217.

Vargo, S. L. and Lusch, R. (2004) 'Evolving to a New Dominant Logic for Marketing', *Journal of Marketing*, Vol. 68, No.1, pp. 1–17.

Exercises

1. What processes do you instigate and follow in order to complete group work to time and to standard? Are these processes efficient and effective? How could these processes be improved?
2. What are the benefits to an FI of defining CRM strategically?
3. How can an FI take steps to minimize customer attrition?

Further reading

www.marketresearch.org.uk/Case study
www.cml.org.uk/cml/home
www.bba.org.uk
www.abi.org.uk
www.gemoney.co.uk/en/about_ge_money/media_centre/index.html

CASE STUDY

Expatriates

A survey questioned 2,155 expatriates (expats) across four continents about the challenges that they face. The term 'expatriate' is often used in the context of westerners living in non-western countries, but, of course, includes anyone who is not resident in their own country. In business, expatriates are often professionals who have been sent abroad by their companies, as opposed to locally hired staff.

Research method

Data were captured by using a virtual survey between February and April 2008. The survey was concerned with a range of topics: lifestyle, earning capacity, issues affecting children, ease of integration into the community. The sample consisted of 2,155 expats living in more than 48 countries, but only findings from countries with over 30 respondents are included.

Expatriate existence

The most luxurious place to live is Singapore, which is followed by the United Arab Emirates. The respondents were asked to provide information as shown in Table C5.1.

Table C5.1   Lifestyle criteria

Highest rated country	Rating criteria	Determinant of high score for each country
For lifestyle	Longevity (of residence)	Attracts new expats and where expats settle
	Earn and save	Where expats can earn over £100k and increase their savings
	Luxurious	The biggest increase in luxury across 11 categories
	Accommodation	An increase in the quality of accommodation

The results to this ranking are presented in Table C5.2. Each criterion was measured on a score from 1–15, where 1 is minimum and 15 the maximum score.

Table C5.2   Expat lifestyle rating

Country	Longevity	Earn and save	Luxury	Accommodation	Mean score
Singapore	10	14	14	15	13
UAE	9	13	15	12	12
United States	13	12	10	14	12
Belgium	12	7	11	13	11
Hong Kong	11	14	12	4	10
Germany	14	4	5	11	8
Netherlands	15	9	3	5	8
Canada	8	7	6	10	8
India	1	15	13	1	7
Australia	2	7	7	10	6
China	3	7	9	6	6
Spain	4	1	8	8	5
France	5	2	4	7	5
United Kingdom	6	8	1	3	4

Singapore scores highly as expatriates are not only able to earn and save money but they also have high-quality accommodation and a high level of luxurious living. The United States scores well too, but is beaten in terms of longevity of stay by the Netherlands and Germany. India has the highest score for ability to earn and save, but expats spend less time there than anywhere else, possibly owing to the poor-quality accommodation. Although France and the United Kingdom have low mean scores, French accommodation is significantly better.

Expats in Hong Kong and India earn the highest salaries, with half of the respondents earning over £100,000 per annum (49 per cent). Figure C5.1 presents information about the earnings of the expats in the survey. More than half earn over £60,000 per annum.

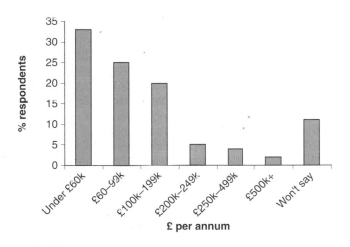

| **Figure C5.1** | Expat salaries

Not only are earnings high, there are also increased opportunities for saving. Low living costs in India, for example, allow 82 per cent of expats to save more than they were able to in their country of origin. Overall, 58 per cent of expats invest and save more; more than half (52 per cent) spend more on food, 49 per cent spend more on shopping and 45 per cent more on socializing.

One of the rating criteria is luxury in lifestyle (where the United Kingdom scores poorly). The items measuring this criterion were: access to private health care, owning more than one property, private education for children, owning a pool and employing staff. The UAE was the most luxurious destination, followed by Spain and Singapore, which were about even. Men reported higher ratings of experiences of luxury than women. As far as accommodation is concerned, scores were highest for Singapore (74 per cent), the United States (61 per cent) and Belgium (59 per cent).

The United Kingdom was the most expensive expat location for accommodation, with 85 per cent of respondents revealing that their living costs had increased. Only 19 per cent of respondents reported an increase in the quality of accommodation.

Offshore offspring

Expats, in many cases, have children, so a part of the survey was dedicated to seeking information about the challenges of raising children in the host country. Respondents were asked to rate the host country in:

- Time that their children spent outdoors
- Time the children spent studying
- Cost of raising children
- Number of languages spoken by their children
- Whether their children would remain in the country

Consistent with earlier findings, the United Kingdom was the most expensive location to raise children, followed by the UAE and Hong Kong. Spain, India and China were the cheapest. Almost half of the respondents reported that their children spent more time outdoors in the host country, with Australia (80 per cent) well ahead of Spain (59 per cent) and France (57 per cent). A third of parents said that their children studied more since relocating; over half (56 per cent) said that this stayed the same. Expat children living in Europe learn the greatest number of languages, with 94 per cent of expat children living in Spain speaking two or more languages; there are also high figures for this in Germany and France. Language learning in Singapore and Hong Kong appeared to be less likely. The issue of likelihood of children remaining in the host country or returning to country of origin generated some interesting responses. Some expats in Canada, for example, expected their children to stay in Canada (33 per cent), but 43 per cent expected their children to return home. Other high expectations for remaining were the United States (25 per cent) and Germany (23 per cent). Expectations about returning home were 42 per cent in Australia.

Expat experience

Expats were finally asked about their experiences in relocating to a new country. They were asked about: making friends, joining the local community, learning the language and buying property. Table C5.3 presents the responses on a country by country basis, with 1 rating the highest and 14 being the lowest; Germany emerges as the country where these four criteria attract the best overall score.

Table C5.3		Expat experience		

Country	Local friends	Community group	Learned language	Bought property	Ranking
Germany	2	1	1	9	1
Canada	1	3	10	2	2
Spain	7	10	2	3	3
France	9	8	5	1	4
Belgium	12	6	2	5	5
Netherlands	10	7	4	6	6
Hong Kong	7	2	8	10	7
United States	6	3	13	4	7
United Kingdom	4	8	12	10	9
Singapore	13	3	9	12	10
India	5	13	7	14	11
Australia	3	14	14	8	11
UAE	14	10	11	7	13
China	11	12	6	13	13

Expats living in Europe were most likely to learn the language of the host country – Germany (75 per cent), Spain (70 per cent) and Belgium (70 per cent). Expats from the Americas were most likely to learn the local language (United States 51 per cent), with figures for Brazilians at 50 per cent. Expats in France were most likely to buy property (64 per cent), followed by Canada (55 per cent) and Spain (52 per cent). About a quarter of respondents started up businesses in Singapore, Spain and France. About a third had children in Belgium, Germany and the UAE. The responses to joining a local community group are presented in Figure C5.2.

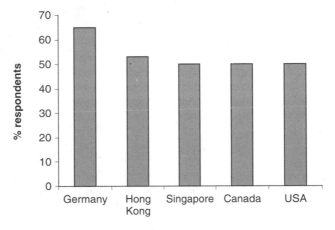

Figure C5.2		Joining a local community group

In Australia, just 38 per cent reported that they had joined a community group, although Australia scored highly in ease of making friends. Expats in Australia tend to be younger (51 per cent are 18–34 years old) and therefore may find it easier to make friends without joining a formal group. German expats were the least likely to join a group (32 per cent).

Questions

1. Why might expats be of interest to a global bank?
2. Comment on the research design? Who was sampled? How representative is the sample? How was the sample compiled?
3. Looking at Table C5.2, which financial services might expats living in Hong Kong and Singapore be interested in?
4. How might an FI assist an expat family with the high cost of raising children?
5. What are the implications of expats' experiences in Europe for financial services (see Figure C5.2)?

Compiled by Jillian Dawes Farquhar, from material in HSBC Bank International Expat Explorer Survey, 2008.

6

Relationship marketing in financial services

Contents

Learning outcomes

At the end of the chapter, the reader will be able to:

- Appreciate the role of relationships in financial services marketing

- Embed relationship marketing within the strategies for economies of scale and scope

- Understand the key marketing actions that contribute to the creation of customer loyalty

Introduction

relationship marketing: when marketing is designed to engage customers in ongoing purchases through the establishment of a dialogue

In this chapter, one of the key strategies that have been adopted by financial service providers over the last decade – **relationship marketing** (RM) – will be explored. RM has been widely researched by academics and has been taken up by many organizations with varying degrees of success. In this chapter, we will be looking at the key components of relationships in a business context and exploring how these concepts can be applied in the marketing of financial services. In addition, we will be looking at how RM is an example of a marketing strategy that is integrate closely with segmentation, as it builds upon knowledge of customer behaviour.

Relationship marketing

When consumers purchase a service, as opposed to a good, they undergo an experience that centres on the simultaneous delivery and consumption of the service. It is at this point that customer perceptions are formed and judgements made on the nature of the experience and the opportunity for relationships to be initiated or enhanced. RM is a process (Grönroos 2000) that consists of having long-term relationships with customers, usually on a one-to-one basis, and forms the strategy that underpins relational exchanges. These relationships are stabilizing elements, which can address the challenges of market fragmentation and lack of differentiation of service offerings (O'Malley et al. 1997). RM forms the bridge between the organization and the customer, by means of reinforcing linkages, responding to customer needs and serving micro segments (Hennig-Thurau 2000). The buyer and the seller are theoretically of equal importance in the relationship, as they are both active parties in a multidimensional exchange process where genuine interaction between the parties takes place over time.

However, in certain sectors – and banking is one of them – the provider often has greater power in the relationship, which is based on superior knowledge and skills, so the customer may be more dependent on the financial institution (FI). There are many advantages for FIs to engage in RM. Customers have a lifelong need for financial services; financial transactions are conducted on a continuous basis to such an extent that customers talk about 'my bank' (O'Loughlin et al. 2004), although this is not necessarily an indication of a favourable view of 'my bank'. In spite of this apparent evidence of some degree of relationship, do consumers want to have relationships with all of their financial providers? If not, do they want a relationship with their main provider? How is this relationship envisaged by the consumer? Is it the same vision as that of the FI? Lastly, and perhaps most importantly, one of the main reasons that FIs are interested in maintaining relationships with customers is that, overall, keeping existing customers is usually cheaper than going out to look for new ones. The benefits of forming relationships between sellers and buyers appear desirable, but how can these benefits be achieved in the financial services sector? From a strategic perspective, there are elements around which RM can be built (Berry 1983).

Developing a central element to the relationship

There have to be clear benefits to the customer to enter and remain in a relationship; the offer has to be of value to the customer over a period of time. FIs should understand what the customer wants, both from their offerings and from the relationship, and ensure that those dimensions are understood at the highest level in the company. It is also important to understand that customers, both personal and business, will in many cases have a number of financial service providers and each provider will be striving to have some indication of their share of the customer's wallet. Customers base judgements about any relationship formed and their value on experiences.

Personalize the relationship

Many FIs count their customers in millions (for example, Grupo Santander has 69 million customers worldwide), so personalizing the relationship, for many customers, has to be defined in ways underpinned by technology. Early RM literature presupposed the existence of a personal relationship, but changes in the way that branches are organized – for example, the use of ATMs for routine tasks – mean that personal exchanges with customers have been reduced. Customer willingness to use a range of multiple channels tends to suggest that the personal element in financial services can be traded off for the benefits for convenience and control that are present in non-personal channels (Farquhar and Panther 2007). This trade-off has strong implications for the quality of customer service, where customer preferences conflict with the pressure to reduce costs. Three-quarters of customers (76.4 per cent) preferred to discuss their financial affairs with trained staff face-to-face (Keynote 2007). In high-credence or high-involvement services, where a personal element remains and is important, the FI needs to ensure that customers are very well cared for so that trust can be gained. Although expertise from the FI staff is important, the personal element of the exchange is such that a high level of personal skills is required (Bell and Eisingerich 2007), which may influence recruitment and development policies within FIs. Financial companies should integrate customer education into the relationship marketing philosophy. They need to be aware of the changing nature of customer perceptions, as education contributes to customer expertise over time. Therefore, FIs need to view customer relationships as dynamic, with customers focusing more on the technical elements of the service offering (Bell and Eisingerich 2007).

Increasing the central element by offering extra benefits

Relationship marketing, like the rest of marketing, recognizes the dynamic nature of the marketplace and that the customer may expect more from the relationship as it continues. As well as the core benefits of a business account, for example, the business may also look for speedier cheque processing, more competitive credit card charges or more dedicated advice. Against this, the FI has to consider the value of the customer to the organization and whether it is worthwhile offering additional benefits.

Making employees aware that they are immediately responsible to the customer

The role of employees is central to financial services at all levels, not just front-line staff. Gummesson (1987) recognized the importance of all staff in the service delivery process, prompting the label of 'part-time marketer' for all staff in an organization. In an increasingly systems-driven banking and insurance sector, the design and maintenance of systems, the managers of call centres and, of course, senior management who develop and resource strategies all play important, although differing, roles in RM. It can also be argued that the net of those responsible for maintaining the relationship can be widened to include a range of stakeholders, such as suppliers (see Figure 6.1).

As can be noted from the way that the elements (Berry 1983) are integrated with financial services marketing, there are tensions. It has been recognized that RM is of particular value in organizational and services marketing contexts, but there may be occasions and business sectors when RM is inappropriate (e.g., Smith and Higgins 2000). There are situations in financial services where RM might work well – for example, with large businesses where mutual dependence can be achieved. However, in consumer financial services, generic offerings such as insurance and current accounts may offer little scope or even value for relationship building. Repeat business may have to be achieved by a variety of means such as building in switching costs for the customer and competitive pricing. RM should only be adopted when it offers or contributes to a company's competitive advantage (Morgan and Hunt 1999). Moreover, there are so many interpretations, both theoretical and empirical, of what constitutes RM that a number of difficulties arise when companies try to execute RM strategies. It is clear that RM is more complex than might have been understood by companies and, in order not to squander scarce resources, the dimensions of relationships need to be appreciated (Ward and Dagger 2007).

Relationships with stakeholders

Although RM is often thought of as a relationship between the business and the customer, the idea of a relationship consisting of a number of stakeholders is increasingly acknowledged (for example, Buttle 1996, Payne *et al.* 2005). The stakeholder model of relationships consists of a number of different parties in the relationships as follows (Payne *et al.* 2005):

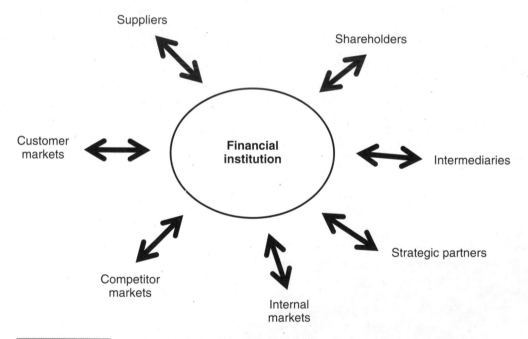

Figure 6.1   Relationships in financial services
Source: Adapted from Payne *et al.* (2005).

- customer markets consist of existing as well as potential customers
- influence markets include consumer groups, financial intermediaries, the press, the family and are highly important in financial services
- supplier and alliance markets could include traditional suppliers, such as IT companies, but also strategic allies for joint ventures (see Exhibit 6.1)
- internal markets consist of staff, managers, departments, subdivisions of the FI. When FIs merge, attention needs to be paid to ensuring that staff are well integrated into the new company – for example, the new Lloyds Banking Group
- competitor markets are very significant in financial services, as many initiatives flow from competitor activity
- government and regulators have the role of ensuring that FIs 'play according to the rules', at the same time maintaining the healthy state of financial services. Failure in this relationship has clearly occurred.

A particular value of the stakeholder model is its contribution to planning and analysis which reminds or even makes companies aware that a focus on the customer is insufficient for competitive activity in today's marketplace. By looking more widely at their markets, they may be able to identify important stakeholders whom they can draw into their strategy development – for example, other FIs in a strategic alliance.

EXHIBIT 6.1

HSBC and Aviva get hitched

HSBC Bank plc and Aviva plc plan the creation of a joint venture, under the 'HSBC Insurance' brand, that aims to be a top-ten player in the UK general insurance industry.* Under the terms of the planned joint venture, HSBC Bank plc and Norwich Union Insurance, the UK general insurance arm of Aviva plc, will underwrite and distribute general insurance products to HSBC's 10.2 million customers in the United Kingdom. Approximately one-fifth of all UK consumer spend on financial services goes to insurance products and the general insurance industry generated £36 billion in premiums in 2005. It is claimed that the proposed joint venture will bring together, in HSBC and Norwich Union (cited as two of Britain's most trusted brands HSBC's distribution network and Norwich Union's underwriting and customer management capabilities to create one of the best general insurance services the market has to offer. Norwich Union and HSBC have had an underwriting relationship for 23 years. At present, HSBC distributes protection, home, travel and car insurance products created by Norwich Union. The planned joint venture will strengthen and deepen this relationship. Customers are increasingly turning to trusted brands for their insurance needs and by leveraging the HSBC brand a significant new force will be created in the UK insurance market. HSBC has set a target to double the contribution to global profits made by insurance operations, and the creation of pre-ferred strategic partnerships with leading general insurers is a key element of that plan. All of the proposals remained subject to finalization of defini-tive documentation, as well as regulatory and other consents. For example, Aviva now provides travel insurance for HSBC customers.

*Target of top-ten UK general insurer ranking based on projected gross written premium.

Compiled by the authors from information at www.hsbc.co.uk.

This joint venture provides a number of examples of marketing in finan-cial services. First, the two FIs will be in a position to optimize any selling opportunities and gain the trust of consumers through existing brands. Second, the key advantages of the alliance are the use of the HSBC net-work for distributing the insurance products and the underwriting skills and experience of Aviva, which will provide both FIs with economies of scale.

Business relationships

business relationships: where relationship marketing started. Relationships with consumers followed when the benefits of relationships between businesses became evidents

Value is enhanced readily in **business relationships** through pooling of knowledge, matching competences and acting collectively, all of which deter a partner from acting opportunistically (Hollendsen 2003) or in such a way to damage the relationship. Existing customers are easier to work with as lines of communication are established; a rapport or understand-ing exists as boundaries between the two organizations begin to blur and, of course, costs are lowered through retaining customers. Relationships take time to build and there can be a number of phases in the devel-opment of the relationship (Hollendsen 2003). There may be a courtship phase, where the financial institution is approached by a start-up com-pany; the courtship may last for sometime while the company develops and starts making a profit. The following exhibit is an indication of the global service provided to a business customer with partner privileges.

EXHIBIT 6.2

A business package with partner privileges

This FI offers free consultation on a wide range of international banking, treasury management and trade finance services through a global markets division, including: foreign exchange risk management, loans, deposit products (currency deposits, demand/ fixed deposits) and trade finance (letters of credit, documentary collections, bonds and guarantees).

Financial advisory services

The specialized team of 'whole of market' financial advisers are available to assist with your personal and business financial planning needs. The advice is fully independent and tailored to each individual business, giving you confidence that any product recommended will be the most suited to your needs, delivered in a tax-efficient way. An initial consultation is made available to new account holders without charge.

With Business Essentials, the customer will have access to valuable discounts, support and advice from the FI's expert partners. They are among the leading providers of business services in national insurance today and can offer legal advice, design services, consultations with communications partners, free audit of insurance arrangements and free accounts software.

Compiled by the authors from a number of different bank websites.

The bonds between the provider and the business are not strong and should the company not succeed or switch to another bank, then losses to the provider are financial and may be recoverable. The relationship phase may then follow; for small and medium enterprises (SMEs) a well-formed relationship with their bank is essential if they are to respond to changing conditions. Businesses and their managers are motivated to improve their own understanding and knowledge of financial management to facilitate the forging of the relationship between themselves and the bank. Additionally, the banks need to appreciate that SME confidence in any formalized process will be greater where small firms' own representatives are seen to be involved with and have endorsed that process and have set up clear contingencies to overcome any relationship problems where trading difficulties arise (Binks *et al.* 2006). The final phase of partnership may begin when difficult times have been successfully handled, the experience of the company has grown and symmetry in the relationship through respect and trust has been achieved. The bond is strong and a personal/social relationship may also occur. The financial provider may have to consider how to resource the relationship in terms of continuity of staff to allow the social bonds to develop. Within a relationship, a number of different types of exchange take place: service exchange, information exchange, financial exchange and social exchange. Social exchanges reduce the perceptions of risk and facilitate assessments of each partner's capabilities, negotiation and adaptability.

The size of the client organization or, more precisely, the strategic importance of the client to the FI will also drive the nature of the relationship; there is growing interest in key account management (KAM). KAM practice in financial services is distinctive because of the regulatory environment, the size and diversity of the sector, the high degree of intermediation, product diversity and complexity and uncertainty of product performance (Hughes *et al.* 2004). The activities that could be offered to key accounts are special pricing, customization of products and services, information sharing and taking over business processes for the client. The larger banks offer specialist industry services – for example, Barclays Bank has a dedicated Local Authority Unit that covers waste, transport, fire and police financing expertise (www.business.barclays.co.uk), which is staffed by a specialist team. From a theoretical perspective, KAM has often been viewed as an activity sitting within personal selling; we mention KAM in later chapters, but research has argued for KAM to be integrated with RM (Homburg *et al.* 2002). While this may seem an argument with little practical significance, the 'ownership' of a particular business function will affect the way that it is viewed within the organization and the way that it is implemented. If KAM is seen as RM, then the relationship should supersede any individual selling efforts through the long-term perspective of RM. If KAM is part of a traditional sales function, then it is possible that the emphasis may fall on a monthly sales target, which may not necessarily be supportive of a longer-term relationship.

Cross-cultural relationships

trust and commitment: both these constructs are central to the establishment of relationship marketing

Managing relationships across the globe within banking and financial services is increasingly important as banking has become a global industry and many customers equally operate across frontiers and continents. A study (Dash *et al.* 2006) aimed to measured cultural value and verified the role of national culture in B2B relationships, based on Indian and Canadian samples. The authors found that high mutual and symmetric interdependence in a dyadic buyer–seller relationship is a critical factor in building **trust and commitment**. As interdependence asymmetry increases, relationship commitment decreases, supporting other studies that have suggested that the degree of prevailing power distance affects the nature of business relationships. Therefore the possibility of cultural differences in buyer–seller relationships should be considered carefully while developing international service strategies. The culture of a country has long been acknowledged as a key environmental characteristic that underlies systematic differences in consumer behaviour, cultural norms and beliefs which influence the functioning of cross-national buyer–seller interactions (Dash *et al.* 2006). To build commitment and trust in global business banking relationships, high mutual and symmetrical interdependence is necessary. Power distance is a concept that captures the extent to which less powerful members accept that power is distributed unequally in the relationship. FIs can reduce power distance by adopting culturally appropriate communities.

Corporate banking relationships are often long lasting, with considerable investment from the partners or actors in the relationship, although the power in the relationship often lies with the bank. Relationships are not static, nor do they all resemble each other, with two opposite behaviours of purchasing having been noted: transactional and relational. Transaction-oriented companies regard each exchange as new and an opportunity for replacement or an alternative. Relational-oriented companies tend to consider one or two buying alternatives only and look at each exchange as an ongoing or new relationship. It is thought that companies need to abandon a transaction-oriented approach to be able to utilize suppliers more effectively. Proença and Castro's study (2005) into Portuguese banks showed that the relationships between the banks were long lasting but that they were subject to short-term instability as a result of internal events in the actors' organizations. The short-term instability can lead to stress in the relationship, which is considered inevitable. Understanding the source of the stress is important in recognizing its potential threat to the relationship. Stress can arise from the client's relationships with other banks, a situation comparable to personal banking relationships where the customer is 'multibanked'.

Relationship outcomes

outcomes: are customer loyalty and positive word-of-mouth communication.

A key driver for building relationships is that costs can be lowered through the retention of existing customers. FIs are aware that not all retained customers generate revenue and therefore seek a stronger outcome from relationship marketing such as customer loyalty. Loyal customers exhibit two attractive behaviours for FIs, firstly, they tend to purchase more and secondly, they also recommend FIs to friends and family. In order for FIs to encourage loyalty, they need to appreciate the complexities of relationship drivers and **outcomes** to allow appropriate resourcing. Although there is considerable debate about which marketing variables will drive or determine the outcomes of a relationship, such constructs as customer satisfaction and trust and commitment are widely accepted.

Customer satisfaction

customer satisfaction:
originally the aim of
marketing. Customer
satisfaction does not
necessarily lead to
profitability

Customer satisfaction appears to influence relationship length, so customer satisfaction needs to be monitored over time through customer 'touches' – that is, any contact between the FI and the customer. For a customer to stay in a relationship, there have to be discernible benefits that impact on customer satisfaction. Customers gain satisfaction, according to Molina *et al.* (2007), from benefits that include, first, confidence, but, further, three other dimensions – frontline employee satisfaction, accessibility and service policy. Confidence refers to a combination of psychological benefits in relation to trust in the marketer, reduction in perceived operations risks and a decrease in anxiety. Maintaining or even developing customer confidence in the provider was found to be an important influence on customer satisfaction in a Spanish study (Molina *et al.* 2007). The study also showed that accessibility, in terms of hours of business, branch location and environment, and service policies – for example, the range of services – were significant.

External pressures from regulatory bodies such as the FSA also appear to have resulted in significant progress in promoting customer service to consumers; the focus on customer-centred services also matches the expressed aims of FIs. A recent report believes that a delicate balance has been achieved between the interests of shareholders and customers, which may be sustained over the next five years. However, FIs must continue to focus on training staff, and the financial education of consumers (requiring funds and moral support from the government, as well as from industry groups) is a necessity if the fair market is to achieve long-term strength (Keynote 2007). Trust and confidence are thought to be closely related (Hennig-Thurau *et al.* 2002), with the combination having a powerful effect on customers' satisfaction (see Figure 6.1).

Trust and commitment

If partners in the relationship or network are committed, then, clearly, they are less likely to abandon it (Morgan and Hunt 1994). Trust may be conceptualized as a belief that a trusted party will deliver on the promise that has been made and not take unfair advantage of a situation. It has been proposed that there are three determinants of trust: integrity, benevolence and credibility (Arnott 2007). Table 6.1 provides some suggestions about how FIs might put some of the determinants into practice.

Research by the Financial Services Authority (www.fsa.gov.uk) examined consumer trust in the financial services industry by means of a survey of just over 1,000 respondents. The responses suggested that:

Table 6.1	Operationalizing trust

Trust	Operationalization
Integrity	Fulfilling agreements, treating stakeholder information with care, developing and following ethical practices, treating customers fairly,
Benevolence	Regarding stakeholders as equal partners, seeking to do good for stakeholders, developing systems that are customer-focused, offering services that are appropriate for customers
Credibility	Pricing strategies that are readily understood, eliminating penalty charges, recovering service failures, making statements that stakeholders can believe in

1. Most financial services firms treat their customers fairly
2. Most financial firms will mislead their customers if they can make more profit by doing so
3. Financial firms sell the product that pays the most commission, not what is best for you

First, it is worth noting how valuable it is in consumer research to ask a number of questions about a particular matter in order to arrive at a good understanding of how the respondents feel. Just considering the responses to the first question would suggest that there is no problem, whereas the responses to questions 2 and 3 indicate that customers are disillusioned with FIs. Second, it would appear the respondents believe that FIs do not always act in the interests of their customers. A partner or a stakeholder in a relationship will make a commitment based on his perception of the other party's commitment, on pledges made by the other partner and such factors as communication, reputation and relationship history. According to the data shown here, it would appear that there is little chance of commitment when consumers perceive that there may be little commitment on the part of the FIs. Since commitment is seen as dedication to the continuation of the relationship and a pledge of continuity, implying some future positive behaviour, it is a critical element in a relationship. One of the key objectives, post-credit crunch, is to address this issue of trust. The complexity of the responses to the FSA investigation suggests that it is another one of these constructs that has a number of different dimensions.

Relational benefits

Stakeholders seek to derive some benefit from staying in the relationship, either from the core service or from the relationship itself (Hennig-Thurau *et al.* 2002). It is suggested that these benefits might include confidence benefits, which refer to perceptions of reduced anxiety and comfort and which have some application in financial services. The second set of benefits is the social benefits, which relate to the emotional part of the relationship and are characterized by personal recognition of customers/stakeholders by staff or familiarity with staff. Finally, there is a category of special treatment benefits, which might take the form of special deals in terms of pricing or bundling of services. The ideas in this model (see Figure 6.2) reveal the elements of a relationship that customers or stakeholders might seek. The arrows show the paths between the various constructs that are significant in the research by Hennig-Thurau *et al.* (2002) across a range of services in the United States, including financial.

The results show strong associations or linkages between satisfaction, commitment, word of mouth and customer loyalty. Social benefits relate both to commitment and directly to customer loyalty and confidence benefits impact on satisfaction. The challenge for FIs is to investigate further the importance of these social benefits and where these benefits are most appreciated by stakeholders/customers. Special treatment benefits relate only weakly to commitment and it seems that social benefits, certainly as far as this research is concerned, might be the key benefit in RM.

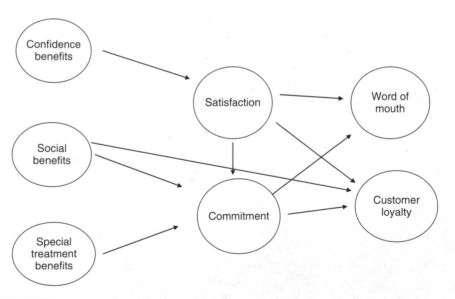

Figure 6.2   Relationship marketing drivers and outcomes
Source: Adapted from Hennig-Thurau *et al.* (2002).

Internal marketing

If social benefits are a key driver in relationship marketing, then how might these benefits be offered to FI customers? As suggested in the stakeholder model of RM above, the employee/manager/staff member is part of the stakeholder network. Even if the stakeholder model of RM is not seen to be compatible with the current strategies of an FI, the importance of the staff in achieving customer satisfaction, with all the vital outcomes (see Figure 6.2) that it achieves, is evident. **Internal marketing** usually refers to a set of practices that engages staff and management in delivering service quality and hence customer satisfaction. It has been understood for some time that, in services marketing, the inseparability of services usually means that much of the service consists of an interaction between staff and the customer. Both trust and commitment can be strengthened by the staff/customer interaction, as well as the creation of bonds; internal marketing is a process in which relationships are built throughout the FI to ensure that all customer touches generate customer satisfaction.

Views of internal marketing vary. One perspective is that the employees should be considered as customers on the basis that they have needs and wants that need to be met; if staff members' needs are met, then they will be in a position to meet the needs of the customer. Recent interpretations of internal marketing, however, focus on the engagement of staff and stakeholders; the mechanism that seeks to achieve this is the corporate brand. Internal marketing has been promoted as a philosophy (Ahmed and Rafiq 2003) that focuses attention on the fit between staff needs and the needs of the other stakeholders. For example, in order to retain staff, there needs to be career progression within an FI, but this progression needs to bear in mind the relationships that particular staff members have built up during the course of their tenure in their present positions. The FI needs to ensure that plans must be in place for those relationships to be maintained and hand-over to the new staff to be smooth. Staff also need to be able go 'the extra mile' to achieve customer satisfaction and to feel similar levels of trust in the FI as core to RM theory (see above). Ahmed and Rafiq (2003) suggest a higher-level interpretation of internal marketing which this type of engaged behaviour might support; the employee needs to feel 'psychologically safe' (p. 1181) so that they can act without fear, share their knowledge and feel valued.

FIs need to identify and encourage behaviours that lead to satisfaction for stakeholders. Looking at Figure 6.2, constructed from customer data, the model can be applied to a range of stakeholders and certainly to employees. Benefits for staff can manifest themselves as: confidence – in the way employees do their job and in employees' faith in their employers, equipment and colleagues; social – a good working environment with other stakeholders; and special treatments - when staff perform well above expected levels. These benefits will then lead to commitment and satisfaction, and subsequently to loyalty and word of mouth (brand advocacy). The cross-functional capacities of FIs are tested in harnessing human resource strategies and policies, reward strategies, managing resources to maximize stakeholder value, adopting a long-term vision and rethinking sales within the context of stakeholder value. It has also been suggested that negative feelings from customers towards FIs is related to weakened customer relationships caused by staffing policies such as rotation of staff, staff reduction or enforced routing through lower-cost call centres (O'Loughlin *et al.* 2004). Even though customers may live with these feeling's of dissonance, they cannot contribute to broadening or deepening the relationship between customer and FI.

Relationship lifecycle

Relationships can be envisaged in terms of their length, depth and breadth. The length of a relationship is how long the customer stays with a company and phases of relationships have been proposed (Beloucif *et al.* 2006). Although the relationship in Table 6.2 shows a cyclical relationship based on a 12-month renewal period, it provides a useful illustration of how a B2B relationship can be formed and indeed how it could break down at any time. Consumer relationships vary according to the nature of the product, with pension and annuity products being of a long duration and some current accounts being held for long periods as well, although without necessarily with the FI making any money out of the service that they are providing. Relationships have dimensions other than length with implications for marketing. The depth of a relationship would normally be reflected in the frequency of the service usage – for example, how often a customer uses an ATM, visits a branch or phones the call centre, all of which result in a cost for the FI. If the FI wants increasing the depth of the relationship so that some revenue is generated from this customer, it might try to persuade the customer to open a fee-paying current account rather than the free version. FIs in the United Kingdom offer attractive interest rates to customers if they switch to one of these accounts (e.g., www.alliance-leicester.co.uk). The breadth of a relationship is exemplified in cross-buying services such as the purchase of house and contents insurance from a mortgage provider. Relationships with customers and, to a certain extent, stakeholders may constitute dimensions of length, depth and breadth. Where FIs need to focus some attention is on the benefits that stakeholders might gain from a deeper and broader relationship, or the reciprocity in these extended relationships (Palmatier *et al.* 2005).

Table 6.2   Relationship between insurance broker and corporate client

Relationship development and time scale	Main characteristics	Management issues
Stage 1 – Pre-relationship: days or occasionally years	Clients obtained through referrals or recommendation. Client referred to as a 'prospect'. Often informal and face-to-face	How was client obtained? Why was previous relationship terminated? What service are they looking for? How does new client fit with existing portfolio?
Stage 2 – New business	Client still a 'prospect'. Initial programme discussed: business type, size of organization, risk profile. Appropriate insurers contacted	Is this relationship to be continued? Criteria for continuance include: cost–benefit analysis, credit rating, business philosophy
Stage 3 – Initiation stage: usually 2–6 months	Instruction given to go ahead with proposals. Underwriters instructed. Documentation received from insurers and checked. Now referred to as a client. Name of client used in full, no abbreviations yet	Account handler assigned to client on day-to-day basis, depending on experience and work load. Premium financing agreed. Opportunity to cross-sell may arise
Stage 4 – Involvement: final 6 months of first year.	Clients' name abbreviated and known throughout as such. Contact can vary dramatically from daily to very rarely, depending on size of client organization. Claims and policy changes notified by letter or fax	If claims higher than anticipated risk assessment, actions can be considered. Proactive approach favoured
Stage 5 – Full relationship and pre-renewal (2 months to renewal)	Obtain financial and business projections for next 12 months or possibly longer-term plans. Updated information passed to insurers to allow renewal terms to be obtained on correct basis. Agreed documentation for next 12 months issued by insurers	Renewal submission made to clients, often at face-to-face meeting. Review of premium financing options. Opportunity to cross-sell. Ensure that covers in place and that documentation is correct
Return to stage 3. Problem claim or complaint	Communication levels increase dramatically	If claim handled effectively, can enhance relationship. If claim handled badly or gaps in risk programme, relationship can be harmed. Can be opportunity to cross-sell or effect covers that client initially unwilling to consider. Opportunity for management to uncover causes of poor service

Source: Adapted from Beloucif *et al.* (2006).

Customers may choose to leave the organization, employees find new jobs and other stakeholders may seek other opportunities elsewhere, leading to the relationships terminating or dissolving. Is losing a stakeholder an indication of a failure in a relationship? What losses are incurred with the dissolution of that relationship? There are two scenarios for FIs with relationship dissolution. The first to be considered is the loss of a valued stakeholder – for example, a profitable customer, a gifted manager or an efficient and effective supplier. What information does the FI have that the relationship was worth saving and what were the indications that the relationship might have been troubled? Is there anything that can be done to revive the relationship (Tähtinen and Havila 2004)? If not what lessons can be learned and actions taken to prevent a repetition? For example, as suggested in the discussion on internal marketing, are the staff rotation policies consistent with the needs of staff work/life balance? Were relationships with the supplier based on mutual respect or was there undue pressure for the supplier to drive down prices and up service levels? Was there reciprocity in the relationship? As Morgan and Hunt (1999) have stated, RM should only be pursued when competitive advantage can be derived. Therefore, when the long-term costs of existing relationships and the resources shared in those relationships outweigh the long-term benefits and those relationships cannot be salvaged, then efforts need to be made to dissolve them with minimal damage to all parties.

The second scenario is the loss of a stakeholder who may be bringing little or insufficient value to the relationship, as illustrated in Exhibit 6.3. As this particular case demonstrates, it is not yet considered acceptable for FIs to end relationships that fail to generate the revenue required, although, in principle, a relationship that does not yield the benefits desired to both parties should be open to this kind of action. FIs, however, have to have an awareness of the interpretations of their actions and they also need to acknowledge that they do tend to attract negative criticism.

EXHIBIT 6.3

Credit card cut-up

Egg Bank has refused to back down in the row over its cancellation of the credit cards of 161,000 customers. The firm sent letters in February 2008 to around 7 per cent of its 2 million customers warning them that their cards would stop working within 35 days. Many of those customers who received letters insisted that they always paid their bills on time and had excellent credit ratings. There have been accusations that the Internet bank made the move because the customers did not make it enough money, which Egg strongly denied. This is the first time that a bank has cancelled such a large number of cards in the United Kingdom. There are fears that other firms may scrutinize their books as the credit crunch continues. Profit margins are getting tighter, which means that credit card companies are trying to avoid bad debt; one way of doing so is by dumping unprofitable customers who never pay interest charges. Rival banks have not cancelled as many cards, but some have introduced flat fees for people who hardly use their credit cards. Others have reduced the interest-free period for those who pay their balance in full each month.

Egg had reviewed its 2.3 million credit card accounts after it was taken over by Citibank the previous year. 'The review was based upon a large number of variables and studied the level of risk inherent in groups of customers, rather than every individual,' said a spokesman. 'So while some customers in that group may be up to date with their payments and have a good record with credit reference agencies and so on, the probability of them becoming a higher-risk customer in the future is higher than we wish to accept.' The spokesman explained that, although someone might not be in default on their card, the bank could tell that they might be heading in that direction in the future. To detect this Egg looked at changes in the way customers used their cards, such as applying for more cards or changing their spending pattern on existing cards. Complaints about cancelling the cards have been made to the Office of Fair Trading, but the regulator has yet to decide if they will be investigated. Egg's decision to cancel the credit cards, in an attempt to stem further bad debts, was seen as an astonishing own goal, even in an increasingly difficult credit card market, as customers struggle to repay debts.

Compiled by the authors from www.bbc.co.uk and the *Daily Telegraph*.

This is an example of badly handled relationship dissolution where a company has made a decision not to serve a particular group of customers, made worse by the number of customers affected by the closures (161,000) and the relatively short notice (35 days) given. A formal review of relationship dissolution is advisable (see Figure 6.1), which should be considered within the context of a stakeholder network – for example, how to address influencer markets (Tähtinen and Havila 2004). One question that other Egg stakeholders may be asking is 'Who is next?'

Digital relationships

Earlier RM literature stresses the importance of personalizing relationships and this has often been envisaged as a personal interaction in the relationship. One of the strengths of the high-street provider was the personal links that customers used to have with particular members of staff. However, the advent of non-personal channels has meant that FIs' relationships with consumers and businesses need to be re-envisaged so that

electronic channels:
non-personal channels
such as the Internet and
mobile devices

they can be maintained via **electronic channels**. Customer relationship management (CRM) is the way in which FIs manage their relationships with their stakeholders, as discussed in Chapter 5. Here we will consider how relationships can be maintained in a digital environment.

Managing business accounts

The use of information technology (IT) is well established in business relationships, with further potential to strengthen them by improving customer service levels, increasing customer switching costs, increasing the geographic reach of their relationships and displaying technological leadership (Mulligan and Gordon 2002). A key advantage of technology in the relationship is the instant access to services, which global companies (and increasingly global consumers) need. On the other hand, personal/social interaction and bonds may occur in business relations which enhance the relationship. However, in spite of the importance of the social nature of relationships, the advantages of IT are such that FIs have made significant investment in centralizing their operations and using non-personal channels where possible. Threats to existing relationships have been observed, such as loss of client control and 'personal touch', and the commoditization of the offering (Mulligan and Gordon 2002); without any personal exchange the product becomes just like any other offering in that class – a commodity. Additionally, threats to security could harm relationships in the move to the adoption of technology, such as loss of data through hacking or theft of data storage devices, along with systems failure. A way forward in the move towards technologically driven service is the integration of systems providers into the network of stakeholders to create systems that are closely linked to and reflect the RM strategies of the FIs.

Connecting with consumers

It has been thought that the impact of non-personal channels would weaken relationships with consumers owing to the absence of the personal interaction and the reduction in opportunities for social interaction. On the other hand, it has been argued that customers can establish a relationship with their FI via non-personal channels, although these relationships may differ from those envisaged in earlier conceptualizations of RM. Consumers seem prepared to engage in some form of trade-off where speed and convenience are substitutes for the personal interaction. It may also be the case that personal interactions may only be of use in certain situations; increasingly, consumers seem prepared to purchase a range of services remotely. The use of mobile services is thought increasing direct relationship investments by building an emotional relationship with customers, particularly through striving to be an important part of the customers' daily lives (Nysveen *et al.* 2005). It is thought that the adoption of mobile banking will follow a similar growth to that of Internet banking.

Mobile banking, though, is more an extension of on-line banking, rather than an entirely new channel, using a smaller screen but with voice prompts and text-to-voice capabilities, providing scope for a range of interactions (onlinebankingreport.com 2007). Customers (whether B2B or B2C) will make the decisions about how they choose to use these devices in ways to enhance their mobile lifestyles. Research has suggested that there are benefit bundles in the use of m-services or mobile-life enhancers (MLEs), one of which applies to financial services. Items that were included in this particular enhancer are as follows: advanced banking services, sending of insurance damage reports, taking part in on-line auctions, trading stock, purchasing products, booking tickets, making payments in shops, access and use of transaction services and currency exchange. Mort and Drennan (2005) also found clusters of consumers with various propensities to use various m-services; for financial services both innovators and techno-confidents were the most likely to use m-services. For financial services, m-services offer considerable potential but the research emphasizes that customers will use mobile devices in ways that suit their lives and that there are some customer groups more disposed to using these devices for financial services than others.

There are many good reasons for FIs to adopt and maintain relationships with not only customers, but also stakeholders, as depicted in Figure 6.1. However, the impact of the credit crunch and its revelations about the way in which many FIs ignored the best interests of their customers has been negative. For FIs, the immediate task is to demonstrate, by their actions within a stakeholder environment, that they value their relationships and that they will work to ensure that all the positive dimensions of relationships, such as satisfaction, trust and other relational benefits, are delivered.

Summary

In this chapter, the following key points have been discussed:

- The nature of relationship marketing (RM): strategies and contexts for developing relationships, both interpersonally and in digital environments, using mobile devices and the Internet.
- Relationship marketing extends beyond the FI and the customer to include a range of stakeholders, such as employees and suppliers.

- Relational drivers, including customer satisfaction and trust and relational benefits.
- Creating relationships with stakeholders – for example, suppliers and referral markets – as a means of enhancing customer satisfaction and internal markets.
- Relationships with consumers and businesses: similarities and differences. Does RM work in consumer markets?

References

Ahmed, P. and Rafiq, M. (2003) 'Commentary: Internal Marketing Issues and Challenges', *European Journal of Marketing*, Vol. 37, No. 9, pp. 1177–86.

Arnott, D. (2007) 'Trust: Current Thinking and Future Research', *European Journal of Marketing*, Vol. 41, No. 9/10, pp. 981–7.

Bell, S. and Eisingerich, A. (2007), 'The Paradox of Customer Education: Customer Expertise and Loyalty in the Financial Services Industry', *European Journal of Marketing*, Vol. 41, No. 5/6, pp. 466–86.

Beloucif, A., Donaldson, B. and Waddell, M. (2006), 'A Systems View of Relationship Dissolution', *Journal of Financial Services Marketing*, Vol. 11, No. 1, pp. 30–48.

Berry, L. (1983), 'Relationship Marketing', in L. Berry, G. L. Shostack, G. Upah (eds), *Emerging Perspectives in Services Marketing*, Chicago, IL, AMA.

Binks, M., Ennew, C. and Mowlah, A. (2006) 'The Relationship between Private Businesses and their Banks', *International Journal of Bank Marketing*, Vol. 24, No. 5, pp. 346–55.

Buttle, F. (1996) 'Relationship Marketing', in F. Buttle (ed.), *Relationship Marketing: Theory and Practice*, London, Paul Chapman.

Dash, S., Bruning, E. and Guin, K. (2006) 'The Moderating Effect of Power Distance on Perceived Interdependence and Relationship Quality in Commercial Banking', *International Journal of Bank Marketing*, Vol. 24, No. 5, pp. 307–26.

Dwyer, F., Schurr, P. and Oh, S. (1987) 'Developing Buyer–Seller Relationships', *Journal of Marketing*, Vol. 37, pp. 39–47.

Farquhar, J. and Panther, T (2007) 'The More the Merrier? An Exploratory Study into Managing Channels in UK Retail Financial Services', *International Review of Retail, Distribution and Consumer Research*, Vol. 17, No. 1, pp. 1–14.

Grönroos, C. (2000), *Service Management and Marketing: A Customer Relationship Management Approach*, Chichester, Wiley & Sons.

Gummesson, E. (1987) 'The New Marketing: Developing Long-term Interactive Relationships', *Long Range Planning*, Vol. 20, No. 4, pp. 10–20.

Hennig-Thurau, T. (2000), 'Relationship Quality and Customer Retention through Strategic Communication of Customer Skills', *Journal of Marketing Management,* Vol. 16, pp. 55–79.

Hennig-Thurau, T., Gwinner, K. and Gremler, D. (2002) 'Understanding Relationship Marketing Outcomes: An Integration of Relational Benefits and Relationship Quality', *Journal of Service Research*, Vol. 4, No. 3, pp. 230–47.

Hollendsen, S. (2003), *Marketing Management: A Relationship Approach*, Chelmsford, FT Prentice Hall.

Homburg, C., Workman, J. and Jensen, O. (2002) 'A Configurational Perspective on Key Account Management', *Journal of Marketing*, Vol. 66, April, pp. 38–60.

Hughes, T., Foss, B., Stone, M. and Cheverton, P. (2004) 'Key Account Management in Financial Services: An Outline Research Agenda', *Journal of Financial Services Marketing*, Vol. 9, pp. 184–93.

Keynote (2007) *Customer Services in Financial Organizations*, March, London, Keynote.

Molina, A., Martin-Consuegra, D. and Esteban, A. (2007) 'Relational Benefits and Customer Satisfaction in Retail Banking', *International Journal of Bank Marketing*, 25, 4, 253–271.

Morgan, R. and Hunt, S. (1999), "Relationship-Based Competitive Advantage: The Role of Relationship Marketing in Marketing Strategy", *Journal of Business Research*, Vol. 46, pp. 281–90.

Mort, G. S. and Drennan, J. (2005) 'Marketing m-services: Establishing a Usage Benefit Typology Related to Mobile User Characteristics', *Database Marketing & Customer Strategy Management*, Vol. 12, No. 4, pp. 327–41.

Mulligan, P. and Gordon, S. (2002) 'The Impact of Information Technology on Customer and Supplier Relationships in Financial Services', *International Journal of Service Industries Management*, Vol. 13, No. 1, pp. 29–46.

Nysveen, H., Pedersen, P., Thorbjørnsen, H. and Berthon, P. (2005) 'Mobilizing the Brand: The Effects of Mobile Services on Brand Relationships and Main Channel Use', *Journal of Service Research*, Vol. 7, pp. 257–76.

O'Loughlin, D. and Szmigin, I. (2006) 'Customer Relationship Typologies and the Nature of Loyalty in Irish Retail Financial Services', *Journal of Marketing Management*, Vol. 22, No. 2, pp. 265–93.

O'Loughlin, D. Szmigin, I. and Turnbull, P. (2004) 'From Relationships to Experiences in Retail Financial Services', *International Journal of Bank Marketing*, 22, 7, 522–539.

O'Malley, L., Patterson, M. and Evans, M. (1997), 'Intimacy or Intrusion? The Privacy Dilemma for Relationship Marketing in Consumer Markets', *Journal of Marketing Management*, Vol. 13, No. 6, pp. 541–60.

O'Malley, L. and Tynan, C. (1999), "The Unity of the Relationship Metaphor in Consumer Markets: A Critical Evaluation", *Journal of Marketing Management*, Vol. 15, pp. 587–602.

onlinebankingreport.com (2007), accessed 13 August 2008.

Palmatier, R., Dant, R., Grewal, D. and Evans, K. (2005) 'Leveraging Relationship Marketing Strategies for Better Performance: A Meta-analysis', *MSI Reports, Working Paper Series*, Vol. 3, pp. 107–32.

Payne, A., Ballantyne, D. and Christopher, M. (2005) 'A Stakeholder Approach to Relationship Marketing Strategy', *European Journal of Marketing*, Vol. 39, No. 7/8, pp. 855–71.

Proença, J. and Castro, L. (2005) '"Stress" in Business Relationships: A Study on Corporate Banking Services', *International Journal of Bank Marketing*, Vol. 23, No. 7, pp. 527–41.

Richarme, M. (2004), Business Segmentation: Emerging Approaches to More Meaningful Clusters, www.decisionanalyst.com, accessed 20 October, 2008.

Smith, W. and Higgins, M. (2000) 'Reconsidering the Relationship Analogy', *Journal of Marketing Management*, Vol. 16, pp. 81–94.

Tähtinen, J. and Havila, V. (2004) 'Editorial: Enhancing Research in Exchange Relationship Dissolution', *Journal of Marketing Management*, Vol. 20, pp. 919–26.

Van del Poel, D. and Larivière, B. (2004) 'Customer Attrition Analysis for Financial Services using Proportional Hazard Models', *European Journal of Operational Research*, Vol. 157, pp. 196–217.

Ward, T. and Dagger, T. (2007), 'The Complexity of Relationship Marketing for Service Customers', *Journal of Services Marketing*, Vol. 21, No. 4, pp. 281–90.

www.sheilaswheels.com, accessed 14 December 2008.

Exercises

1. Think of additional ways in which the determinants of trust can be operationalized (see Table 6.1).
2. Looking at Figure 6.1, what recommendations would you make to an FI about areas that might contribute to positive word-of-mouth and customer loyalty?
3. Consider three positions in an FI and note down how each of the three staff members contributes to the satisfaction of the customers.
4. What are the main points about RM in a digital environment for financial services?

Further reading and references

Berry, L. (1983) 'Relationship Marketing', in L. Berry, G. L. Shostack, G. Upah (eds), *Emerging Perspectives in Services Marketing*, Chicago, IL, AMA.

Hooley, G., Saunders, J. and Piercy, N. (2003), *Marketing Strategy and Competitive Positioning*, 3rd edn, Chelmsford, Prentice Hall.

Morgan, R. and Hunt, S. (1994) 'The Commitment–Trust Theory of Relationship Marketing', *Journal of Marketing*, Vol. 58, pp. 20–38.

www.fsa.gov.uk

www.santander.com

www.newbusiness.co.uk/articles/banking-finance

Managing customer relationships in Irish retail banking

The Irish financial services sector has received increased attention over the last few decades but continues to pose challenges for marketers. In recent years, this traditionally highly concentrated market has witnessed unprecedented turbulence due to deregulation and heightened competition between financial institutions, which has had a critical impact upon consumer behaviour and marketing success. Faced with these new developments, Irish financial service practitioners have had to re-evaluate their marketing strategies, including reassessing their approach to relationship marketing.

The Irish banking market

The Irish financial services marketplace has seen similar developments to international environments wherein deregulation and technological advances are amongst the main developments generating recent competitive pressures (Government of Ireland 2001). Analysis of the market shows that contribution of the banking sector to GNP is 5 per cent, with employment at 80,000 (IBF 2007). Irish retail banking has traditionally been significantly more concentrated than other markets, with only five clearing banks until recently owning approximately 90 per cent of all bank branches (AIB, Bank of Ireland, National Irish Bank, Permanent TSB and Ulster Bank). The new legislative environment has lowered entry barriers to the sector, blurred the business boundaries between different types of financial services and created unprecedented competition between FIs. A whole new vista has opened for the customer in terms of choice of suppliers with the entrance of new UK financial providers such as Halifax, on-line financial suppliers such as Rabo Direct and Northern Rock and non-traditional financial suppliers, including retailing outlets such as Marks & Spencer and Tesco. Mirroring its foreign counterparts, the Irish retail financial services sector has undergone a significant technological transformation in terms of delivery channels, which have evolved from relatively high-touch, interpersonal-oriented encounters to high-tech interaction. Hence, the adoption of high-technology services by Irish consumers, including tele-banking and Internet banking, represents a key technological development, with 40 per cent of 25–34-year-olds banking on-line (Sunday Business Post 2007). In a marketplace comprising of foreign providers and new entrants from non-traditional spheres, changing consumer behaviour and delivery channels and rapidly emerging new services and packages, all players in the Irish retail banking sector have had to establish their most viable competitive position and adjust their marketing and customer relationship management strategies.

The role of relationship marketing within financial services

Relationship marketing (RM), the process of 'attaching, maintaining and enhancing customer relationships' (Berry 1983), has profoundly influenced marketing thought and practice. It is claimed that the RM approach is particularly applicable to the banking sector as financial services can be characterized as complex, high-risk, continuous and long-term purchases. Therefore, relationship formation and participation have been traditionally central to service delivery within banking. However, operational problems have been associated with RM, raising questions about its appropriateness for all customers, particularly in sectors where the nature of interaction and service delivery has changed. Indeed, retail banking is a good example of a sector in which personal relationships have become much weaker as a result of automation of bank branches and de-skilling of bank manager tasks; the long-term future of the traditional branch banking is uncertain. Since the introduction of on-line banking, customers have begun to use a combination of IT channels to interact with their financial services provider, which affects the nature and quality of relationships. A more technologically savvy and less loyal customer base has emerged, evidenced by over 20,000 Irish consumers switching banks in 2005 under the Personal Switching Code (IBF 2006). Consequently, financial providers nowadays have to compete for customers they traditionally had the luxury of taking for granted. On the other hand, some experts emphasize that banks still operate in a high-contact business; the nature of buyer–seller interactions and establishment of long-term relationships based on confidence and trust directly affect customer recruitment and retention. Regardless of whether relationship marketing is an appropriate approach to retail financial services, there is no doubting that the significant internal and external changes have affected financial service delivery and quality and impacted upon opportunities for customer relationship building and management.

The nature and diversity of relationships held by consumers with their banks has recently been explored within an Irish context (O'Loughlin and Szmigin 2006). The majority of consumers hold several different and distinct relationships with a variety of financial services providers in meeting their financial product needs, which include current accounts, savings and investment products, credit cards and loans, mortgages and pensions. More importantly, the types of relationships held by customers include: first, purely transactional, non-personal dealings with counter staff, known as *transactional experiences*; second, goal-oriented, opportunistic relationships with key personnel, termed *outcome-focused relationships*; third, *interactive friendships* with counter staff; and, fourth, highly close *personal relationships* with senior managers in the bank. As illustrated in Figure C6.1, each of the four types of relationship can be depicted along a continuum, from pure *transactional experiences*, which reflect a transactional approach to marketing, to highly *personal relationships*, which can be categorized under the relationship marketing approach.

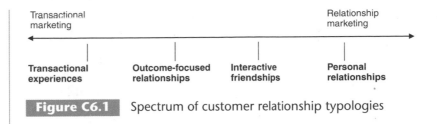

Figure C6.1   Spectrum of customer relationship typologies

Transactional experiences with front-line staff

Some consumers have a purely *transactional experience* with their primary bank. Being in an early stage of the lifecycle, some consumers may not have yet taken out a mortgage or embarked upon investment decisions and have limited financial experience. Consequently, due to the limited level of contact between consumer and provider, these customers have transactional experiences with their bank, involving non-personal transactions with non-specific staff at the front line. Hence, consumers in this category, whether by choice or design, tend not to know anybody personally in their bank branch and prefer to use tele-banking or bank on-line. Moreover, transaction-based encounters may not only apply to the consumer's primary bank where key current and savings accounts are held, but may even apply more so to secondary bank accounts, such as investments and mortgages, which tend to be more transactional in nature and involve even less contact with the bank. This may be attributable to lower-transaction secondary accounts requiring less communication between consumer and supplier than high-transaction accounts such as current and main savings accounts. Indeed, after the account set-up stage, these transactional experiences with secondary suppliers do not appear to develop into more close, intimate relationships over time; instead, most consumers are satisfied 'to let them work away' without feeling the need to be in regular contact with the supplier. Hence, opportunities for relationship building are minimal.

Outcome-focused relationships with key personnel

Consumers who could be categorized in the middle-income and more financially experienced group tend to hold *outcome-focused relationships*, involving business-focused relationships with staff or management. Unlike the relationships in the *transactional* category, these relationships are with key staff or middle/senior management in the branch. These outcome-focused relationships are highly functional in nature and the majority of consumers in the group are primarily goal-oriented, using the relationship to 'get access to loans' and 'get the best deal', such as quick approval or a favourable interest rate on a mortgage or loan. Moreover, the majority of consumers tend to exhibit little or no allegiance to their bank despite developing these relationships and instead view their dealings with the bank as opportunistic, believing that 'business is business'. In addition, consumers in this category are generally capable of outlining the main motives for developing these relationships, including becoming known by the manager and obtaining a good service or expert advice. Hence, these relationships are focused on outcomes for the consumers and, therefore, lack the personal characteristics and deep social bonds associated with closer relationships.

Interactive friendships with front-line staff

Another type of relationship held by consumers can be classed as *interactive friendships*, which involve friendly interactions with financial services staff, mostly at front-line level. Although these relationships involve more interpersonal communication and personal interaction than *transactional* and *outcome-focused relationships*, this type of relationship is predominantly formed with junior-level or front-line staff as opposed to with key staff or management. Due to the social, friendly dimension to these relationships, they tend to be held by older, female consumers who have the time to visit the branch often, who personally know most of the 'people behind the counter' and value these 'friendships', placing importance on staff helpfulness, courtesy and empathy. While these older female consumers may be familiar and even friendly with personnel in the branch, most do not have a key contact in the branch and would not ask for or seek out any one person in particular. Importantly, as these friendships tend to be with front-line staff or junior staff who may possess minimal influencing power, customers in this category are unable to use these contacts to redress more serious customer issues or problems. On the other hand, as most of the consumers holding these interactive friendships have relatively uncomplicated financial needs, the level of influence of their front-line contacts in the bank does not appear to matter.

Personal relationships with key personnel

A minority of consumers, particularly in the high-income category, fall into the *personal relationship* category, enjoying a truly personal relationship with one or more key senior people within their bank. These consumers may have a unique set of circumstances, which necessitate the development of a personal relationship with key personnel in their bank. For example, consumers such as farmers and those who are self-employed perceive the importance of a personal relationship with their bank in order to accommodate the uniqueness of their financial situation, with irregular income and fluctuating credit and overdraft facilities needs. For other customers, the relationship can take precedence over all other decision criteria, with some customers unaware or unconcerned by their bank's level of competitiveness, stating that they 'wouldn't even think about the rate'. A third type of personal relationship is held by private banking customers, who enjoy the highest level of personal relationship and tailored banking available to retail banking customers. Interestingly, these customers perceive the bank as 'working for them' and 'keeping their interests at stake', a perspective not shared by other consumers. In general, these 'privileged' consumers in the *personal relationship* category enjoy many associated tangible benefits, including better rates, tailored service, good advice and flexibility, in addition to psychological advantages such as feelings of trust and security.

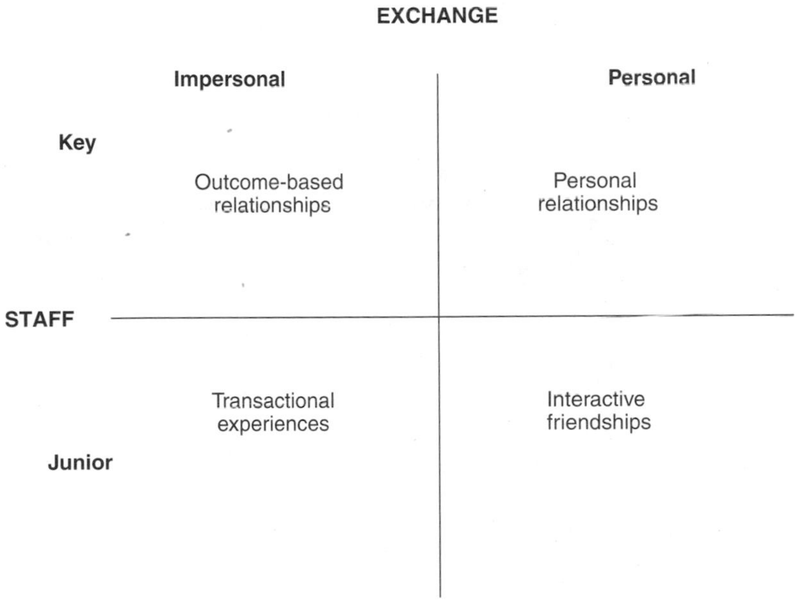

EXCHANGE

	Impersonal	Personal
Key	Outcome-based relationships	Personal relationships
STAFF		
Junior	Transactional experiences	Interactive friendships

Figure C6.2   Customer relationship typology matrix

As illustrated in the matrix in Figure C6.2, these four types of relationships can be differentiated across two dimensions: front-line or key personnel as relationship partners and personal or impersonal exchanges. Transactional experiences involve impersonal exchanges with front-line staff, whereas interactive friendships represent personal exchanges with front-line or junior staff. In addition, although outcome-focused relationships are held with key personnel and managers, they can be differentiated from personal relationships, as they are mostly impersonal and business- or goal-focused in nature and do not reach the deeper personal levels associated with personal relationships.

Meeting different relationship needs

The majority of consumers hold multiple relationships with different financial institutions, ranging from transactional experiences to close personal relationships. Importantly, these relationship types do not appear to be mutually exclusive and most customer relationships appear to be multidimensional in nature. For example, depending on the particular transaction involved, a customer could have an autonomous transactional experience on one level with their bank – for example, when completing an on-line transaction – and a close personal relationship with key personnel in the same bank – for example, when discussing investment product options. Despite the introduction of technology and alternative channels, banking in Ireland remains, for many customers, a high-contact business in which the service agent or employee appears to play a key role in creating positive interactions and forging relationships with customers. In addition, it appears that personal relationships are still favoured by many respondents, young and old, who recognize their inherent advantages. Therefore, a challenge for all financial service providers will be to define current customer requirements with regard to banking relationship type and look to ways to incorporate this in new forms of service delivery and customer experience.

Questions

1. Discuss the main internal and external developments within the Irish financial services sector.
2. Identify the key challenges facing financial services marketers in implementing a relationship marketing approach.
3. Recommend an appropriate customer relationship management strategy for financial services providers in light of current diverse customer relationship needs.

References

Berry, L. (1983) 'Relationship Marketing', in L. Berry, G. L. Shostack, G. Upah (eds), *Emerging Perspectives in Services Marketing*, Chicago, IL, AMA, pp. 25–34.

Government of Ireland (2001) *Banking Sector: Some Strategic Issues, Report of the Department of Finance*, Central Bank Working Group on Strategic Issues facing the Irish Banking Sector (on-line). Available at: http://www.irlgov.ie/finance/publications/otherpubs/bankingsector.htm.

IBF (2007) 'About Banking', Issue 5, Irish Bankers' Federation (online). Available at: http://www.ibf.ie/pdfs/About_Banking_June_2007.pdf.

IBF (2006) 'The Competitiveness of the Irish Financial Services Sector', Irish Bankers Federation Fact File (on-line). Available at: http://www.ibf.ie/pdfs/Fact File_May_2006.pdf.

O'Loughlin, D. and Szmigin, I. (2006) 'Customer Relationship Typologies and the Nature of Loyalty in Irish Retail Financial Services', *Journal of Marketing Management*, Vol. 22, No. 2, pp. 276–93.

Sunday Business Post (2007) 'Banking Online is a Growing Trend', 30 September.

Walsh, S. (2002) 'Integrating the Activities Required to Recruit and Retain Profitable Customers in Contemporary Retail Banking', *Irish Marketing Review*, Vol. 15, No. 1, pp. 24–37.

This case was written Dr Deirdre O'Loughlin, Senior Lecturer in Marketing, Kemmy Business School, University of Limerick, Limerick, Ireland.

The material in the case has been drawn from a variety of published sources, interviews, archival records and research reports.

7

Building and sustaining the financial services brand

Contents

Learning outcomes

At the end of this chapter, the reader will be able to:

- Appreciate how branding theory applies to the marketing of financial services

- Contribute to developing branding strategies in financial services

- Describe the key branding issues that apply to financial services, such as corporate branding and corporate communications

Introduction

Branding is one of the more visible and one of the most exciting aspects of marketing to which financial institutions (FIs) devote significant proportions of their marketing budgets. At the same time, it is not well understood by many organizations and FIs have found branding to be an extremely challenging area. In Interbrand's 2008 ranking of global brands, American Express is the highest ranked at 15 and HSBC comes in at 27 (www.interbrand.com). Investment banks focus on international capital markets and multinational customers with brands such as Merrill Lynch and JPMorgan, which have dropped down from their previously high rankings in the Top Global Brands as they have fared extremely badly in the credit crunch. Seven of the ten top 50 brands that fell in value in 2008 were banks. Between them, their brands lost more than $10 billion (£5.5 billion) of their value. As far as branding is concerned in retail banking, this remains largely a national business. Indeed, in some important markets (including Germany, Italy, Spain and the United States), retail banking remains to varying degrees a sub-national business, with regional and local banks continuing to be significant. Most retail bank brands, therefore, do not meet the Interbrand global criteria, but the FI described in Exhibit 7.1 is an exception, with a ranking of 86 in 2008.

---

strategy: plans the allocation of resources to enable the FI to meet its organizational objectives.

> ### EXHIBIT 7.1
>
> # A global financial services brand
>
> ING is a global financial services company providing banking, investments, life insurance and retirement services. The company serves more than 85 million customers in Europe, the United States, Canada, Latin America, Asia and Australia. They have a broad customer base, comprising individuals, families, small businesses, large corporations, institutions and governments. ING's strategic focus is on banking, investments, life insurance and retirement services. The company provides retail customers with the products they need during their lives to grow savings, manage investments and prepare for retirement with confidence. The successful execution of the **strategy** is underpinned by continued efficient reallocation of capital through redeploying that which the company generates in mature markets to high-growth businesses, or returning it to shareholders. With this strategy, ING focuses on creating value for its shareholders, rewarding them with a better total return on investment than the average among peers in the financial sector over the longer term. ING conducts business according to clearly defined business principles. In all activities, it carefully weighs the interests of various stakeholders: customers, shareholders, employees, business partners and society at large. ING strives to be a good corporate citizen.

> ING wants to pursue profit on the basis of sound business ethics and respect for its stakeholders. Corporate responsibility is therefore a fundamental part of ING's strategy: ethical, social and environmental factors play an integral role in our business decisions.
>
> Compiled by the authors from material on www.ing.com.

What is a brand?

Classical descriptions of branding focus on name, symbol and design, which all communicate the values that a particular brand offers the marketplace. The meaning of the brand is defined as a mental picture or image in the customer's mind that is associated with the market offering. The image of the brand, therefore, exists in the consumer memory as knowledge (Iacobucci 1998), creating a summary of all the information related to the brand and funnelling it down to a useful size and meaning. Brands provide consumers with a means of evaluating offerings in the marketplace and providers with the capacity to distinguish themselves from their competitors. A dissenting voice to this view is that of Kapferer (2001), who has stated companies need to use the 'source effect', which he describes as the key credibility factor in persuasive communication. To achieve this effect, brands need to be managed like companies so that they can inject meaning into the services that they provide to meet the expectations of the questioning and critical consumer.

Brands are usually envisaged as having at least two elements. The first element focuses on the functions of the brand such as ability to purchase on credit offered by a credit card. The second element of the brand is concerned with its appeal to emotions so that a unique and welcoming experience is offered to its stakeholders (De Chernatony *et al.* 2006). As Palmer (2008) has observed, the emotional or non-functional elements of the brand are becoming more important owing to their capacity to position the brand along such dimensions as liking, trust or aspiration. Brands should therefore represent a distinctive value system that is relevant to customers. The brand needs to indicate the origin of the offering, so enabling the building of relationships between customer and FI based on trust (Dall'Olmo Riley and De Chernatony, 2000).

Branding in financial services

A strong identity and reputation of the company as a brand is a crucial way of enhancing consumers' perceptions and trust in the range of services. There are numerous advantages for organizations in having a strong brand, including an increased likelihood of repurchase and – importantly, for financial services – an increased likelihood of extending the number of purchases. Existing customers may respond favourably to being offered new products because of familiarity with the brand. Communicating with the chosen audience is more effective as the brand has already established a key or focal message. In certain circumstances, the brand may allow a premium pricing strategy; although this is a route that financial services would dearly love to be able to follow, there are few examples of this being successfully achieved other than in private banking. New entrants to financial services seek some form of differentiation in this extremely crowded and competitive marketplace. While there are clear benefits for building brands in this field, competitive advantage will probably not be gained from the functional benefits of a brand. An exception to this was Direct Line who managed, in the short term, to offer insurance over the phone. Their distinctiveness was soon copied by their competitors, as is often the case in services. There have been attempts to appeal to customers' aspirational desires by offering various types of current accounts and credit cards. Increasing customer instrumentality (that is, choices made on the basis of price from a set of undifferentiated suppliers), deregulation and increasing technological development mean that branding has to be relevant, meaningful and implementable (O'Loughlin and Szmigin 2007). The diminishing brand loyalty demonstrated by customers (Veloutsou *et al.* 2004) is further exacerbated by the absence of any personal bonding through face-to-face interactions, as financial services shift inexorably away from the branch to remote channels. Figure 7.1 demonstrates the situation that financial brands face, losing any ability to price themselves based on differentiation and descending towards commodity markets.

For specialist services such as investment, it has been argued that brand building is best achieved through the establishment of a good reputation, strong industry rankings and favourable media reviews. Marketers of this type of service should, therefore, stress objective sources of information rather than the use of advertising or even word-of-mouth, which are subjective media. A reliance on reputations calls for relationship building with public relations professionals, so that favourable events are publicized and less favourable ones 'managed'. From a theoretical perspective, for certain high-involvement financial services, intrinsic cues such as corporate reputation are more important than extrinsic cues such as price and referrals are more influential in purchase decisions (Brady *et al.* 2005).

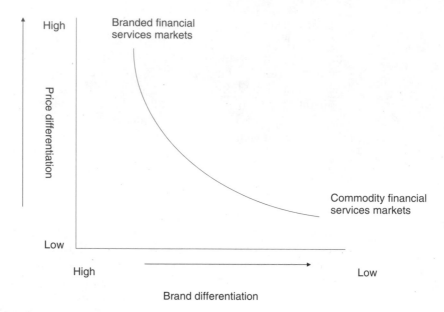

Figure 7.1 Brand decay in financial services
Source: Adapted from Knox (2000).

Developing the brand

Brands provide evidence of consistent standards, particularly where the company has not been able to build a strong relationship. The aim of the brand here is to limit the search activities of customers, encouraging them to discount other products that do not come with the statement of values that this particular brand does (Palmer 2008). Brands should aim to act as a proxy for a personal relationship and simplify decision-making process by trying to provide a sense of security and consistency that may not exist outside a relationship. Brands originally sought to offer a means of differentiation, which Kapferer (2001) has argued against. The culture of 'me-too' in financial services, that is a tendency to copy what the competition does whether it offers the best strategic option or not, can impact on ways of creating genuine distinctiveness that offer value to the customer. Differentiation can be best achieved by doing something that the competitors are not doing, but that takes courage. FI culture can be risk-averse and struggles to look at things from a new perspective. Another consideration is that customers may not look to their financial service provider for innovation. The relationship between institution and customer is based on solidity, duration and a lack of risk, although not necessarily trust. Interbrand's study (2001) provides a very interesting perspective on branding

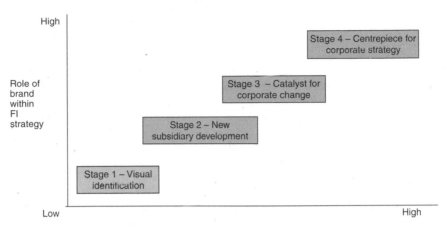

High

Role of
brand
within
FI
strategy

Stage 4 – Centrepiece for
corporate strategy

Stage 3 – Catalyst for
corporate change

Stage 2 – New
subsidiary development

Stage 1 – Visual
identification

Low High

Value of brand to FI

Figure 7.2 Branding approaches
Source: Adapted by the authors from Interbrand 2001.

approaches in financial services in which, based on interviews with banks, they identify the four stages of branding as shown in Figure 7.2.

Stage 1 of branding is for the companies who are at the first level of brand development; visual identification is the only role described for the corporate brand. These companies have traditionally placed a lower priority on developing and associating values with the brand and have focused on it principally as a naming device, which raises customer/prospect awareness. In so doing, much of the brand's potential value has been unexploited by not clearly defining a brand personality or a relationship with all stakeholders, especially employees. The second level of branding occurs with a brand that is established for a new type of service (e.g., telephone or Internet banking, or insurance like that offered by Smile, Egg or Cahoot). The rationale for this strategy appears to be that while the personality, style and culture of the overall organization is too entrenched for a radical change, a new service can be developed which is managed in a completely different way and kept separate from the parent. In each instance, the new sub-brand is an integral part of the intended relationship between the brand and its stakeholders. In these cases the corporate brand continues to be confined to a name and a visual identity for external communication, as described at stage one. In telephone and Internet-based operations, the sub-brand is heavily used for both internal and external explanation of the service and is seen to be central to the development of the new business, enabling the new service to be strongly differentiated from the parent organization and brand. The critical change occurring is that FI operations staff of the new service – not just the marketing staff – see the brand as conveying the underlying service promise.

The aim of branding is to communicate the values and nature of the service or services on offer, and the nature of the relationship between the brand and the customer and stakeholders. In so doing, it is also informing employees about what they should seek to deliver to customers and encouraging behaviours that reflect the new sub-brand's values. The difficulty these new branded services face is that they remain part of a parent institution that sees brand solely in terms of visual identity and has a contrasting vision and set of values. The resulting clash of values and behaviours, sometimes within the same offices, limits the effective delivery of the new brand and the maximization of brand value. To address this clash, the sub-brand can be separated completely from its parent and given its own premises, policies and tailored IT systems, which support its brand vision and values. The preferred option is to realign the corporate brand so that its vision and values, and consequently its policies and systems, are consistent with those of its successful sub-brand.

The third type of brand use is as a catalyst for a significant organizational and cultural change programme where companies have identified a need to improve the competitiveness of their service, primarily though raising their standards of customer service. Powerful retail brands entering the market are using their association with value and consistent service to challenge traditional players. Company brands in this category have high awareness, but need to convey stronger relationship characteristics of quality customer service and personality if they are to resist the competition from new entrants. The brand is given a more central, strategic role in the parent business and is positioned as an emblem of the vision and values of the whole company, emphasizing the importance of customer relationships to the business. It is used to motivate staff, to communicate with customers and it is managed by a cross-functional team, who have a long-term, business-based perspective on its development. This is, however, a transitional stage *en route* to the highest level of brand management, with the brand at the centre of the business strategy. The critical issue for these organizations is whether they can sustain the momentum behind the new brand-driven culture until it is universally accepted. About 25 per cent of the companies surveyed in the Interbrand study describe a management structure and range of activities which indicate that their master corporate brand is at the centre of their business strategy, corresponding to our top level of brand development. In these companies, the top management team developed and agreed the corporate brand strategy and positioning at the same time as the business vision and strategy. So, for these organizations, the brand has become the embodiment of the company vision and direction and the brand mission and values serve as the lenses through which proposed changes and improvements are filtered. What are the practical implications of positioning the brand at the centre of corporate strategy? These companies have a brand-driven organizational infrastructure, comprising visibly brand-committed senior management teams leading a workforce who live and breathe the brand vision and values in their regular activities.

Only a few FI brands seem to have achieved an emotional appeal; arguably UK examples may be First Direct and the Co-operative Bank. The lack of success in financial services with creating this type of appeal may be because managers another FIs are overly concerned with building brands' functional values. They should, instead, be aiming for a symbiotic relationship between functional values and non-functional values. Non-functional or emotional values can be developed through initiating relationships within the FI that are aimed at building shared knowledge. Brand is conceived of as a cluster of functional and emotional values and relationship built with customers through interaction with staff 'forging a bond'. Brands represent a distinctive value system, but in complex contexts such as financial services, a strong identity and reputation of the company as a brand needs work to develop trust in the range of services. To achieve this, it has been stressed that it is vital to obtain employee buy-in (Dall'Olmo Riley and De Chernatony 2000). Research into technological aspects of branding has suggested that, in terms of building or strengthening the emotional values of the brand, mobile phones can play a part through regular messaging of account details, as mobiles are very personal (Nysveen et al. 2005). Two-way personal communication that is relevant and time-sensitive between the customer and the company may strengthen the emotional relationship and hence reinforce the brand's emotional values (Nysveen et al. 2005).

Extending the brand

If a strong brand has already been developed, then a process of building on a strong brand can be undertaken, which is known as line or brand extension, depending on the nature of the new offering. The aim is to introduce usually related offerings to existing customers, which is very much consistent with the cross-selling that financial companies often strive to achieve, or to engage new markets. In some cases, the extensions can be quite a leap; the Virgin group has been particularly courageous at extending their brand into completely new areas such as transport, financial services and cosmetics (www.virgin.com). Extending the brand is not based on a product range, however successful, but on a recognition that there is a segment or segments of customers in the marketplace who identify with that brand and are therefore predisposed to jump to new product ranges owing to their favourable attitude to the brand.

As considerable effort has already been established in creating functional and emotional values, there are advantages to be had from extensions to a brand. Laforêt (2007) summarizes arguments about brand extensions by stating that perceived fit, risks and brand trust would appear to be relevant in horizontal brand extensions. Perceived fit in brand extensions refers to the cohesiveness between the existing products in the brand and the new extensions that consumers of the brand (that is stakeholders) see in the horizontal extensions. An insurer, for example, specializes in providing cover for events that involve loss or cost to the policy-holder, therefore extensions that insure against losses or costs may convey a 'fit' between the existing product range and new additions. As can be seen by the Virgin example, that cohesiveness is not always a pre-requisite. Work conducted in the Irish banking sector (O'Loughlin and Szmigin 2007) revealed that consumers perceived little difference between the brands or 'an identity crisis' (p. 443), which could be attributed to the absence of a cohesive brand image or ineffective brand appeals. The salience of functional values over emotional, with competitive rates being the most important issue, is even further weakened by evidence that suggests that banks are even failing to differentiate themselves across functional values. Trust continues to be a problem in financial services and since the credit crunch has become even more elusive.

Sustaining the brand

Much of the branding that has occurred within the fast-moving consumer goods (fmcg) sector has occurred at product level, with large multinational companies such as Premier Foods, which has an extensive range of food brands. Product branding works well with the aim of reducing consumer search activities so that repurchase of particular items becomes likely. However, leading brands offer more than a means of short-circuiting decision-making; they offer something intangible or, as Kapferer (2001) suggests, a bonus or gift that transcends mere exchange consisting of aspirational values. For brands that have established a relatively strong appeal in financial services, such as First Direct or Cater Allen (the private banker who has managed to target a niche market), capturing the aspirational values of the customers may be quite achievable. For mass-market brands such as Lloyds, conveying values is much more challenging owing to the extent of the markets and number of segments that the bank targets worldwide. To a certain extent, Tesco faces a similar challenge owing to the size and rapid diversification of its activities that includes financial services. Financial service providers therefore have a balancing act to effect of achieving economies of scale through being a global player and yet at the same time understanding the needs of segments or groups of customers with a brand that identifies with them.

Brands offer the means of establishing an identity through four dimensions: physical dimensions, personality dimensions, values and implicit relationships or associations. Consumers of the brand construct their own identity through the last two dimensions of values and implicit relationships (Kapferer 2008). Luxury brands are a particularly good example of this construction and, at the same time, highlight how difficult it is for the larger FIs to achieve strong brands. An argument can be developed, therefore, for having a stable of brands, so that if a customer wearies of a brand or if his/her circumstances change, there is the opportunity to introduce this customer to another brand that the company provides. Again, observations from practitioners gathered by the authors about branding in financial services are as follows:

- the effectiveness of brands used exclusively or mainly for marketing insurance varies according to type and operating model of the insurer, with direct personal brands generally faring better than life insurance and pensions brands;
- it is generally the case that brands that fall into a bottom quartile for overall brand effectiveness are those for which awareness levels are lower or which are oriented towards use in conjunction with marketing of retail lending or payment cards;
- the performance of new financial brands, defined as those launched in the United Kingdom during the 1995–2005 period, varies significantly from one firm to another, with Egg, ranked eighth in terms of overall brand effectiveness, finishing well ahead of its closest rivals;
- brands that create value for their owners are those that possess a well-balanced set of attributes, scoring in the top quartile for the majority of the factors used to evaluate brand effectiveness – for example, Visa, RAC, Halifax, Nationwide and MasterCard.

For FIs, these assessments are not very encouraging. Egg, in spite of ranking relatively highly, is likely to have suffered owing to its decision to jettison certain customers.

Corporate branding and identity

Service organizations have to ask themselves whether they wish to build their brand around a product or around the company as a whole (McDonald *et al.* 2001). A further consideration, especially post-credit crunch when this becomes even more pressing, is how the acquired brands fit with the new parent company when mergers and takeovers have taken place. The financial services sector offers examples of global

Table 7.1	Brand name spectrum or hierarchy		
McDonald *et al.* (2001)	**Laforêt and Saunders (2005)**	**Example**
Company as a brand name	Corporate branded	Nationwide
Strong company endorsement	Endorsed+	Santander and Alliance & Leicester
Weak company endorsement	Dual brand	Royal Sun and More Than
Individual brand name	Branded	RAC

corporate branding: where the company is the dominant brand, e.g., HSBC, instead of product brands or sub-brands

branded giants such as HSBC and AXA, **corporate branding** at regional level such as Zurich and BNP Paribas, as well as examples of local brands such as Dunfermline Building Society. Developing a new division or business can often be based on the identification of new segments that offer the parent company potential but not with the existing brand or be a result of convergence in the industry. HBOS a few years ago acquired Birmingham Midshires Building Society, which now targets particular segments of mortgage customers under the former building society brand. Further examples can be seen in Table 7.1.

Consumers can contribute to the development of a corporate service brand; although their level of participation may vary, it can be a fundamental aspect of service brands (McDonald *et al.* 2001). Balmer and Grey

Table 7.2	Corporate brand categories in financial services		
Corporate brand category	**Explanation**	**Suggested financial services example**
Familial	Sharing of same corporate brand by two former separate entities	HBOS
Supra	Quasi arch-brand used to supra endorse company brands. Derived from several rather than single corporate entities	Santander with Abbey
Multiplex	Multiple uses and/or rights of a corporate brand in a variety of industry sectors	Virgin
Federal	Creation of a new corporate brand by separate companies who pool resources in a joint venture	May arise from credit crunch

Sources: Adapted from Balmer and Grey (2003) and Lambkin and Muzellec (2008).

(2003) propose corporate brand strategies, which have been adapted for the financial services sector (see Table 7.2).

Similarly to corporate branding, corporate identity was initially defined in terms of graphic design as a corporate logo, where the aim was to represent the organization via a symbol, behaviour and communication (Van Riel 1995). He and Balmer (2005), in their investigation into generic identity, criticize this approach, believing it to be too narrow and generally to fail to capture the identity of the organization. The identity of an organization is concerned with 'Who are we as an organization?' and 'What are we as an organization?', which then draws the discipline of organizational behaviour into the strategy. FIs have begun to talk about 'living the brand' and 'living the values', where the whole organization shares a vision of the brand and the values that they are trying to convey to their customers. Corporate identity is concerned with those attributes that make an organization distinctive.

Building societies, owing to their history, have had an identity as an industry distinct from other FIs (Meidan 1996). Since the 1980s liberalization of the financial services marketplace, which enabled building societies to compete with banks, some loss of identity has occurred. The study has implications for identity in financial services, both corporate and generic (He and Balmer 2005). Generically, building societies are perceived by the UK public to be trustworthy, traditional and equitable. Corporate identities evolve at an increasing rate as the power of the consumer grows. There are now multiple interpretations of mutuality, so each society needs to build a distinct identity for itself. The implication of this research for the wider financial services industry, particularly post-Northern Rock, is to understand that a generic identity of high-street banks probably exists, but that this identity is not necessarily one that the FI would choose. Efforts at brand building and corporate identity for each organization need to be directed at building on those distinctive qualities that are valued and understood by all stakeholders. Adopting a historical perspective may be necessary when attempting to comprehend an organization or industry's identity. Understanding an individual organization's identity may also involve understanding the identity of the industry. This last point is particularly important for brand managers in financial services as a whole.

Product branding

re-branding: when a company chooses to either strengthen an existing brand or to use a single brand instead of a number of sub-brands, e.g., Aviva

Many of the brands in the financial services sector are corporate brands; for example, Aviva is **re-branding** Norwich Union to strengthen its aim to become a global financial service provider. One exception to this norm is Royal Bank of Scotland, which owns a number of brands, including Direct Line, the insurer. Some banks have attempted to brand certain products – for example, branding of current accounts. Barclays offer an Additions account and a Premier account, and Halifax offer an Ultimate Reward current account. These accounts differ from ordinary current accounts as the customers pay a monthly fee or have to meet certain wealth criteria. In return for the fee, certain benefits such as phone insurance are offered. It is not clear exactly how these accounts fit the branding criteria that have been described above. It is possible that certain segments of customers may value the functional benefits that these accounts offer, but it is less clear what emotional values these accounts offer. It is possible that customers of these accounts are fulfilling aspirational needs but it may just be that the banks providing these accounts are optimizing revenue.

Own label

'Own label' refers to the practice of retailers selling products with their brand, such as Sainsbury's cheese or orange juice. Retailer brands operate at the level of value – for money and aim for loyalty across a single horizontal brand. Owing to the success of this practice, retailers have moved into financial services. In Exhibit 7.2, loans (*prêts*) offered by Carrefour are briefly described. Although Carrefour is a global organization, the financial services at the core of its business are available only in France. **'Pass'** is the name of their financial range of products, which includes a credit card.

EXHIBIT 7.2

Carrefour

PRÊT PERSONNEL PASS: des taux attractifs pour tous vos projets! Acheter un nouveau véhicule, préparer les prochaines vacances, refaire la déco. Pour réaliser les projets qui vous tiennent à coeur, profitez des taux attractifs du Prêt Personnel PASS. Choisissez votre montant et prenez le temps de rembourser!

carrefour.com/cdc/press/

This section of the Carrefour website offers familiar benefits such as buying a new car (*véhicule*), holidays (*vacances*) and refurbishing (*refaire la déco*). Retailer branding in financial services is not new and has come about partly as a response to the limited growth options that characterize saturated markets. One of the key factors that underpin the entry of own label brands into financial services has been the recognition that these retailer brands are just like any other brand in the marketplace and therefore consumer perceptions of product quality are affected by these brands (Collins-Dodd and Lindley 2003). A key issue in considering the extension of a retailer or own label brand into financial services is that customers face a shift from low-risk purchases, usually tangible, to high-risk, intangible offerings. Nonetheless, a study of Sheffield (United Kingdom) consumers showed that trust was transferred from the parent brand to the extension (Laforêt 2007). Laforêt also concludes that the stronger the corporate brand, the greater the likelihood of unrelated products to the brand will be recognized and accepted. The reverse is also likely in weaker brands, with the added disadvantage that the brand overall may be diluted. Nonetheless, retailers are being drawn into this market and are seeking to 'add value' by providing a wide range of services and products.

The marketing of financial services in supermarkets and other stores is conducted under the process known as 'white labelling'. It involves an agreement with an FI to provide the FI's products under the label of the supermarket (i.e., the label is blank or white until the name of the supermarket is inscribed). This approach has allowed the company comparethemarket.com to enter into a number of white-label agreements, using third-party financial service providers, but with services presented under the comparethemarket.com branding. The company's white-label partners are Simply Business (SME services), PMI (health insurance), Motley Fool (loans), Xelector (utilities) and The Idol (travel insurance). White labelling may also help some of the FIs whose brands may have suffered through association with toxic debt to maintain sales.

Partnerships

There is scope for brands to work together to endow both brands with superior value. Nectar was launched in January 2005 as the United Kingdom's first large-scale business to business loyalty programme. The Nectar credit card was launched in 2005 too, allowing Nectar collectors to 'double dip' at Nectar partners, as well as earning Nectar points on all other credit card expenditure. The credit card is co-branded with Amex (www.amex.co.uk). By bringing these two brands together, the aim is to mutually enhance both brands through the association. Other instances of **co-branding** in financial services are affinity cards – for example, Visa operates a card for the RSPCA which has brought in £1 million to the charity. The choice of partner is critical in these ventures, with the need to harmonize the functional and emotional attributes and values that underpin strong brands.

co-branding: bringing two or more brands together to mutually enhance all the brands through association

Re-branding

Re-branding occurs from time to time as the dynamics of the marketplace change, in particular as the financial services industry responds to the demands of globalization. Exhibit 7.3 provides an interesting example of re-branding in just one part of a very large business.

EXHIBIT 7.3

Re-branding at the top!

BNP Paribas Wealth Management is the new brand for the private banking business of the parent company. BNP Paribas is a major player in the private banking sector, employing more than 4,500 professionals in 30 countries, and managing assets valued at nearly €150 billion at the end of June 2008. BNP Paribas' strategy for the wealth management business is to tailor its services to its clients' individual needs, offering private clients a wide array of financial instruments and investment options. The new name, BNP Paribas Wealth Management, is a more accurate reflection of the universal dimension of BNP Paribas' private banking client relationships. It also carries a guarantee of security by being part of a strong global banking group, together with an ability to innovate and offer new investment techniques and products. BNP Paribas Wealth Management will comprise two business lines: Wealth Management Networks (WMN), supported by the future Retail Banking Group, and joint venture Asset Management and Services (AMS).

Compiled by the authors from www.bnpparibas.com.

In spite of its size and the range of its activities, this bank does not yet feature in the Interbrand global ranking. By developing this brand, it may be seeking to strengthen its presence in smaller but clearly more lucrative segments.

Stakeholders

Branding is much more than an activity that occurs purely between the company and its customers. It is increasingly recognized in marketing generally, and in branding, that there are a number of interested parties or stakeholders involved in marketing. FIs need to be aware of the extent and the power of these stakeholders. Just as segmentation is concerned with identifying groups of customers based on shared characteristics who might be interested in the company's offer, so there is a range of people who may, for some reason, have a 'stake' in the brand. Whether all brand managers have caught up with this thinking remains debatable, as Rust and his colleagues have observed: 'Brand management still trumps customer management in most large companies and that focus is increasingly incompatible with growth' (Rust *et al.* 2004: 110).

In this section, the wider audience of brands is explored so that a greater understanding of to whom brands appeal to can be gained.

Communities

There are other audiences in branding, such as business partners, prospective employees and media. The media have become very influential in shaping consumer belief and understanding of financial markets and it has been proposed that company attempts at branding are being subverted by groups or **brand communities** that provide information and support to members and/or consumers. There are a number of complaint websites that have been set up to complain about banks; FIs have been slow to adjust to a world where branding has to operate almost by consent. Brands can be built around segments (see Exhibit 7.3), identifying the variables that shape and define these, but, at the same time, balancing economies of scale with individual customer needs (Rust *et al.* 2004). If branding strategies are going to reach a wider audience, Rust and his colleagues recommend a change in reporting structures for brand-related decisions so that there is direct contact with top management. There also needs to be an emphasis on a quantitative culture to enable metrics to be developed for measuring the success of the brand (Kapferer 2008). Branding strategies need to be seen within the wider context of growing customer equity, which is the sum of lifetime values of all the customers across the brand. As a result of these changes in the way that branding is thought of, management have to rethink the goals, metrics and roles associated with a well-managed brand (Rust *et al.* 2004). A brand needs to reflect the identity of the customers rather than the financial service provider, making a significant switch from aggrandizing the brand to maximizing customer value.

brand communities: often referring to online consumers who share a passion, or even a hatred, for a brand

Banks, particularly those that have a community of on-line customers, have the advantage of customers who visit the website to conduct transactions, where the opportunity for building and sustaining a relationship via the brand is presented to them. Increasingly, as reality becomes virtual, brands become the only point of reference where the power has shifted to the consumer – for example, with the provision of on-line comparison sites (the rise of the infomediary). There are a number of questions that FI management might care to ask themselves.

- Is your brand mediactive – that is, does it reach its target audience across a range of media?
- Is the brand hyper-relational – that is, is it open to true dialogue? It is not enough for channels of communication to be from seller to buyer; the buyer must have a means of responding to the messages to engage in the sustainability of the brand.

- Is the brand capable of permanent learning? Nothing is static, everything is on the move and brands can be left behind if they do not learn how to adapt and to evolve.
- Is the brand connective in that it fosters virtual communities or partnerships? A brand cannot act in isolation and the contributors to branding, such as Kapferer and De Chernatony, believe that strong brands prosper in communities and partnerships.

Branding to the customer

Mitchell (2001) has argued that a number of factors will impact significantly on the brand. Brands need to be on the customers' side; marketing to customers needs to happen in an organized and professional way. There is no longer a place for a sales perspective; instead, brands will work to acquire a meta- or supra-status and aim to assemble what is best for the customer (Mitchell 2001). One of the key advantages to the supplier in being able to develop a strong brand is that it reduces customers' search costs by identifying the offerings that they seek quickly and accurately. From the customers' perspective, a recognized brand reduces perceived risk by providing an assurance of quality and consistency. If this risk reduction is reinforced by consistent quality, the supplier is then in a position to be able to develop new offerings that may interest the customer and which convey the same messages of reduced risk. However, the customer learns about the values of the service through their holistic experience of the brand and, as De Chernatony *et al.* (2006) find, each 'touchpoint' with the brand echoes a clue about the brand's values. Consumers do not draw on a single source to understand the brand, so managers need to monitor the jigsaw of information cues that consumers and other stakeholders use to check for consistency.

Branding responsibly

Most FIs have statements on their websites that relate to their corporate social responsibilities (CSR), which will extend to branding and brand values. Brands only target those customers within the segments of their marketing framework, which raises the important question of the impact of brands on wider society (Kapferer 2008). This question has particular relevance in the aftermath of the Northern Rock débâcle; not only were customers of the bank affected by its high-risk strategy, but also whole countries, such as Iceland and Latvia, as a result of the effect it had in the context of the credit crunch (news.bbc.co.uk/1/hi/business/7761066.stm). To meet CSR requirements, the strategy needs to be considered increasingly subservient to customer relationships; within the organization, responsibility needs to be placed on managers charged with relationship building (Rust *et al.* 2004). The popularity of a brand not only increases the customer's trust that the offering will perform as required, and indeed promised, but also contributes to customer's social needs – for example, private banking. Brands, therefore, need to achieve economies of scale with individual customer needs (Rust *et al.* 2004), but balance that against a tighter focus that sends the message 'This brand is for you!'. It is important to ensure that there is no gap between the expectations projected through advertising and customer experience (O'Loughlin and Szmigin 2007). Additionally, the reputation of the banks is currently being viewed in entirely negative terms based on reckless behaviour in investment and retail markets, undermining all the messages being communicated via the brand.

Figure 7.3 presents the responses of a sample of consumers to a question about branding in financial services. As the chart show, 49 per cent of the respondents consider that branding is an important influence in the choice of FI. These findings do not necessarily weaken assertions about the commoditization of financial services, as there may be some interplay between brand and price, but indicate that branding is only 'quite important' to less than half the respondents. Branding managers and the FIs as a whole will want to try to improve those figures.

Branding appeals to a customer's levels of trust by reducing risk and because it avoids the need to evaluate a range of alternatives. As far as financial services are concerned, customers above everything else seek trustworthiness and ability to offer value for money when considering a brand (Finaccord 2006). Brands found to score highly in a range of attributes are Visa, RAC, Halifax, Nationwide and MasterCard. Financial services legislation has, to some extent, eroded the need of consumers to trust in strong brand because a level of protection exists across the

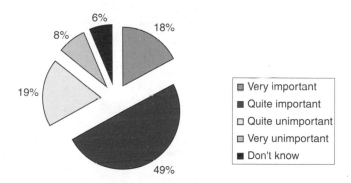

Figure 7.3   Brand metrics: consumer research: breakdown of responses to a question asking how important branding is as an influence on choice of financial services
Source: Adapted from data on Finaccord (2006).

whole sector (Palmer 2008). The credit crunch has tested this trust and has undermined the ability of legislation to protect the customer from questionable global financial practices.

Stakeholder branding

Brands are increasingly animated by a range of stakeholders that might include staff, suppliers and even competitors. Many FIs note the vigour of the First Direct brand, for example. It has been recognized for some time that staff strengthen the brand with additional support from good internal communication, scripting and training. These are used to reinforce the internal corporate culture and increase employees' service delivery motivation (Dall'Olmo Riley and De Chernatony 2000). Additionally, the role of senior management in 'living the brand' cannot be overlooked. If senior

| **Table 7.3** | Stakeholder relationships of the FI brand |

	Stakeholders	Description
Financial institution brand	Internal	Employees, managers enact the brand values
	Shareholders and money markets	FI has commitments to a range of investors which may not be entirely harmonious with branding
	Regulators and governments	A relationship existed but has been reinforced by government bail outs. Scope for strengthening the stakeholder relationship further through the brand
	Suppliers and alliance partners	Suppliers provide a range of services such as products, alliances generate questions about shared brand values
	Competitors	Competitors play a key role in branding decisions
	Influencers	A diverse group consisting of intermediaries, families, journalists
	Customers: new and existing	Traditional focus of branding but note the distinction between the two customer groups

Source: Adapted from Farquhar (2008).

management do not fully appreciate the importance of the emotional aspects of branding and how they may be co-created with customers and other stakeholders, then branding efforts will be hollow. This notion of a number of stakeholders in branding is taking hold and a preliminary list of stakeholders model can be developed from relationship market-ing with a number of stakeholders, including competitors and suppliers (Farquhar 2008). The aim of adopting this model is to develop the idea of a brand experience for all those in the stakeholder or brand environment.

Through 'living the brand', the service and whole brand experience can be sustained and, over time, take the development of the brand for-ward. Brand citizenship is a construct that describes a set of behaviours that enhance the brand identity (Burmann and Zeplin 2005); it is driven by the extent of psychological attachment of stakeholders and influences willingness to exert effort in reaching the goals of the brand.

Branding in a digital environment

The advent of Internet banking has brought about a significant change in branding, shifting branding away from advertising and personal inter-action to an environment where the brand is interpreted remotely. The advantages of being on-line are significant to FIs, mainly in lowering costs. FIs have pursued two alternative approaches in on-line provision, either launching a separate on-line brand such as Cahoot (Abbey) or Smile (Co-operative Bank) or retaining their physical brand (e.g., Barclays). How does a brand function without a physical presence? The brand of an FI needs to convey messages about the high level of security and trust in the processes and technology. The brand is the primary information mech-anism on which the promises are made and informs customers about what they can expect through the electronic experience by acting as a point of connection (Davis *et al.* 2000). It helps to build dialogue and strengthen the motivation of consumers to the offering through the value of the on-line marketing relationship. Branding therefore plays a more important role in the electronic environment than it does in the physical, acting as a mirror for the physical space in the consumer's memory. If the brand is weak in the first place, taking it into the **digital environment** is likely to expose its deficiencies without the repair mechanisms of personal interaction.

digital environment: as opposed to the physical environment, usually refers to the Internet, but increasingly to mobile devices, televisions etc.

Brands in a global environment

Although the digital environment may have exposed some weaknesses in the brand, it has equally enabled FI branding in a global environment by removing the geographic and cost barriers to global distribution

(Wright 2002). Technology enables good internal systems via the Internet and intranet. The question about standardizing or customizing the brand seems to have been largely addressed by HSBC, whose message of 'the world's local bank' embraces the essence of a global FI player (www.hsbc.com). Good FI websites reinforce the brand and allow the institution to offer a portal that gives customers access to a branded banking community. An earlier prediction that there will be global masters in the banking world, perhaps about a dozen, with smaller financial institutions being niche players or product specialists, is in the throes of being fulfilled, but possibly not with the names that might have been anticipated. Exhibit 7.4 provides an example of how a major insurance company has restructured to manage a consistent brand image with economies of scale.

EXHIBIT 7.4

Zurich Financial Services

Zurich Financial Services Group launched its Global Industry Specialization Programme in spring 2008. The group-wide programme enables Zurich to leverage its existing knowledge base and expertise in general insurance and to expand its risk insights into specific industry sectors. The programme aims at improving the way Zurich serves its customers and distributors by developing differentiated customer propositions and offering tailored risk management solutions. The programme is an integral part of Zurich's Customer and Distribution Management Strategy, which is focused on efforts to make Zurich a more customer-centric organization while leveraging its many distribution channels. The Global Industry Specialization Programme will effectively function as a global practice leadership, where leaders from Zurich's various divisions, functions and geographies can share knowledge and build upon expertise gained from their various experiences. As such, they will develop far-reaching insights on current and future trends that may impact on the industry, as well as the capability to respond quickly with people, products and information resources to a changing risk environment anywhere in the world.

Compiled by the authors from www.zurich.com.

The credit crunch has further concentrated the provision of financial services amongst the remaining FIs and they will seek to achieve economies of scale by operating globally. It is not a question of whether 'to go global', it is 'when and how quickly and effectively?'. Figure 7.4 shows how technology supports branding in a global environment in both the industry (supply) side and the customer (demand) side.

The left-hand side of the figure represents supply-side drivers with demand-side drivers on the right. Although the figure suggests some

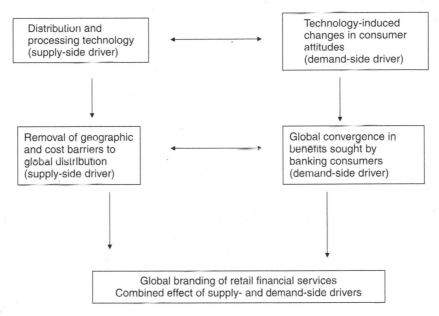

Figure 7.4 Technology-enabled global branding
Source: Adapted from Wright (2002).

interesting applications of technology, branding, as argued above, extends beyond a simple supply- and demand-side interpretation. The stakeholder view of branding anchors branding strategies to those of building relationships, which is a more robust strategy for the post-credit crunch period.

Brand equity

No matter the environment, the value of a brand is highly individualized and, like all communications, its message can be interpreted in many different ways; in other words, brands, like beauty, are in the eye of the beholder. Virgin's growth in the financial services market might be attributable to the power of its branding, which, to particular groups of customers, succeeds in conveying a set of values. Brand equity attempts to evaluate the brand, traditionally focusing on the assets and liabilities of the brand (Aaker 1991), such as:

- Loyalty: a premium price might obtainable through consistently achieving high levels of customer satisfaction
- Perceived quality of the brand: strong leadership to ensure that quality is consistently delivered

- Associations/differentiation: perceived value, brand personality, organizational associations
- Awareness of the brand: putting the brand in the forefront of consumer/stakeholder memory
- Market behaviour: affecting market share, price and distribution indices.

Balmer and Grey (2003) believe that corporate branding imparts long-lasting value by giving the company some advantage over its competitors, but for FIs the identification of the that advantage has proved elusive. An assessment of brand health can use indicators that assess changes in direction in brand equity and the key issues to be addressed. Examples of health measures include whether: the brand stays relevant and consistent, brand managers understand what brand means to consumers and the brand portfolio (e.g., RBS) makes sense (Cravens and Piercy 2006). Brand equity, as conceived of by Aaker (1991), provides the basis for an argument for non-marketers within the organization that investing money in branding yields financial benefits for the company. Although there is often a relationship between market share and profitability, market share may not govern profitability in financial services; therefore, using market share as a measure for brand equity may not be as reliable or even as desirable as previously argued. Nonetheless, a study of financial services in New Zealand has been able to show that the best measures of brand equity in terms of correlation with market share remained brand awareness issues, such as brand recall and familiarity, widely used in goods markets (Mackay 2001).

Since branding still proves challenging in FIs, these organizations may need to look to brand evangelists such as Kapferer and Mitchell, who have moved thinking in branding forward. They argue that branding is not a company-driven activity to sell more, but the creation of an identity that excites and enthuses customers and a wider audience of interested parties. FIs, like many other companies, have metrics and measures in place that may take time to adapt to the environment. Developing metrics that hard-headed members of the wider brand community, who may not have marketing backgrounds, can appreciate may be the challenge that marketers in financial services face in the future if they are to develop the brands that do engage the communities that they seek to reach.

Branding for FIs continues to be problematic and at the same time an imperative if FIs are seeking to differentiate themselves in a very crowded marketplace. In addition to differentiation, branding also provides organizations with the means of building loyalty through emotional attachment. However, FIs have not been able to achieve the brand strength that they aspire to. Once more, the period after the credit crunch provides FIs with the opportunity to reassess their branding thinking so that it can contribute to building trust and confidence. The stakeholder approach to branding provides a valuable template of taking branding forward from the rather uninspiring approaches currently adopted.

Summary

- There is a great deal of work to be done in financial services in achieving differentiation in a commoditized marketplace.
- In an increasingly virtual world of communications, where consumers have a growing role in branding, managers have to be aware of the consumer influence. The value of services is defined in terms of value-in-use by the consumer and stakeholders, with implications for managing the brand.
- A brand may need to reflect the identity of the customers/stakeholders and their communities rather than the FI itself, making a significant switch from aggrandizing the brand to maximizing customer value.
- UK and US FI brands have been weakened in the credit crunch, leaving European brands in a strong position to capitalize on their limited involvement in the toxic debt fall-out. If FIs are really seeking a brand that is relevant to a rapidly changing environment, then the credit crunch should prompt some radical action.

Exercises

1. Study the websites of Royal Bank of Scotland and NFU Mutual. What are the key branding approaches adopted by these organizations? What are the aspects of the brand that convey value-in-use to customers? Are there other stakeholder audiences with whom the website is communicating? Try to account for the similarities and the differences between the two brands? What are the challenges that each of these organizations face when developing branding strategies?
2. How would you advise a new entrant to the financial services marketplace to develop a brand?
3. What can be learned from the take-over or merging of FIs from a branding perspective?

References

Aaker, D. (1991) *Managing Brand Equity: Capitalizing on the Value of a Brand Name*, New York, Free Press.
Balmer, J. and Gray, E. (2003) 'Commentary. Corporate Brands: What are They? What of Them?', *European Journal of Marketing*, Vol. 37, No. 7/8, pp. 972–97.

Brady, M., Bourdeau, B. and Heskel, J. (2005) 'The Importance of Brand Cues in Intangible Service Industries: An Application to Investment Services', *Journal of Services Marketing*, Vol. 19, No. 6, pp. 401–10.

Burmann, C. and Zeplin, S. (2005) 'Building Brand Commitment: A Behavioural Approach to Internal Brand Management', *Brand Management*, Vol. 12, No. 4, pp. 279–300.

Collins-Dodd, C. and Lindley, T. (2003) 'Store Brands and Retail Differentiation: The Influence of Store Image and Store Brand Attitude on Store Own-brand Perceptions', *Journal of Retailing & Consumer Services*, Vol. 10, No. 6, pp. 345–52.

Cravens, D. and Piercy, N. (2006) *Strategic Marketing*, 8th edn, New York, McGraw Hill.

Dall'Olmo Riley, F. and De Chernatony, L. (2000) 'The Service Brand as Relationships Builder', *British Journal of Management*, Vol. 11, pp. 137–50.

Davis, R., Buchanan-Oliver, M. and Brodie, R. (2000) 'Retail Service Branding in Electronic-Commerce Environments', *Journal of Service Research*, Vol. 3, pp. 178–86.

De Chernatony, L., Cottam, S. and Segal-Horn, S. (2006) 'Communicating Service Brands' Values Internally and Externally', *Service Industries Journal*, Vol. 26, No. 8, pp. 819–36.

Farquhar, J. (2008) 'Branding for Stakeholder Relationships in High Street Financial Services: In Words and Pictures', Academy of Marketing Services Special Interest Group, University of Westminster, 7–9 November.

Farquhar, J. D. and Rowley, J. (2006) 'Relationships and Online Consumer Communities', *Business Process Management Journal*, Vol. 12, No. 2, pp. 162–77.

Finaccord (2006), *Brand Metrics: Consumer Awareness of and Attitudes Towards Brands in UK Financial Services*, London.

He, H.-W. and Balmer, J. (2005) 'The Saliency and Significance of Generic Identity: An Explanation of UK Building Societies', *International Journal of Bank Marketing*, Vol. 23, No. 4, pp. 334–48.

Iacobucci, D. (1998) 'Cognitive Networks of Services', *Journal of Service Research*, Vol. 1, No. 1, pp. 32–46.

Interbrand (2004) *Integrated Brand Communications: A Powerful New Paradigm*, Canada, Interbrand.

Kapferer, J.-N. (2001) *[Re]inventing the Brand*, London, Kogan Page.

Kapferer, J.-N. (2008) *The New Strategic Brand Management*, 4th edn, London, Kogan Page.

Knox, S. (2000) 'Branding and Positioning', *Marketing Management: A Relationship Marketing Perspective*, Cranfield School of Management, Basingstoke, Macmillan Business.

Laforêt, S. (2007) 'British Grocers' Brand Extension in Financial Services', *Journal of Product & Brand Management*, Vol. 16, No. 2, pp. 82–97.

Laforêt, S. and Saunders, J. (2005) 'Managing Brand Portfolios: How Strategies Have Changed', *Journal of Advertising Research*, September, pp. 314–27.

Lambkin, M. and Muzellec, L. (2008) 'Rebranding in the Banking Industry Following Mergers and Acquisitions', *International Journal of Bank Marketing*, Vol. 26, No. 4/5, pp. 328–52.

McDonald, M., De Chernatony, L. and Harris, F. (2001) 'Corporate Marketing and Service Brands', *European Journal of Marketing*, Vol. 35, No. 3/4, pp. 335–52.

Mackay, M. (2001) 'Application of Brand Equity Measures in Service Markets', *Journal of Services Marketing*, Vol. 15, No. 3, pp. 210–21.

Meidan, A. (1996) *Marketing Financial Services*, Basingstoke, Macmillan.

Mitchell, A. (2001) *Right Side Up: Building Brands in the Age of the Organized Consumer*, London, HarperCollins.

Nysveen, H., Pedersen, P., Thorbjørnsen, H. and Berthon, P. (2005) 'Mobilizing the Brand: The Effects of Mobile Services on Brand Relationships and Main Channel Use', *Journal of Service Research*, Vol. 7, pp. 257–76.

O'Loughlin, D. and Szmigin, I. (2007) 'Services Branding: Revealing the Rhetoric within Retail Branding', *Service Industries Journal*, Vol. 27, No. 4, pp. 435–52.

O'Loughlin, D. Szmigin, I. and Turnbull, P. (2004) 'From Relationships to Experiences in Retail Financial Services', *International Journal of Bank Marketing*, Vol. 22, No. 7, pp. 522–39.

Palmer, A. (2008) *Principles of Services Marketing*, 4th edn, London, McGraw Hill.

Rust, R., Zeithaml, V. and Lemon, K. (2004) 'Customer-Centered Brand Management', *Harvard Business Review*, September, pp. 110–18.

Taylor, S., Hunter, G. and Lindberg, D. (2005) 'Understanding (Customer-based) Brand Equity in Financial Services', *Journal of Services Marketing*, Vol. 21, No. 4, pp. 241–52.

Van Riel, C. (1995) *Principles of Corporate Communication*, Hemel Hempstead, Prentice Hall.

Veloutsou, C., Daskou, S. and Daskou, A. (2004) 'Are the Determinants of Bank Loyalty Brand Specific?', *Journal of Financial Services Marketing*, Vol. 9, No. 2, pp. 113–25.

Wright, A. (2002) "Technology as an Enabler of the Global Branding of Retail Financial Services', *Journal of International Marketing*, Vol. 10, No. 2, pp. 83–98.

Further reading

www.interbrand.co.uk
www.virgin.com

CASE STUDY

Re-branding a major Russian financial group – the Alfa Banking Group

Alfa Banking Group is one of Russia's largest privately owned banking groups in terms of equity, assets, branches, retail deposits and funds under management. Alfa Banking Group has 304 offices across Russia and abroad. The group also operates through subsidiary banks, affiliates and branch offices in Kazakhstan, the Netherlands, Cyprus, the United States and the United Kingdom and serves more than 2.65 million individuals and other clients. Alfa Bank has won numerous awards, including Best Bank and Best Russian Brand 2006 (*Business Week*), Best Trade Finance Bank in Russia 2007 (*Global Finance*) and Best Bank in Russia 2007 (Euromoney).

In the summer of 2005, our consultancy was approached by the Alfa Banking Group to develop a single, unified brand to replace the different brand identities used by subsidiaries and divisions – retail, corporate and investment banking. While there was logic and strategic advantage in operating the different Alfa business under one signature, there was concern as to whether the changes would be positively accepted by clients and stakeholders. The process was made particularly difficult because of a massive, relatively recent investment that Alfa had made to create their retail bank, Alfa Express. The 'A' logo and name, developed by Wolff Olins, had become a well-known signature for the retail activities and branches in Moscow and across Russia. However, this awareness and developed equity was not necessary appropriate for the business and corporate investment parts of Alfa, who used the well-established corporate Alfa Group brand identity. Although this admittedly needed some updating, it had significant and widespread recognition, clearly differentiating it from the retail bank activities.

We observed and listened to the views of key people involved, as well as the Alfa Board, and quickly realized we could fall into the classic trap of attempting to design an amalgamated 'camel' in an attempt to combine everyone's interests. However, for logical and political reasons, we embarked on an exploration of the current identities, attempting to extract the common features and the essence of each brand symbol concept. Migration strategies were quickly rejected, as there seemed little point in any phased transition. Painful but short, sharp change surgery are favoured rather than a lingering death by transition to balance different faction interests. Careful migration is sometimes necessary and easier in addressing the interests of acquired or merged parties being asked to 'lose' previous identities. The 'advantage' the Alfa management had was the fact that the group is run by Mikhail Friedman, a Russian oligarch. His autocratic style meant decisions would be forthcoming. The possible bad news was that it would be up to the rest of us to ensure change would be received positively by all interested parties – the essential component in any change strategy. His views became very clear; the Bank had spent a lot of money investing in the retail 'A' brand and he was in no mood to invest in a new brand identity – he favoured building on the retail mark. Potential negative implications for other group divisions were clear – analogies of 'the tail wagging the dog' – the retail brand taking over the main group brand were cited. Not surprisingly, group directors were less the enthusiastic about a retail image being applied to their investment operations and raised questions regarding their credibility and authority as serious corporate players. The challenge for us as consultants was to satisfy the group people that we could design their media and communications to maintain their differentiation from their retail colleagues. Equally, we had to rationalize the 'A' symbol media presentation so it could maintain, on the one hand, the retail equity of Alfa Express for retail operations, but, on the other, be suitably rationalized and presented as a corporate umbrella mark for the group operations. 'Express' was dropped for the retail brand and careful nuances of the 'A' mark then developed across key applications, introducing different combinations of backgrounds, image and message to reinforce the relevant operations, functions and ethos.

It was indicative of Russian management style that discussions on brand vision and values were seen as a purely Board-level matter – the results would then be disseminated to the rest of the company. It did not matter how much we lectured and advised on the concepts of empowerment and engagement, ultimately old habits and a refusal to 'let go' (a basic requirement of empowerment) kick in when more democratic initiatives are proposed. With the design principles agreed, for some this was the end of the exercise. It was October and the launch was to be at the beginning of the New Year for branches and offices across Russia. Logistic discussions and plans for briefing contractors and suppliers could start. Unfortunately, it was left to us to remind everyone gently the most important launch was nothing to do with signage and printing but everything to do with inner customers – the Alfa Group staff. Now the real challenge started, which made the agreement on the new brand identity a relatively simple process, despite the politics and commercial pressures. While key people understood the need for staff engagement, it was seen as purely a marketing and communications exercise. We were highly aware of the complexities of cutting through department silos and distance logistics. Trying to make Vladivostok staff, with a seven-hour time difference to Moscow, feel involved in what could appear to be a remote central office initiative 6,500 kilometres away was an interesting challenge!

The command-led management style of many Russian companies has been slow to embrace the need to facilitate, innovate and inspire their employees. While the theories of 'walking the talk' and the concepts of interdepartmental coordination, staff empowerment, etc. are recognized, practice is something different. A glance at Alfa Bank's offices, with typically management cellular offices and closed doors, offers a far cry from the open-plan transparency principles of a modern democratic workplace. Alfa had a quarterly internal magazine, *Alfa Navigator*, distributed to all bank employees, with an on-line digital version continuously available together with the company intranet. Monthly circular letters from the CEO and Chairman of the Board, plus internal process releases, provided basic top-down communication, with bulletin boards and posters kept continuously updated. The key was to organize a coordinated cascade of information appropriate to the media and messenger. While there were CEO meetings for 20 per cent best-performing managers every month, video and physical conferences, one of the most important elements was face-to-face coffee talk opportunities at branch level. It was fascinating to review a wide range of staff interaction opportunities at a local, region and head office level. Team-building exercises, special events and celebrations provided a range of situations where the reasons and 'good news' about the unifying group brand could be explained and discussed.

Russians are used to distances and the challenge of covering 54 cities, from Kaliningrad in the west to Vladivostok in the east, was not an issue. The real challenge was achieving credible top-down, bottom-up and, most difficult, cross-departmental and -division communication. While everything had to be organized very quickly to meet the Christmas deadline, fast-track opportunities, decisions and actions utilizing already-planned visits, events, reviews and activities enabled a quick dissemination of information and messages across all levels of the company. Working in a less politically correct culture environment allows fast, simple transmission of message and issues. I suspect such an exercise in a more 'sensitive' western organization would have taken six months plus, not the three months we were faced with. The culmination was the Christmas party in Moscow and in the regions, where Alfa's 15th anniversary and the 'official' announcement of the new group brand launch were combined and celebrated. It was an ideal event to launch a symbol of a unified group and communicate the potential of being part of a successful, proactive organization. 'Bringing the brand to life' is a too-often quoted cliché, but it does sum up the vital element for any successful brand development initiative. Understanding, whatever your job function, that someone wants to know what you think and what you need to make your specific job better for the company and yourself is a great start. This is a classic 'listening' management initiative, but the danger is then of broken promises and lack of action. Interestingly, it was the speed and momentum of the new Alfa brand development that created a buzz and a positive internal perception before it hit the streets and screens of Russia in January 2006.

Questions

1. What dangers can arise from listening to everyone when developing a brand?
2. What distinctive approaches did the bank leadership bring to the re-branding task?
3. What did the consultancy team perceive to be the key problems of the re-branding task?
4. What are the key cultural issues that arise from this case?

Written by Clive Woolger of Woolger Associates.

8

Creating value: The financial services product

Contents

Learning outcomes

At the end of this chapter, the reader will be able to:

- Understand the nature of the financial services product and the difficulties of achieving differentiation

- Suggest how value is created in financial services products

- Comprehend the key issues of product development in financial services

- Appreciate service bundling, the role of service quality, service failure, service recovery and affinity marketing as part of managing the service offering

Introduction

Marketers of financial services are faced with a number of problems relating directly to the products that they sell. It is difficult to create meaningful differentiation between their range of products and those of their competitors. Customers, therefore, find it hard to distinguish between products and usually make a decision based on price. This commoditization or the transformation of branded products into undifferentiated products is a severe problem for financial institutions (FIs). Although FIs may try to build into their products some distinguishing features, these differences may be of little significance to their customers. To give some idea of the number of products that are available in UK retail banking alone: there are over 150 current accounts, almost 1,000 individual fixed-rate mortgage products and over 1,500 instant access savings accounts on the market (www.moneyexpert.com). The retail consumer accordingly has an extensive, if not a totally bewildering, choice of financial products.

The financial product

One of the key axioms in marketing is that customers buy a product for the benefits that it offers and this is very much the case in financial services; for example, a current or cheque account offers a customer a convenient means of managing their income and their outgoings. Financial services are intangible, which means that evaluating the service is difficult (Lovelock 2001). How do customers assess the 'fitness for purpose' of a financial service, such as travel insurance? As discussed in Chapter 3, financial services consist of experience or credence qualities that customers either find out about when using them or have to trust the provider. The assessment is going to be even harder for more complex products, where the role of FIs is to discuss and suggest services that are suitable for an individual customer. Customers may not be, generally, in a strong position to make an informed evaluation of any particular financial service. This situation often arises because of an asymmetry of information, which means that the providers of the service understand more about the product than their customers. The provider could, and perhaps should, try to reduce the asymmetry, but this has not always been the case in financial services. Customers may feel dissatisfied with the amount of meaningful and useful information that accompanies financial products, but this may only happen long after the product was actually purchased. Customers may not have fully appreciated that the performance of financial services is often dictated by global factors, which can be the result of natural disasters, political changes, warfare or, indeed, reckless behaviour on the part of FIs.

Marketers can begin to introduce some level of differentiation into financial product through the creation of number of levels or layers: a core **offering**, some distinction offered by the brand plus an element of a relationship. The core product can be quite standard – for example, an unsecured loan. Figure 8.1 demonstrates three possible levels of a financial product that starts with its core benefits.

At the core benefit level, a loan – for example, for business or a personal purposes – has standard features such as amount and repayment options. At the next level, the brand or reputation of the lender is usually a consideration, the interest charged and the level of services, such as the speed of arrangement, also occur at this attribute level. The final level of support is particularly important in financial services as, in many cases, the FI is keen to initiate or maintain a relationship. Therefore, the scope of a financial service extends well beyond the core product. The arrow on the right-hand side of the figure refers to the capacity of the offering for differentiation, which may contribute to higher levels of customer satisfaction and opportunities for co-creating value with the customer (Vargo and Lusch 2004).

offering: a term that covers both the product and the way in which it is delivered to the customer

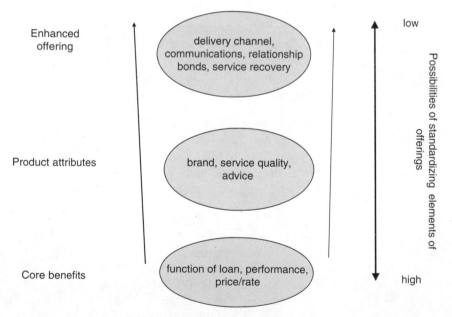

Figure 8.1   Levels of offering for a loan
Source: Adapted from Hollensen (2001).

Value and benefits

A further issue that has to be considered with financial services is the nature of the products themselves itself. Going shopping may be contemplated with varying degrees of anticipation, but the purchase or acquisition of a credit card, the arrangement of a loan or car insurance is usually considered to be functional or utilitarian consumption. It is very important to be aware that financial products are not purchased as an end in themselves but are purchased to achieve some other outcome. For marketers in the industry, it is vital to understand this aspect of their offering – how and why their customers desire and use their products. Additionally, some financial products are purchased to avoid an undesirable outcome, and as such are often described as averse products. With these products, it is even more important to convey the benefits that the purchase of this product brings (see, for example, www.tescocompare.com/travel/why-get-travel-insurance.shtml).

A service will only be successful if the benefits that it offers are of value to the customer; for example, a business requires a means of managing its cash, paying its suppliers, credit to cover times between making and receiving payments, credit card services and advice. Large businesses require dedicated and customized services that allow them to meet their organizational objectives. These benefits are almost taken for granted by customers and yet the provider has to maintain and develop systems to offer these services, respond to customer needs and enquiries and maintain delivery channels. To many UK customers, a current account is free, although many high-street current account providers are trying to persuade their customers to upgrade to a premium banking services post-credit crunch. A number of FIs have developed a value-added current account for consumers that offers the traditional elements, such as receiving salary payments and cash withdrawals, but also includes travel insurance, theatre tickets and other 'goodies'. The consumer pays a monthly charge for this service (for example, Lloyds TSB Platinum account). It is not easy to see quite where these accounts sit in the model in Figure 8.1 as it can be argued that they do not actually add value as far as customer perceptions are concerned. Many customers may prefer to buy their own travel insurance and theatre tickets at prices that they can compare. In financial services, an expansion in the means of delivering financial services has been spurred on by the Internet, mobile phones and even ATMs, offering customers additional benefits. Daily text messages on cheque account balances via mobile is an example of a service which does appear to offer value that customers appreciate.

Bundling

Customers may, in many instances, view financial services in packages or bundles. Even a current account can be considered a bundle of services in that the customer usually has a range of services attached to it, such as direct debits, use of ATMs and provision of overdraft facilities. Bundling a number of services together in a sector where products are largely homogeneous provides FIs with the means of differentiating their services from those of their competitors and can be compared with the three levels of offering in Figures 8.1 and 8.2. It is critical, however, to design the product bundles to satisfy both the bank's and its customers' interests. From the bank's perspective, a combination of attractive and slightly less attractive services helps the sale of the latter. From the customer's perspective, the bundle needs to offer particular benefits and in order for this to be successful, bundles need to be developed that are targeted towards specific segments (Koderisch *et al.* 2007).

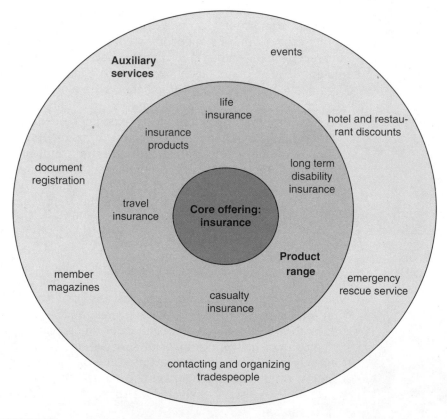

Figure 8.2   Bundling insurance
Source: Adapted from Koderisch *et al.* (2007).

For the bundling to be successful, a balance of offerings needs to be achieved that is integrated with relationship and loyalty strategies, which should assist further in differentiation. Tracking and monitoring bundling approaches across the customer groups will provide the bank marketers with the information to develop and refine product bundling.

The service performance

If the service is viewed as a performance, several of the difficulties of delivering a consistent level of provision can be addressed, as the analogy focuses on the activity nature of services (Fisk *et al.* 2004). An excellent performance relies on a cast of performers, technical and presentational design, the curtain rising and falling at times advertised and peripheral services such as interval drinks. Bringing drama into banking services may sound a little alarming, but if transactions are regarded as performances then the 'back office' systems that are so critical to financial services are integrated with the customer's role to create a more satisfactory delivery. Many bank branches have been redesigned to encourage a more relaxed and intimate atmosphere, with furniture, colour schemes and layout that support the performance concept. Although there is limited scope for customizing the service performance in retail banking, private banking and corporate banking develop offerings in line with specific customer requirements. Underpinning the service performance is the service script, which is a chronologically ordered representation of the steps that make up the service performance from the customer's perspective (Fisk *et al.* 2004). A simple script is exemplified by the use of an ATM, where customers are led through the stages in using the required service. A more complex script is offered to help customers open a new current account on-line. Whether simple or complex, the strength of the script is greater when large numbers of customers are involved and where the provider wants to minimize human interaction.

Service setting

servicescape: the environment in which the service is delivered/consumed

The '**servicescape**' (Bitner 1992) includes all the aspects of the physical environment in which the service provider and the customer interact. Although the servicescape has been usually conceived of as the provider-owned or -managed premises – for example, restaurants, hotels or bank branches – the concept can be extended into other arena where interaction occurs between the customer and the provider. The value of the servicescape is to manage tangible cues that the customer uses to evaluate the quality of the service. Bank branches are often in nineteenth- or early twentieth-century buildings, which convey the solidity of the bank and, therefore, its suitability for the savings or cash of the customer. The consumption of financial services now takes place in other locations than a bank branch and, as Fisk *et al.* (2004) suggest, there are a number of other *-scapes* or spaces – for example, postalspace, telespace or cyberspace – for services. All of these spaces need to be designed not only to facilitate the efficient delivery of the service, but also for the customer's convenience, as well as with security in mind. The role of the brand in creating tangible evidence is, of course, vital, particularly where consumption occurs in virtual spaces. A number of financial service providers have informative websites where a range of information is made available to customers and other surfers. These provide good examples of cyberspaces where interaction between the provider and the user occurs and which the provider can use not only to promote products directly, but also to build relationships, build the brand and create virtual communities.

The customer experience

The customer experience is particularly important to marketers, who recognize that customers can consume an offering over a period of time and that satisfaction with the product can include a number of attributes or even apparently unrelated elements.

EXHIBIT 8.1

Getting to a branch

You are going ski-ing in about two weeks and you need some euros. So how do you get to your branch to get your foreign exchange? Think about it. You work out of town and there isn't even an ATM handy, but euros are not yet dispensed at ATMs in any case. Parking in the city is very tough, with traffic wardens known to materialize out of thin air. You are at work when the bank is open. Your bank has, however, started to open again on a Saturday. So the choice is take some time off (not the dentist again!) or combine going to the bank with some Saturday morning shopping – along with the rest of the planet. Then you remember that M&S do foreign exchange and that their opening hours are much more flexible – they are even open on Sundays!

The core marketing concept here is that it is the experience that generates value to the customer rather than the product itself (Holbrook 1999), which, again, has implications for marketers regarding understanding and mapping the customer experience, as well as appreciating the benefits and sacrifices that a customer is prepared to make to obtain value.

Figure 8.3 A model of the customer experience in financial services
Source: Adapted from O'Loughlin *et al.* (2004).

In co-creating value, the organization then contributes, at the very least, to minimizing sacrifices and raising the level of benefits. In Figure 8.3, O'Loughlin *et al.* (2004) provide a model of the customer experience in financial services that builds on that described in Exhibit 8.1. The model shows that an experience consists of both negative and positive forces that can take place within the bank environment but could be extended to consider a wider context. Although FIs may argue that these wider forces may be beyond their control, as far as the customer is concerned these circumstances actually are part of their experience and cannot be discounted so readily. US banks have long offered drive-in facilities; although this model is not consistent with current environmental concerns, it does recognize the dominant role of the car in many customers' lives and, by implication, the parking problems that arise from the role. O'Loughlin *et al.* (2004) propose that there are three levels of experience, which are interrelated and together contribute to customer satisfaction. The negative forces, they argue, arise from internal FI practices and policies of depersonalization and automation, which reduce opportunities for interpersonal interaction.

FIs, like many other organizations, are constantly trying to lower costs and yet increase the levels of services to cater for customers' needs and expectations. One way that they try to address this is through ongoing investment in technology solutions. They work with other specialist companies to try and develop solutions that achieve these objectives, as seen in Exhibit 8.2.

EXHIBIT 8.2

Transforming customer service operations

A global consultancy has helped to transform ABN AMRO's customer service operations across Europe, the Middle East and Africa by consolidating local client service activities into regional **service quality** centres and establishing a dedicated group of client representatives to service the bank's highest-need customers. The transformation began with consultants designing a strategy for business change, then overseeing the project during the consolidation and implementation of CRM and telephony. The centres are supported by the latest contact-centre technologies and will help the European bank achieve the necessary economies of scale and efficient standardized processes needed to lower costs per transaction without sacrificing service levels. The bank is further developing its account management capabilities through the centres and has established a client service consultant group, which is accountable for the company's relationship with its top 250 corporate clients. ABN AMRO is owned by RBS, Santander and, until recently, by Fortis bank.

---

service quality: usually refers to the gap (or lack of one) that may occur between the customer's expectation of the service and their perception of it

There is a careful balancing act to be maintained between lowering costs through economies of scale and generating the levels of customer satisfaction that contribute to loyalty. It is easier to demonstrate that savings have been made than to show that customers are loyal, so the metrics used in these scenarios need to reflect the short- and long-term outcomes of decisions.

value co-creation: where consumers are enabled by the service provider to use the offering in such a way that they can create their own value

Value co-creation

Previous ideas in marketing are giving way to new interpretations such as service-dominant logic (S-DL), as articulated by Vargo and Lusch (2004). One of their foundational marketing premises is that a company can only make a value proposition, meaning that the customer gains value from the way in which they put the offering or product to use (value-in-use). The customer is then part of the production process, as it the customer who actually puts the product into service. To some extent this has been happening in financial services anyway, as the product is generally used to achieve some other end – for example, a credit card enables immediate purchase of an item or the management of finances, depending upon the customer. The variety of credit cards offering different benefits such as balance transfers, low interest rates or charity donations recognizes this. However, the S-DL view would probably argue that this does not go far enough and that a customer could acquire a credit card and then choose the benefits that they want rather than selecting a card that more or less offers them what they want. As part of developing strategies for the post-credit crunch recovery, FIs should be thinking of identifying ways in which they can make value propositions to their customers as a means of seeking competitive advantage. An enduring problem with services is that they are easily copied by the competition, making it difficult to gain any lasting advantage.

New product development

New product development is a key aspect of marketing, but in financial services the situation is quite distinctive, principally owing to regulation and the competitiveness of the sector. Entirely new products in financial services are quite rare; innovation is usually achieved through other means, such as delivery – for example, Direct Line's entirely branchless insurance operation. Much innovation in financial services has been an extension or imitation of a financial product that is in existence in another country. Technology has, however, spurred three waves of innovation (Matthews and Thompson 2008):

- Application of technology in bank organization, although this is not specific to banks but occurs in all service sector organizations and applies to the ordering, storing and dissemination of information (e.g., rating agencies)
- Application of telecoms and computer information technology to improvements in money management methods for the consumer
- The advent of the customer information file, which enabled the FI to gather information about the spending pattern of their client and offered them the opportunity to 'get closer' – that is, understand customer needs better.

New additions to existing product categories are quite common and Exhibit 8.3 describes a new insurance product that responds to a 'new' crime.

EXHIBIT 8.3

Identity protection

Identity theft occurs when a criminal is able to gain access to someone's personal details, enabling them to perform a number of illegal acts, varying from using their credit card details to make purchases to making withdrawals from their account or even creating a new identity. Research in the

United Kingdom has indicated that one in four British adults either had been affected by identity theft or knew somebody who had, with 100,000 people per year being affected and costing victims £1.3 billion per year. According to the credit-scoring firm Equifax, it typically takes a UK identity theft victim up to 300 hours to clear their name. A new product that has been developed to address people's worries about having their personal details accessed has been developed by Goldfish, which provides insurance of up to £50,000 and provides the service of alerting customers about suspicious activities on their credit report though a continuous monitoring service.

Compiled by the authors from www.identitytheft.org.uk and www.goldfish.com.

Although it is generally believed that the success rate for new products in the marketplace is as low as 50 per cent, it has been argued that a market-oriented approach to new product development improves the likelihood of good product performance (Langerak *et al.* 2004). It is axiomatic in marketing that financial services, like any other product, need to be developed with customer needs in mind and that the product should be targeted towards a segment that 'needs' the offering – for example, people concerned about identity theft. Slattery and Nellis (2004) point to the difference between a customer's expressed need and their latent needs. A latent need is one that customers are unable to articulate; an organization's ability to respond fully to customer requirements would, therefore, be inhibited if it did not investigate their latent needs. An understanding of a customer's latent needs is important in financial services; uncovering them requires skilled sales staff. Other products may have been developed as a means of tapping into customer insecurities or as a result of an imperfect knowledge of the precise financial circumstances of a particular customer. Payment protection, for example, is a product developed to cover mortgage customers in situations where they might be unable to meet their mortgage payments. However, financial services are also subject to regulation, both nationally and in EU legislation, covering such areas as the management of risk, conduct of business with retail customers, prevention of money laundering and the reporting of financial performance. A disadvantage of tight regulation, it has been suggested, is that the organization focuses less on customer needs, although this does not sound particularly convincing. Figure 8.4 shows the sources of pressure on financial service providers in the United Kingdom.

The UK Financial Services Authority (FSA) does not have a role in the development of new products, but aims to protect and educate consumers. The Treasury in the United Kingdom, however, focuses on the design and cost of products rather than the behaviour of the product providers (Slattery and Nellis 2004). Pressure also comes from UK government, although it has been accused, along with the FSA, of not watching

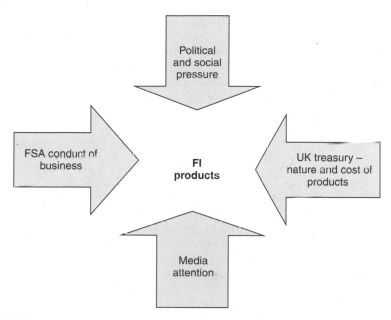

| Figure 8.4 | Pressure in the United Kingdom on FI products |

Source: Adapted from Slattery and Nellis (2004).

the industry carefully enough in the period leading up to the credit crunch. Media attention on financial service providers, however, is relentless (see, for example, bbc.co.uk/blogs/thereporters/robertpeston/) and post-credit crunch there is pressure from consumers on FIs to reconsider their business practices, including products. FIs are also under pressure to sell products and developing new products is often seen as a means of increasing sales. The following exhibit provides an example of an insurance product that has been developed with a number of benefits to both purchaser and the purchaser's employer.

EXHIBIT 8.4

Pet insurance

A specialist area of pet insurance is that for exotic pets, which provides owners with financial assistance should their exotic pet fall ill, get lost or be stolen. Policies are specifically tailored to cover the insurance needs of a pet, whether it is an exotic bird, mammal or reptile. The majority of insurance providers will cover veterinary costs up to a specified annual limit, which is usually dictated by the type of exotic pet insured. Insurers will pay out an agreed amount on the theft, loss or death of an exotic pet.

The value of each pet insured is usually agreed prior to the start of a policy and third-party liability cover is also likely to be included; this will protect the policy-holder financially if damage is sustained to property or individuals as a result of the actions of the exotic pet. Most insurers will offer customers policies that enable multiple exotic pets to be insured on the same policy, which can attract a discount if the pets are the same species. The level of cover can be extended to include transportation of the pet to exhibitions or shows. The benefit of insuring the exotic pet collection with a comprehensive level of cover is that the policy-holder will have financial support to pay for veterinary or legal fees should the unexpected occur.

Overall pet bereavement costs UK businesses £8.3 million a year, as staff pull 'sickies' to get over the death of their pets. One in four pet-bereaved Brits have been too upset to go into the office. Rather than admit to their bosses, 12 per cent of those staying off work say that they are sick. In addition, nearly half of pet owners (42 per cent) use holiday time to grieve for a beloved pet, of whom 18 per cent say that they could not tell their boss the real reason for their absence from the office. More than a third of bereaved owners who did not take time off (35 per cent) admitted they had been upset and unproductive in the office. One in five (19 per cent) said that they could not concentrate, with a similar proportion (18 per cent) revealing that they wanted to get home as quickly as possible. The research identified the severity of the emotional cost of losing a pet. More than one in three owners (39 per cent) grieved for their lost dog as severely as for their best friend or relative, while a further one in four (24 per cent) revealed that they didn't feel they would ever get over it.

Compiled from by the authors from www.money.co.uk/pet-insurance/exotic-pet-insurance.htm and www.directline.com.

Customers participate in new product development by supplying new ideas or even co-producing the product. In corporate marketing, as opposed to consumer marketing, the customer's role is more important and extensive as services in this sector are characterized by high customization to customer needs, adding to their complexity. Larger companies have specific needs and require particular products that address problems and, of course, provide the benefits that they need. Athanassopoulou and Johne (2004), in their investigation into effective communication in the development of new banking products, found that more successful product developers kept levels of communication high and constant through the development process. They also argue that it is important who is used in the communication process; the selection and use of 'actors' in the process – that is lead customers, teams of multifunctional specialists and internal management – contributes to the success of a new product.

Doyle (2002) describes an innovative product as offering four benefit criteria: important, unique, sustainable and marketable; even then he

Table 8.1   Developing a product

Steps	Key issues/decisions	Learning actions/tools
Identification of environmental changes	Interpretation of information and development of hypotheses	Data gathering, internal and external, inferences, exploring and testing
Emergence of idea	Strategic intent, vision, choice of vocabulary, determining threats and opportunities, competitor evaluation, internal capabilities,	Creation of broad frame of thinking, sharing of vision. Sharing of vocabulary, informal and formal discussion, convergence of interpretation, create 'champions', involvement of customers
Official birth of development process	Create organization to support development, define priorities, create common understanding, motivate middle management, start process	Internal communication, exchange of ideas, work to achieve consensus
Composition and management of development team	Create project leaders, allocate responsibilities, create time frame and methodology, relationships with selected customers	Anticipate difficulties, select different competences, cross-functional communication, problem-solving system
Defining the new offering: content and process	Value to client? Benefits and attributes of offering, design of supporting information system, staff training	Determine customer expectations and demands, competitor monitoring, progressive refinements of offer, tests, simulations, trial and error, delivery scenario, prototyping, adjustments to offer
Adapting the organization	Reviewing organizational chart and business processes	Adaptation of job descriptions, creation of new departments/teams, re-engineering, training sessions for staff
Implementation	Assuring acceptance by and uniformity across distribution network,	Freezing specifications and behaviours, memorization of sequences, internal/ external communication and promotion

Source: Adapted from Athanassopoulou and Johne (2004) and Stevens and Dimitiradis (2005).

points out that few innovations are truly new products and are in many cases not new to the world. Entirely new products are riskier and involve the bank in greater resourcing, whereas products with minor adaptations can provide revenue with considerably less exposure to risk. Services are, however, easily replicated and even a rapid assessment of the financial services market reveals that there are very few products that are particular to any single provider. If a service is introduced by a bank or building society, there is very little to stop a competitor offering the very same service the following day. Many products offered in the sector are the result of copying the competition and are frequently referred to as 'me-too' products. Papastathopoulou *et al.* (2006) studied new-to-market and 'me-too' products in Greek retail financial services. They found that genuinely new offerings were greatly supported by the marketing function in the bank concerned, whereas the 'me-too' products were generated by the IT or electronic data processing function. Stevens and Dimitriadis (2005) studied the role of learning in the development of new financial products. The development process of the product did not follow any formal, well-defined and step-by-step process, which they observed is consistent with studies into service innovation projects. Managers experience and manage new products as a sequence of problems, issues and questions to which they have to find solutions (see Table 8.1). The conclusions from this study are that decision-making and problem-solving activities are much more effective when learning actions and loops are allowed to happen.

The greening of the environment has prompted a number of opportunities for companies to develop offerings for customers who seek to reduce their carbon emissions, lower levels of pollution or just save the planet. Exhibit 8.5 shows how a leading global bank has responded to the green revolution.

EXHIBIT 8.5

New product development (NPD) and the environment

In the summer of 2008, Barclays Bank introduced Barclaycard Breathe, a credit card that rewarded consumers who bought greener products and then donated half its profits to carbon reduction projects. Customers receive their statements on-line, therefore eliminating paper statements and packaging; they have access to a dedicated website informing them about Barclays environmental projects, which also offers customers ways to save money with the bank's latest offers and discounts. Finally, customers can receive marketing literature on-line. The card itself is made with a material more environmentally friendly than a traditional PVC card.

The bank guarantees that, for the first year, it would make a minimum donation of £1 million to environmental projects. The bank also offers a corporate card equivalent – Barclaycard Business Sustain – for all corporate customers. The bank claims that it is the first business card designed to help companies offset the carbon emissions of business air travel.

Compiled by the authors from material on www.barclays.com.

Product elimination

There comes a time when a service no longer fulfils customer needs and should be removed or eliminated from the providers' offerings. Whilst much has been written about the development of new offerings, there is considerably less about the elimination of products. It has been argued that eliminating products can improve the financial and operational performance of an organization's portfolio (Avlonitis 1993). Financial products that may require elimination could be identified by changes in delivery systems – for example, from a personal delivery to an IT-based delivery – compliance with changes in legislation and an improved ability to calculate the financial contribution of a product. By eliminating a product, the organization benefits through being able to use the resources freed up by this process more effectively. Elimination has also been used widely to recruit new customers, where offerings have been developed with a fixed capacity, such as amount available for home loan borrowers, or when environmental circumstances change, such as the credit crunch, where mortgages of 125 per cent were withdrawn in 2008. Harness and Marr (2004) looked at the process and outcome success measures for **product elimination**, with a particular focus on the customer. They found that, looking across the heterogeneous financial service range, pensions investment and insurance products were influenced greatly by regulation. For simpler products, such as savings and money transmissions, the management of systems is important.

product elimination: a process where products that no longer generate value to the FI are removed from the product portfolio

Service quality and delivery

Lovelock (2001) highlights basic differences between goods and services, noting that other people may form part of the product, a factor which has often been the case in financial services. Generally, the more complex the service, the greater the likelihood that there will be interaction between at least two people (the buyer and the seller), although the increase of technology in the delivery of financial services has reduced the amount of personal interaction. Service quality (SQ) in banking has been heavily researched but it remains questionable whether customers, particularly retail consumers, receive the levels of SQ that they might expect. It has been argued that SQ contributes to customer satisfaction, without which FIs would find it hard to retain customers or create loyalty. It is less certain whether SQ provides a basis for differentiation. Poor SQ does not necessarily lead to customer defection (see Chapter 3). It is likely that SQ is a necessary rather than a sufficient condition in marketing, and it is hard to see how a meaningful relationship can be maintained in its absence.

Given that SQ is key in customer satisfaction, how can quality in the service be discerned? According to Grönroos (1984, 2000), good functional, as well as good technical, quality contributes to the overall image of the service and the company itself. The technical components of the service refer to its abilities to perform to the levels specified; functional components focus on the interaction between the service provider and the customers, such as advice and assistance. Another perspective on service quality is the SERVQUAL instrument, developed by Parasuraman, Zeithaml and Berry (1985, 1988). SERVQUAL continues to be the basis for many investigations into the quality of service provision in financial services, although it has attracted criticism (for example, Buttle 1996). Parasuraman, Zeithaml and Berry (1988), or PZB as they are often known, identified five dimensions of service quality: tangibles, reliability, responsiveness, assurance and empathy; banks were included in their study. There is some overlap with the technical/functional approach to service quality – for example, reliability and responsiveness could be seen as similar to technical service quality and the remaining three with functional SQ. In an increasingly global market, the delivery of SQ across a range of cultures has become a concern for financial services. Tsoukatos and Rand (2007) investigated the influence of culture on SQ and satisfaction in the Greek insurance market. Using GIQUAL, which the authors built around the dimensions of the original SERVQUAL scale, they found that service expectations are affected by cultural profiles and that culture determines the importance of service quality dimensions to customers. They suggest that financial services management should turn to culture as an aid to their decision-making process, especially in relation to allocating quality efforts and resources. In their study, reliability in particular, followed by responsiveness and assurance, had the greatest impact on customer satisfaction. FIs expend a great deal of effort in measuring customer satisfaction but there are indications still that customer satisfaction levels vary.

Service recovery

The variability of a service is acknowledged and many companies have developed strategies for putting things right when a mistake is made. Interest in recovering service failures arises from the role that recovery can play in retaining customers (Roos 1999), preventing unfavourable word of mouth (Swanson and Kelley 2001) and influencing perceived service quality (Gronroos 2000). Companies unable to put right breakdowns in service place themselves at a disadvantage in achieving customer satisfaction and gaining customer loyalty and it has been argued that companies gain by facilitating complaints about service (Bearden and Teel 1980, Vorhees *et al.* 2006). As service forms an increasingly dominant component in many contemporary marketing exchanges, the encounter between provider and customer, whether real or virtual, is vulnerable to variability (de Ruyter and Wetzels 2000), so the way in which failure is recovered by a company can contribute significantly to levels of customer satisfaction (Smith *et al.* 1999, Swanson and Kelley 2001). Recovering service failure should not only address putting things right when they go wrong, but extend to preventing the error happening in the future (McCollough *et al.* 2000). Although **service recovery** has been described as a short-term activity that should, in the long term, be embedded within reliability (Boshoff 1999), the argument that it forms a cornerstone of a customer satisfaction strategy (Tax and Brown 1998) appears stronger when service recovery is considered within the context of customer satisfaction and loyalty.

service recovery: a process in which an FI attempts to put right a service mistake or error in order to satisfy the customer

Customer satisfaction with service recovery efforts is influenced by a number of factors – for example, whether the failure is core to the service or offering (Keaveney 1995), how critical the failure is to consumption (Hoffman and Kelley 2000) and the magnitude of the failure (Smith *et al.* 1999). The literature is somewhat divided about the impact of negative service encounters. A single instance of service failure can permanently lower customers' overall satisfaction (Hocutt and Stone 1998); conversely, customers' cumulative satisfaction can be substantially enhanced by situations that involve failure and subsequent recovery (Smith and Bolton 1998). Service providers, therefore, have the opportunity not only to satisfy their customers, but also to create loyalty through repeated satisfying experiences, where cumulative evaluations of service quality are particularly valuable predictors of loyalty (Olsen and Johnson 2003) – and customer loyalty is, of course, something that financial service providers would dearly love to have. Sadly, however, there seems to be little evidence that service recovery efforts in high-street banks generate customer satisfaction, whether complaints are made in the branch or over the phone (Jones and Farquhar 2007). The most successful way of recovering from a service failure is to make things right, eliminating the cause of dissatisfaction with the initial service. Generally, respondents were not unreasonable about their expectations of service recovery. Staff need to be knowledgeable about how to put right service failure. Not all complaints are voiced, therefore complaints need to be facilitated. Analysis of service failures and complaint data identifies areas for improvement with, of course, appropriate training for staff.

EXHIBIT 8.6

Customer complaints

Overall, the number of mortgage and banking disputes has more than tripled, with a record total of 123,089 new complaints, a 30 per cent rise from 2007–8. Payment protection insurance complaints increased six-fold, with most cases now related to how policies were sold rather than rejected claims. The Financial Services Ombudsman (FOS) says over 95 per cent of businesses that fall under its umbrella received no complaints, while six of the United Kingdom's biggest financial services groups were involved in half of the total number of cases. A spokesman says the companies will not be named at this point but adds that their anonymity is being reconsidered as part of Lord Hunt's review of the ombudsman. The FOS saw a ten-fold increase in complaints about banks' charges on current accounts. The ombudsman says this is probably due to the current legal test case in the High Court involving the Office of Fair Trading and eight current account providers. The ombudsman was hoping for an overall reduction in case numbers but the economic climate has led to a record number of new complaints. The FOS welcomes the broadening diversity of consumers using the service, saying that 'Making our service accessible to everyone is a top priority identified by Lord Hunt in his recent review of the openness and transparency of the ombudsman service.'

Compiled by the authors from www.moneymarketing.co.uk.

Nonetheless, this sort of increase in complaints suggests that current systems are not working and that the larger banks appear to lack commitment to service recovery and, indeed, preventing service failure in the first place.

Affinity marketing

Affinity marketing links the marketing activities of a company with the revenue-generating activities of a non-profit organization with the aim of enhancing the appeal of the commercial organization's offering by differentiating it in a competitive marketplace. The aim of affinity marketing is to capitalize on the goodwill that consumers have towards a group to which they belong or have a positive attitude (Horne and Worthington 2002). The premise is that by linking specific products, such as credit cards, to a respected and credible cause or organization the product offering will be more attractive to consumers. Two distinct sets of benefits underpin the value proposition to the consumer. First, such schemes are based on the provision of group benefits – that is, payments to the non-profit organization in return for members or donors adopting or using the product. These group benefits offer consumers a cost-free, or perhaps low cost, and simple way of contributing to the cause. Second, there are individual tailored benefits offered to the consumer for adoption and use of the product. The second set of benefits can relate to functionality (a better-performing product) or image. These benefits are summarized in Figure 8.5.

Many schemes offer both sets of benefits. However, there is considerable variety in the benefits that consumers seek from affinity cards, with individual benefits scoring highly. Indeed, consumers reported uncertainty and scepticism about the real value of the group benefits of the affinity cards (Mekonnen *et al.* 2008).

The extensive range of financial services available to consumers and businesses is not necessarily an indication of FIs understanding and meeting customer needs. There is pressure from a number of sources for FIs to develop new offerings that conform to regulation, to make the lives of customers more straightforward and, of course, to generate profit.

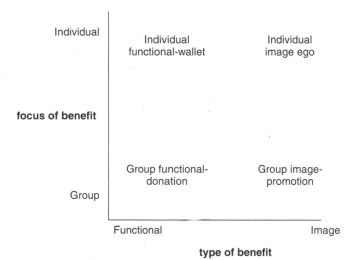

Figure 8.5 Typology of affinity product benefits
Source: Adapted from Mekkonen *et al.* (2008).

Summary

- A customer rarely goes shopping for a financial service; instead a product or offering is acquired and consumed for the benefit or value. They may also be purchased to avoid a particular outcome.
- New interpretations of marketing emphasize that customers seek value and that all a company can do is make a value proposition; the customer will derive value-in-use from the product/offering.
- New product development is more successful if the process is built around teams and involves a loop process.
- Service quality and service recovery are important parts of the offering as they form part of the customer experience.
- Products are eliminated from the product range when they cease to meet customer needs.
- Affinity cards offer opportunities for FI and customers, where a number of benefits can be amalgamated.

Exercises

1. Go to the Barclays website (www.barclays.co.uk) and note the range of services available to personal customers. Then go to the HSBC website (www.hsbc.co.uk); which of the services available on this website differ from those on the previous website?
2. How does Santander (www.santander.co.uk) use its website to address the intangibility of its products?
3. Select four affinity cards (moneysupermarket.com) and then, using the affinity typology (Figure 8.5), analyse which particular benefits each credit card offers.
4. Go to Britannia Building Society's website (www.britannia.co.uk) and note the services that this building society offers. How does its range compare with larger competitors? What conclusions can you draw from its product range?
5. What opportunities for value co-creation have you identified in your use of financial products?

References

Athanassopoulou, P. and Johne, A. (2004) 'Effective Communication with Lead Customers in Developing New Banking Products', *International Journal of Bank Marketing*, Vol. 22, No. 2, pp. 100–25.

Avlonitis, G. (1993) 'Project Dropstrat: What Factors Do Managers Consider in Deciding Whether to Drop a Product?', *European Journal of Marketing*, Vol. 27, No. 4, pp. 35–48.

Bearden, W. and Teel, J. (1980) 'An Investigation of Personal Influences on Consumer Complaining', *Journal of Retailing*, Vol. 56, Autumn, pp. 3–20.

Bitner, M.-J. (1992) 'Servicescapes: The Impact of Physical Surroundings on Customers and Employees', *Journal of Marketing*, Vol. 56, April, pp. 57–71.

Bloemer, J and Kasper, H. (1995) 'The Complex Relationship between Consumer Satisfaction and Brand Loyalty', *Journal of Economic Psychology*, Vol. 16, pp. 311–29.

Bloemer, J., de Ruyter, K. and Wetzels, M. (1999) 'Linking Perceived Service Quality and Service Loyalty: A Multi-dimensional Perspective', *European Journal of Marketing*, Vol. 33, No. 11/12, pp. 1082–07.

Bolton, R., Lemon, K. and Verhoef, P. (2004) 'The Theoretical Underpinning of Customer Asset Management: A Framework and Propositions for Future Research', *Journal of the Academy of Marketing Science*, Vol. 32, No. 3), pp. 271–92.

Booz Allen Hamilton (2003) *Implementing the Customer-Centric Bank: The Rebirth of the Forgotten Branch*, www.boozallen.com, accessed 6 September 2005.

Boshoff, C. (1999) 'RECOVSAT: An Instrument to Measure Satisfaction With Transaction-Specific Service Recovery', *Journal of Services Research*, Vol. 1, No. 3, pp. 236–49.

Buttle, F. (1996) 'SERVQUAL: Review, Critique, Research Agenda', *European Journal of Marketing*, Vol. 30, No. 1, pp. 8–32.

Cobanoglu, C. and Cobanoglu, N. (2003) 'The Effect of Incentives in Web Surveys: Application and Ethical Considerations', *International Journal of Market Research*, Vol. 45, No. 4, pp. 475–88.

Dekimpe, M., Steenkampe, J.-B., Mellens, M. and Abeele, P. (1997) 'Decline and Variability in Brand Loyalty', *International Journal of Research in Marketing*, Vol. 14, pp. 405–20.

Dick, A. and Basu, K. (1994) 'Customer Loyalty: Toward an Integrated Conceptual Framework', *Journal of the Academy of Marketing Science*, Vol. 22, No. 2, pp. 99–113.

Doyle, P. (2002) *Marketing Management and Strategy*, 3rd edn, Harlow, FT Prentice Hall.

Farquhar, J. and Panther, T. (2007) 'The More the Merrier? An Exploratory Study into Managing Channels in UK Retail Financial Services', *International Review of Retail, Distribution and Consumer Research*, Vol. 17, No. 1, pp. 43–62.

Fisk, R. Grove, S. and John, J. (2004) *Interactive Services Marketing*, 2nd edn, Boston, Houghton Mifflin Company.

Gremler, D. and Brown, S. (1999) 'The Loyalty Ripple Effect: Appreciating the Full Value of Customers', *International Journal of Service Industry Management*, Vol. 10, No. 3, pp. 271–91.

Grönroos, C. (1984) 'A Service Quality Model and its Marketing Implications', *European Journal of Marketing*, Vol. 7, No. 3, pp. 59–71.

Grönroos, C. (2000) *Service Management and Marketing: A Customer Relationship Approach*, Chichester, Wiley.

Gruber, T., Szmigin, I. and Voss, R. (2006), 'The Desired Qualities of Customer Contact Employees in Complaint Handling Encounters', *Journal of Marketing Management*, Vol. 22, pp. 619–42.

Harness, D. (2004) 'Product Elimination: A Financial Services Model', *International Journal of Bank Marketing*, Vol. 22, No. 3, pp. 161–79.

Harness, D. and Marr, N. (2004) 'A Comparison of Product Elimination Success Factors in the UK Banking, Building Society and Insurance Sectors', *International Journal of Bank Marketing*, Vol. 22, No. 2, pp. 126–43.

Hart, C. Heskett, J. L. and Sasser, W. O. (1990) 'The Profitable Art of Service Recovery', *Harvard Business Review*, Vol. 68, No. 4, pp. 148–56.

Hocutt, M. and Stone, T. H. (1998) 'The Impact of Employee Empowerment on the Quality of Service Recovery Effort', *Journal of Quality Management*, Vol. 3, No. 1, pp. 117–32.

Hoffman, K. D. and Kelley, S. W. (2000) 'Perceived Justice Needs and Recovery Evaluation: A Contingency Approach', *European Journal of Marketing*, Vol. 34, No. 3/4, pp. 418–32.

Hogan, J., Lemon, K. and Rust, R. (2002) 'Customer Equity Management: Charting New Directions for the Future of Marketing', *Journal of Service Research*, Vol. 5, No. 1, pp. 4–12.

Holbrook, M. (1999) *Consumer Value: A Framework for Analysis and Research*, London, Routledge.

Hollensen, S. (2001) *Global Marketing: A Market Responsive Approach*, 2nd edn, Harlow, FT PrenticeHall.

Horne, S. and Worthington, S. (2002) 'The Relationship Rhombus: A Quadratic Relationship', *Journal of Market-Focused Management*, Vol. 5, No. 2, pp. 127–34.

Jones, H. and Farquhar, J. (2007) 'Putting it Right: Service Failure and Customer Loyalty in UK Banks', *International Journal of Bank Marketing*, Vol. 25, No. 3, pp. 161–72.

Keaveney, S. (1995), "Customer Switching Behavior in Service Industries: An Exploratory Study", *Journal of Marketing*, 59, April, 71–82.

Koderisch, M., Wuebker, G., Baumgarten, J. and Baillie, J. (2007) 'Bundling in Banking: A Powerful Strategy to Increase Profits', *Journal of Financial Services Marketing*, Vol. 11, No. 3, pp. 268–76.

Langerak, F. Hultink, E. and Robben, H. (2004) 'The Impact of Market Orientation, Product Advantage and Launch Efficiency on New Product Performance and Organisational Performance', *Journal of Product Innovation Management*, Vol. 21, pp. 79–94.

Lovelock, C. (2001) *Services Marketing*, 4th edn, Upper Saddle River, Prentice Hall.

McCollough, M., Berry, L. and Yadav, M. (2000) 'An Empirical Investigation of Customer Satisfaction After Service Failure and Recovery', *Journal of Service Research*, Vol. 3, pp. 121–37.

Matthews, K. and Thompson, J. (2008) *The Economics of Banking*, 2nd edn, Chichester, John Wiley & Sons.

Mekkonen, A., Harris, F. and Laing, A. (2008) 'Linking Products to a Cause or Affinity Group', *European Journal of Marketing*, Vol. 42, No. 1/2, pp. 135–53.

O'Loughlin, D. Szmigin, I. and Turnbull, P. (2004) 'From Relationships to Experiences in Retail Financial Services', *International Journal of Bank Marketing*, Vol. 22, No. 7, pp. 522–39.

Oliva, T., Oliver, R. and MacMillan, I. (1992) 'A Catastrophe Model for Developing Service Satisfaction Strategies', *Journal of Marketing*, Vol. 56, July, pp. 83–95.

Oliver, R. (1999) 'Whence Consumer Loyalty?', *Journal of Marketing*, Vol. 63, Special issue, pp. 33–44.

Olsen, L. and Johnson, M. (2003) 'Service Equity, Satisfaction, and Loyalty: From Transaction-Specific to Cumulative Evaluations', *Journal of Service Research*, Vol. 5, No. 3, pp. 184–91.

Papastathopoulou, P., Gounaris, S. and Avlonitis, G. (2006) 'Successful New-to-the-market Versus "Me-too" Retail Financial Services', *International Journal of Bank Marketing*, Vol. 24, No. 1, pp. 53–70.

Parasuraman, A., Zeithaml, V. and Berry, L. (1985) 'A Conceptual Model of Service Quality and its Implications for Further Research', *Journal of Marketing*, Vol. 48, Autumn, pp. 41–50.

Parasuraman, A., Zeithaml, V. and Berry, L. (1988) 'A Multiple-item Scale for Measuring Consumer Perceptions of Service Quality', *Journal of Retailing*, Vol. 64, No. 1, pp. 12–40.

Payne, A. (2000) 'Customer Retention', in *Marketing Management: A Relationship Marketing Perspective*, Cranfield School of Management, Basingstoke, Macmillan Business.

Reichheld, F. (1996) 'Learning from Customer Defections', *Harvard Business Review*, March/April, pp. 56–69.

Reichheld, F. (2003) 'The One Number You Need to Grow', *Harvard Business Review*, December, pp. 46–55.

Reinartz, W., Thomas, J. and Kumar, V. (2005) 'Balancing Acquisition and Retention Resources to Maximize Customer Profitability', *Journal of Marketing*, Vol. 69, January, pp. 63–79.

Roos, I. (1999) 'Switching Processes in Customer Relationships', *Journal of Services Research*, Vol. 2, No. 1, pp. 68–85.

Sivadas, E. and Baker-Prewitt, J. (2000) 'An Examination of the Relationship between Service Quality, Customer Satisfaction and Store Loyalty', *International Journal of Retail & Distribution Management*, Vol. 28, No. 2, pp. 73–82.

Slattery, D. and Nellis, J. (2004) 'Product Development in UK Retail Banking: Developing a Market-oriented Approach in a Rapidly Changing Regulatory Environment', *International Journal of Bank Marketing*, Vol. 23, No. 1, pp. 90–106.

Smith, A. and Bolton, R. (1998) 'An Experimental Investigation of Customer Reactions to Service Failure and Recovery Encounters: Paradox or Peril', *Journal of Services Research*, Vol. 1, No. 1, pp. 65–81.

Smith, A., Bolton, R. and Wagner, J. (1999) 'A Model of Customer Satisfaction with Service Encounters Involving Failure and Recovery', *Journal of Marketing Research*, 36, pp. 356–72.

Stephens, N. and Gwinner, K. (1998) 'Why Don't Some People Complain? A Cognitive-Emotional Process Model of Consumer Complaint Behavior', *Journal of the Academy of Marketing Science*, Vol. 26, pp. 172–89.

Stevens, E. and Dimitriadis, S. (2005) 'Learning During Developing and Implementing New Bank Offerings', *International Journal of Bank Marketing*, Vol. 23, No. 1, pp. 54–72.

Strauss, B. and Neuhaus, P. (1997) 'The Qualitative Satisfaction Model', *International Journal of Service Industry Management*, Vol. 8, No. 3, pp. 236–49.

Swanson, S. and Kelley, S. (2001) 'Service Recovery Attributions and Word-of-mouth Intentions', *European Journal of Marketing*, Vol. 35, No. 1/2, pp. 194–211.

Tax, S. and Brown, S. (1998) 'Recovering and Learning from Service Failure', *Sloan Management Review*, Autumn, pp. 75–88.

Tsoukatos, E. and Rand, G. (2007), 'Cultural Influences on Service Quality and Customer Satisfaction: Evidence from Greek Insurance', *Managing Service Quality*, Vol. 17, No. 4, pp. 467–85.

Vargo, S. and Lusch, R. (2004) 'Evolving to a New Dominant Logic for Marketing', *Journal of Marketing*, Vol. 68, January, pp. 1–17.

Venkatesan, R., Kumar, V. and Bohling, T. (2005) 'Selecting Valuable Customers Using a Customer Lifetime Value Framework', Working Paper Series, Marketing Science Institute.

Vorhees, C., Brady, M. and Horowitz, D. (2006) 'A Voice From the Silent Masses: An Exploratory and Comparative Analysis of Noncomplainers', *Journal of the Academy of Marketing Science*, Vol. 34, No. 4, pp. 514–27.

Further reading

www.hsbc.co.uk/1/2/premier
www.yougov.co.uk
www.moneyexpert.com
www.financial-ombudsman.org.uk

CASE STUDY

Pay as you go or not?

The UK government has made proposals about road pricing that involve replacing road tax and petrol duty with a scheme for road charging or pricing. The key points of the plan are that each driver would be charged for every mile of his or her journey, but the charge would vary according to which roads were used and at what times. For example, a driver would pay premium charges for driving on the capital's motorways, say the M25, at peak times, but for the driver on quiet roads during the day, the charges would be much lower. A feasibility study by the Department for Transport (dft.gov.uk/strategy/futureoftransport) concluded that a national scheme had the potential to cut congestion by about 40 per cent, but would only result in 4 per cent fewer cars using the roads. A key factor in the scheme was the deployment of new technology to monitor driver road usage, ultimately with a view to manage roadspace more effectively.

Pay-as-you-go car insurance

The implications of road pricing have not been lost on the car insurance industry. The Association of British Insurers (ABI) believes that new technology could revolutionize insurance marketing because driving in areas with low traffic density lowers the risk of an accident, which would, then, be reflected in the insurance premium. However, the scheme is not likely to suit everyone. Under pay-as-you-drive insurance, the car owner pays an up-front premium of about a third of a standard policy and then pays a monthly charge on top that is calculated on how far they have driven, the type of road used and the time of each journey.

Product details

A two-year pilot of 5,000 motorists was conducted by the insurers Norwich Union in which a pay-as-you-go insurance product was trialled. The key components of the scheme are that the policy-holder pays an up-front charge for the installation of a GPS (global positioning system) black box, the size of a DVD case, to be fitted to the car. The box collects, stores and transmits information about when and where the car has been travelling. Details of journeys are sent back via the mobile phone network to the insurer, where the monthly bill is calculated and the sum then taken by direct debit from the policy-holder's account. The insurer will, therefore, have information on exactly when, how far (and at what speed) the car has been driven, as the GPS monitors each journey.

The scheme has the advantage of being tailored to the behaviour of individuals, which, it is argued, can result in lower motoring costs. Insurers state that there is a maximum payment, which is a similar amount to what a driver might expect to pay for an 'unmetered' policy. Norwich Union offered two policies. First, one for young drivers aged 18–23, who receive a 100 free miles a month, after which they will be charged according to their driving habits. They may have to pay as much as a £1 a mile during the high-risk accident time between 11pm and 6am. The second policy is for those aged 24–65, who pay as they go from the start. The insurer prices road trips so that driving at 70mph on a motorway or dual carriageway is 10 per cent of the price of driving at 30mph on an urban road, calculated on the data of accident probability. All policies discourage night-time driving. Under this policy, younger drivers could save significant sums – perhaps as much as £2,000 a year. However, there are some other considerations with this type of policy. The black box records a driver's speed as well as the exact location. Insurers have provided data at the request of the police following two serious accidents. Drivers who were speeding at the time of an accident will find that the data available will affect any claims made. Advantages of having a GPS box in the car have been cited as the ability to call for help in the event of a breakdown or emergency, access to congestion information on payment of a supplement and the ability to track the car should it be stolen. A major advantage for the wider community is that pay-as-you-drive insurance may encourage people to leave the car at home.

Price structure

Drivers pay a small advance payment, plus £50 for the installation of the GPS, although they can get cover instantly and pay a flat daily fee until the black box arrives. Policy-holders pay a fixed monthly fee that covers risks such as fire and theft and a payment per mile. As with normal insurance practice, if the policy-holder has convictions and/or a poor insurance record, then the he/she will pay more. Where the policy-holder lives (postcode), where the car is parked, the type of car, any modification etc. will all affect the price charged. Policy-holders will receive an itemized bill, much like a mobile phone bill, which breaks down usage by when and how much driving has been done, and on what type of road. No privacy between the people that drive the same car then!

And so?

Some drivers could make significant savings with pay-as-you-go car insurance. Insurers have stated that drivers who do less than 8,000 miles per year and those who mainly use motorways and dual carriageways are likely to save money. Young drivers who are willing to forego night-time driving will also save money. The scheme should also reduce motor accidents, as people adapt their habits to drive less, and at safer times and on safer roads. Ideas of budgeting may have to change as costs may vary from month to month. For example, some policy-holders may pay more in the winter as they abandon other forms of transport in cold, dark commuting conditions.

Pay-as-you-drive insurance withdrawn

In spite of high levels of initial interest, Norwich Union, Britain's biggest insurer, has suspended its flagship car insurance scheme less than two years after its roll out. Norwich Union hoped that by encouraging people to drive less at rush hour and late at night it would pay out less in claims, meaning it could offer lower premiums. The company said too few customers had joined, and blamed a slow take-up rate of the technology amongst car makers. Norwich Union had set a target of 100,000 drivers. The company would not reveal exactly how many people had signed up, but said it was 'not less than 10,000'. Norwich Union is writing to customers to inform them of the change. It says no one will be left without insurance, and that it will offer policy-holders a discount on its standard insurance policies. The insurance industry had been closely watching the scheme's progress. The suspension of pay-as-you-go car insurance could have repercussions beyond just car insurance. Any road-pricing scheme introduced by the government is likely to use similar technology to send back data on road, therefore it is important to discover the key reasons for the lack of success for this particular trial.

Questions

1. Where did the stimulus of the scheme originate? Which other aspects of environmental change contributed to the scheme?
2. Analyse the advantages and disadvantages of the pay-as-you-go car insurance scheme.
3. Did the scheme meet any criteria of SD-L interpretation of marketing?
4. What evidence is there in the case to support NPD theory?
5. What evidence is there in the study to explain the withdrawal of the scheme?
6. What marketing lessons can be learned from this case?

Written by Jillian Dawes Farquhar with information from www.bbc.co.uk, www.guardian.co.uk, www.fool.co.uk, www.moneyexpert.com.

9

Pricing and value in financial services

Contents

Learning outcomes

At the end of this chapter, the reader will be able to:

- Comprehend key pricing considerations in the marketing of financial services

- Evaluate pricing strategies, including cross-selling, product bundling, relationship pricing and customer value

- Critically consider pricing strategies in financial services for different segments

- Appreciate the role of value in the marketing of financial services

Introduction

rates: usually refers to the interest either paid or received on many financial products such as savings accounts, credit cards and mortgages

One of the most important characteristics of pricing in financial services is that direct payment is rarely made for the services that banks and other financial institutions (FIs) offer (Heffernan 2005). The language of pricing is also quite distinctive. Customers tend to pay fees, charges, premiums and **rates**, rather than employing terms such as 'price', 'invoice' or 'bill' used in most other situations. Another important dimension, which can cause dissatisfaction and, sometimes, anger, is that the cost of a service may be deducted or charged directly from an account, leaving the customer with little power in the exchange. The onus is then on the customer, if the charge is disputed or even incorrect, to try and get the money back from the FI, which can be complex and frustrating. Financial services are necessary rather than desirable in themselves; there is not much excitement to be had in insuring the house as compared to buying the latest Apple offering or a pair of Jimmy Choos! There seems, therefore, plenty of opportunity for customers to be dissatisfied in the area of pricing in financial services.

Costs

There are different ways of working out how to price the products that a company sells, but in these calculations the costs of the company have to be taken into consideration. The aim of pricing is to bring in sufficient revenue to cover costs and to meet company objectives. Economies of scale, it is argued, mean that large banks have a cost advantage over small ones. The credit crunch has created even larger high-street FIs, as they have absorbed or merged with those FIs that have encountered difficulties. Economies of scope, on the other hand, suggest that multiproduct banks will be more efficient than a 'financial boutique' (Heffernan 2005) – that is, a provider than specializes in a small range of offerings, such as a niche insurer. Empirically, there is little evidence to support these assertions, with considerable variation in the studies conducted. Heffernan (2005) found that one profit-maximizing strategy was to set highly competitive deposit and loan products alongside uncompetitive products, aiming to benefit from customer inertia. This is an example of pricing using non-pricing characteristics and, not surprisingly, is unpopular with customers or regulators. Furthermore, the financial services market is both mature and saturated, which allows little opportunity to FIs for pricing practices open to other industries or sectors. Overall, pricing in financial services, rather than the pricing of the services themselves, makes this one of the most contentious areas in their provision to customers, whether personal or business.

As might be expected from the financial services industry, where a grasp of numbers and money should be sound and, generally, better than most of its customers, FIs have developed complex **pricing strategies**. A key question for marketing is whether customers perceive the prices that they pay for the services provided are fair or even acceptable. Customers will not be satisfied or perceive value from products and services which they perceive to be priced unfairly. Most FIs seek to make a profit – for example, banks and insurance companies who have shareholders – but there are other FIs, such as credit unions and building societies, who aim to attract investment so that they then lend on to borrowers. Marketers recognize that there is a tripod of costs underpinning pricing strategies. The first leg of the tripod represents the costs incurred by consumers and by service providers. As well as monetary costs, consumers incur psychological costs when making decisions about the purchase of financial services. Customers are often described as inert, as the costs that they can experience when changing provider (switching) can be high. FIs have relatively high fixed costs, including branches, administrative centres, networks, IT infrastructure, call centres, sales staff, which can be compared, perhaps, to those of other retailers such as food stores. Variable costs, however, are low; for example, the serving of one extra customer does not result in a significant increase in costs. Realizing that many customers could be served without increasing costs may have contributed to larger banks believing that they could serve a mass market.

It might have been reasonably assumed that the advent of technology might have offered economies through the reduction in staff costs, but even some early research has shown that the introduction of ATMs has not necessarily reduced costs overall. Although ATMs are cheaper for banks than a staff transaction, US data suggest that customers tend to use those more, which then raises overall costs. Technology offers an improved service for customers but has a neutral effect on bank costs (*American Banker* 1990); this would appear to be the case for multiple channels as well. The introduction of multiple channels has not lowered costs for banks or other FIs, as customers seem to like to use a combination that suits them. Customers have resisted bank efforts to 'migrate' them from branch to Internet; instead, they prefer to use the range of channels that suit them. One highly significant cost, particularly to banks and other lenders, is the cost of money. FIs borrow and lend money to each other on the wholesale money markets; in Exhibit 9.1 the role of the wholesale markets in financial services is demonstrated.

pricing strategies: covers a range of approaches that an FI can adopt for pricing

---

EXHIBIT 9.1

Wholesale exposure

An important measure of banks' stability in these troubled times is the extent to which their loans are funded by their deposits. If the money the banks lend out has come from the deposits of other customers, then they can, to an extent, ignore the upheaval in the wholesale money markets. In the period leading up to the credit crunch, many banks lent money out the 'front door' to customers, both personal and business, and tried to borrow it back through the 'back door' from wholesale financial markets. These markets have dried up as banks and institutional investors have become increasingly unwilling to lend to each other. As a result, the banks that are most dependent on wholesale funding found themselves in vulnerable positions. The figures show the ratio of deposits to loan of 118 per cent for Standard Chartered represents a relatively healthy position of higher deposits to loans. However, Northern Rock at 31 per cent, Bradford & Bingley and Alliance & Leicester at 58 per cent all have a much lower ratio, indicating that they are highly dependent upon wholesale money markets, which effectively dried up in 2008. Northern Rock has been nationalized and Grupo Santander has acquired all or part of the other two FIs.

Compiled by the authors from www.bbc.co.uk, *The Independent on Sunday, The Observer.*

The second leg of the tripod is concerned with the competition. As branding strategies have not been as successful as FIs may have wished, the customer often makes choices based on the price of the financial service that they seek. Car insurance is frequently bought purely on basis of the price of the premium, or customers may decide to stick with their current provider owing to high switching costs. FIs, therefore, need to acquire a customer in the first place and then hope that this customer may be sufficiently satisfied (not necessarily loyal) to skip the cognitive, physical and emotional costs of finding another provider. In order to capture the customer in the first place, the price of the service has to be acceptable, which generally means about the same as similar services in the marketplace. FIs cannot, unlike restaurants or hotels, charge premium prices for their largely commoditized services.

The final leg of the tripod is customer demand. Demand for financial services is subject to little fluctuation, as customers, both B2C and B2B, need them for day-to-day life. The wealthier the population, the greater the demand for financial services as people look for loans, insurance, investments and pensions. As a consequence of this healthy demand, even in times of the credit crunch, there are plenty of providers in the marketplace. The UK financial services marketplace has been so fertile that new entrants such as Grupo Santander and Tesco have invested heavily in growing their presence. One of the reasons that the UK marketplace has proved so attractive is the relative lack of regulation in the financial services sector. The regulator for personal finance in the UK is the Financial Services Authority (FSA) which has been roundly criticized for its supine overseeing of the personal financial services sector; it remains to be seen whether this authority will continue. A more vigorous body might expect to play a greater role in the pricing of financial services, especially with regard to some of the fees charged.

Pricing objectives

It is as important in pricing to set objectives as it is in other areas of marketing and there are several options that will ultimately determine the pricing that an FI adopts and which are discussed below.

Increase market share

Acquiring customers has long been a key objective of the larger banks and they have used many approaches to achieve this aim, usually involving targeting a particular segment.

Profit maximization

Profits are maximized by charging as much as the market will bear. Banks, in particular, are unhappy with offering free banking and seek to recoup the costs involved in this service by high charges for overdrafts. They also tend to make money through cross-subsidies; one product may not be making a profit but another is more than covering any shortfall.

Product quality leadership

In mass-market financial services – that is, retail banking and insurance – this is not really a realistic objective, as customers generally perceive little difference between providers. As financial services have become commoditized, customers tend to seek the lowest offers that fit with their perceptions of the value of the service.

Having finalized the objectives, the FI is in a position to develop the strategy that will enable the objective to be achieved.

Pricing strategies

The pricing strategies that a company adopts should be those that enable it to achieve its corporate objectives, such as quality leadership, which would then allow it to pursue premium pricing. For most financial services, there seems to be little scope for premium pricing and, in this highly competitive sector, there are limited pricing choices for FIs. FIs faced with this situation tend to place a great deal of emphasis developing prices according to their competitors' current prices and strategy (Avlonitis and Indounas 2006). Customers are willing to choose their financial services according to the price they pay. This situation can be attributed to the lack of strong brands in the marketplace and the utilitarian nature of the products themselves. Overall, pricing should have the following characteristics:

- market segments should be charged differentially to maximize profit from each segment
- if a single product is aimed at a range of market segments, the pricing should not unduly subsidize some segments at the expense of others (e.g., new and existing customers)
- price needs to be communicable – that is, clear and readily understood by the relevant segment.

A selection of strategies that can be taken for pricing in the financial services sector is now discussed.

Penetration or low pricing

If an FI seeks to grow its market share as an objective, then it can set prices that undercut those of its competitors, which might involve offering attractive loans or investment rates to attract customers. In a saturated market, new customers are usually acquired from the competition by offering inducements to switch. FIs have traditionally used low pricing or free banking facilities to attract new student customers. Once the student has opened a cheque account with the bank (frequently one of the large high-street banks in the United Kingdom), it is likely that he/she will remain with that bank for some time, even years in some cases. This approach may work for current accounts, which offer the FI a fulcrum for building a relationship with a customer. FIs that do not offer this account have a different experience. Research by one of the authors found that one FI attracted customers by frequently being in the 'Best Buy' tables that appear in the financial section of newspapers. This FI found that many of the customers that responded to their attractive offers were customers of very short duration and would switch to obtain better rates when they became available (Farquhar and Panther 2007). These customers are price-sensitive and, in financial services 'speak', known as 'rate chasers'; they actively seek products that offer the most attractive rates. They could be considered the opposite of inert customers, prepared to incur in the non-price costs (e.g., cognitive) to save money. The FI in question reconsidered its pricing, adjusting to 'be alongside the competition', and this was proving to be more successful.

Price bundling

Many FIs price defensively to prevent competitors eroding their market share. By bundling two or more services together it makes it difficult for the prospective and repeat purchaser to compare across the providers. **Price bundling** also allows FIs to improve their profitability as they can achieve some economies of scale and scope (Koderisch *et al.* 2007). Price bundling enables the FI to achieve some degree of differentiation in the way that the bundle of services is packaged and the segment at which the bundle is targeted. Exhibit 9.2 provides an example of price bundling in insurance.

price bundling: where a number of products are grouped together to the customer in which some of the products generate revenue for the FI and some do not

---

EXHIBIT 9.2

Extra cover and discounts!

Axa, the global insurance company, enables customers to choose a Home Plus version of their house insurance, depending on the level of insurance cover required. The 'Essential' version covers the basics, but Home Plus cover provides extra piece of mind with some accidental damage cover as standard. Additionally, the company also offers a range of options such as family legal protection, home assistance, accidental damage cover, pedal cycle cover, personal possessions cover, plus the option to pay your home insurance premium monthly. A 20 per cent discount is available for getting a home insurance quote on-line, and even more by buying buildings and contents insurance together.

Source: Adapted from www.axa.co.uk/media.

It is quite difficult to compare this product with others in the marketplace as Axa is rolling up a number of different products together; there is even a discount for Internet enquiries and purchase, which saves a consumer those costs mentioned above. There are four steps involved in putting together a bundle of services. The first step is to design a bundle that satisfies both the needs of the target customer and the FI, which combines attractive products with ones that are less so. If customers are loyal then it is easier to achieve this type of bundling. The bundle of course must be tested using conventional market research techniques, such as focus groups and expert judgement. The pricing of the bundle can be based either on a single price that covers all components or a building block system (for an example, see www.rac.co.uk for breakdown cover). The internal infrastructure also needs to be in place for this kind of approach to work, as the price of the bundle is usually less than the sum of its parts, which may lead to internal conflict with regard to share of revenue (Koderisch *et al.* 2007).

Relationship pricing

FIs attempt to build relationships with their customers in order to offer them relevant financial products and to encourage them to be loyal. In spite of the importance of building relationships with existing customers in terms of lowered costs and improved selling opportunities, penetration pricing, aiming to attract new customers, has often undermined efforts to retain customers. Loyal customers have noted that they are paying higher prices than prices offered to new customers, leading them to question the wisdom of being loyal. FIs can use price as part of building relationships through price bundling, as mentioned in the previous section, offering customers advance warning of particularly good rates, targeting new products with special discounts for repeat purchases – in other words, recognizing the value of these customers to the organization. FIs sustain lower costs with existing customers as the organization already holds information about their purchases, their purchasing behaviour and their creditworthiness. The value of these customers seems to be have been overlooked in the past, as FIs pursue growth in market share through the acquisition of new customers, usually with the offer of low prices.

relationship pricing: a pricing approval limit around an individual customer satisfaction.

    The idea of **relationship pricing** opens up the possibility of charging different groups of customers different prices, as relationship marketing relies upon robust segmentation. It is important in relationship pricing to identify the service element; for example, is it an individual service, such as an insurance policy, or is it the bundle of services that a customer receives, say, from a private bank? An insurance policy for a car is almost a commoditized product, meaning that one offering can be easily substituted by a competitor product. It is relatively straightforward for customer to switch if the price of the service is not consistent with the perceived value of the product. With a more complex offering, where a relationship or loyalty may 'buffer' the value (Kasper *et al.* 2006), comparisons are harder to make, substitutes are less easy to discern and the consumer may be willing to pay a higher price. For business, private and corporate clients, pricing is more fluid and designed around individual situations, where the value of the client can be considered with respect to the prices charged. There is some indication that small businesses perceive that they pay excessive prices for the services that they consume (see Exhibit 9.3).

EXHIBIT 9.3

Free banking for Federation of Small Businesses (FSB) members

Research conducted by the Co-operative Bank revealed that as many as 40 per cent of small business bosses believe that one of the biggest problems they face is the uncertainty and confusion around bank charges. According to their own research, the 185,000 members of the FSB could be paying more than £65 million each year in bank charges, including fees for depositing cash over the counter in bank branches. Many banks impose limits on the number of cheques and the amount of cash that can be deposited in business accounts each month. The Co-operative Bank is famous for its ethical stance whereby all customers have a say in where their money is invested and are safe in the knowledge that the bank will turn away business from companies or organizations that it considers are unethical. The bank is offering FSB members a new promise of free banking, without complicated terms and conditions. The Co-operative Bank is committed to providing FSB members with more value for money, making the account a must-have for small businesses. Sandy Harris, FSB Member Services Chairman, said: 'Small businesses have £44 billion on deposit with the banks and it is high time that they received the service they deserve. The FSB is delighted to have teamed up with the Co-operative Bank to provide its members with an account where it is crystal clear what is on offer – genuinely free banking.'

Compiled from material from www.presswire.co.uk (2005).

This free banking account is the result of collaboration between the Co-operative Bank and the Federation of Small Businesses, which appears to offer benefits to all parties (see Table 9.1). The FSB membership will increase as businesses join to access the account; the Co-operative Bank gains customers and the customers have access to free banking, which is even more valuable during the credit crunch period. Relationship building also leads to an important activity in financial services – cross-selling. FIs, especially those with a wide product range such as the high-street banks, examine their customer information systems to identify 'prospects' – that is, those whom the FI's analysis indicates are likely to respond positively to being offered a particular product. Based on the information that the FI has

| Table 9.1 | Comparison between FSB Business Banking and main competitors |

	Abbey Free Banking Forever £	Barclays Business Tariff £	Lloyds TSB Business Extra £	NatWest Standard £	FSB Business Banking £
£4,000 cash	5.00	20.00	20.00	19.60	0.00
8 counter charges for manual credits	0.00	6.00	5.60	5.36	0.00
3 standing orders and direct debits	0.00	6.00	5.60	5.36	0.00
Credit 10 cheque credits	0.00	2.50	2.70	2.80	0.00
Monthly fee	0.00	0.00	2.50	5.75	0.00
Total monthly cost	5.00	34.44	36.42	40.07	0.00
Annual cost	60.00	413.28	437.04	480.84	0.00

Note: Assumes 20 working days per month, one branch visit made twice a week to pay in £500 cash and cheques. Limit of £4,000 cash deposited per month.
Source: Compiled by the authors from information on www.fsb.org.uk.

about a customer, it is able to model the propensity or inclination of that customer to purchase that particular product. For example, if the FI has information about whether the customer has a pet from home insurance details, then the customer can be sent details about pet insurance. FIs only have access to their own data about a customer and they cannot access or share details with other FIs about individuals (see www.ico.gov.uk).

A more sophisticated approach to relational pricing would be for FIs to look at the overall value of a particular customer to the organization across the services taken up in that case. Based on this evaluation, the FI could decide how valuable the relationship is to it and consider how to manage it accordingly through flexible pricing over time. Research suggests that pricing does not yet appear to be differentiated across customer groupings, in spite of customer data that would support this type of pricing (Avlonitis and Indounas 2006). Banks, in particular, make money from customers in many ways other than charges, such as interest they earn on customer deposits and clearing times for cheques, all of which could contribute to a more customized approach to pricing.

Risk and pricing

Relationships in marketing are often based around segments and different segments can be characterized by risk, as the lender apportions it to that particular group. Exhibit 9.4 reports research conducted by one of the authors into a high-risk segment in 2004.

EXHIBIT 9.4

High risk and high rates!

One lender, a former building society, now part of a larger FI, was targeting a particular group of borrowers, whom it described as sub-prime. This is a term used to describe the market where loans or mortgages are supplied to people with lower credit ratings; it is based on data about the borrower, which could mean the postcode, earnings, marital status, frequency of moving house and previous experience in managing debt (current borrowings, for example). There is little standardization of what exactly constitutes sub-prime, but it can cover a whole range of situations. Some lenders consider a house buyer with less than 5 per cent deposit to be sub-prime, or those needing to borrow more than 3.5 times their annual salary. The self-employed can be regarded as sub-prime, regardless of their wealth, because their income is never guaranteed. At the lower end of the scale, sub-prime also includes borrowers with a history of bad debt management or county court judgments. It was this lower level that the lender was targeting. The lender charged a higher rate to these borrowers to cover the extra risk involved in lending to these people with less than perfect credit ratings.

This exhibit shows that rates are also affected by the lenders' calculations about the risk with a particular segment. So that they do not lose money, FIs lending or serving higher-risk segments will raise their the rates at which they lend. Not all FIs have the option of cross-subsidizing prices as do the larger banks. Building societies that concentrate on home loans have a number of constraints when they price up their offers. Originally, building societies only lent money that investors had lodged with them, but many now borrow money on the wholesale market, which they lend on in the form of mortgages. The rate that they offer for mortgages is affected not only by the rate at which they have managed to secure the wholesale funds, but also other internal and external factors, as shown in Figure 9.1.

The wholesale or base rate is the rate at which the society or the lender has borrowed the money. The internal factors refer to the costs of the

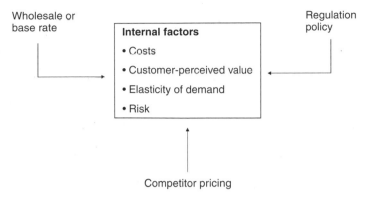

Figure 9.1 Mortgage pricing
Source: Adapted from Meidan and Chen (1995).

FI and levels of risk consistent with the segments targeted. Customer-perceived value refers to the value that a consumer attaches to the product. Elasticity of demand is an important determinant in pricing generally and refers to the uncertainty in the marketplace about responses to price change. The formula for price elasticity is:

$$\text{Price elasticity of demand} = \frac{\% \text{ change in quantity demanded}}{\% \text{ change in price}}$$

If demand falls by 5 per cent when a seller raised his price by 1 per cent, price elasticity is −5 (minus sign confirms inverse relation between price and demand). As price elasticity is affected by demand; when customers are less price-sensitive or when the product is unique or highly distinctive comparison is not easy. This is generally not the case in financial services; therefore, it can be argued that demand is elastic and that FIs will keep prices relatively low in these situations. Regulations in financial services are in place mainly to protect the consumer, but the FSA has come under severe criticism for its role in the lead-up to the credit crunch. FIs will include a factor in the pricing based on an assessment of risk involved in serving that particular segment.

This practice extends to insurance, where high-risk customers of car, health, travel and life insurance will pay higher premiums than lower-risk segments. Pricing for insurance involves assessment of risk or the probability of making a claim; therefore, customers who present lower levels of risk generally pay less for their insurance. Insurance companies manage their costs through a rigorous process of loss adjusting to minimize fraudulent claims, which would result in an increase of premiums.

Pricing by channel

FIs are aware of the options of pricing their products according to the channel through which customers access them. FIs are also motivated by a desire to 'migrate' customers away from the branch to the Internet, so have priced remote channels lower than branches to achieve this migration. However, this is a rather simplistic way of optimizing revenue because customers have a complex set of needs and wants, which includes a preference for using more than one channel (Lee, 2002; Black *et al.* 2002 Thornton and White, 2001) and varying the channel according to the nature of the transaction or purchase. Straightforward transactions and products are accomplished on-line, whereas more complex exchanges may occur in an environment where there is a personal interaction, such as the branch, where slight differences in price may be offset by lower emotional costs such as risk reduction. This choice of channel provides an example of value-in-use (Gronroos 2006), where the customer gains value from the services through managing their financial matters according to their own preference and convenience. An Internet-only provider has lower costs than a lender who has a branch network to run.

In home loans, pricing will also be determined by the channel. The broker plays an important role in the distribution of mortgages and FIs will price mortgages sold in this way differently from those sold through their own direct channels, sometimes developing a different brand for this purpose. Yorkshire Building Society, for example, has developed an intermediary.

Fixed pricing

Customers pay charges for the services that they consume, but a contentious area is the penalty charges that customers pay for unauthorized overdrafts or for late payments for credit card bills. Credit card companies have a set of charges as shown in Table 9.2.

Charges vary from one credit card company to another, but the data in Table 9.2 were common across three credit card companies operating in the United Kingdom. Consumers can avoid paying any of these charges, so reducing incomes for the credit card companies or any of the FIs that have these fixed charges. Revenue is generated instead by customers who do not pay off their bill in full at the end of the month and so incur interest payments in the region of 15.6 per cent (ASDA credit card, December

Table 9.2	Charges for fee free credit card	
Fees	Cash advance	3.00%
Charges	Paper copies of statements	£3.00
	Overseas transactions (including cash transactions)	2.75%
Default charges	Late payment	£12.00
	Administration fee for returned cheques or direct debits	£12.00
	Over credit limit	£12.00
	Trace fee (applied if change of address not notified and company has to trace customer)	£25.00

Source: Compiled by the authors from a selection of fee-free credit cards.

2008). Intervention from regulatory bodies has resulted in some changes to charging practices as described in Exhibit 9.5.

EXHIBIT 9.5

Banks battle it out for customers

A string of high-street names, including First Direct, Alliance & Leicester and Lloyds TSB, has announced they are making significant changes to the way that many of their current accounts and overdrafts operate. FIs are keen to retain current account customers because they believe them to be integral to the long-term health of their businesses. The current account provides a useful platform for cross-selling and helps to build relationships with customers because current accounts give a great insight into their behaviour. But, while levels of interest from in-credit accounts have been the focus of these marketing efforts in the past, banks and building societies now appear to be more concerned about preventing the Office of Fair Trading (OFT) imposing tough sanctions. Earlier this year, the regulator launched investigations into whether current accounts are sufficiently transparent and provide value for customers; it also examined whether unauthorized overdraft charges and fees for returned items are fair. Tens of thousands of complaints about charges have been received by the county courts and the Financial Ombudsman Service, which have prompted FIs to take this pre-emptive action. Overall, the recent changes across the market will only cause additional confusion in a market that is already hard to compare. While some fees have seen reductions, many of the other fee changes are less clear cut. Fees have changed names, now have tiered levels and have moved from monthly to daily, while interest rates have even changed to daily fees. For some customers, this may be a welcome change, but many others, such as those who fail to keep within the agreed terms and conditions, will see much higher fees.

Compiled from Moneywise, December 2007.

Bank charges contribute to customer dissatisfaction to a very significant degree, with findings from a study showing that 63 per cent of customers contacting their bank about bank charges stated that would not be likely to continue their custom with the bank (Jones and Farquhar 2007).

The customer

There has been some shift in the balance of power between FIs and customers as customers gain confidence, both in understanding financial services and realizing that the competitive environment provides extensive choice. They are fully aware that if one FI does not provide them with the product they require at an acceptable price, then they can try for a better offer from a competitor. Customer awareness of pricing in financial services, nonetheless, still lags behind that of other services, owing to the relative complexity of financial services (Estelami 2005).

New and existing customers

As customers are increasingly price-sensitive and willing to shop around, FIs are aware that they have to offer competitive rates for their products to gain new customers. Savings accounts will be offered at an attractive rate of interest so they feature in the 'best buy' columns of newspapers and other information sites. FIs usually fix a target for these accounts – that is, they aim for fixed number of accounts to be opened; when they reach that target, the account is then taken off the market. This is similar to a standard retailing practice, as a product offered at a low price will sell out quickly. Customers respond to the promotion of these accounts and then apply to open accounts through the appropriate channel. Usually, the attractive rate will run for a period of three or six months, after which the rate will fall so the customer receives a less attractive return on their savings. In the meantime, a new savings product will be launched to attract new customers at a higher rate. Existing customers feel disadvantaged and may choose to exit; more likely, however, is that they will leave their money where it is through inertia; but they will feel dissatisfied and may well 'voice' their complaints.

Perceptions and awareness

Not only do consumers and customers incur monetary costs in the purchase and use of financial services, they also incur other non-financial costs as well. FIs to understand these costs so that they recognize when the customers may encounter difficulties. They can provide information to 'ease' the customers through the process.

Figure 9.2 shows three costs incurred by customers arising from the purchase of car insurance: search costs, acquisition costs and after costs. Search costs constitute cognitive, physical and emotional costs. First, the consumer has the cognitive costs in comparing products – for example, the amount of excess, whether breakdown cover is included and how

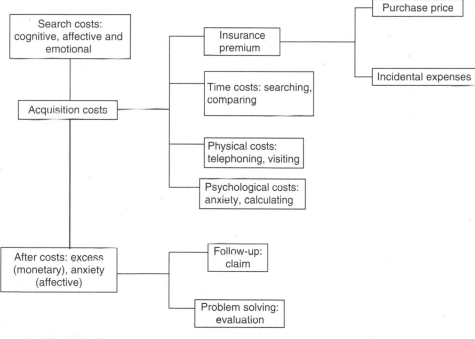

Figure 9.2 Customer costs in purchasing car insurance
Source: Adapted from Lovelock (2001).

many drivers are on the policy. There may be physical costs such as visiting branches or offices, although the Internet and phone have had an impact here. Customers may also feel emotional costs arising from increased perceptions of risk if changing provider. All these costs are in addition to the monetary cost of the product that they are purchasing. The consumer incurs search costs in evaluating the different insurance packages. These costs would be significantly reduced if he/she did not change the company that already insures the car. The insurance company needs to convey to the consumer, at this point, the benefits of remaining with them and they need to have demonstrated the benefits of being insured with them in any contact about claims. It should also be stated explicitly in the renewal notice that the insurer recognizes that the customer is loyal, by offering a loyalty discount. In addition to the search costs that the prospective purchaser of car insurance expends, there are costs attached to the purchase itself.

Time costs are incurred in arranging the purchase, such as the supply of information to the provider, whether on-line, visiting or phoning the insurer or broker. Physical costs may similarly be experienced if travelling to premises is required or rooting out information. The final box refers to costs that are incurred after the premium has been paid, such as excess that has to be paid by the customer in the event of an accident. High excess charges may allow a low premium to attract particular customers. The insurance company has access to data on motoring that allows the calculation of the probability of certain segments' exposure to accidents and, thus, has calculated how much excess it needs to charge to offset lower premiums. Insurers could reduce after costs with the prompt despatch of the insurance documents, with appropriately branded stationery and a small gift such as a tax disc holder – again appropriately branded.

Based on the amount of effort expended in merely insuring a car, this figure gives some indication why customers can be inert – that is, often stay with their existing provider – and why insurance websites have become so popular.

Evoked set

Although the financial services market appears to be highly competitive, customers, when comparing prices, have a set of preferred FIs in mind. Avoidance of risk, familiarity with the brand or company may jostle for place in the mind of the prospective purchaser or customer, with decisions based on a number of different elements in addition to price. It is vital for a company to be on the first page of any search results, if that is the way that they choose to compete, as customers are not prepared to search further. Direct Line, the first insurance company to rely on remote channels, chooses not to be listed on price comparison sites. The implication is, of course, that its prices are higher than its competitors; however, it believes that its brand is appreciated by the segments it serves. Customers may also have a list of companies that may be excluded from consideration, based on either their own experience or that of others. The existing provider must be in the evoked set, which means that it must have avoided service failures in the relationship to date. If service failures have occurred, then appropriate service recovery procedures must be in place.

Price satisfaction

Overall satisfaction with a product will include an appraisal about whether the consumer has paid a 'fair' price. Exploring customers' perceptions of pricing in financial services, Matzler *et al.* (2007) applied theories of customer satisfaction, using a three-factor model. This model states that 'dissatisfiers' (basic factors of customer satisfaction) are minimum requirements; if these factors are not catered for adequately they will cause dissatisfaction, but, even if they are catered for, they will not lead to satisfaction. 'Satisfiers' increase customer satisfaction but do not cause dissatisfaction if not delivered; these can generate delight. Performance factors lead to satisfaction if performance is high and dissatisfaction if performance is low This three-factor model has been developed based on the notion that customers display a loss aversion where losses loom larger than gains, revealing an imbalance in perceptions. This research in Austria found that price fairness strongly influences overall price satisfaction when customers consider that they have been treated unfairly. However, owing to the asymmetry in the satisfaction theory above, price fairness does *not* increase customer satisfaction if customers believe that they are being treated fairly. The writers conclude that price fairness is a necessary but not sufficient condition for high levels of satisfaction and which has implications for bank charges as discussed above.

As recognized in the services marketing literature (e.g., Lovelock 2001), the intangibility of the service makes it hard for customers to make an evaluation regarding how well it meets their needs. This difficulty is particularly pertinent with the bundles of service that many customers receive. How does a customer judge whether being able to get cash 24/7, access to advice for 12 hours a day, free credit cards and overdrafts is fair to the parties in the exchange? The concept of **transparency** plays a role in arriving at assessments of fairness. There are two types of transparency: price transparency and transparency of

transparency: availability or disclosure of information to market participants

the service. When both types of transparency are low, the provider of the service has the greatest freedom in setting the price. Price comparison sites appear to have raised levels of transparency in financial services, making both price and service comparable to customers. The burden remains on the customer to be able to decode the products and their pricing sufficiently to allow accurate comparisons. If the customer chooses a product inadvertently that does not offer the attributes or product qualities that they really need, the provider will not meet any shortfall.

Banks provide 'free banking', or so they argue, but it is less well known that they make money from the money held in the thousands of current accounts through aggregating the sums in these accounts and accessing capital on the wholesale banking markets (Mitchell 2001). Table 9.3

Table 9.3   What customers pay

Aggregate revenue of banks from personal current accounts (PCAs) was approx £8.3 billion, or £152 per active account

personal current accounts generate more revenue for banks than savings and credit cards combined

'insufficient fund' charges have increased by an average of 17 per cent in real terms between 2003 and 2007

when banks were asked to calculate how much a hypothetical customer would have to pay in a given scenario (which included exceeding an agreed overdraft limit), the reported charges varied from £0 to £260

the average daily unarranged overdraft balance in 2006 was £680 million. Paid item and maintenance fees totalled some £1.5 billion – which would equate to a return of over 220 per cent on the average balance

there is significant potential for slight errors in financial management to result in hundreds of pounds of charges

over 12.6 million accounts (23 per cent of active accounts) incurred at least one insufficient funds charge in 2006

those consumers who incurred a charge were more likely to incur at least six charges rather than just one

4 million accounts incurred charges of over £200 in 2006, of which 1.4 million accounts incurred charges of over £500

in a survey conducted for the study, over a fifth of consumers were unaware of the existence of charges until they had incurred one

Source: www.oft.gov.uk/news/press/2008/84-08.

presents information about the revenue from customers that banks derive from personal current accounts.

Some customers have been so dissatisfied with the fees that they have been charged and the unwillingness of FIs to address their dissatisfaction that they have become activists in campaigning for consumer rights. Websites, such as www.penaltycharges.co.uk, show other customers how to complain, even providing templates for letters to send to their FI. Even though there is a vocal group of complainers, there are, equally, many customers whose response to charges and fees is passive and, although unhappy, they are not inclined to act either by switching provider or by complaining. Although there is considerable confusion and anger about the prices set by FIs, pricing in financial services could respond to more marketing-derived principles, as we discuss in the following section.

Perceived value and consumption

Value is inherent in the theory of exchange, where the participants trade so that each obtains something of value. In contemporary marketing, value is recognized as both a significant and dominant determinant of consumer loyalty (Sirdeshmukh et al. 2002), as well as an important constituent of relationship marketing (Ravald and Grönroos 1996). Interest in value has largely come about because customer satisfaction has not proved a reliable antecedent of customer loyalty. While the importance of delivering value for organizations is acknowledged, the relevance of value is that it provides a framework for a customer-based means of pricing in financial services. Value is a trade-off between the gains to the consumer through the acquisition or consumption of a product and the price paid, or whether the benefits of the product outweigh the sacrifice. In services research, the interrelationships between product quality, perceived value and customer satisfaction have been more or less agreed. Woodruff (1997) also draws attention to the evaluation of the user experience of an offering and points out that the desired value of an offering consists of the product's attributes, the performance of these attributes and the consequences related to its use. Value and the co-creation of value has increased significantly as the key component or outcome of marketing (e.g. Vargo and Lusch 2004).

If CPV is considered from a relationship marketing perspective (e.g., Grönroos 2000), it then adds to the emotional bond between the provider and customer and strengthens the level of commitment between provider (Ravald and Grönroos 1996). Value plays a mediating role in trust/loyalty relationships (Sirdeshmukh *et al*. 2002). Although value can be assessed on the basis of a single encounter, it can also be the result of an enduring global perception (Rust and Oliver 1994); perceptions of value can change over time, possibly differing between the time of purchase, when using the product and after use. Usefully for financial services, this extends the perceptions of value to an experience rather than a single encounter or purchase, as most financial products are consumed over a period. Consumer use of attributes in decision-making is widely recognized in consumer behaviour, but its relevance in discerning value is often restricted to the time of purchase.

Recent thinking has begun to approach marketing from the angle of delivering value or offering the customer value propositions (Vargo and Lusch 2004). This approach has a number of advantages in that it reminds the marketer that customers generally seek value from the whole service experience, which is itself customer-derived. Perceptions about the price that has been paid for the financial service will be based on the customer's evaluation of value. Where customers perceive higher value, then there is scope for the provider to charge higher prices; FIs might like to consider how they can create higher value for their customers in their products and services.

It has been understood for some time that quality may often be inferred from the price of a service, leading to assumptions that the higher the price the better the quality of the offering. Chen *et al*. (2005) argued that the importance of price may diminish in assessments of quality where there are other cues as to the quality of a service. They measured the relationships between the cues of price, brand and their impact of service quality, perceived risk and customer value and found that brand cues affect customer value through perceptions of service quality. Price cues affect customer choice through a customer's perception of the risk of the service. Risk perceptions play an important role in the consumer's view of services. This research demonstrates the importance for financial services of discovering the cues that customers use to assess the service and the relative significance of the cues. These cues can be internal (product improvements) or external (marketing). Due to the quality inferences that consumers draw from price, certain financial service categories could be raised higher than convention might suggest. A positive relationship between advertising and price awareness suggests that advertising not only helps develop the positioning of the brands but also helps to educate consumers about product attributes including price (Estelami 2005).

Pricing approaches and the prices that customers pay for their financial services have provoked high levels of customer dissatisfaction. In this period of the credit crunch, FIs could respond by increasing the transparency of their pricing as part of an overall strategy to (re)gain customer confidence in the industry and the relationships that they have with their customers. The arguments for price transparency are compelling, as customers are earning very little on their investments and are therefore looking for lower prices. Banks are probably the most culpable here; they might argue that they need to make some money somewhere, but 'unfair' charges are not the means of doing this. Cost reductions will have to be achieved elsewhere, such as by rationalizing product portfolios, refining technology and perhaps reconsidering senior management remuneration.

Summary

- Pricing in financial services quite often involves fees deducted from customer accounts, leaving the customer disempowered. FIs operate in mature and saturated markets with little opportunity for creative pricing strategies.
- Attempts to build relationships are undermined if customers face charges that they perceive as being unfair. FIs may be tempted to behave opportunistically in pricing owing to lack of transparency in the services.
- Customer expectations are now that price is a major determinant when choosing a financial service, although customers remain less aware of pricing in financial services.
- There is scope for FIs to think more creatively about pricing, especially within a framework of corporate and marketing objectives, asking how they may integrate pricing into strategies for retaining and acquiring customers.
- A value-based approach to pricing in financial services may generate more flexibility in pricing based on brand cues and perceptions of risk and quality.

References

American Banker, 6 October 1990.

Avlonitis, G. and Indounas, K. (2006) 'Pricing Practices of Service Organizations', *Journal of Services Marketing*, Vol. 20, No. 5, pp. 346–56.

Black, N., Lockett, A., Ennew, C., Winkelhofer, H. and McKechnie, S. (2002) 'Modelling Consumer Choice of Distribution Channels: An Illustration from Financial Services', *International Journal of Bank Marketing*, Vol. 20, No. 4, pp. 161–73.

Booz Allen Hamilton (2003) *Implementing the Customer-Centric Bank: The Rebirth of the Forgotten Branch*, www.boozallen.com, accessed 6 September 2005.

Chen, T., Chang, P.-L. and Chang, H.-S. (2005) 'An Investigation of Personal Influences on Consumer Complaining', *Journal of Retailing*, 56, Autumn, pp. 3–20.

Cronin, J., Brady, M. and Hult, G. (2000) 'Assessing the Effects of Quality, Value, and Customer Satisfaction on Consumer Behavioral Intentions in Service Environments', *Journal of Retailing*, Vol. 76, No. 2, pp. 193–218.

Estelami, H. (2005) 'A Cross-category Examination of Consumer Price Awareness in Financial and Non-financial Services', *Journal of Financial Services Marketing*, Vol. 10, No. 2, pp. 125–39.

Farquhar, J. and Panther, T. (2008), 'Acquiring and Retaining Customers in UK Banks: An Exploratory Study', *Journal of Retailing and Consumer Services*, Vol. 15, No. 1, pp. 9–21.

FSA (2002) 'Young are Storing up Last Minute Pension Panic', Financial Services Authority, www.fsa.gov.uk/pubs/press/, accessed 14 November 2003.

Grönroos, C. (2000) *Service Management and Marketing: A Customer Relationship Approach*, Chichester, Wiley.

Grönroos, C. (2006) 'Adapting a Service Logic for Marketing', *Marketing Theory*, Vol. 6, No. 3, pp. 317–33.

Heffernan, S. (2005), *Modern Banking*, Chichester, John Wiley.

Jones, H. and Farquhar, J. D. (2007) 'Putting it Right: Service Failure and Customer Loyalty in UK Banks', *International Journal of Bank Marketing*, Vol. 25, No. 3, pp. 161–72.

Kasper, H., van Helsdingen, P. and Gabbott, M. (2006) *Services Marketing Management: A Strategic Perspective*, 2nd edn, Chichester, John Wiley.

Koderisch, M., Wuebker, G., Baumgarten, J. and Baillie, J. (2007) 'Bundling in Banking: A Powerful Strategy to Increase Profits', *Journal of Financial Services Marketing*, Vol. 11, No. 3, pp. 268–76.

Kotler, P., Armstrong, G.,Wong, V. and Saunders, J. (2008) *Principles of Marketing*, 5th European edn, Harlow, Financial Times/Prentice Hall.

Lee, J. (2002) 'A Key to Marketing Financial Services: The Right Mix of Products, Services, Channels and Customers', *Journal of Services Marketing*, Vol. 16, No. 3, pp. 238–58.

Lovelock, C. (2001) *Services Marketing: People, Technology, Strategy*, 4th edn, Upper Saddle River, Prentice Hall.

Matzler, K. Renzl, B. and Faullant, R. (2007) 'Dimensions of Price Satisfaction: A Replication and Extension', *International Journal of Bank Marketing*, Vol. 25, No. 6, pp. 394–405.

Meidan, A. and Chen, A. (1995) 'Mortgage Pricing Determinants: A Comparative Investigation of National, Regional and Local Building Societies', *International Journal of Bank Marketing*, Vol. 13, No. 3, pp. 3–11.

Mitchell, A. (2001) *Right Side Up: Building Brands in the Age of the Organized Consumer*, London, HarperCollins.

Office of Fair Trading (2008) *Personal Current Accounts in the UK: A Market Study*, Office of Fair Trading, www.oft.gov.uk/, accessed 8 August 2008.

Ravald, A. and Grönroos, C. (1996) 'The Value Concept and Relationship Marketing', *European Journal of Marketing*, Vol. 30, No. 2, pp. 19–30.

Reinartz, W., Thomas, J. and Kumar, V. (2005) 'Balancing Acquisition and Retention Resources to Maximize Customer Profitability', *Journal of Marketing*, Vol. 69, January, pp. 63–79.

Rust, R. and Oliver, R. (1994) *Service Quality: New Directions in Theory and Practice*, Thousand Oaks, CA, Sage.

Sirdeshmukh, D. Singh, J. and Sabol, B. (2002) 'Consumer Trust, Value, and Loyalty in Relational Exchanges', *Journal of Marketing*, Vol. 66, pp. 15–37.

Sweeney, J. and Soutar, G. (2001) 'Customer Perceived Value: The Development of a Multi-item Scale', *Journal of Retailing*, Vol. 77, 203–20.

Thornton, J. and White, L. (2001) 'Customer oOrientation and Usage of Financial Distribution Channels', *Journal of Services Marketing*, Vol. 15, No. 3, pp. 168–85.

Vargo, S. and Lusch, R. (2004) 'Evolving to a New Dominant Logic for Marketing', *Journal of Marketing*, Vol. 68, January, pp. 1–17.

Woodruff, R. (1997) 'Customer Value: The Next Source of Competitive Advantage', *Journal of the Academy of Marketing Science*, Vol. 25, No. 2, pp. 139–53.

Zeithaml, V. (1988) 'Consumer Perceptions of Price, Quality and Value: A Means-Ended Model and Synthesis of Evidence', *Journal of Marketing*, Vol. 52, July, pp. 2–22.

Exercises

1. Using one of the comparison websites, choose three potentially attractive and relevant car insurance offers. Carefully note down exactly what each offer actually consists of on a grid. Is the cheapest deal going to offer a package of benefits that is most appropriate for your needs?
2. Check one of the many advertised insurance websites and, using the same set of criteria, obtain a quote for car insurance. How does this quote compare with the quotation obtained via the intermediary website? Why did you choose this website? Analyse as thoroughly as you can your selection criteria. Did this website also appear on the intermediary website?
3. Is the website oriented towards the providers or the consumers? Is there any way of telling?

Further reading and information

Office of Fair Trading: www.oft.gov.uk/
www.penaltycharges.co.uk

www.MoneySavingExpert.com
www.moneysupermarket.com
Data Protection information: www.ico.gov.uk/
www.esure.com/media_centre/thieves_target_student_digs.

CASE STUDY

Price satisfaction in Austrian banks

The Austrian banking sector has one of the most intensive banking networks in Europe, with about 870 main banks, each with several branches. This means that, with about 1,600 inhabitants per branch bank, Austria lies well ahead in an international comparison, although Germany has about 2,200 customers per branch. In the middle of the twentieth century, Austrian banks were rather small scale and fragmented, but during last two decades banking has undergone a wave of concentration and mergers in the country. Table C9.1 lists Austria's largest banks and gives an overview of their size, showing how they rank with other major international banks.

Table C9.1   Austria's ten largest banks (in US$ million)

Rank in Austria	Bank	Rank, top-1000 banks of the world 2007	Core capital	Balance sheet total
1	Bank Austria*	66	11,196	203,154
2	Erste Bank/Sparkassen	93	8,146	239,304
3	Raiffeisen Zentralbank	97	7,443	152,283
4	Österreichische Volksbanken AG	171	3,508	88,805
5	BAWAG P.S.K.	174	3,390	66,912
6	RLB OÖ	304	1,604	28,267
7	Hypo Group Alpe Adria**	396	1,078	28,583
8	Oberbank	454	882	17,413
9	RLB NÖ-W	474	818	17,020
10	RLB Steiermark	490	802	15,388

Source: *The Banker*, 31 December 2006.

Besides the traditional banking, some 'direct banks' have emerged during the last few years. Unlike traditional banks, direct banks have no physical distribution branches but execute the whole business via Internet or phone. Their product range varies from pure investment banking to pure savings and loan products. After continuous growth rates in the beginning (since 1997), the growth stopped in 2007, as, by this time, most traditional banks also offered on-line banking facilities; also the interest rates for instant access accounts were largely similar. In terms of balance sheets, Austrian direct banks, as a whole, to date have about 0.6 per cent share of the banking market in Austria.

Typical products available to Austrian banking customers are as follows:

Savings books The savings book is the Austrians' most popular investment form. At most banks opening a savings bank book is free of
cost, but can exclusively be used for depositing savings; monetary transactions are not possible. Until 2002, the opening of a savings book
could be undertaken anonymously, without any identity verification.
The European Commission claimed that this fostered money laundering
and constrained the tracing of illegal transactions. Since then, identity
verification has been obligatory. There exist several forms of savings
bank books: the most simple form is the savings book, usually instant
access, where customers can deposit and take out money every day, and
the interest rate is variable. Typically, customers are offered rather low
interest rates, although the price range is considerable (between 0.125
per cent and 4 per cent). Most banks offer a wide range of savings
bank books, but even for the simplest form a comparison is complex.
This is due to the many options customers can choose from: savings
books with notice or without; flexible/fixed interest rate; and one-time
deposit/continuous deposit. As an alternative to common savings books,
continuous deposits saving books with a one-time deposit offer fixed
terms and interest rates. Table C9.2 gives an overview of different product offerings of this type (known as a *Kapitalsparbuch*, or capital savings
book) for banks in the southern region of Austria with a one-year deposit
period.

Table C9.2 Comparison of different savings book offers,
one-year notice period

Product name	Bank	Minimum deposit (€)	Interest rate (%)
Kapitalsparbuch (12 Monate)	P.S.K.	12,000	4.375
BKS-Kapitalsparbuch (1 J)	BKS Bank AG	4,000	4.250

Table C9.2 continued

Product name	Bank	Minimum deposit (€)	Interest rate (%)
HYPO Garantie-Sparbuch (12 Monate)	Hypo Alpe-Adria-Bank AG	100	4.250
PremiumKonto 12 Monate (Festgeldkonto)	Generali Bank AG	2,000	4.250
Kapitalsparbuch (12 Monate)	P.S.K.	100	4.125
KAPITALSPARBUCH (12 M)	Sparda-Bank Villach/Innsbruck	100	4.010
SPARDA Kapitalsparbuch	Sparda-Bank Villach/Innsbruck	100	4.010
Vermögenssparbuch (1 Jahr)	Raiffeisenlandesbank Kärnten	100	4.000
Kapitalsparbuch (1 Jahr)	Kärntner Sparkasse AG	0	4.000

In the past, many banks did not automatically adjust the interest rates of simple savings in line with increasing interest rates, only adjusting them downwards. A judgment in the Austrian High Court now obliges banks to revise interest rates in both directions. However, as consumer interest organizations found out, most banks still do not automatically adjust the interest rates for savings, nor do they do this free of charge. Some banks illegitimately charge up to €20 for a belated adjustment, or are even not prepared to perform an adjustment for savings below €15,000. This behaviour by the banks makes consumers loathe to insist on changes, as any benefits from getting a higher interest rate on their savings will be offset by having to pay charges.

Table C9.3 Comparison of different giro account offers

Product name	Bank	Debit interest (%)	Credit interest (%)	Annual costs (€)
Gehaltskonto Pauschalverrech-nung	Sparda-Bank Villach/Innsbruck	8.000	0.125	22.00
ModulKonto	Generali Bank AG	9.125	1.000	48.97

FrfolgsKonto	Bank Austria Creditanstalt AG	13.250	0.125	66.34
Privatkonto Plus	Kärntner Sparkasse AG	12.250	0.125	75.00
BKS Klassikonto Plus	BKS Bank AG	12.125	1.625	75.35
Hypo Inklusivkonto	Hypo Alpe-Adria-Bank AG	11.500	0.125	87.10
Hypo Inklusivkonto Plus	Hypo Alpe-Adria-Bank AG	11.500	0.125	97.10
ErfolgsKonto Plus	Bank Austria Creditanstalt AG	13.250	0.125	99.72
PLUS-Konto	Raiffeisenlandesbank Kärnten	10.750	0.125	124.52
ErfolgsKonto Premium	Bank Austria Creditanstalt AG	13.250	0.125	144.84
ErfolgsKonto Gold	Bank Austria Creditanstalt AG	13.250	0.250	169.56

Note: Results of a query at www.bankenrechner.at (a service representating of employee interests), 22 May 2008, 3.30pm, normal using intensity, with 240 transaction per month. All-inclusive prices.

Giro accounts For giro accounts (see Table 9.3), most banks offer a variety of different packages at inclusive rates. Depending upon the type of giro account (student, salary, pension account) and on the desired services, prices for the annual account range from €22–170; the credit interest rates are equally low at most banks. However, there are considerable differences in the charges for debit interests, which many consumers do not calculate in the beginning.

Table C9.4 compares charges for giro accounts in Austrian banks.

Table C9.4 Detailed comparison of the most and the least expensive giro account offer in Table C9.3

The account type 'Erfolgs-Konto Gold' at Bank Austria Creditanstalt AG contains the following banking services:	Salary account 'Sparda Gehaltskonto' at Sparda bank: zero fees for your giro account
• Account management (all bookings) • Set up, altering and deletion of standing orders	No account management fees • No booking fee, no quarterly fee

Table C9.4 continued	
The account type 'Erfolgs-Konto Gold' at Bank Austria Creditanstalt AG contains the following banking services:	**Salary account 'Sparda Gehaltskonto' at Sparda bank: zero fees for your giro account**
• Maestro Banking Card with cash card function and Quick function (electronic wallet) • VISA Classic Card with insurance coverage • Diners Club Gold or Golf Card, including enduring bonus • All self-service account statements • Heightened credit interest • Telephone banking • On-line banking • 24h service line • Individual shopping reserve • Finance check • Bank Austria ticketing • Reduced service charge for private financing	• No fees for standing orders • Free assignments (domestic/EU) • Free telephone banking (SPARDAfon) • Free Internet banking • Free home and office banking • (Telebanking without Internet access) Charge for the Maestro banking card with cash function, €22
Price per quarter €42.39	**Price per year:** €22

Loans Loans for housing are very common in Austria, as in the rest of Europe, but a loan is one of the most complex products for customers to evaluate as banks charge a variety of different fees. Besides the official loan tax of 0.8 per cent, which is the same for all banks, examples for other one-off charges include: handling fee (fluctuation range between €1,000 and €3,000), property notarization costs (€100–200), fee for registering the property in the land register (€40–100 + 1–3 per cent of the registered property amount) and account management fee (€13–30 per quarter). In order to facilitate the comparison among loan offers for consumers, banks are obliged to provide an effective interest rate, which includes all these fees. However, often banks make use of loss leaders that provide very advantageous conditions for the first few years but then – for the customer unexpectedly – raise prices. A further distortion factor is the lack of clarity of what provides the basis for the interest rate: most banks take the three-month Euribor as a basis, which is usually slightly higher than the one-month Euribor. The Euribor (see www.euribor.org for an explanation of this rate), plus a banking mark-up (ranging from 0.8 per cent to 3 per cent among banks and dependent upon the creditworthiness of borrowers) is the interest rate customers usually refer to when they talk about interest rates. The exact composition of basic Euribor interest rate and banking mark-up is often not recognized.

Satisfaction with pricing

These pricing practices, described for three products, suggest that Austrian banks may not appreciate the impact of charges on customer satisfaction. In marketing terms, the central role of price perceptions is well understood as an influence in customer satisfaction, on the likelihood of switching and recommendation to others (Varki and Colgate 2001, Keaveney 1995). Money-back guarantees, fixed prices and honest pricing (for example, giving the customers open, honest and complete information on products and complex fee structures and finding the best product for them) are some of the tools that aim at increasing satisfaction with pricing policy. However, the examples provided suggest that Austrian banks (and they may not be alone in this) may be more interested in making money through charges than the longer-term goal of customer satisfaction.

Two studies (Matzler *et al.* 2007, Matzler *et al.* 2006) have investigated pricing with particular reference to satisfaction in the Austrian banking market. The studies identified that satisfaction with pricing is a multidimensional construct, with five distinct dimensions as follows:

- *Price-quality ratio*: ratio or trade-off between quality of the service and monetary costs
- *Price fairness*: customer perception of whether the difference between the socially accepted price or another comparative party is reasonable, acceptable, or justifiable
- *Price transparency*: clear, comprehensive, current and effortless overview about a company's quoted prices
- *Price reliability*: fulfilment of raised price expectations and prevention of negative 'price shocks'; customer certainty that the price is favourable
- *Relative price*: price of the offer compared to that of competitor offers.

Over 400 customers of eight different Austrian banks were surveyed and their responses measured by means of a five-point Likert scale, where 1 represented high level of satisfaction/agreement and 5 a high level of dissatisfaction/disagreement.

The findings revealed that on all five price dimensions there is room for improvement on the part of the banks. The mean values for each dimension are given in Table C9.5. Relative price scores least well, suggesting that customers perceive that competitor offerings are priced more favourably, which may mean that they switch providers in the future.

Table C9.5 Mean values of price satisfaction across the dimensions of price satisfaction

	Price reliability	Price transparency	Relative price	Price–quality ratio	Price fairness	Price satisfaction
Mean score	2.1	2.2	2.7	2.3	2.4	2.24

Questions

1. What do you think might be possible reasons for the relatively poor results of Austrian banks on the five dimensions of price satisfaction?
2. What could be done to improve customers' perceptions of these five dimensions? Make concrete suggestions!
3. How do price satisfaction and each of the five dimensions relate to customer satisfaction and loyalty intentions?

References

Austrian National Bank, www.oenb.at

Keaveney, S. M. (1995) 'Customer Behavior in Services Industries: An Exploratory Study', *Journal of Marketing*, Vol. 59, April, pp. 71–82.

Matzler, K., Renzl, B. and Faullant, R. (2007) 'Dimensions of Price Satisfaction: A Replication and Extension', *International Journal of Bank Marketing*, Vol. 26, No. 6, pp. 394–405.

Matzler, K., Würtele, A. and Renzl, B. (2006) 'Dimensions of Price Satisfaction: A Study in the Retail Banking Industry', *International Journal of Bank Marketing*, Vol. 24, No. 4, pp. 216–31.

Varki, S. and Colgate, M. (2001) 'The Role of Price Perceptions in an Integrated Model of Behavioral Intentions', *Journal of Service Research*, Vol. 3, No. 2, pp. 232–40.

Case study written by Rita Faullant and Kurt Matzler.

10

Distributing financial services

Contents

Learning outcomes

At the end of this chapter, the reader will be able to:

- Understand the relationship between the channel of distribution and the financial services offering

- Appreciate the range and drivers of channels in the distribution of financial services

- Propose strategies for managing multiple channels in financial services distribution

- Articulate the key principles for successful multichannel marketing to retail and business markets

- Appreciate the marketing impact of remote channels on banking and customer satisfaction

Introduction

Traditionally, the bank branch has played a pivotal role in the distribution of financial services, not only for the retail consumer, but also, in many cases, for the business customer as well. New technology, changes in lifestyle, constraints on costs for banks and other providers have all contributed to the way that these services now reach customers and, indeed, form part of the service itself. This chapter considers how financial services are distributed and reviews the underlying changes that have supported the introduction and growth of new channels. The role of each channel will be described and discussed with reference to marketing theory and practice. The discussion will then move onto how financial institutions (FIs) manage the range of channels to satisfy their customers and yet contain their costs. FIs have changed their distribution strategies, offering direct services to their traditional channels through the phone and the Internet. Some supermarkets and retailers offer financial services, such as Marks & Spencer in the United Kingdom and Corte Inglés, the Spanish-based department store.

The impact of the Internet, and other forms of what we shall call remote banking, cannot be underestimated on the provision of financial services. Although the uptake or adoption of banking on-line has not been quite as widespread as FIs, especially retail banks, may have hoped, there is little doubt that many people have changed the way that they interact with their FI. This chapter considers first the situation regarding changes instigated by the providers themselves (supply side) and then distribution from the customer perspective (demand side). The issue of multiple channel distribution is considered subsequently.

Distribution

However, customers acquire their purchases, in the end it is more than possible that the purchases themselves have passed through a number of different hands before arriving at their intended final destination. In classical marketing texts, there can be as many as five players in the channel, where goods could, for example, be imported and then fed into a distribution chain via wholesalers. Services are, however, often the outcome of co-production between the consumer and the provider (Lovelock 2001), therefore channels are shorter and the emphasis may fall accordingly on where and how the service can be 'consumed' or, in financial services, accessed. Managers have to make decisions about when and how the service can be made available to the customer, the role of any intermediary in the delivery of the service and how any elements of tangibility can be conveyed to the customer (Palmer 2008).

Channel strategy

channel strategy: the overall approach that an FI adopts in how it interacts and delivers its offerings

In services marketing – unlike retail goods channels, for example – the offering or service is often produced simultaneously between the producer and the consumer, which is frequently referred to as inseparability (e.g., Lovelock 2001). An insurance product, for example, only becomes operational when the policy is bought and signed for by the purchaser. The channel may also feature an intermediary, but this principle of inseparability remains intact. In Figure 10.1, the interaction between the financial service itself and the channel through which it is offered is demonstrated. In remote channels, such as internet banking, the purchaser or consumer almost produces and consumes the offering themselves; for example, they make choices about which product is most suitable for their requirements, select method of payment, read and 'sign' agreements and choose the method of delivery.

Financial services, as discussed in previous chapters, share classical characteristics of services in general; of particular relevance here is that financial services do not take up physical space. The exception to that statement is of course cash, which not only takes up space but also requires continuous security, which is expensive. Many of the

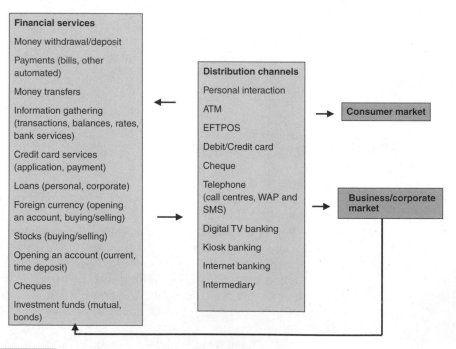

Figure 10.1   Distribution of financial services
Source: Adapted from Akinci *et al.* (2004).

considerations that apply to classical distribution marketing, such as logistics, do not apply to the distribution of financial services – for example, warehousing and transport. Nonetheless, many FIs have a presence on the high street, which is very costly.

Financial services vary in the extent to which they are co-produced; also known as inseparability, this refers to the interaction between the customer and the service provider. This notion of inseparability has been further developed by the service-dominant logic marketing research (Vargo and Lusch 2004), where it is maintained that value is co-created between the provider and the customer. Distribution channels in financial services offer potential for value co-creation – for example, Internet banking, where bills can be paid, investment accounts opened and insurance purchased at any time. FIs are generally pleased to shift the routine transactions over to lower-cost channels such as **ATMs**, where much of the burden of service production falls on the customer through the application of self-service technologies (SSTs). The limited scope for co-production means that financial services can be distributed in a number of different ways according to the requirements, capabilities and preferences of the customer and the resources and inclination of the provider. The downside of this trend is that there is a reduced opportunity for building personal relationships and hence cross-selling.

ATMs: automated telling machines more often referred to as 'holes in the wall', where customers can conduct transactions such as cash withdrawals, pay in money and check balances

Financial services are not generally perishable in the way that airline seats or holidays are, although if a customer misses an appointment with a financial adviser, there is a cost for the FI. Variability is a major consideration in designing channels for financial services, with service quality remaining a major concern for FIs owing to its role in customer satisfaction. A further consideration is the congruence, or fit, between the service being offered and the distribution method. Research was conducted into the perceived attributes of a service and associated information uncertainty. It was found that a consumer's preference for a particular distribution channel was secondary to perceptions about whether the channel is appropriate to the service that is being considered (Morrison and Roberts 1998). It was concluded that managers needed to build up consumer perceptions that new shopping channels are appropriate vehicles for delivering their services rather than trying to boost preference for the distribution method itself. For many customers, it is hard to distinguish between the service itself and the channel through which it is obtained; it is the benefits of the service rather than the service itself, which is important.

Adoption of channels

There is a number of other matters for the marketer to consider when planning distribution of financial services. A prime consideration is that the principal driver of any successful channel is customer readiness to use that channel. In a study of SST trialling, Meuter *et al.* (2005) found that the factors that influenced customer readiness to trial SSTs were clarity of role (knowing what they had to do), motivation (the benefits of using the technology) and their ability to use the technology. Customers who are currently satisfied with the branch service are also less likely to switch channels (Devlin and Yeung 2003), which presents FIs with something of a dilemma if they want to increase the uptake of non-branch channels. Customers using SSTs prefer personal control, time and cost savings, real-time information and evaluation, as well as free research and analysis tools (Ding *et al.* 2007) and the avoidance of personal contact. If customers become dissatisfied with levels of service within the branch, there is no guarantee that they will switch to another channel and stay with the bank; they may just change their bank. Some level of encouragement in the use of non-branch channels may be the only alternative. Readers of the financial pages of newspapers will be aware that there is evidence of differential pricing across channels, with generally the best savings rates available via Internet banking and the most attractive loans and insurance offers also available via remote channels. Most customers consume more than one financial service offering and each of these offerings may be consumed via different channels. Indeed, there is evidence to suggest that there is a complex interplay of product, channel etc. (Black *et al.* 2002). As argued earlier, consumers regard time and effort as resources, often in short supply, and they will choose how to 'spend' those resources according to a set of variables, which, as far as channel research is concerned, involves demographic variables and experience (Schoenbachler and Gordon 2002).

Although, as discussed above, there is scope for co-production in financial services, customers do make choices about the channel based on the type of service and the channel through which the consumer/customer chooses for that particular offering (Howcroft *et al.* 2003). There is additionally, as mentioned in Chapter 3, the proposition that some consumers are increasingly confident about financial services and, as such, are less dependent upon personal interaction with bank staff; this drives use of remote channels such as the phone and the Internet. The second important aspect to the distribution of financial services is the connection between what the customer is aiming to purchase and the channel that is used for the purchase or transaction. Customers will use different channels for different offerings and the rule seems to be the more risky the purchase, the more personal the interaction required for the purchase. Pensions, therefore, are more likely to be purchased from an intermediary, whose advice and impartiality weigh heavily in the consumer decision-making process.

However, what is convenient for the customer may be highly costly for the FI – for example, having a bank branch staffed for seven to eight hours, six days a week. The marketer is, therefore, faced with the tension between meeting the needs of their customers and yet ensuring that the costs of distribution are covered one way or another. Distribution provides little scope for generating revenue, but channels perform key functions as follows:

- Sale and offer of services
- Gathering of information for marketing, planning and improved customer service
- Marketing communications and branding
- Customer acquisition, relationship building

Financial services are generally distributed directly to the consumer/customer, unlike goods which can pass though a number of different stages in the channel; in many instances, the services are acquired from the provider that actually creates the offering (e.g., a personal loan). Intermediaries also figure in the distribution strategies of most financial service providers and have an established role as a conduit for selling the financial services on which the intermediary receives commission from the original provider. This system supports attempts to acquire customers, as the intermediary shares the costs of customer acquisition. However, when attempting to build customer relations, using an intermediary may be less effective as a battle for ownership of the customer between the supplier and intermediary may result (Fitzgibbon and White 2005). Whilst the intermediary or broker brings in new business, FIs have acknowledged that the relationship between the institution and customer is weaker (Farquhar and Panther 2007), with the implication that these customers may be harder to retain in the future. If the FIs are seeking to retain their customers, then they have to promote customer satisfaction and loyalty in circumstances where the intermediary currently 'owns the customer', but the establishment of a close partnership with the intermediary (Brown and Chin 2004) would reduce the potential for customer churn.

Branches

The major change that has occurred in banking distribution is not confined to the financial services themselves and their immediate competitive environment. Customers, users, consumers and all other players in consumption, whether in consumer or business markets, have become accustomed to conducting business, placing orders, gaining information, making decisions using a number of channels – among which the telephone and the Internet are perhaps the best known. The addition of virtual channels to the distribution mix has added to the cost structure of the banks, as consumers tend to avail themselves of a number of channels and conduct more transactions. As a consequence, the industry has been trying to migrate customers to the virtual channels, offering education and training in support (Harrison 2000). However, readiness on the part of customers to embrace new channels, of course, depends on a number of things, including understanding their role in the consumption of the service, their motivation and ability to use the service (Meuter *et al.* 2005). In spite of the efforts of banks to shift business away from branches, the branch has remained pivotal in the distribution mix of financial services, because it is where relationships between provider and customer are forged (Booz Allen Hamilton 2003). Banks also face the problem of servicing customers who are relatively low in value and high in transaction costs; if these customers can be successfully migrated to channels, which are consistent with their worth to the organization, savings can be achieved (Myers *et al.* 2005).

However, migration has proved problematic for the banks, not only from the perspective of customer satisfaction and corporate reputation, but also in an environment that is sensitized to social exclusion. Central to any distribution mix in financial services, the bank branch remains pivotal. Swedish research has suggested that although the number of branches may diminish, their role may be redefined as counselling and relationship-building venues (Yakhlef 2001). Transactions, which are costs to the FI, will play a lesser role and customers will be persuaded to use remote channels, such as ATMs or post. As part of managing the high costs of branches, FIs with significant presence on the high street moved towards a 'hub and spoke' strategy where a central branch provides the full range of services with outlets providing a reduced range of the most commonly required services, such as transactions. Customer requests for specialized services are, then, either passed from outlet to hub or customers are encouraged to use alternative channels, such as the phone or the Internet (Palmer 2008). There are significant advantages to this approach in terms of lowering costs through economies of scale, but the customer may experience a lower level of service and it also may affect the opportunity for cross-selling. The cost of the branch is sufficiently high for high street FIs to have made strenuous efforts to reduce the number of branches as part of lowering costs. This move has, however, prompted vigorous customer resistance and has slowed the rate of closures. NatWest, for example, has made a feature of its branch network in its marketing communications, providing mobile branches in rural areas (www.natwest.com/global/media/y2007). To remain economic, however, there is a need to encourage transactions to be managed by the cheaper channels (Booz Allen Hamilton 2003)

Many bank branches are housed in nineteenth- and early twentieth-century buildings, a situation which has tended to reinforce the image of the traditional banks in town centres in the United Kingdom and the rest of Europe. Over the last 25 years, there has been an extensive rolling programme of redesign and refurbishment to create a more relaxed and welcoming environment for customers. Decisions have also been made about the locations of branches, even though many have been in the same location for many years. The redesign has also been undertaken to facilitate selling in such a way that customers visiting the bank to conduct a transaction are invited to avail themselves of other services on offer which may be of interest. The traditional counter for transactions is now often tucked away in the corner of the branch so that customers and staff can interact more informally, allowing the flourishing of a relationship between the bank and its customers. The resemblance between many bank branches and the shops that flank them is not coincidental as they all have an interest in generating revenue. The cost of refurbishing is very high, so new designs have to be carefully evaluated for their impact on customers. Figure 10.2 provides an overview of how the customer perspective should be incorporated into the design of an FI retail branch.

This very detailed model links the environment of the branch to customer perceptions of design and service quality, their affective responses and outcomes of their behaviour. It describes the sequence involved in environmental-behaviour interaction, from perceptions through to emotional response and behavioural outcome. The left-hand side of the

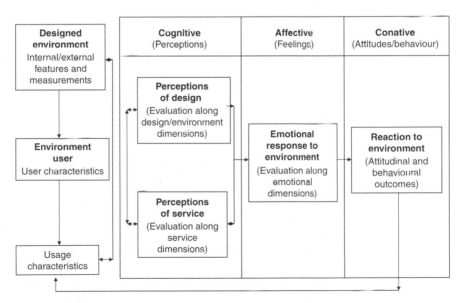

Figure 10.2   Branch environment-response model
Source: Adapted from Greenland and McGoldrick (2005).

model refers to the interaction between the environment and the user, which includes those who also work in the branch. The remainder of the model then refers to familiar concepts in consumer behaviour regarding perceptions (cognitive), emotional response (affective) and then attitudes and behaviour (conative). The value of this model is to embed branch design in understanding of customer behaviour (demand style) rather than a supply-driven model, with a greater chance, therefore, of favourable reception on the part of users – that is staff and customers. This research also found that most modern styles of branch design have a favourable impact on consumer responses to the environment. The absence of bandit screens facilitates the development of customer/staff relationships and tends to allow customers to feel more in control (Greenland and McGoldrick 2005). The branch is valuable in providing tangible evidence to the service, allowing customers to visualize the brand and to provide additional marketing communications. It has been believed widely that the solidity of the branch provides a signal to the customer of the security of the bank in looking after their money and their financial needs.

Financial services intermediary

As illustrated at the beginning of the chapter, the intermediary plays an important role in the distribution of financial services, presenting advantages both to the provider and the customer. As suggested above, services are co-produced and value co-created (Vargo and Lusch 2004), but the intermediary role in services raises a number of issues (Palmer 2008) as follows:

- Services cannot be owned, therefore it is difficult to talk about service ownership
- Pure services are intangible and perishable, therefore stocks cannot exist
- The inseparability of most services should logically require an intermediary to become a co-producer of the service.

Financial services, although intangible, are not perishable and to a certain extent the intermediary acts as a co-producer by offering advice or a more convenient way of accessing a particular service for a financial services consumer. Owing to high levels of perceived risk with many financial services, intermediaries may be in a strong position to be able to offer impartial advice in more congenial surroundings than a bank branch. Insurance products are often sold by intermediaries as well as investment products.

Aggressive selling has taken place in the past in financial services, with the principals (i.e., the banks and insurance companies) pushing their sales down the channel. Traditionally, financial services advisers (FSAs) provide financial services, often home loans and insurance products supplied by existing companies, with a level of advice. Intermediaries (frequently FSAs) are tightly regulated in the United Kingdom by the Financial Services Authority (fsa.org.uk) regarding the advice that they give and the commission that they receive from the company whose products they are selling. They can be 'tied' to a particular provider or be independent, but the customer must be made fully aware of the status of any intermediary and the commission paid by the original provider of the product. The decision about whether to use an intermediary on the part of a financial services provider is essentially one of control and is dependent upon current strategy and, perhaps in some cases, past strategy within the organization itself. Intermediaries provide an efficient way of distributing the providers' services to customers in that the intermediary bears all the operational costs, such as running an office and staff, her own time, any advertising costs etc. The provider pays commission on the 'sale' of the service, which **independent financial advisers (IFAs)** now have to make clear to their customers. The disadvantage for the provider is the lack of control in the service experience and, ultimately, in any relationship that may be initiated and future business. Accordingly, there is some diversity in financial services provider strategies *vis à vis* intermediaries (Farquhar and Panther 2007). Intermediaries are a valuable means of increasing the size of an FI as Exhibit 10.1 shows.

independent financial advisers (IFAs): an important channel in the delivery of financial services to customers (see www.unbiased.co.uk)

EXHIBIT 10.1

BNP's entry into the United Kingdom

European financial group and bank BNP Paribas has revealed its intention to move into the UK market by releasing a range of products aimed at British independent financial advisers. BNP has provided a new web portal for IFAs (ifa.bnpparibas.co.uk), which is aimed at providing easier access to the group's financial services products. In addition, the group will be pulling together its brands in the United Kingdom as part of the drive, as well as providing other new services over the course of the year. According to BNP's UK head of territory, Ludovic de Montille, IFAs will be attracted to the company because the group can be a strong partner in today's uncertain markets. BNP Paribas has developed a range of specialized solutions tailored for UK financial advisers, which it will expand over the coming years. The group is making a strategic commitment to this market as the first step on its growth path. The bank is one of the three strongest in the world; it is undertaking an integration programme across its UK brands and plans to roll out a broad range of IFA-focused services over the coming year. It also hopes to expand its range of investment funds and structured products and offer more white-label and bespoke solutions for IFAs in the near future.

Compiled by the authors from www.bnpparibas.com, www.trustnet.com.

Banks are also aiming to increase their sales by working with supermarkets. Supermarkets offer the financial services of the FI to their customers under their own brand; the benefits to both parties are demonstrated in Exhibit 10.2.

EXHIBIT 10.2

Sainsbury's Bank

Sainsbury's was the first major British supermarket to open a bank, commencing trading in February 1997 in a joint venture with HBOS (now taken over by Lloyds TSB). Sainsbury's Bank provides a range of products, including insurance, credit cards, savings and loans, that are competitively priced, easy to understand and to apply for. Customers can manage their accounts on-line and can make savings deposits in-store, benefiting from the longer opening hours and parking available at the supermarket. Sainsbury's Bank now has almost 1.5 million customers with deposits in excess of £2 billion. The bank has further access to over 16 million customer shopping visits per week. It receives over 5 million customer calls to its call centres every year; and has over 1 million website visits every month. Sainsbury's are not financial experts, which is why the banking arm is only 55 per cent owned by the supermarket with the other 45 per cent is owned by the FI. Customers can gain reward points through the Nectar scheme on the purchase of financial products from Sainsbury's Bank. Sainsbury's Bank combines shopping with personal finance, allowing it to offer a range of competitively priced products. The credit crunch and the loss of confidence in high-street brands may offer supermarket banks the opportunity to increase market share, but this may be dependent upon the strength of the partner FI post-crunch.

Compiled by the authors from www.bank.org.uk and www.sainsburys.co.uk.

Supermarkets add a new and potentially very exciting dimension to the sale of financial services, tending to bracket these services with the offerings more commonly sold in supermarkets, where habit and price advantages dominate consumer decision-making. Financial services are undergoing a process of demystification in which consumers are increasingly predisposed to purchase financial services such as insurance, credit cards and even mortgages. Supermarkets are using their expertise in retailing to leverage brand advantages (e.g., Marks & Spencer), their segmentation expertise and footfall.

Price comparison information

The growing availability of financial services has contributed to the commoditization or lack of differentiation between financial offerings. Consumers are not only prepared to purchase financial services or products from supermarkets, but also they are equally disposed to purchase them on-line using price comparison websites, for example uSwitch and moneysupermarket.com. These sites apparently offer a number of benefits to consumers, although most of them have commercial arrangements with the companies they feature. Some involve a commission fee payable when someone buys through the site, others receive a click-through payment every time a customer clicks from a price comparison site through to a company's own website.

Monthly hits for two popular sites are approximately as follows: moneysupermarket.com – 4.046 million and confused.com – 1.026 million (www.bbc.co.uk). It is therefore important for FIs to manage to appear on the first results page that a consumer accesses on a price comparison site. Other FIs have adopted a completely different approach; for example, UK insurance provider Direct Line makes it clear through its marketing messages that it is not available via these websites.

Remote banking

FIs have quickly realized the advantages of using remote (non-physical) channels; they all offer cost reductions, making them cheaper to run than the traditional high-street branch, which incurs high running and staffing costs. The logic of persuading retail customers to shift from the expensive branch to the less costly remote channels appeared to be very sound to the cost-conscious providers. Shifting customers away from the branch would allow considerable savings to the providers, which could either be passed back to the customers in higher rates of interest on cheque accounts or allow them to increase their profits. Hughes (2006) has remarked upon the carrot and stick approach of encouraging customers to use low-cost channels through offering high interest rates or discouraging high-cost channel use by closing branches. Financial service providers are aware that there is some tension between the pursuit of 'migrating' customers to lower-cost channels and building relationships (Farquhar and Panther 2007).

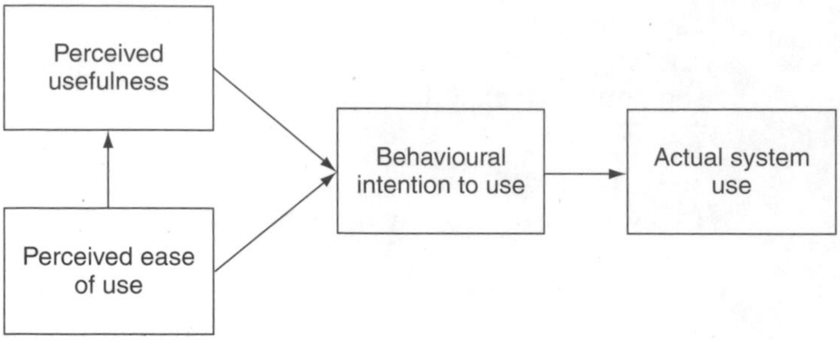

Figure 10.3 Technology acceptance model (TAM)
Source: Davis (1989), Venkatesh *et al.* (2003).

Although many of the new channels in financial services have been introduced by the providers themselves, mainly in order to lower costs, there have been changes in consumer lifestyles and business practices, such as globalization, that have driven customer uptake of these channels. However, the success of remote channels is dependent upon customer acceptance, in particular of new technology. This topic has been the subject of research over several years and one of the dominant models is the technology acceptance model (TAM) which has been widely used and modified to try to explore how consumers interact with technology (Davis 1989).

The TAM model (Figure 10.3) asserts that consumers are more likely to adopt or accept technology if they perceive it to be useful and easy to use. The model has been empirically tested and extended since its inception and has been used extensively to explore the acceptance of technology in remote banking. In one investigation into **mobile banking** using mobile devices, the model was expanded to deal with specific issues that are considered important to the application of the model with reference to banking (Luarn and Lin 2005). The researchers found that trust was a key element in consumer behaviour in banking, so a trust-based construct of 'perceived credibility' was identified; two further resource-based constructs of 'perceived self-efficacy' and 'perceived financial cost' emerged in the research (Luarn and Lin, 2005). This extension to the original TAM model demonstrated that these new dimensions apply to technology in the adoption of mobile banking technology.

mobile banking:
financial transactions that can be conducted via mobile devices

Automated telling machines (ATMs)

The 'hole in the wall' has been an established distribution channel in financial services since the 1980s, and has succeeded in shifting many routine transactions away from staff in branches to automatic transaction.

The advent of ATMs provided consumers with a service accessible at all hours and in a variety of locations. The location of ATMs is dependent on where, when and how consumers want access to their cash, pay in money, have information to their accounts and other routine enquiries or transactions, although the vast majority are located in shopping centres. The role of the ATM in the lifestyle of consumers is illustrated in the following exhibit, which provides information about the network behind many ATMs.

EXHIBIT 10.3

LINK network

LINK is the United Kingdom's national cash machine (ATM) interchange network and the busiest ATM transaction network in the world. At peak times, the LINK switch processes almost 1 million transactions per hour. There are nearly 130 million LINK-enabled cards in circulation from 38 card issuing financial institutions. Over 61,000 ATMs are connected to the LINK network, which is effectively every ATM in the United Kingdom. Cash machines are by far the most popular channel for cash withdrawal in the United Kingdom, used by millions of consumers every week. The number of ATMs connected to the LINK network, transaction volumes and the value of cash withdrawn from ATMs have all grown rapidly since the launch of the network in 1986 and this is expected to continue. The figures for 25 May 2007 indicate the popularity of ATMs; in spite of the poor weather forecast for that bank holiday weekend, the Friday before the weekend was the busiest day of the year for LINK cash machines. A record £513 million was withdrawn in over 7,345,000 withdrawal transactions. At the lunchtime peak of 1.04pm on the Friday, the LINK network was processing 312 transactions each second! The average cash withdrawal was £69.84. The busiest region was London, with over £79 million withdrawn in over a million transactions. This high number of withdrawals was explained by end of the month payment of salaries, preparing for the bank holiday, whether for shopping, entertainment or day trips.

Compiled by the authors from information on www.link.co.uk.

Most transactions using ATMs are free to customers, but it has been predicted that there may be charges at some stage in the future as the larger banks seek to retrieve some of the costs of running free banking. The credit crunch may have delayed any plans for charging in the immediate future as the financial services industry seeks to establish some credibility and consumer confidence in the sector. Equally, there seems to be evidence that premium accounts have been promoted heavily (for example, Alliance & Leicester). However, ATMs are not accessible to everyone and a recent report from the Minister for Rural Affairs in the United Kingdom (January 2008) observed that customers living in the countryside were not well provided for by ATMs. The costs of maintaining ATMs may not always be appreciated by consumers; equally, banks may not fully understand that customers have grown to expect access to basic financial services at all times.

Telephone

Using the telephone in banking is not a new phenomenon; indeed, the first all-telephone bank in the United Kingdom, First Direct, was established in 1985 (www.firstdirect.com) and the first insurance company to abandon traditional channels was Direct Line in 1989, a division of the Royal Bank of Scotland. One of the changes that enabled the adoption of the telephone is the willingness of customers to use the phone in spite of the nature of financial services. The model that First Direct developed has received much attention and it is often cited by managers in competing banks with a degree of reluctant admiration for its strong brand, its high levels of service quality and its affluent customers. Staff are empowered to offer a high degree of personalization and, of course, the bank is 'open' 24 hours a day, seven days a week.

EXHIBIT 10.4

First Direct: key facts and figures

First Direct has 1.2 million customers

- 880,000 of them use Internet banking; 360,000 customers use SMS text message banking
- First Direct sends around 2.6 million text messages to customers every month
- First Direct employs 3,500 people in 3,000 full-time equivalent (FTE) roles at two sites, in Leeds and Hamilton (near Glasgow)
- 46 per cent of First Direct's sales are via e-channels
- More than one in three of First Direct's customers join because of personal recommendation
- Over 80 per cent of customer contact with First Direct is electronic
- First Direct handles around 200,000 telephone calls every week
- First Direct takes over 13,000 calls a day outside working hours
- First Direct takes over 1,400 calls a day from abroad
- First Direct has been in profit every year since 1995

Compiled by the authors from information available on www.firstdirect.com.

A range of financial services is available through using the telephone with the added benefit to the provider of much lower costs. The rise of the call centre, whether based in the United Kingdom or abroad, which ensures longer hours available for customers to contact their bank has proved in the past very attractive to many retail customers as it matches their lifestyles. The phone has been a useful halfway house on the route to the adoption of other remote forms of banking, leading ultimately to the Internet and mobile. Why has the telephone proved so popular? Changing lifestyles, confidence with making routine transactions, levels of service that met the needs of customers have all contributed to the acceptance of phone banking. Nonetheless, expectations of telephone provision have been shaped by experience, in that peak times are avoided, waiting to be put through expected and repeated explanations of 'the problem' anticipated. Call centres do allow FIs to lower costs, but the evidence is that some call centres are insufficiently resourced, resulting in high levels of customer dissatisfaction. Callers may often be transferred from one representative to another, repeating at each transfer their query or request. Some FIs have also been tempted to locate their call centres abroad to lower costs, which have not proved popular with all customers as they have encountered language difficulties.

The speed and convenience of the telephone allows customers to make purchases and access the range of services that their FI provides. Both First Direct and Direct Line based their entire approach on recognition that certain segments of customers were ready and willing to use the phone for conducting either their banking transactions or their insurance purchases/renewals, or both, by phone. The proposition of First Direct and other virtual or Internet-only banks such as Smile and Cahoot in the United Kingdom (there are other European on-line-only banks) is that they are branchless and therefore do not have a physical presence on the high street.

Mobile banking

The telephone, or at least the landline, is a step away from the branch but it is still a restriction in terms of mobility in that customers are restricted to some degree. Developments in distribution tend now towards mobile consumption of financial services and this shift towards use of mobile technology including wireless laptops, PDAs and mobile phones, but take-up or adoption of mobile technology has not been as widespread as predicted. A key factor that was suggested in the research conducted by Luarn and Lin (2005) was the resource issue for the consumer in adopting mobile banking. Laukkanen and Lauronen (2005) conducted a qualitative study that increased understanding of customer-perceived value and value creation on the basis of attributes of mobile services and customer-perceived disadvantages of mobile phones in the electronic banking context. The advance of any form of technology-based service – banking in particular – is based on willingness to use the 'channel', based on the perceived costs to the user, including whether the service delivered this way is of value to them. Value can be very simply seen as 'costs +/– benefits = value' from the perspective of the consumer and the consumer will perceive costs in a very individual way. The industry believes that mobile banking offers many opportunities to providers in their efforts to build relationships, if this is carried out in a way that is in tune with the needs of the customer. Once more, the advantages of being able to conduct transactions and even make purchases from any location in the world are benefits that an increasingly mobile marketplace may favour.

Internet

Not only do customers use the Internet for straightforward banking transactions, they are increasingly disposed also to use the Internet to purchase financial services such as car and travel insurance and share dealing. In the EU27 (the 27 states in the European Union) in 2008, nearly 30 per cent of individuals used Internet banking, with 60 per cent of households having Internet access, compared with 54 per cent during the first quarter of 2007; 48 per cent had a broadband Internet connection, compared with 42 per cent in 2007. Household Internet access ranged from 25 per cent in Bulgaria to 86 per cent in the Netherlands. In 2008, the proportion of households with Internet access was three-quarters or more – in the Netherlands (86 per cent), Sweden (84 per cent), Denmark (82 per cent), Luxembourg (80 per cent) and Germany (75 per cent). The lowest levels were registered in Bulgaria (25 per cent), Romania (30 per cent) and Greece (31 per cent). The proportion of households with a broadband connection in 2008 was also highest in the Netherlands and Denmark (both 74 per cent) and Sweden (71 per cent).

The suitability of the Internet for financial services consumption is that it removes any requirement for physical distribution and it provides access 24/7, often from the consumer's house or business premises. Claims about the impact of the Internet have varied wildly from a paradigm change to a new business model or the addition of a new distribution channel (Stewart 2002). It is, however, the customer's view of the impact of the Internet and the context that has the most importance for the marketer. No matter the potential that the Internet has for the provider, the extent to which it can be used will be constrained by its adoption by the customer, as discussed above with reference to the research based on TAM. Research into the bricks and mortar concept of banking suggests that two of the most important factors in the adoption of e-banking are consumer trust and consumer socio-demographic traits (Flavián *et al.* 2006) – for example, profession and age. Interestingly, though, research has indicated that Internet adoption is influenced by customer perceptions of the bank branch; the greater the satisfaction with the branch, the greater the likelihood that on-line services will be adopted (Montoya-Weiss *et al.* 2003). Furthermore, perhaps unsurprisingly, perceptions of security risk have significant negative effects on on-line channel use in financial services. The Internet provides significant benefits to small businesses, allowing owners to access their bank at times to suit them. According to the British Banking Association, 43 per cent of small businesses bank on-line and this is a figure could continue to grow. However, FIs are not necessarily meeting their side of the bargain. Internet banking lowers their costs significantly but the exhibit below suggests that FIs are not resourcing Internet banking sufficiently.

EXHIBIT 10.5

All is not well with Internet banking

In spite of the benefits of Internet banking, a study of 52 leading European financial services companies found that UK banks and building societies often provided poor levels of on-line customer service. The study revealed significant shortcomings in the on-line customer service experience, with UK FIs offering only limited web self-service options and failing to respond to e-mail queries. Researchers tested the quality of on-line customer service offered by each FI by attempting to find the answer to a typical customer query through the available on-line channels. Simple queries were used, such as 'What savings accounts do you offer? What are the interest rates?' or 'How do you ensure that the Internet banking you provide is secure?'. In the United Kingdom, 53 per cent of financial institutions failed to correctly answer a simple enquiry through any on-line channel, either providing an incorrect answer or no answer at all. Meanwhile 35 per cent of those surveyed did not provide a contact e-mail address on their website and 18 per cent did not respond to an e-mail enquiry at all. The mystery shopping exercise also reveals that more work needs to be done to provide channels that protect modern consumers; with only 29 per cent of banks surveyed providing encrypted and secure communication channels and over two-thirds providing non-encrypted communication, leaving consumers vulnerable to on-line theft.

Compiled by the authors from information provided by www.InternetRetailing.net.

A barrier to banking on-line remains concerns about security; other potential Internet users are content with their existing channels and see little reason to change. As a result, uptake of the Internet for banking is beginning to stall (Forrester Research 2005). In the opinion of the 38 per cent of people in the United Kingdom who bank on-line, the Internet is a very secure and convenient way to access their bank's services. However, banksafeonline.org.uk remind Internet users that it pays to be on the lookout for scammers who try to gain access to bank accounts, usually by attempting to persuade Internet users to hand over security information such as user names, passwords and memorable information (www.banksafonline.org.uk).

Multichannel banking

Multichannel banking: the provision of financial services via a number of different channels; the customers choose such channels they wish dependent in the service/time, etc. access

Banking, and retailing more generally, has witnessed an explosion in the number of channels through which services and goods are being made available to customers. The challenge for FIs is not managing a long vertical chain from supplier to customer but managing the breadth of channels that customers use for their financial services. Since the aim of any FI is to have customers purchase as many of their services as possible, it is likely that customers will use a number of different channels for their banking needs. A business customer, for example, may have a personal adviser whom she contacts via the telephone early in the morning, she may then also have a personal account with the same bank, which she uses either during a brief break in the day or via the Internet late in the evening, and via her personal digital assistant (PDA) she receives updates on her personal and business account. FIs have been surprised to note that customers do not choose just to use one channel and are, in fact, increasingly disposed to use a range of channels. **Multichannel banking** has been available for some time. Devlin (1995) recognized that distribution channels offer providers a means of catering to a number of segments. In this case, an FI would use a mix of distribution rather than a product mix to achieve some level of differentiation. The larger FIs offer multiple channels, which are becoming almost a necessary condition for operating in the financial services environment.

Managing multiple channels

It seemed to be entirely logical that FIs should try to persuade their customers to use the lower-cost remote channels, especially the Internet which has the lowest costs of all. Indeed, it has been suggested that the provider can influence behaviour regarding choice of product and channel (Black *et al.* 2002) by managing the reputation of the organization, including brand image, size and longevity, as well as the range of channels that the organization makes available to its customers. The challenge for the providers is integrating the channels *across* the organization, whereas more traditional distribution is often concerned with managing the different stages in a vertical channel. Kumar and Reinartz (2006) have observed that people have changed their channel habits as a response to the explosion in channels as they derive different benefits from the various channels. They go on to develop the idea of multiple channels within the strategy of customer relationship management (CRM), as shown in Table 10.1.

As Table 10.1 demonstrates, the increase or proliferation of channels can enable companies and FIs with a mixture of benefits and tests. In these circumstances, a clearly articulated strategy throughout the organization, with carefully considered objectives that minimize opportunities for conflict, helps to reduce the barriers to success. Looking at the first line in the table, multiple channels do allow for access to larger numbers of customers – for example, through intermediaries or smaller organizations, such as UK building societies reaching out to new geographic areas. But are new customers necessarily the best way to grow the business?

Table 10.1 Emerging channel environment in financial services

Opportunities	Challenges
Access to a larger number of customers	IT systems must be re-engineered each time a channel is introduced
Multichannel habits of customers. Increasing numbers of customers derive different benefits over different channels	Message dissonance occurs over different channels
Direct and customized interaction with customers over different channels. Nurtures differentiated customer relationships	Multichannel conversation with the consumers – interchannel co-ordination problems, problems in managing integrated marketing communications, threatening relationships
Customers self-select into channels – individualization and segmentation	Channel conflict – multichannel interaction with consumers can lead to conflict of interest among the competing channels for the same share of customer contact or service
Channel specialization, each performing a different channel function, can mitigate channel conflict	Possible rise in consumer expectation of service and/or quality

Source: Adapted from Kumar and Weinartz (2006).

The costs of introducing new channels have to be set against the revenue that new customers generate for the organization. Readers of the book will no doubt be familiar with uncoordinated information systems where companies are unable to share information across channels, thus requiring customers to repeat information several times. The integration of the information systems that link the various channels requires significant ongoing investment to meet customer expectation and competitor levels of integration. A further challenge is to manage the conflict that can arise for the share of the customer. Farquhar and Panther (2007) found that branch staff were unhappy about losing commission on sales to telephone and Internet channels. In another institution, managers of channels were competing among themselves to achieve the best performance for their channel, which, overall, was undermining company performance. To address this conflict, Kumar and Reinartz (2006) note that a system of 'coopetition' is emerging where a balance is achieved in competing for the customer share of wallet and yet managing the relationship. The message to draw from the interesting proliferation of channels is that, ultimately, success is dependent upon the strategy that underpins the expansion. However, the one essential part of the equation is the 'preparedness' of the customer to use these remote channels.

Consumers and multiple channels

The background to the consumer in the multichannel environment, as suggested by Baker (2003), lies with the shift from a production-driven to a consumer-led economy leading in turn to the rise of the 'new consumer', who seeks new experiences (Stuart-Menteth *et al.* 2006). Their research suggests that experience consistency, although difficult to define, is an important aspect for the customer. Lee's (2002) research into customer preferences found considerable variation in customer preference for particular channels of delivery across the types of financial product. Credit cards, for example, were often purchased through direct means, but mortgages were usually obtained face-to-face. The research into channel usage (Black *et al.* 2002, Thornton and White 2001, Wan *et al.* 2005) has indicated the importance of grouping customers, whether by demographics or other variables such as lifestyle. Self-service channels have higher current and future usage rates amongst those customers who have favourable attitudes towards convenience, change, technology and feel knowledgeable about methods of accessing their money (Thornton and White 2001). Customers who prefer service and require reassurance (Wan *et al.* 2005) prefer face-to-face interaction. Studies (e.g., Farquhar and Panther 2007, Forrester Research 2005) have shown that 'better' customers use remote channels, with less valuable and older customers generally ignoring SSTs.

The power of the customer in any transaction or relationship cannot be ignored; customers will not restrict themselves to their current channels, preferring to channel surf (Nunes and Cespedes 2003). These writers prefer to describe channels as pathways and warn against trying to fetter customers to a particular channel or pathway. They urge companies never to get between customers and their preferred channel. Montoya-Weiss *et al.* (2003) find that multichannel service evaluations have complementary effects on customers' overall satisfaction with the service provider; both on-line and branch service quality perceptions have positive effects on overall satisfaction with the financial service provider. However, alternative channel service quality perceptions have competitive affects on customers' use of the on-line channel; branch service quality perceptions have a negative effect on on-line channel use. Multiple channels potentially broaden the customer's exposure and access to the service provider's offering.

Summary

- FIs now use a range of distribution channels, from the branch to the Internet, but the way in which the customer accesses it is part of the service itself.
- Customers will use different channels for different financial services, often based on what they consider to be convenient. Channel adoption depends in a range of variables that may include convenience, perceived usefulness or perceived ease of use. Multichannel banking is concerned with understanding and managing customer interactions across a range of channels.
- Purchases of financial services equally take place through diverse channels, either owned by the provider or via an intermediary. As the distribution of financial services becomes increasingly remote, providers face the challenge of building relationships that are based less on the personal interaction that occurs in the branch. Supermarkets are well poised to increase their status in personal financial services post-credit crunch.
- Earlier haste to migrate customers to cheaper channels has given way to promotional activities that feature phone numbers of local branches and call centres in the customers' own country. Indeed, the role of the branch is being redefined, although financial service providers may choose alternative approaches to how the branch 'fits' in a multichannel environment. Crime, or the perceived level of crime, inhibits the penetration of alternative channels in the United Kingdom.

- Service quality remains as important as ever in managing channels and distribution. Remote channels may not be adequately resourced by FIs, with e-mails often unanswered.

Exercises

1. Visit the local branch of an FI. Make an evaluation of its design, based on Figure 10.2, regarding the way the design has addressed the consumer's cognitive, affective and conative dimensions.
2. Investigate how friends and family use their mobile phone for banking purposes. What do they find appealing about the service offered and is there anything that they dislike?
3. Looking at Figure 10.2, what behaviours do FIs seek to elicit from their customers in a retail branch? How can the branch environment encourage appropriate staff behaviours?
4. Using the TAM model (Figure 10.3), develop a set of questions (no more than 12) that might uncover customer responses to adopting Internet banking.

References

Akinci, S., Aksoy, S. and Atilgan, E. (2004) 'Adoption of Internet Banking Among Sophisticated Customer Segments in an Advanced Developing Country", *International Journal of Bank Marketing*, Vol. 22, No. 2/3, pp. 212–32.

Baker, S. (2003) *New Consumer Marketing: Managing a Living Demand System*, Chichester, Wiley.

Black, N., Lockett, A., Ennew, C., Winkelhofer, H. and McKechnie, S. (2002) 'Modelling Consumer Choice of Distribution Channels: An Illustration from Financial Services', *International Journal of Bank Marketing*, Vol. 20, No. 4, pp. 161–73.

Booz Allen Hamilton (2003) *Implementing the Customer-Centric Bank: The Rebirth of the Forgotten Branch*, www.boozallen.com, accessed 6 September 2005.

Brown, S. and Chin, W. (2004) 'Satisfying and Retaining Customers Through Independent Service Representatives', *Decision Sciences*, Vol. 35, No. 3, pp. 527–50.

Davis, F. D. (1989) 'Perceived Usefulness, Perceived Ease of Use, and User Acceptance of Information Technology', *MIS Quarterly*, Vol. 13, No. 3, pp. 319–39.

Devlin, J. (1995) 'Technology and Innovation in Retail Banking Distribution', *International Journal of Bank Marketing*, Vol. 13, No. 4, pp. 19–25.

Devlin, J. and Yeung, M. (2003) 'Insights into Customer Motivations for Switching to Internet Banking', *International Review of Retail, Distribution and Consumer Research*, Vol. 13, No. 4, pp. 375–92.

Ding, X., Verma, R. and Iqbal, Z. (2007) 'Self-service Technology and Online Financial Service Choice', *International Journal of Service Industries Management*, Vol. 18, No. 3, pp. 246–68.

Eurostat (2008), news release, December.

Farquhar, J. and Panther, T (2007) 'The More the Merrier? An Exploratory Study into Managing Channels in UK Retail Financial Services', *International Review of Retail, Distribution and Consumer Research*, Vol. 17, No. 1, pp. 1–14.

Fitzgibbon, C. and White, L. (2005) 'The Role of Attitudinal Loyalty in the Development of Customer Relationship Management Strategy within Service Firms', *Journal of Financial Services Marketing*, Vol. 9, No. 3, pp. 214–30.

Flavian, C., Guinalíu, M. and Torres, E. (2006) 'How Bricks-and-mortar Attributes Affect On-line Banking Adoption', *International Journal of Bank Marketing*, Vol. 24, No. 6, pp. 406–23.

Forrester Research (2005), 'How UK Consumers Use Banking Channels', Cambridge, MA, Forrester Research.

Greenland, S. and McGoldrick, P. (2005) 'Evaluating the Design of Retail Financial Environments', *International Journal of Bank Marketing*, Vol. 23, No. 2, pp. 132–52.

Harrison, T. (2000) *Financial Services Marketing*, Harlow, FT Prentice Hall.

Howcroft, J., Hewer, P. and Durkin, M. (2003) 'Banker-Customer Interactions in Financial Services', *Journal of Marketing Management*, Vol. 19, pp. 1001–20.

Hughes, T. (2006) 'New Channels/Old Channels: Customer Management and Multi-channels', *European Journal of Marketing*, Vol. 40, No. 1/2, pp. 113–29.

internetretailing.net, accessed 12 December 2008.

Kumar, V. and Reinartz, W. (2006) *Customer Relationship Management: A Databased Approach*, Hoboken, NJ, John Wiley.

Laukkanen, T. and Lauronen, J. (2005) 'Consumer Value Creation in Mobile Banking Services', *International Journal of Mobile Communications*, Vol. 3, No. 4, pp. 325–38.

Lee, J. (2002) 'A Key to Marketing Financial Services: The Right Mix of Products, Services, Channels and Customers', *Journal of Services Marketing*, Vol. 16, No. 3, pp. 238–58.

Lovelock, C. (2001), *Services Marketing: People, Technology, Strategy*, 4th edn, Upper Saddle River, Prentice Hall.

Luarn, P. and Lin, H.-H. (2005) 'Toward an Understanding of the Behavioral Intention to use Mobile Banking', *Computers in Human Behavior*, Vol. 21, No. 6, pp. 873–91.

Meuter, M., Bitner, M.-J., Ostrom, A. and Brown, S. (2005) 'Choosing Among Alternative Service Delivery Modes: An Investigation of Customer Trial of Self-Service Technologies', *Journal of Marketing*, Vol. 69, April, pp. 61–83.

Montoya-Weiss, M., Voss, G. and Grewal, D. (2003) 'Determinants of Online Channel Use and Overall Satisfaction With a Relational Multi-channel Service Provider', *Journal of the Academy of Marketing Science*, Vol. 31, No. 4, pp. 448–58.

Morrison, P. and Roberts, J. (1998) 'Matching Electronic Distribution Channels to Product Characteristics: The Role of Congruence in Consideration Set Formation', *Journal of Business Research*, Vol. 41, No. 3, pp. 223–9.

Nunes, P. and Cespedes, F. (2003) 'The Customer Has Escaped', *Harvard Business Review*, November, pp. 96–105.

Palmer, A. (2008) *Principles of Services Marketing*, 4th edn, London, McGraw Hill.

Schoenbachler, D. and Gordon, G. (2002) 'Multi-channel Shopping: Understanding What Drives Consumer Choice', *Journal of Consumer Marketing*, Vol. 19, No. 1, pp. 42–53.

Stewart, K, (2002) call for papers on a special issue on Internet banking, *International Journal of Bank Marketing*, www.emeraldinsight.com/ijbm/call.htm

Stuart-Menteth, H., Wilson, H. and Baker, S. (2006) 'Escaping the Channel Silo: Researching the New Consumer', *International Journal of Market Research*, Vol. 48, No. 4, pp. 415–37.

Management Review, Autumn, pp. 75–88.

Thornton, J. and White, L. (2001) 'Customer Orientation and Usage of Financial Distribution Channels', *Journal of Services Marketing*, Vol. 15, No. 3, pp. 168–85.

Vargo, S. and Lusch, R. (2004) 'Evolving to a New Dominant Logic for Marketing', *Journal of Marketing*, Vol. 68, January, pp. 1–17.

Venkatesh, V., Morris, M. G., Davis, G. B. and Davis, F. D. (2003) 'User Acceptance of Information Technology: Toward a Unified View', *MIS Quarterly*, Vol. 27, No. 3, pp. 425–78.

Wan, W., Luk, C.-L. and Chow, C. (2005) 'Customers' Adoption of Banking Channels in Hong Kong', *International Journal of Bank Marketing*, Vol. 23, No. 3, pp. 255–72.

Yakhlef, A. (2001) 'Does the Internet Compete with Bricks-and-mortar Bank Branches?', *International Journal of Retail & Distribution Management*, Vol. 29, No. 6, pp. 272–81.

Further reading

www.banksafeonline.org.uk
www.internetretailing.net
www.link.co.uk

CASE STUDY

Crédit Agricole – a multichannel mutual bank

Crédit Agricole is the first French banking group with 28 per cent of the consumer market. The group is also the first European banking group in terms of retail banking revenues, and the eighth world banking group in terms of shareholder's equity. Crédit Agricole is a mutual banking group, which means that it is characterized by a decentralized decision-making system, even though it has a cohesive financial, commercial and legal organization. This cohesion is ensured by Crédit Agricole SA (CASA), which represents 'all group business lines and entities, and serves the entire spectrum of customers, from personal customers right through to large international groups'. Nearly three-quarters (73 per cent) of CASA's capital is held by the 39 Crédit Agricole Regional Banks, the capital of which is owned by 2,573 local banks that form the core of the group's mutual organization (the remainder is held by the general public and group employees). According to the most recent figures available from Crédit Agricole (for 31 December 2006), overall, it has nearly 7,160 branches that serve 20 million individual, professional and small business customers. This network is supposed to 'combine a dynamic commercial approach with strong local relationships and a high-quality service, and represents a major competitive advantage'. However, the development of information and communication technologies also enabled Crédit Agricole, as any of its competitors, to develop many new distribution channels over the last few years. Hence, inbound and outbound call centres, mobile phones services, websites, more and more advanced ATMs, etc. are now at the disposal of their customers who need or want to access the bank's services anywhere, at any time.

Crédit Agricole's multichannel distribution strategy: definitely not without branches!

The '2008 Bank–Customer Relationship Barometer', which analyses customer behaviour within the nine main French banks, shows that 80 per cent use different channels to access the services of their bank. However, if, in global terms, customers are satisfied with Web services, many are not with the quality delivered by call centres. They consider that these interactions are dehumanized, that call-centre employees are not flexible enough, do not show initiative and do not understand customers' needs. Even though these results are not specific to Crédit Agricole, it is something that this bank has been trying to address over the last few years. The bank has a very active multichannel distribution and communication strategy. As an example, eight of its regional banks, which grouped together in a GIE (*Groupement d'Intérêt Économique*, an association for developing commercial interests), have developed a common tool to manage their multichannel communication campaigns. The objective is to be able to send the customer a personalized message (in other words, a commercial offer), adapted to the period or a particular event in his or her life, through the most appropriate channel (branch advisers, call-centre adviser, mail, website, e-mail or SMS/MMS).

The proliferation of the number and the nature of these channels raises a major problem for the bank: what should be the place of the branch in this new distributive architecture? Hichem Jaballah, deputy manager of Crédit Agricole Ile-de-France, considers it a priority: 'The branch is at the core of our multichannel distribution strategy. Our model "Click, Phone and

Mortar" aims to open up these three channels to give the customer the opportunity to interact with her bank through the channel most adapted to function of the context. Obviously, we also offer her the possibility to mix them. The branch must continuously be informed of the customer's actions in order to turn these contacts into sales opportunities.' This quote is best illustrated by the slogan adopted by Crédit Agricole in September 2005: '*Une relation durable, ça change la vie!*' (A lasting relationship changes your life!).

Yet, if multichannel distribution can enhance the global bank–customer relationship, it does not come without any drawbacks. First, many customers have been complaining that these new channels, especially the call centres, aim to limit their interactions with their branch. Reaction is the same to ATMs (Crédit Agricole has 11,300 of them) that prevent the customer from entering the branch. The multichannel was initially mainly considered as a source of productivity and cost reductions; the change of perspective (i.e., the actual development of closer relationships) is relatively recent. A second example of the risks of multichannel development is the rising use of the Internet to compare prices, which increases the pressure on pricing and service quality. Indeed, the customer can now compare their own bank with its competitors; relationship is not preferred over better prices. At the European level, 58 per cent of retail banks' customers declare that they use the Internet to find better prices. Once again, this legitimates the importance of both the branch and the interpersonal face-to-face relationship between the customer and her financial adviser. As Hughes Brasseur, in charge of CASA's individual customers market, states: 'A model of transactional banking is emerging, pulled by prices, but where the quality of the relationship makes the difference.' In such a context, the use of geomarketing tools becomes essential to optimize the branches network. In addition, to keep growing and face these consumer behavioural evolutions, Crédit Agricole began to offer new kinds of services to nurture the relationship with its customers. As a consequence, it launched real-estate agencies under a new brand called Square Habitat, plus a dedicated website (www.squarehabitat.fr). By the end of 2007, 25 regional Crédit Agricole banks had developed this new activity, with 485 agencies in France.

Developing local innovations and distribution strategies

Given the mutual structure of the bank, not all the products or services sold in the regional banks are identical. Furthermore, customers often discover when they move or go on holiday in another region of France that they may become 'nonexistent'. In fact, since they do not have the same information system, a customer of Crédit Agricole Nord de France may have problems withdrawing cash in a branch of Crédit Agricole Midi-Pyrénées if she does not have a card to use in an ATM. This situation has been evolving over the years, as the number of regional banks in the group dramatically declined from 94 in 1988 to 39 in 2007. Many regional banks have already merged, whereas some others have merely grouped some resources together. In this case, information systems are either merged or interconnected, financial resources are pooled, multichannel distribution strategies are aligned, new products are sold in the same different regional banks, etc. However, the aim is neither to have one global information system for the whole group, nor to merge all the regional banks together. Hughes Brasseur even explains that one interesting benefit of the existence of many regional banks lies in the fact that innovations can be tested and, if they prove promising, be generalized subsequently to the entire group ('Le multicanal bouscule les mutualistes' 2007).

Thus, at the end of 2007, the Regional Bank des Savoies was experimenting with a health insurance virtual adviser, as well as conferences with many customers based on Internet Protocol technology. The Regional Bank of Centre-Ouest was testing a completely virtual local branch, and 60 per cent of the regional banks offered their customers a 'Web call-back' service (the customer has to click on a button on the website to be called back by the bank). Hughes Brasseur also claims that Crédit Agricole was the first bank in France to sell banking products on-line, from the beginning to the end, without asking the customer to come to the branch to complete the transaction. To skip what used to be a necessary step, Crédit Agricole enables its customers to use an electronic signature, legalized in 2006 in France. Products sold this way are still relatively basic, but it is planned to sell more and more complex products in the future. Launched in August 2007 by the Regional Bank of Provence Alpes Côte d'Azur, this new service was relatively successful, and has been progressively implemented in many other regional banks ever since. For instance, the Crédit Agricole Ile-de-France sold about 400 products between November 2007 and January 2008, without any advertising targeted at Internet users. The aim is to generalize this to the whole group by the end of 2008.

A last innovation example dates back to late October 2007, when the Regional Bank of Aquitaine launched a simulator of consumer credit available via mobile phones (for the first time in France). This tool enables a customer to fill in a form, and then get an assessment of her monthly payments. In the hour that follows, a call-centre adviser calls the customer to get some more information, in order to confirm (or not) the credit. This innovation is scheduled for generalization later to all the other regional banks, to enable CASA to further improve its leadership in the consumer credit market (figures released in September 2007 show that CASA had €15.9 billion of a total market of €134 billion at the end of 2006). Its hope is to have this simulator used by at least 15 per cent of French people; they hope it will prove popular as a result of the possibility for the users to send information to their friends.

Pauline and Louis want to buy a house...

(The names have been changed, but this account is based on the actual experience of a Crédit Agricole customer.)

In June 2007, Crédit Agricole decided to launch a multichannel campaign aimed at young working people. These represent 60 per cent of its 18—24-year-old customers, and more than 90 per cent between 25 and 29 years old. The idea was then to go beyond traditional segmentation criteria (in this case, the age), and to identify key moments in customers' lives.

In this context, Pauline (26 years old) and Louis (27), who had met three years before, intended to buy a beautiful house with which they had fallen in love. They had decided that it would be there that they would raise their children to come, as the neighbourhood was very nice, quiet and not so far from where they worked. Accordingly, since Pauline had been a client of Crédit Agricole from more than 12 years, she immediately made an appointment with her financial adviser. She was slightly disappointed when she learned that the adviser who had been in charge of her account over the last six years had left her branch three months before, but she thought: 'Well, anyway, I'm pretty sure that service quality will be the same. I know this bank so well, I do not want to go somewhere else.' Hence, she did not even look at the competition and decided to meet her new adviser, whose name was Bernard. At least, she tried to meet him. She had called the call centre to make the appointment. Apparently, however, the call-centre employee in charge of her call had not correctly scheduled the rendezvous in the electronic timetable of the branch adviser. Hence, when she arrived in the branch, the latter was not available to meet her. She then had to return three days later, very anxious because she knew many people were interested in the same house she and Louis wanted so much.

When she finally met Bernard, he made a simulation to establish whether she and Louis could borrow enough to buy the house. He told her, after a long wait, that it should be OK. However, he explained to her that he needed supporting documents to confirm his decision. Pauline returned the following day to give them to him, but learned that he was not there, and that he would not get them for at least three days. Still very concerned about the house, Pauline called three days later and asked the call-centre adviser whether she could speak to Bernard. This was impossible because he was having an appointment with another customer. Although the call-centre adviser proposed to take care of Pauline's demand, once she had explained the situation, he told her that he could not help her, and that she would have to wait for Bernard's phone call. Two days later she still had no news, so she phoned again, and was finally put through Bernard. He told her that it the loan had been confirmed and that they could buy the house. Pauline was delighted to hear that, but she was a little bit disappointed by the interest rate. She and Louis tried to negotiate as much as they could, but they could not have less than 5.2 per cent, plus insurance. She had hoped that being a loyal customer might have helped, but in fact it made no difference. As Bernard told them: 'You know, I would really do something if I could, but I swear, I can't. It's the system, you know, the computer decides this.'

Some days later, however, Pauline got a call from a Crédit Agricole call-centre adviser, supposedly on Bernard's behalf. He wanted to know whether she planned to buy a house in the following months. She was shocked, first, because the person on the phone did not know she was in the process of taking out a loan to buy a house And, second, she was even more stunned that the adviser told her that he could offer her a special interest rate, given her age and professional situation. This rate was 4.8 per cent, plus insurance, which was very interesting. When she asked for more information, Pauline understood that Bernard should have offered her this promotion. Very angry, she called him immediately. When he heard this, Bernard sounded very surprised and promised her that he had not tried to swindle her. He swore that he would make some phone calls to get more information, and would call her within the day. Some hours later, Pauline received a call from him; he explained to her that the 4.8 per cent rate was reserved exclusively for the outbound call-centre promotional campaign. Nevertheless, given the situation, he had been authorized to offer it to her. What's more, to compensate for the disagreement, he also had been authorized to deduct 50 per cent from the loan management charges. This reassured Pauline, who had been thinking of leaving her bank.

Questions

1. How does Crédit Agricole rely on its multichannel distribution strategy to keep growing?
2. Do you think the mutual organization of the bank is an advantage or a drawback? Compare this with other banks you know.
3. Analyse the problems Pauline and Louis encountered. How would you solve these dysfunctions? Based on this example, what can you say about customer satisfaction in a multichannel context?

This case was written by Loïc Plé, IÉSEG School of Management (Lille, France). It is intended to be used as a basis for class discussion rather than to illustrate either effective or ineffective handling of a management situation. It was compiled from published sources.

References

'Les banques cherchent à mieux valoriser leurs réseaux d'agence', *Les Échos*, 9 April 2008.

http://www.Crédit-agricole.com/banking-:-account-bank-and-business-banking-171/about-us-172/organisation-173/Crédit-agricole-s.a.-177/profile-571.html, accessed 21 May 2008.

http://www.Crédit-agricole.com/banking-:-account-bank-and-business-banking-171/about-us-172/organisation-173/index.html, accessed 21 May 2008.

'Les caisses bretonnes du Crédit Agricole inventent l'union sans fusion', *L'Agefi Quotidien*, 26 February 2008.

http://www.letelegramme.com/gratuit/generales/economie/credit-agricole-les-bretons-se-rapprochent-20080226-2596417_1233914.php, accessed 22 May 2008.

'Crédit Agricole lance un simulateur de crédit à la consommation sur portable', *l'Agefi Quotidien*, 25 October 2007.

'Le multicanal bouscule les mutualistes', *l'Agefi Hebdo*, 27 September 2007.

'Des campagnes de prospection géolocalisées', *Marketing Direct*, 1 April 2007.

'Des campagnes de marketing multicanal complexes', *l'Agefi Hebdo*, 26 April 2007.

Crédit Agricole: Rapport d'activité 2006.

Crédit Agricole: Rapport d'activité 2007.

'Quelques pistes sur le rôle de l'agence bancaire de demain', *Banque & Informatique*, 1 July 2007.

http://www.relationclient.net/3eme-Barometre-de-la-relation-banque-client-Alertes-sur-la-relation-bancaire-!_a3164.html, accessed 21 May 2008.

'2007, l'an I du décollage des ventes de produits financiers par Internet', *Les Échos*, 7 January 2008.

'Une clientèle jeune difficile à séduire', *l'Agefi Hebdo*, 21 July2007.

'L'impact de l'Internet sur le comportement d'achat de services financiers', December 2007, in partnership with Capgemini, Crédit Agricole, Efma, Microsoft and Novamétrie.

11

Communicating in the marketing of financial services

Contents

Learning outcomes

At the end of this chapter, the reader will be able to:

- Appreciate the interaction between the sender and recipient of marketing messages

- Define marketing communications objectives

- Provide an overview of major communication strategies in the marketing of financial services

- Appraise the key strengths of marketing communication channels in terms of strategic objectives, particularly new communications channels

Introduction

Marketing communications is the high-profile aspect of marketing; financial institutions (FIs) are heavy users. Advertising, public relations or direct mail all form part of a wider range of activities; an *integrated marketing communications* (IMC) *strategy*. The credit crunch has resulted in an overall drop in advertising spend of 9.1 per cent in 2009 (ipa.co.uk) and it may be that more conventional forms of marketing communications may not be appropriate post-credit crunch. Experts have recommended that banks and other FIs embrace new media such as Twitter (the-banker.com/news). The prime goal of IMC is to affect the customer's perception of value and their behaviour through directed communication. The development and diffusion of IMC is closely associated with the rapid technological advancement of a global and deregulated marketplace (Holm 2006). At the same time, customers are increasingly predisposed to demand and expect individualized services and are very willing as well to articulate this desire and complain if the service does not meet an expectation or an ideal. Marketing practitioners are aware that they need to use a carefully selected blend of promotional tools to achieve their **communications objectives**. Financial services, of course, are an intangible offering with the additional challenges of being complex and purchased to achieve another end. Communicating the service, therefore, in these circumstances can almost become part of the offering itself, especially considering the notion of value-in-use – that is, how the offering is going to be used by the consumer. Marketing communications are also inextricably entwined with the management of the brand; all messages communicate something about a firm and its goods and services (Gronroos 2000). New media present new opportunities for FIs, as shown in Exhibit 11.1.

communications objectives: setting clear aims for communicating with target groups

---

EXHIBIT 11.1

Twittering financial services

US commentators believe that financial institutions can no longer afford to ignore or resist the latest social-networking phenomenon sweeping the world. Everyone seems to be talking about Twitter, which now has more than 10 million users. Twitter is rapidly emerging as a major source of financial innovation. A short message service for mobile and Internet users, limiting a posting to 140 characters maximum, it also allows users to share web addresses for useful information. As a result, it is a fantastic knowledge-sharing resource, with the majority of users over the age of 35. With this number of users, the financial services sector should take note of the Twitter. Its particular strength is catching customer dialogue and responding. There are already financial sites that are growing around it, such as TwitPay, Tweetwhatyouspend, StockTwits and FXTwits. These all offer some form of payment or finance service through Twitter. Some innovative banks, such as ING Direct and the Co-operative Bank, are responding, so it would seem that FIs need to twitter too. Compiled by the authors from www.thebanker.com/news/fullstory.php; www.twitter.com; www.cooperativebank.co.uk, www.ingdirect.com

The communications loop

communications loop: a communications model that illustrates the importance of feedback in effective communication

Underpinning successful communications is an understanding of the circular process of communication, emphasizing the importance of getting feedback on how the message is received. Marketing messages need to be designed in accordance with this loop (see Figure 11.1), otherwise there are problems with gauging the effectiveness of the message.

Message sender and recipient

A sender will transmit a message usually to a carefully defined audience. The audience then decodes the message according to how it perceives the message. Members of the audience, on receipt of the message, provide some form of feedback, which can take a variety of forms and might be no action or response at all. In terms of marketing communications to large audiences, such as in advertising, an awareness of the way in which messages will be decoded by the target group and the importance of being able to capture the feedback are critical but have often been problematic for the organizations. Noise in a message represents the interference that occurs in the transmission and the reception of the message; this

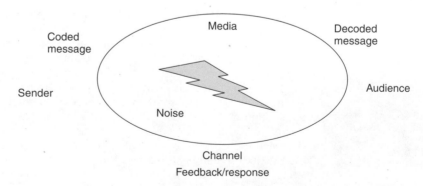

Figure 11.1 Communications loop

can consist of a lack of interest or some element in the construction of the message that interferes with the target audience decoding it in the intended way. There is an increasing array of media through which marketing messages can be sent, including TV, print, Internet, direct mail and mobile phone. There is also a choice of channels that can be used for sending messages, such as in the branch, by post, ATMs and, of course, the Internet as a direct contact.

The message originators have to be aware that the decoding of the message is performed by the target audience and will, as such, be influenced by personal and social factors. A well-researched understanding of the target audience is therefore a prerequisite in developing marketing messages. There are other considerations for the message sender. Current views of the workings of marketing communications are that the attitudes of the target audience play a critical role in decoding. Think, for example, how the credit crunch has impacted on consumer and business attitudes to FIs? An attitude, in a formal sense, consists of three separate components, as follows:

- cognitive (reflecting knowledge and belief)
- affective (feelings associated with the object)
- behavioural (action readiness).

To appreciate how these attitude components interact, consider this example of a customer who has a preference for a particular local building society (affective component) because it is locally based, has a good image in the community and she knows the staff. Moreover, the customer notices that the society is offering a particularly good rate on a savings account (cognitive component). She is therefore ready to respond to the good offer on the savings account (behavioural component). Messages, therefore, for this particular FI can build on the favourable attitudes that existing and prospective customers have of their organization and continue to build on this through a marketing communications strategy working across a number of channels.

Selecting the target audience

Marketers use similar techniques when deciding to whom the message is aimed as they deploy for analysis of segmentation. Messages must, therefore, take into account the following (Palmer 2008):

- Socio-demographic characteristics, such as age, area of residence and occupation
- Level of involvement in the service, such as those who are merely aware or those who may be directly affected by any changes in rate or conditions

- Frequency of use; many financial services are continuously used, such as the cheque account or a regular savings account, others less so, such as previously acquired ISAs or premium bonds
- What are the benefits sought by the target audience? For the marketer it is essential that he/she understands how the offering is going to be used. A business account provides the means of managing cash flow and payments efficiently but it is even more important to understand how the aspects of the service are going to be used by that particular business. For example, what role the FI can play in enabling the business to grow or achieve its organizational objectives over a period of years?

Marketing communications have to convey a message that is of value for the audience; this value consists of the content as well as the channel for delivering the information, otherwise the communication can add or destroy value (Heinonen and Strandevik 2005). Continuing with the example of the business, does a time-pressed businesswoman want to spend time opening direct mail (assuming that it meets the criteria of 'direct') or receive phone calls when there is a customer that needs to be served? The FI has to think when that businesswoman may have a favourable attitude for receiving messages – this may be on the way to and from work, listening to the car/van radio.

Source and interpretation of message

The marketer also needs to consider how the target audience views the source of the message and whether the interpretation of the message is consistent with its style? Celebrities and sports stars have been used extensively by FIs as sources of marketing messages – for example, Lewis Hamilton for Santander. However, for FIs, the maintenance of an image consistent with the marketing of financial services is paramount and celebrities cannot always be relied upon to maintain squeaky-clean images. In spite of the huge benefits that can be derived from successful relationships with celebrities, FIs have generally fought shy of using 'real' people with some exceptions – for example, Nationwide Building Society have run a series of TV advertisements using the comedian Mark Benton as a manager for a nameless competitor in the advertisements.

If the organization wishes to use a personality to deliver messages, how can the purity of the spokesperson be maintained? This objective can be achieved by creating a character that is not real and exists only for the purposes of the communications and brand. For consumers who focus on brand information, marketers can obtain considerable benefits through the introduction of and consistent use of characters that target audiences perceive as being as more relevant. There should be a degree of fit between the spokescharacter and the advertised product; the symbols need to convey key attributes that are relevant to advertised brands (Garretson and Burton 2005). The authors claim that the use of spokescharacters can generate superior brand attribute recall and more favourable brand attitudes. A further advantage is that the spokescharacter can address some of the problems inherent in financial services offerings. An example of a spokescharacter is the dog in the Churchill communications who uses a combination of humour and plain-speaking to decode financial products.

EXHIBIT 11.2

Churchill

Churchill insurance (part of the RBS group) has been able to create a spokescharacter that conveys a degree of tangibility for insurance services, which are bought to offset the outcomes of undesirable events. Competitive pricing adds further value to the offering, particularly pertinent as insurance is a service that customers do not actively desire. Further attributes that the bulldog character are conveyed by the straight-talking northern accent and the bulldog with the virtues of that breed tying in with the name of the British prime minister during the Second World War. All these convey a solidity and no-nonsense approach to financial services. The dog even has a nodding head, which implies that he will agree to requests. In July 2006, Churchill took to the road with the 'Challenge Churchill' campaign, urging people to challenge him to save money on their car and home insurance. The initiative has significantly increased unprompted awareness of the brand.

Compiled by the authors from www.churchill.co.uk.

Did it work for you?

Closing the message loop involves an evaluation of the success of the message that has been sent. When developing the message, the desired outcomes have to be clearly specified and a system of measurement created – for example, by establishing how many loans the FI wants to make or how many ISAs it wants to sell, as well as what the ratio of enquiries to actual sales made turns out to be. The marketer seeks a response to that message and needs to consider how to facilitate that response through the provision of free phone numbers or minimum number of clicks on an Internet site. Extensive research has been undertaken into the responses to advertisements, as this is the most expensive medium and the hardest to measure effectively. Tests for effectiveness can be experimental. One example of this is a sophisticated physiological test that takes place under experimental conditions to measure the effects of marketing stimuli on the body through looking at the dilation of the pupil in the eye (De Pelsmacker *et al.* 2005). The more the pupil dilates, the higher the level of arousal. Less invasive methods of measurement consist of assessing unprompted awareness, or unaided or spontaneous recall, when people are asked about advertisements that they have noticed recently. Similarly, customer attitudes towards products or advertisements can be measured. Advertisements are also pre-tested to assess whether or not they can achieve their desired outcome; they can even be tested midway through a campaign to enable adjustments to be made. For example, the Nationwide campaign is being modified in the light of the credit crunch with the objective of casting the building society, and financial services generally, in a more favourable light. In the post-testing of advertisements, the subject's recall of the advertisements that they have seen is investigated, which is where the Churchill dog seems to have been successful.

Marketing communication objectives

Successful communication will depend on having a clear idea of what you are trying to achieve. There are a number of possible objectives that will determine the way the programme of marketing communications is put together which have been based, in this case, on the conventional consumer decision-making model (Cravens and Piercy 2006).

Needs recognition

This is the stage where is a customer need is triggered; with financial services the trigger may be external – that is, a legal requirement such as car insurance. Many financial services fall into the category of 'averse or avoidance products', so a need is often expressed as a desire to avoid a particular situation. Insurance products, for example, enable the policy-holder or members of the scheme to avoid lengthy delays in obtaining health treatment or losing money at major outdoor events through bad weather. Customers often require particular financial services at certain times of the year – for example, just after Christmas, when they are often trying to manage their finances by consolidating their credit card debt. Consequently, credit card companies offer attractive rates for balance transfers at this time of year.

Finding customers

In many of the financial services markets these days there are a limited number of new customers; encouraging customers to switch from one FI to another has thus become an objective of marketing communications. At the same time, FIs are becoming more selective about which customers they actually seek and those which they seek to retain. Recently, staff at a large FI in the United Kingdom were incentivized to encourage customers who were already running businesses to switch to the bank's business account, not those seeking business start-up funds. The risk arising from customers already running a business is less than that incurred in backing new businesses, which have a relatively high failure rate. Customers for a particular offering can also be found within the existing customer base. FIs are always seeking to increase their share of the customer's wallet – that is, to encourage the customer to buy more financial services from them. An FI can identify from its information system which products a customer is likely to purchase and send that customer details of that offering with a regular mailing such as a credit card bill. The FI may note that the customer uses the credit card for foreign travel and so send that customer details of the FI's foreign currency service.

Building the brand

Branding has become a very important aspect of marketing, with significant sums of money spent on the development and maintenance of the brand. It is, however, evident that both of these activities are supported through communication. Branding in financial services is a real challenge for the FIs as there is little to distinguish one provider from another, or what they offer. In order to dissuade customers from making choices of financial services based on price alone, FIs engage in communicating messages about their brand and what the brand offers to customers.

Overcoming alternatives

The aim of this marketing objective is to ensure that the brand is considered in some way superior to its rivals. As with branding, mentioned in the previous section, this is hard for FIs to achieve – all the more so since there are so many products in the marketplace. The comparison websites are one way in which FIs have sought to achieve this objective, as these websites allow customers to select exactly which product features are important to them. These websites also allow FIs to lower their costs as the customer does much of the work. Being on a website does allow direct comparisons to be made and can undermine the brand. It is not surprising that Direct Line, the first remote UK insurer, has made a decision not to participate in Web comparison sites, instead advertising to potential customers with an invitation to contact them directly via phone or Internet through advertising. This is an interesting decision from a marketing perspective and the outcome of this decision is not yet known.

Deciding to purchase

With a comparison website, the decision to purchase is facilitated by means of clicking through to the provider of the product, where the transaction can be completed in a few minutes. The purpose of communication at this point is to reassure the customer about the 'rightness' of the product for them, the ease of concluding the transaction and also the supplying of information, which is either legally required or recommended as good industry practice. However, there are other financial services where personal selling may play a role, especially when the product is complex and the consequences of making a decision are well into the future. The low uptake of pensions and/or provision for later years in the United Kingdom and in Europe is causing governments considerable concern as they seek to reduce their involvement in this area. Customers of this type of product require advice, support and sometimes encouragement to make a purchase.

Retaining customers and relationships

Just as many financial service providers encourage customers to switch from their competitors, so there has to be equal emphasis on encouraging the profitable customers to stay. Making customers feel valued should be embedded in any marketing communications strategy; however, this needs to be set against assessing the value of the customer to the FI. In research conducted by Farquhar and Panther (2008), they found that one building society managed the level of marketing communication according to the actual and projected value of the customer to the society. Using sophisticated information systems, the society modelled the value of a customer to the organization over a period of time; the society then developed a relationship with that particular customer based on that calculation of value. In practice, this meant that customers receive quite different levels of service, with low-value customers receiving few direct mailings and better 'prospects' receiving carefully targeted offers. Customers do want to hear from their FI if they consider the communication to be proactive and appropriate; furthermore, the quality of the communications is important (Madden and Perry 2003). Communications should aim to be personalized, relevant and timely. FIs generally seem to have learned this lesson and have reduced mailings, ensuring that those that remain meet the above criteria and demonstrate the value that the FI attaches to the customer.

Marketing communications strategy

integrated marketing communications: interlinks a set of communication media to achieve an overall objective.

Although marketing is often regarded simply as advertising, it does not take much thought to realize that advertising forms just one element of marketing, and, upon even further reflection, a sub-component of marketing communications. The practice of **integrated marketing communications** is an attempt to pull together, within the term, all the different types of marketing communications, with the emphasis on interlinking the communications channels so that the strengths of each one are harnessed to maximize the message sent to the target audience. Marketing communications is commonly considered to consist of a mix, rather like the marketing mix. In this case, the following elements are involved: advertising, personal selling, direct marketing and on-line marketing, sales promotion and publicity or public relations. IMC recognizes the need to integrate a carefully chosen combination of these quite disparate promotional activities with the remit of lowering costs but in no way reducing effectiveness. Hartley and Pickton (1999) comment that, although the integration of marketing communications undoubtedly takes place, the degree of integration is often minimal; IMC presents its own 'working model' (see Figure 11.2). The degree of success with which marketing communications is integrated may be open to debate, but figures show that communication budgets have shifted away from advertising to a more varied mix (Holm 2006).

This working model of IMC identifies three levels of communication (corporate, marketing and customer) and illustrates which activities may be appropriate for each level. Many FIs have a strong corporate identity and image in a global marketplace, such as HSBC or Zurich, and they maintain this by product advertising at marketing level and branch or local sales at customer level. Marketing communications within the channels of financial services should include support for intermediaries or brokers, who play a vital role in the selling of many financial services. The model also shows the nature of the dialogue, which at customer level is two

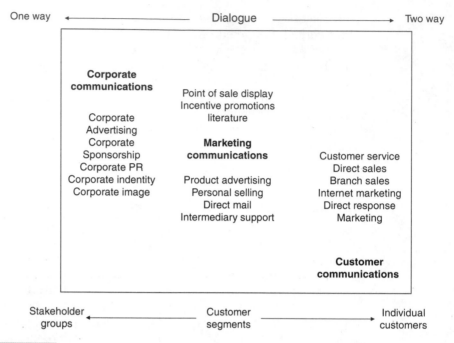

Figure 11.2 Working model of IMC

Source: Adapted from Hartley and Pickton (1999).

way. The targets for the communications again vary according to the level of communication. At corporate level, the groups are diverse but will probably have some interest or 'stake' in the FI, including staff, shareholders and suppliers. This concept of 'stakeholder' is becoming more acknowledged in marketing; the focus is not exclusively on the customer but extends to other groups who contribute directly or indirectly to the organization.

Marketing communications strategies in financial services are often founded on three key activities, known as the three Ps, which are – pull, push and profile (Fill 2006). Strategy is concerned with the direction, approach and implementation of an organization's desired marketing communications with a selected audience. In financial services, one of the key issues that FIs have to address is the maintenance or even the re-creation of trust, owing to a number of well publicized mis-selling scandals such as pensions in the 1980s, mortgage cover insurance and, most recently, the credit crunch. A further issue for marketing communications is the intangibility and complexity of financial services, as well as the problem of rather indirect benefits of the financial services themselves. In planning any marketing communications strategy, whatever model is deployed, the needs of the target market should be understood, as discussed in Chapter 4; the identification of appropriate segmentation variables is critical.

Pull strategy

Pull strategies are directed at creating demand from target end-users of financial services that results in a pull demand for the product/brand created. For example, medium-sized businesses might be looking for an FI to provide them with an injection of money to allow them to grow. Pull strategies would have as objectives the creation of awareness or a stimulus to action or to cross-sell. The FI that lends the medium-sized business the funds to grow might also seek the opportunity to sell relevant insurance products. With this strategy, the formulation of the core message proposition is key. For example, Aviva, the global insurance company, aims to provide prosperity and peace of mind for its customers; therefore, the marketing messages will build on this corporate vision. Both of these aims have been have been carefully considered because insurance products are usually developed to avoid unpleasant outcomes or to yield some form of payout at the end of the product – for example, term assurance. Customers, as always, seek the benefits of these products; the marketing communications are thus concerned with making these benefits explicit and relevant to the target market

Push strategy

A second type of target audience for marketing communications is the focus for the second strategy of push. This audience does not actually consume the products themselves but is in a position to add value to the product (Fill 2006), usually through the offer of expert independent advice. The independent financial intermediary (see www.unbiased.co.uk) plays a significant role in the provision of financial services and FIs devote significant resources to maintaining a relationship with intermediaries, who are also referred to as brokers or introducers. As the logo of the professional body that represents independent financial intermediaries suggests, the key value that they offer is independent and unbiased advice. Customers have to be advised about the commission or incentive that the intermediary receives for selling the financial product.

Intermediaries work in personal, business and corporate markets, in partnership, to communicate and ultimately address the needs of the end-users. The provider is in direct communication with the intermediary to update them with product information and to encourage, maintain and build the relationship. The intermediary has valuable information about the marketplace so systems need to be in place to capture these data and act upon them, reinforcing the need for a communications loop. Communications will also consist of materials to ensure that the intermediary is in the best position to reach his/her market and may consist of product information, sales incentives or promotional materials, all of which are designed to communicate the brand values of the supplying organization (e.g., bank, insurance company or investment bank). Financial service intermediaries and their supplying organizations also have to comply with guidelines and regulations laid down by regulating authorities, such as the Financial Services Authority in the United Kingdom, for personal banking. FIs have dedicated teams for the creation and maintenance of relationships with intermediaries.

Profile strategy

A profile strategy recognizes the various stakeholders of an organization and that they need different messages or perhaps similar messages but in different formats. There are overlaps with branding at this (often corporate) level; messages are concerned with development of corporate image and reputation to stakeholders such as intermediaries.

As Fill (2006) argues, these strategies are not mutually exclusive; indeed an integrated marketing communications involves all three acting in harmony. What will change according to environmental changes, strategic objectives and organizational development and learning is the emphasis that is placed on any one of these three Ps.

Communications and quality

A particular issue for services marketers is the role of quality in the provision of the service. The aim of quality initiatives is to address variability or heterogeneity. In financial services, the quality of offering is usually subject to regulation or guidelines. However, the level of service quality that an FI provides to its customers could be a means of differentiating itself from its competitors. Fieldwork conducted by one of the authors found consistently that First Direct bank in the United Kingdom is seen by its competitors as an aspirational target for the levels of service quality in the sector. For this enviable situation, First Direct must have communicated quality standards to everyone connected with the production and consumption of the services, including customers. The same notions of continuity and evaluation need to be applied throughout the FI so that front-line staff are able to deliver the service that customers

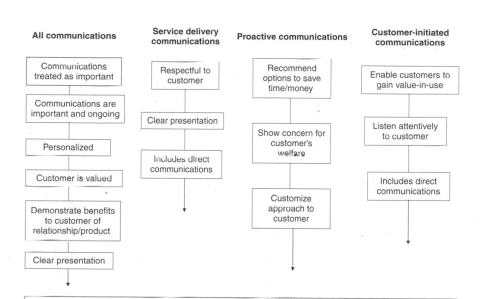

Figure 11.3   Main characteristics of ideal communication
Source: Adapted from Madden and Perry (2003).

expect. According to Madden and Perry (2003), customers generally have an ideal for the type of communications that they have with their financial institution, as shown in Figure 11.3.

In this figure, the four columns relate to communications between FIs and their customers: the first to all communications between FI and customer, the other three to particular categories of communications. Some examples of the ideal apply across other categories – for example, clear presentation. However, the latter could be considered a base-level requirement; if the FI is seeking to create loyalty then more sophisticated communication that demonstrates concern for welfare through a personalized approach is required. Communications are important both inside and outside service delivery. Customers want to hear from an FI outside service delivery through proactive and customer-initiated communications; the quality of the communication with that FI is important to them (Madden and Perry 2003). Well-timed communications keep customers up to date with new products and offerings and keep them informed about the FI and its developments, thus fostering loyalty. It is important to remember that communications do not take place just between the provider and the customer; there are other stakeholders to be considered, such as intermediaries and employees, so messages need to consistent and unequivocal to all possible audiences – whether the prime target of the message or not.

| EXHIBIT 11.3 |

Plain English

An Office of Fair Trading (OFT) market study reinforces complaints that the Plain English Campaign receive about bank charges. The OFT finds that lack of clarity in some FI communications is a major reason for poor relationships with customers. Banks know that plain language enables better financial management for both themselves and their customers. Yet there is an obvious need for legislation in this area to ensure consistency. FIs have a responsibility to their customers; clarity of communication is an example of a way in which honouring that responsibility can empower the customer. The finance industry already recognizes the valuable contribution that clear language offers in preventing the confusion around unnecessary and excessive charges. The current financial climate has highlighted that unclear and misleading information can cause people financial hardship. For instance, recent customer marketing from one major bank claims to counteract the effects of the 'credit crunch' by offering emergency funds. On closer inspection, these funds are no more than an additional overdraft facility at a hugely inflated interest rate.

Adapted by the authors from www.plainenglish.co.uk.

Multichannel marketing will continue to have a significant effect on marketing communications as distinctions between channels of delivery and communications are eroded. There is considerable evidence that information gained across channels is used to develop strategies for targeting and communicating with customers in a multichannel environment (Thomas and Sullivan 2005). The value of this information lies in the fact that it is already within the FI; the most important thing, therefore, is having the capacity to assimilate information gathered from various channels. Once assimilated, the information is used to develop appropriate strategies that target customer segments of differing value to the organization with appropriate communications (Farquhar and Panther 2008).

In terms of choice of media, there are considerable differences in profiles for different media (Heinonen and Strandevik 2005); traditional direct mail, for example, had higher communication value than e-mail and SMS messages. The implications for banks and other financial service providers are that they need very carefully to consider and measure the effectiveness of their selected media. The research also found that value can be decreased through the selected medium, with as yet lower responsiveness to new interactive media in spite of the benefits of immediate and easy feedback or reply.

Determining budgets

Advertising and marketing messages are a cost for the FI so it is important to set budgets for marketing communications. There are a number of criteria for setting a budget, which will be discussed. Using *percentage of sales* as a means of setting the budget has both advantages and disadvantages. It is simple and based on tradition; it assumes that marketing communications is directly related to sales, but, as discussed above, there may be other objectives for marketing communications. Using this budgeting method is also inappropriate when there is a downturn, during which time stimulating awareness may be more critical than usual. Similarly, setting a budget according *affordability* neglects market conditions and looks inward rather than out towards the customer/stakeholder base. Therefore, the FI may miss valuable opportunities that a more outward-looking focus may achieve through adopting a more flexible approach. Financial services is a highly competitive environment and the larger banks and major building societies have been heavy spenders, so *matching the competition* (or 'me-too') in the setting of the budget may be entirely understandable. As with *affordability*, this method of setting budgets is not market-driven; furthermore, of course, what suits a competitor may not suit you. The FI that adopts a 'me-too' budget could end up bombarding its customers with inappropriate messages that stand a good chance of being ignored or, at worst, creating negative attitudes.

The most rational method for setting a marketing communications budget is to *set objectives and cost the tasks* required to implement them. Farmers, for example, run businesses and therefore are interested in ensuring pensions for themselves, as well as providing advice and support for their employees. FIs in this specialized business, such as NFU Mutual, will be aware that the business of pensions for farmers is a relatively small market where advice and support from specialist staff for prospective customers will be a large part of the product. In this way, serious consideration is given to the target audience, the nature of the messages and the optimum way or ways of reaching the desired audience, focusing on the market. From the options for setting a budget suggested above, affordability may be considered, but this is a highly specialist market, which this particular FI is well suited to exploit. Relying on affordability as a decision-making tool with regard to establishing an advertising budget might result in its missing an excellent opportunity to be a market leader. Setting objectives offers a much better probability of meeting the needs both of the marketplace and the institution (www.nfumutual.co.uk/business/business-pensions/index.htm).

Marketing communications mix

marketing communications mix: the various components that make up marketing communication, such as advertising and increasingly powerful digital communication

Once the marketing communications strategy (for example, push or pull) has been developed and the budget set, the tools to achieve the objectives of the strategy can be considered. The choice of tools in the communications mix is more extensive than the marketing mix itself and we will give here just a sample of what is available to the financial services marketer and the agencies with which he/she will work. Technology has increased the number of channels through which messages can be transmitted, as noted above, but the mix of communications at the disposal of the financial services marketer remains relatively stable. The diverse means of communication available to support FI brands (e.g., TV, print and interactive advertising; trade and consumer promotions; arts, sports, and cause sponsorships) means that marketers must understand what various marketing communication options have to offer and how they should be combined to optimize their marketing communications programmes (Keller 2001).

Advertising

There are two main categories of media for advertising campaigns, essentially – print and audiovisual – to which can be added the use of new technology in marketing communications. Consistent with budget setting above, clear objectives for the advertising must be developed, such as building the brand. Financial services constantly try to create differentiation, or encourage desired responses by sending specific messages, but without a great degree of success. An advertising platform is pivotal to this strategy since it has to convince consumers/customers to undertake some kind of outcome – for example, switching to that FI or taking up a loan. As mentioned previously, the struggle for financial services is due to the nature of the offering (being intangible, functional and sometimes motivated by avoidance); therefore, the challenge is to convey the message in such a way that demonstrates to the target market that this offering will meet their needs and ultimately offer other benefits. The challenge is for FIs and their creative teams is to come up with ideas for communicating these benefits and the best way to express their message. At the same time, qualities such as trustworthiness, integrity and credibility that may transcend any product attributes need to be conveyed. Advertisements make both rational and emotional appeals to the consumer. Rational appeals will consist of information – for example, about attractive interest rates on loans. Emotional appeals may offer the means of caring for your family through the purchase of a particular insurance product. FIs can strengthen emotional appeal through careful selection of actors to do voice-overs to advertisements. Humour has also been used (see www.newsroom.barclays.com/imagelibrary) and also music.

Large amounts have been devoted to the advertising of financial services; for example, More Than, a large insurance company, has in the past spent at least £20 million annually. Barclays has been reported as 'slashing its TV ad spend', but still spent £11 million on product-based advertising in 2007. The change in direction by Barclays is interesting and their rationale for this change is that it will allow greater flexibility and a wider selection of media. Overall, it suggests that TV advertising, which has long been favoured by FIs, may be losing its appeal. Reducing spend on TV advertising may also be an acknowledgement that the 'fit' between financial services and TV advertising is questionable, as FI brands have not achieved the results for which they had hoped. The way in which consumers watch TV has also changed; they channel-hop, skip through adverts and have well-developed psychological barriers to advertising messages. It may be that digital TV presages the end of conventional high-spend TV advertising campaigns to mass, that is undifferentiated, audiences. Print media may allow FIs to concentrate on making a rational appeal based on the detail of the product rather than less specific messages about the value of the brand. It may also allow more precise targeting of messages through careful selection of newspapers, journals and magazines. Nonetheless, TV advertising amongst the larger FIs, especially those on the high street, is still common, even after the credit crunch has started to bite, as indicated in Exhibit 11.4.

EXHIBIT 11.4

The chequered flag

ING launched its 2008 global advertising campaign, featuring ING Renault F1 Team driver and double F1 World Champion Fernando Alonso. The campaign aired initially in 30 countries globally, in 30–45 second spots, both on those national TV stations broadcasting Grand Prix (GP) races and via international broadcast media, during each race weekend in the GP calendar. The broadcast campaign was supported by a print media roll-out, and an on-line presence in leading news, on-line print and F1 portals. The commercial was screened to coincide with beginning of the ING Australian Grand Prix weekend. The campaign provided media support to ING's business objective for year two of its F1 sponsorship, which was designed to build awareness and, using the F1 platform, to drive business into the FI. The advert sits alongside ING's title sponsorship of the ING Renault F1 Team, title sponsorship of the ING Australian, ING Hungarian and ING Belgian Grand Prix, global sponsorships of Fernando Alonso and Nelson Piquet and on-track branding at 13 of the 18 Grand Prix. The commercial uses ING's F1 sponsorship to illustrate ING's central message in which ING acknowledges that financial services can be complex, and by 'cutting through the clutter', ING makes managing financial affairs easier for its customers, allowing them to focus on what really matters. In the commercial, this message is illustrated by Fernando Alonso, and is reinforced visually by a number of post-production filming techniques. The campaign was created with the London-based advertising agency, Iris.

Compiled by the authors from www.ING.com.

The exhibit provides an interesting example of a global multimedia campaign that consists of national TV, press, PR and electronic media, and the way branding, sponsorship and advertising all come together with a vigorous message to the consumer.

Direct mailing

The take-up of direct mail or marketing by financial service providers has been prodigious – for example, building societies' use of direct mail increased by 18.8 per cent in 2007. A total of 15.92 million mailings were sent by building societies in the last quarter of 2006, up from 13.4 million in the same period in 2005 (news.royalmailgroup.com/news). According to Royal Mail, these figures illustrate the importance of direct mail to the financial sector for driving sales and boosting customer retention. This growth can also be attributed to the number of new product launches and services, along with the growing need to treat customers fairly and communicate the impact of interest rate rises on mortgages, savings and loans. The insurance sector also experienced a small increase in direct mail volumes for the October to December period, from 83.44 million items in 2005 to 83.87 million in 2006. There was also a rise in the volume of direct mail sent to the 55—64-year-old age group. In addition to being responsive to direct mail, this generation is particularly important to the financial sector as they approach retirement, complete their mortgages and see investments come to fruition.

The concept of direct marketing is based on the idea of direct communication with the customer without the intervention of the third party (De Pelsmacker *et al.* 2005) such as a financial intermediary. A key difference between advertising and direct marketing is the one-to-one element of the message and the response. Instead of segmenting and targeting a group of customers according to a set of variables or characteristics, the financial services marketer develops a message that is appropriate to this customer's needs, derived from information that they hold on this customer. In practice, a group of customers is identified from an analysis of the information system and a mailing/messaging organized and dispatched, based on the likelihood of those customers taking up the offer. The response rate to direct mailings can be measured precisely, providing clearer evaluation than available for more traditional forms of advertising. The responses generated by the direct mailings, whether positive or negative, are then assimilated in to the information system, adding further to the profile of the customer. The figures from UK Royal Mail above refer to hard copy direct mail, but direct mail also includes e-mail. It is important to remember the concept of direct at this point, where the aim is to maintain and grow a relationship. Therefore the context and the relevance of using e-mails for marketing communications has to be carefully understood and has led to the term 'precision marketing', which emphasizes the focus on the individual with the aim of obtaining a favourable response and supporting brand values.

M-technology

The impact of m-technology on marketing has been defined as the use of the mobile medium as a communications channel between a brand and an end-user (Michael and Salter 2006). The penetration of the mobile phone is three times greater than computers; it is in use all day and every day (Riivari 2005). Mobile marketing for financial services is concerned with strengthening interactive one-to-one communication as part of a coherent integrated strategy. Mobiles are currently used by FIs to convey information about their accounts. RBS, for example, offers its business customers a mobile banking service (www.rbs.co.uk/business/banking) with mobile transactions and balances. Mobile banking presents a good example of the blurring of the functions of channels and communications in marketing, allowing a relationship to flourish based on individual customer needs. The FI does not need to send conventional marketing messages, but offers a personalized service at that customer's disposal 24/7. As part of a shift from supply-driven modes of communication such as advertising, the mobile phone can offer considerable potential to FIs, providing that this technology is used in a non-invasive manner.

Sponsorship

Sponsorship takes the form of an investment in an activity in return for access to the commercial potential associated with this activity. A FI is able to promote its brand by tying it to a specific and meaningful event. FIs are heavy users of sponsorship, hoping that it provides a means of strengthening their poorly differentiated brands. Sponsorship activities include, in the United Kingdom: the football premier league by Barclays;

and Nationwide sponsorship of the national football teams of Wales, Scotland, Northern Ireland and England, under 15 cricket and an art prize (www.nationwide.co.uk/sponsorship). There may also be philanthropic motives behind the sponsorship. Sponsorship performs two of the objectives of advertising in that it raises awareness of the company and promotes positive messages about the company (De Pelsmacker *et al.* 2005). Sponsorship consists of a relationship between the sponsor and the organization that is being sponsored (sponsee), which requires maintenance as well as funding. When considering a sponsorship arrangement, the public's perception of the organizations (both separately and how they interact in the mind of the target audience) has to be considered – in other words, the suitability or harmony of the relationship. What is the message that is being conveyed by the 'relationship' and is this message consistent with the the company's other CRM activities?

EXHIBIT 11.5

'Royal' sponsorship

Royal Bank of Scotland quite understandably sponsors Scottish sporting teams and individuals. Golf 'north of the border' is taken very seriously and RBS has been involved in golf for over a century. The bank is associated with the spiritual home of golf – the Royal and Ancient Golf Club of St Andrews. RBS has strengthened its links with golf through their 'ambassadors', Jack Nicklaus, Luke Donald and Paula Creamer. RBS has a strong relationship with the governing bodies of golf both in Europe and the United States. The bank also sponsors the Williams F1 team, believing that no other sport pushes the envelope in quite the same way. From driver down to the pit crew, every aspect demands total focus and commitment. Sponsorship also includes the Scottish rugby team, where the bank logo is painted on the pitch at every fixture. The intense rivalry and passion of the players on the pitch is matched only by that of the fans. The Royal Bank of Scotland Group are proud to sponsor the Six Nations tournament. Finally, and most excitingly if you are tennis fan, RBS supports Andy Murray, a player of tremendous passion, focus and drive. Andy Murray has made a spectacular entrance to the world of international tennis. His meteoric rise up the world tennis rankings has firmly established him in the top ten of the tennis elite.

Note that the sponsorship activities of RBS may be constrained by its late 2008 bail-out by the UK government, as indeed may other sponsorship deals with FIs who have been exposed to high levels of toxic debt.

Compiled by the authors from www.rbs.co.uk.

Word-of-mouth

In a saturated financial service market, positive word of mouth (WOM) is seen as a powerful influence on the behaviour of other people (Gremler and Brown 1999). Positive WOM, or advocacy, can generate new business either through gaining new customers or existing customers buying more. Just as positive WOM is persuasive in influencing other people, so the power of negative WOM should not be underestimated. In spite of negative experiences, either their own or others, customers do not switch from one FI to another readily, resulting in customer inertia that has characterized the sector, but negative WOM may deter new customers. Nonetheless, negative comments about financial service providers abound, particularly with reference to charging, and there seems to be little public relations activity to counter this. FIs are aware of the importance of positive WOM and at marketing level make it a priority (Farquhar and Panther 2008). However, at corporate level, other actions undermine marketing, such as bank charging and senior staff bonuses. WOM extends beyond an immediate FI/customer dimension into a wider perspective that includes a range of other stakeholders such as staff, suppliers and competitors.

Personal selling

In spite of the increasing adoption of remote channels by many financial services customers, personal selling remains a critical channel or means of communicating and ultimately selling financial services. Financial service providers can increase the revenue from their customers by increasing the number of products that each customer has (known as 'product holdings'). Some products can be 'sold' to many customers with little personal interaction, particularly such low-involvement products as home contents insurance or credit cards. This type of product, though, tends to induce little loyalty and many customers are quite prepared to switch providers in this area. Other financial services, such as pensions and more complex investment products, benefit from consultation and advice from either direct employees of the provider or an intermediary. These can be classified as high-involvement offerings and customers usually perceive higher levels of risk, which FIs can offset with feelings of reassurance or trust in the provider or seller. It is with this type of offering, therefore, that personal selling comes into its own. A professional financial services study showed that effective communications are critical in impacting on perceptions of technical and functional quality, trust and relationship commitment, both formal and informal (Sharma and Patterson 1999). It goes on to suggest that effective communication when providing advice about investments (selling) consists of:

- displaying empathy and listening skills
- accurately explaining fees and charges
- setting realistic expectations about risks and returns
- educating clients along the way so that they can make more informed decisions
- explaining investment options in jargon-free terms
- explaining how various investment portfolios work
- regularly reviewing clients' portfolios.

Underpinning these suggestions lies an understanding of the importance of training and development, not only in the technical aspects of the financial offerings that are being made available, but also in high-level interpersonal skills. Not only are these professionals required to generate revenue from their clients, but they also play the central role in retaining the clients through relationship building. Homburg *et al.* (2002) investigated key account management (KAM), focusing on the organizational structure that enables companies to respond and supply their key customers. They identify four areas of KAM – activities, actors, resources and approach formalization – that they argue require an appropriate internal design in the organization. KAM is too important to be left to the sales teams, but there does not need to be a formal KAM programme.

Public relations

Public relations (PR) is concerned with managing the company's reputation, usually by means of managing relationships with key stakeholders such as journalists as a planned, sustained effort. According to the Chartered Institute of Public Relations (CIPR), the aim of PR is to close the gap between the way a company wishes to be seen and how it is seen by its key stakeholders or publics. PR professionals are concerned with building relationships with key stakeholders, opinion formers, financial analysts and investors. Financial services seem, from time to time, to be rocked by events that undermine the whole sector; managing crises is a sub-component of PR. The Northern Rock story has not only impacted on the company but on the sector, the Financial Services Authority and even the city of Newcastle itself. Société Générale (SocGen) suffered a huge loss at the hands of one of its employees, who lost the company £3.5 billion. What characterizes these events is the way in which these companies have failed to manage related communication, although it is difficult to see how any good can be extracted from either situation. Public relations may be an area to which, as yet, many financial institutions are still to pay sufficient attention. There seems to be an inherent inconsistency in spending millions of pounds/euros in advertising when events and news undermine the messages that the advertising is aiming to transmit. Journalists are often the target of public relations activities, as opinion formers. However, a glance in the newspapers will show the reader that many financial journalists are, in fact, highly critical of many high-street financial service providers, offering exhortations to switch to lower-cost providers.

Blogging

Blog is a contraction of 'Web log' and usually refers to an on-line journal where an individual makes regular entries about matters that interest him or her. A celebrated blog in the financial services sector is that of Robert Peston, the BBC financial journalist who broke the news about the impending collapse of Northern Rock (www.bbc.co.uk/blogs/thereporters/robertpeston). Peston has been reporting regularly on the credit crunch and the changes that have been taking place in the sector. Ray Boulger is a well-known commentator on the mortgage industry and he blogs on this topic (www.charcol.co.uk/knowledge-resources/ray-boulgers-blog). Blogging, it is believed, allows companies to go beyond press releases and traditional media coverage and to extend the brand experience. Currently, however, FIs appear not to be engaging in blogging, although it presents an opportunity for their experts to respond to the comments in other financial services blogs and counter some of Peston's commentaries.

Communicating in a global marketspace

Many FIs operate in international markets – for example, the full name of HSBC is Hongkong & Shanghai Banking Corporation.

As Solberg argues (2002), one of the key issues in marketing management is the trade-off between economies of scale that result from standardizing strategies and adapting to the local cultural requirements. **Globalization** trends have tended to encourage managers to centralize marketing decisions because they seek control of the strategy and to maximize the global appeal of the brand, but this can lead to tensions with the need to recognize local conditions such as consumer culture. The term 'glocalization' has been adopted to describe the strategies that seek to blend global and local requirements. Figure 11.4 seeks to show in more detail how these possible tensions may be addressed. The key strategic dimensions in the figure are, first, HQ knowledge of local market

globalization/global marketing communications: communications that can transcend national, regional and cultural boundaries

Influence on marketing communication decisions

Mainly local representative   Mainly HQ

	Mainly local representative	Mainly HQ
Deep	**Confederation** Conscious development of local communications strategies Some learning and control	**Federation** Global strategies in cooperation with local representatives Learning and control
Shallow	**Local Baronies** Disparate profiles of FI in different markets Limited learning and control	**Civil war** Standardized marketing without local marketing knowledge Source for conflict between local and HQ

(HQ knowledge of local market conditions)

Figure 11.4   FI governing strategies in global marketing communications
Source: Adapted from Solberg (2002).

conditions, which is depicted as either deep or shallow, and, second, the decision-making centre, which is located either at HQ or locally.

In Figure 11.4, the four approaches to marketing communications are shown – confederation, local baronies, federation and civil war – which suggest mechanisms for managing communications across the globe. As the figure indicates, shallow knowledge at HQ combined with main influence of HQ can result in civil war between local and HQ managers in the management of marketing communications. On the other hand, deep knowledge about the market conditions with local influence on marketing decisions may result in confederation where both local and global considerations are met. A further consideration for marketing strategists is the possible prevalence of western values in advertising and marketing communications. Consumers respond to advertisements that match their culture; communications compatible with their culture are generally more effective, so should be adapted to meet **cultural values**. Advertising appeals, in Asia for example, are dominated more by western values than eastern, although it is not clear what is preferred by eastern audiences; it appears to depend upon the product. Consumer cultural values are a powerful force in shaping consumer motivations, lifestyles and choices

cultural values: different groups will interpret images and words according to their upbringing/education etc.

(Gram 2007). HSBC seems to recognize cultural values in its marketing communications (see hsbc.com/1/2/about-hsbc/advertising).

Again, the credit crunch provides an opportunity for FIs to rethink how they communicate with their customers. Advertising spend may never recover from the low of 2008 – 9, but in the meantime the advent of Twitter and the existence of social networking sites present exciting alternatives. It is even more important that FIs think about the messages that they need to convey and how to restore confidence and trust in the sector, focusing on being in tune with changes in customer attitudes and behaviour and re-establishing some credibility.

Summary

- Marketing communications is a major marketing activity in financial services, but there is a shift from supply-driven advertising to demand-driven marketing solutions.
- There are three key strategies that underpin marketing communications activities – pull, push and profile – which interact and which will change in emphasis according to circumstances.
- Marketing budgets are best set by defining clear communication objectives that are measurable.
- The marketing communications mix consists of a number of different promotional activities, from advertising to public relations, and once more an integrated campaign will consist of a 'mix' of these activities.
- Going global requires an awareness of cultural matters, with particular attention to any imposition of western values. Glocalization is one strategy that recognizes that brand and promotional messages need to manage marketing communications both at global and local level.
- The credit crunch could enable FIs to rethink their IMC strategies and how they can re-engage their customers.

Exercises

1. Government in the United Kingdom has been particularly exercised in trying to encourage people to take responsibility for provision in their old age, which has raised the question of how to advertise pensions. What are the marketing communications considerations involved in developing a campaign to encourage the purchase of pension schemes?
2. What are the key issues that face a financial services marketer with a pull strategy? Provide an example of how these issues have been addressed.

3. How has technology changed marketing communication, both in detail and in strategy?
4. How does sponsorship contribute to the marketing of financial services? In what way are the benefits of sponsorship measurable to the company?
5. What are the key messages that FIs need to covey and to which audiences post-credit crunch? Evaluate some of the new media's strengths for FI communication.

References

Booz Allen Hamilton (2006) *The Future of Advertising: Implications for Marketing and Media*, New York, Booz Allen Hamilton.

Cravens, D. and Piercy, N. (2006), *Strategic Marketing*, 8th international edn, Boston, McGraw Hill.

De Pelsmacker, P., Geuens, M. and Van den Bergh, J. (2005) *Foundations of Marketing Communications: A European Perspective*, Harlow, FT Prentice Hall.

Farquhar, J. and Panther, T. (2008), 'Acquiring and Retaining Customers in UK Banks: An Exploratory Study', *Journal of Retailing and Consumer Services*, Vol. 15, No. 1, pp. 9–21.

Fill, C. (2006) *Marketing Communications: Engagement, Strategies and Practice*, Harlow, FT Prentice Hall.

Garretson, J. and Burton, S. (2005) "The Role of Spokescharacters as Advertisement and Package Cues in Integrated Marketing Communications', *Journal of Marketing*, Vol. 69, October, pp. 118–32.

Gram, M. (2007),'Whiteness and Western Values in Global Advertisements: An Exploratory Study', *Journal of Marketing Communications*, Vol. 13, No. 4, pp. 291–309.

Gremler, D. and Brown, S. (1999) 'The Loyalty Ripple Effect: Appreciating the Full Value of Customers', *International Journal of Service Industries Management*, Vol. 10, No. 3, pp. 271–91.

Gronroos, C. (2000), *Service Management and Marketing: A Customer Relationship Management Approach*, Wiley & Sons, Chichester.

Hartley B. and Pickton, D. (1999) 'Integrated Marketing Communications Requires a New Way of Thinking', *Journal of Marketing Communications*, Vol. 5, No. 2, pp. 97–106.

Heinonen, K. and Strandvik, T. (2005) 'Communication as an Element of Service Value', *International Journal of Service Industry Management*, Vol. 16, No. 2, pp. 186–98.

Holm, O. (2006) 'Integrated Marketing Communications: From Tactics to Strategy', *Corporate Communications: An International Journal*, 1Vol. 1, No. 1, pp. 23–33.

Homburg, C., Workman, J. and Jensen, O. (2002) 'A Configurational Perspective on Key Account Management', *Journal of Marketing*, Vol. 66, pp. 38–60.

Keller, K. (2001) 'Mastering the Marketing Communications Mix: Micro and Macro Perspectives on Integrated Marketing Communication Programs', *Journal of Marketing Management*, Vol. 17, No. 7–8, pp. 819–47.

Madden, K. and Perry, C. (2003) 'How do Customers of a Financial Services Institution Judge its Communications?', *Journal of Marketing Communications*, Vol. 9, pp. 113–27.

Michael, A. and Salter, B. (2006) *Mobile Marketing*Oxford, , Butterworth-Heinemann.

Palmer, A. (2008) *Principles of Services Marketing*, 4th edition, London, McGraw Hill.

Plain English (2008) No. 73, p. 2, High Peak.

Riivari, J. (2005) 'Mobile Banking: A Powerful New Marketing and CRM Tool for Financial Services Companies all over Europe", *Journal of Financial Services Marketing*, Vol. 10, pp. 11–20.

Sharma, N. and Patterson, P. (1999) 'The Impact of Communication Effectiveness and Service Quality on Relationship Commitment in Consumer, Professional Services', *Journal of Services Marketing*, Vol. 13, No. 2, pp. 151–70.

Solberg, C. (2002) 'The Perennial Issue of Adaptation or Standardization of International Marketing Communication: Organizational Contingencies and Performance', *Journal of International Marketing*, Vol. 10, No. 3, pp. 1–21.

Thomas, J. and Sullivan, U. (2005) 'Managing Marketing Communications with Multichannel Customers', *Journal of Marketing*, October, pp. 239 51.

Further reading

www.moneymadeclear.fsa.gov.uk/about/financial_advertising.html
www.zurich.co.uk/home/Welcome/livingbritain/presspack.htm
www.ipa.co.uk
www.asa.org.uk
www.oft.gov.uk

CASE STUDY

The ASA and Alternative Finance Group Ltd

Channel S broadcast an advertisement for Alternative Finance Group, in a mixture of English and Bangladeshi. Channel S was voted the most popular Bengali channel outside Bangladesh in 2006. A recent UK survey also found Channel S as the most-viewed Bengali television channel in the

United Kingdom. According to Channel S, over 70,000 households in the United Kingdom watch the channel and the average Bengali household has around 4.8 people. Channel S is the only Bengali-language channel in the United Kingdom and Europe, and the channel claims that there is something for everyone. Programmes are produced not only in Bengali, but also in English and Sylheti to cater for the unique needs of the British Bangladeshis. The demographic of the audience for the channel breaks down as follows: 5–15 years old: 15 per cent; 16–24 years old: 28 per cent; 25–44 years old: 39 per cent; 45–64 years old: 10 per cent; and over 65: 8 per cent.

The advertisement referred to the ASA featured a male presenter speaking straight to the camera with a computerized image of a city skyline in the background. The presenter said in Bangladeshi, 'What would you think if I tell you that you can buy a house without any down payment...', while on-screen text stated, 'Buy property with no down payment, deposit or fees'. The presenter continued, '...you can get up to £50,000 cash back', while on-screen text stated, 'up to £50,000 cash back per investment deal'. The advertisement showed bundles of money piling up on-screen. The advert then showed small, round inset images of several properties, while the presenter said, '...you can build a property portfolio of about £1 million within only two years'. On-screen text stated, 'Develop £1 million property portfolio within 2 years'. The advert showed £50 notes falling on the presenter, while he continued, 'You can even earn an extra £50,000 within two years', and, at the same time, on-screen text stated, 'develop an annual income of £50,000 per year'. While he held a tree in the palm of his hand, the presenter went on to ask, 'Would you tell me that money does not grow on trees?' and the advert showed more £50 notes falling from the tree. On-screen text was stating, '100 per cent satisfaction guaranteed with full refund policy'. The presenter pointed to the viewer and said, 'Well, if you became a member of Alternative Investment Club, money will grow in your pocket.' The on-screen text invited viewers, 'Join the property investment club now! OFT Licence No 561669'. The ad concluded with an image of the company logo and the text 'Alternative Finance Group. 0871 xxxxxx. Other attractive products and services are available'. A woman's voice, speaking in Bangladeshi said, 'To find out more about our attractive products and services or to get more details, contact AFG on 0871 xxxxxx.'

Challenge

ASA monitoring staff challenged whether:

1. the advert offered an investment opportunity for an unregulated product;
2. the claimed earnings and rental return could be substantiated;
3. investment would result in a £1 million property portfolio value in two years;

4. investment in the properties would be possible without 'down payment, deposit or fees';
5. the advertiser implied it was licensed by the Office of Fair Trading (OFT) because of the reference to 'OFT Licence No xxx'.

Response

Channel S submitted a response from Alternative Finance Group Ltd (AFG) – doing business as Alternative Estates, who said the advert was for an 'Alternative Investment Club' – to the ASA challenges as follows:

1. Alternative Estates said AFG did not offer 'investment or financial products' directly and did not provide 'investment or financial advice to its members'. They explained that it offered access to independent financial advisers who could offer services to an investor and that it was up to the investor to source a mortgage or finance required to buy a property. They were designed to 'develop informed and educated members in property and property investment' and said the Alternative Investment Club afforded members 'Tailor-made training programmes', explaining, 'The Club also provides essential resources that are required for successful property investment, which includes access to finance, mortgages, legal and tax advisors.' They added that the club sourced below-market-value properties for its members.
2. and 3. Alternative Estates did not respond in writing but asserted that they had evidence to support the claims, which they did not submit. They said they had withdrawn the advert as a goodwill gesture.
4. and 5. Channel S did not comment.

Assessment

The first challenge was upheld. The ASA noted Alternative Estates' assertions that they did not offer investment or financial products but provided training programmes for successful property investment. The ASA pointed to rule 9.5 (c), which states, 'Any advertising which implies that, for example, a collectors' item or some other unregulated product or service could have investment potential would normally be unacceptable (investment is used in its colloquial sense in this note.)'. The ASA considered that the advert made several specific references to the financial advantages of investing in properties and implied those advantages would be gained as a direct result of becoming a member of the Alternative Investment Club. It was considered that the advert offered an investment opportunity for an unregulated product and so breached the Code. The advert breached CAP (Broadcast) TV Advertising Standards Code rule 9.5 (Unacceptable categories). Challenges 2, 3, 4 and 5 were also upheld. In the absence of evidence to substantiate them, the ASA considered that the claims were misleading. The advert breached CAP (Broadcast) TV Advertising Standards Code rule 5.1 (Misleading advertising) and 5.2.1 (Evidence).

Action

The ASA concluded that the advertisement was not to be shown again in its present form and that the product should not be advertised without adequate substantiation for the claims made for it.

Questions

1. What is the relevance of the viewing statistics that Channel S provides for marketing communications?
2. What was the key message that the advertisement was communicating and who was the audience?
3. What is the role of Channel S in broadcasting the advertisement from a marketing perspective? What lessons could the channel learn from this adjudication? Who are its stakeholders?

Compiled by the authors from www.asa.org.uk and www.chsuk.tv.

12

Marketing strategies in financial services

Contents

Learning outcomes

At the end of this chapter, the reader will be able to:

- Provide an overview of the principal components of marketing strategy and planning

- Outline key aspects of financial services marketing strategy and planning

- Review arguments for evaluating marketing practices and strategies

- Discuss marketing approaches for financial institutions (FIs) post-credit crunch.

Introduction

In this chapter, we will be looking into the strategic planning that financial institutions (FIs) might undertake. Through developing marketing plans, FIs can manage their resources most effectively in fast-moving competitive environments. Although we have looked at a number of different strategies, such as branding and marketing communications, we have yet to consider how the strategies are located within marketing planning.

EXHIBIT 12.1

Planning a brand

Plans for Aviva to become the customer brand for the Aviva Group worldwide were announced in early 2008. Aviva became the new name for the former CGNU in July 2002, which had been formed in 2000 by the merger of Norwich Union and CGU, itself the result of the merger of Commercial Union and General Accident in 1998. The change to Aviva is part of the group's planned journey towards being recognized as a world-class financial services provider. The Aviva brand brings together more than 40 different trading names around the world, creating further opportunities for the group to harness the benefits of its size and international capabilities. The aim is to create a new and powerful international financial services brand; the Aviva name tested positively in consumer research, being associated with life, vitality and living well. The Norwich Union brand, under which Aviva, the United Kingdom's biggest insurer, does most of its business in its home market, is very well known in British insurance but, within the next two years, this name will be abandoned and replaced by the Aviva name. It is considered that the brand advocacy of Norwich Union is not as high as some other financial services companies. The one exception to this strategy will be for motoring, where Aviva will continue to operate under the RAC brand. Senior management believes that the RAC brand has a motoring heritage in the United Kingdom. In Ireland, the 'Hibernian' name will go and, in Poland, so will the Commercial Union name. The rebranding will allow Aviva to expand its business and enter into deals with new distribution partners. The insurer was prepared to make a 'significant investment' to boost the Aviva name – £9 million. The move is part of a global push by the company to unify its branding under the Aviva name.

Compiled by the authors from Aviva plc, FT.com.

Exhibit 12.1 demonstrates how rebranding forms part of the insurance company's strategy to become a global provider of insurance services and how critical branding is as part of that strategy. Many FIs seek to achieve economies of scale – that is, lowering costs by producing or selling more – but, as part of building relationships and loyalty, strong branding must also occur.

What is strategic marketing?

stakeholders: a group of organizations or people to whom a company has some kind of responsibility or duty. Includes shareholders but recognizes that there are other groups, such as employees

TOWS analysis: a straightforward, popular way of analysing the capabilities of the organization and its responses to the current environment

Strategic marketing seeks to create the capability of an organization to adapt to changes in the marketing environment. The aim for an FI in planning its strategic marketing is to meet the needs of its customers and **stakeholders** through creating value more effectively than its competitors. In order to achieve this, an FI or any other organization requires a flexible and responsive organizational structure and culture that encompasses these stakeholders. An organization will usually conduct a thorough analysis of the environment in which it operates, usually consisting of a grouping all the variables in its environment under the heading of: threats, opportunities, weaknesses and strengths. This analysis is referred to as a SWOT or, as we prefer, a **TOWS analysis**. The value of a TOWS analysis is derived from its evaluation of external variables and a subsequent look at internal capabilities in the light of the external forces. This way round there is more likely to be a better 'fit' between what is happening or likely to happen outside the organization and its internal capabilities. For FIs, post-credit crunch, a TOWS analysis could look as represented in Table 12.1.

Looking at the threats that FIs face, the first is the control that governments, regulators and the European Union have gained in the financial services sector. In the longer term, there is also a strong possibility of a tighter legislative environment, although how tight that is going to be is not known yet. The Financial Services Authority (FSA) in the United Kingdom was not keeping a close enough eye on the activities of FIs and, as a result, the authority will probably be replaced or strengthened soon. The United States is planning to set up a financial services watchdog for consumers in the aftermath of the credit crunch. Weaknesses that FIs should consider include an over-emphasis on short-term growth and shareholder value, as both of these probably contributed to the demise of FIs such as Northern Rock. There is also the risk of increasing pressure from non-bank competitors, such as Virgin in the United Kingdom and Corte Inglés in Europe. Opportunities for FIs arise from the fact that there are fewer competitors, as weaker or more reckless institutions have been acquired by their stronger brethren. Both Grupo Santander and Nationwide have made some potentially valuable acquisitions at 'knockdown' prices, at the same time eliminating some of the competition. For brave FIs, there is also the opportunity for radically changing the way that they carry out their business. In particular, FIs could consider

Table 12.1   Post-credit crunch TOWS analysis

Threats	Opportunities
Government control	Fewer competitors
Loss of confidence: consumers, competitors, industry, media	Government loans
Competition from new entrants	Pressure to do things differently and achieve some differentiation or distinction
Increased cynicism and scrutiny	IT capability
Poorly differentiated marketplace	
Low margins	
customer spending down	

Weaknesses	Strengths
Short term outlook	Established position
Entrenched practices and thinking	Well known and alternative providers not known
Lack of customer focus	
Focus on market growth rather than customer growth	Expertise and knowledge
	Systems
Emphasis on shareholder value	Customer inertia
Weak brand	

shifting from maximizing shareholder value to reflecting on stakeholder approach, which would also support their social marketing objectives. The strength of FIs is derived from the key role that they play in global, regional and national economies, as evidenced by the government support that was provided when a number of them were on the brink of failing. Stakeholder thinking will be discussed in more detail later in the chapter.

There is, as yet, little evidence to suggest that the big banks are considering radical changes. In spite of the public outrage at the bonuses paid to senior staff, there are signs that bonuses are back with Goldman Sachs, the investment bank planning to pay large bonuses in 2009 (observer.co.uk). In not responding to the opportunities, FIs are probably displaying their characteristic short-termism and entrenched position. Many will be quietly biding their time and waiting for all the fuss to die down so that they can get back to doing things the way that they have always done them. To be fair, there seems little incentive for them to change. Governments have bailed them out, there have been few conditions to these bail-outs and we are all highly dependent on the banking and insurance infrastructure and the services that it provides – and that includes governments!

An essential part of strategic planning is the formulation of objectives, which fall into the three categories, as suggested in Table 12.2.

Table 12.2	Financial institution objectives, performance criteria and metrics

Objectives	Performance criteria	Metrics
Profit and financial objectives	Profitability	Profit Profit as percentage of sales Return on investment
	Contribution to shareholders	Earnings per share Price–earnings ratio
	Utilization of fixed assets	Capacity utilization Fixed assets as a percentage of sales.
Growth objectives	Per cent yearly growth	Sales Unit sales Profits
	Competitive strengths	Market share, share of wallet Brand awareness Brand preference
	Contribution to customers	Price relative to competition Customer satisfaction, value Customer retention Customer loyalty
Social responsibility objectives	Contribution to employees	Career development Reward packages, work–life balance
	Contribution to society	Support for community activities and charities
	Contribution to the environment	Reduction of carbon footprint

Source: Adapted from Hollensen (2003).

The first priority for profit and financial objectives is to look at the revenue that the FI is generating; the contribution of marketing to these objectives is significant. It has long been thought, and there may be pockets of this thinking still, that marketing is something of an extravagance, meaning that it has constantly been required to provide evidence of return on investment (ROI). Although ROI is useful in situations for the marketing mix and where the total marketing budget is fixed, more broadly Ambler (2003) argues that the concept is flawed. Instead he puts the case for discounted cash flow (DCF), which can be crudely described as payback – that is, how long it will take to recover the cost of the investment. More formally, DCF is a method of estimating an investment's current value based on the discounting of projected future revenues and costs. The further into the future the flow occurs, the more heavily it will be discounted (www.cim.co.uk). The example of corporate objectives also contains growth objectives that impact on marketing strategies. Many FIs, along with other companies, have been very concerned with achieving growth through mergers and acquisitions (M&A). Growth has often been achieved through the take-over or absorption of other FIs. Grupo Santander, for example, the Spanish-based FI, looked at the financial services market in the United Kingdom, noting particularly its relative freedom from financial regulation, and has made three acquisitions – Abbey, Alliance & Leicester and part of Bradford & Bingley, the last two as a result of the credit crunch.

Competitive strategies

When viewing the competitive arena from a traditional perspective, an important model was developed by Michael Porter, which has stood the test of time. Porter (1980) advocated three main ways of achieving competitive advantage: cost leadership, differentiation and focus. Cost leadership involves a very tight control of the costs within the FI through such activities as economies of scale, maximizing customer value and a constant re-evaluation of costs across the organization in relation to its organizational objectives. The attempts by FIs to migrate customers over to the Internet for their banking are an example of lowering costs. However, there is a significant difference between lowering costs and achieving cost leadership through having the lowest cost base and there is little evidence of any FI achieving this. At the same time, service quality levels need to match target market expectations and the value of employee skills and knowledge be fully appreciated. The problem of differentiation in financial services is ongoing. FIs have tried to achieve differentiation through branding, but, as discussed elsewhere, branding is not well understood by FIs, thus a means of creating differentiation has been missed. A focus strategy requires a company to maintain such close links with its customers/target market that no other competitor can intervene. This sort of strategy is suitable for smaller organizations. There is certainly some evidence that smaller building societies have pursued this strategy, where they believed that they could meet the needs of a local or regional community with a relatively narrow range of products. The dwindling number of smaller building societies may suggest that this strategy, or the way that it was implemented, has not proved successful.

Whilst financial services is a highly competitive industry, there is always the danger that competition may come from an unexpected direction and catch the industry unawares. First Direct was the first non-branch bank and its vision and strategy are benchmarks in the financial services industry. In the meantime, practically all FIs now offer on-line or telephone banking, but First Direct, through an understanding of its target market, has managed to hold onto its premium position in the marketplace. Porter (1985) later developed an equally enduring model that maps the forces that impact on the competitive arena of any sector (Figure 12.1).

In considering these five forces, Porter encourages managers to think about a wider competitive framework that enables them to defend and attack more effectively than if they just focused on existing rivalry. There is always a danger that, in a highly competitive marketplace, resources are devoted to responding to or overcoming the immediate competition and the core business of the company can be forgotten. The 'five forces' model is a potent one that encourages strategists to think more creatively about ways to compete. For the FI sector, the threat of new entrants is very real, as the case study for this chapter argues. Food retailers across Europe see that offering financial services is a means of growth beyond the retailing of foods, furniture

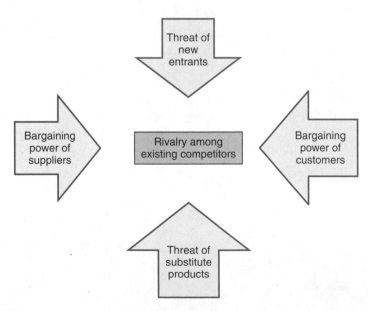

Figure 12.1 Five competitive forces in financial services
Source: Adapted from Porter (1985).

and all the other areas into which they have expanded. The entry of new competitors increases the power of customers and the loss of confidence in traditional FIs may encourage more customers to switch. Business and corporate customers are not as able as consumers to move away from the specialist services that FIs provide, such as insurance and credit facilities. Nonetheless, some of these customers are in a strong position to bargain, owing to the size of the business that they bring to FIs. Smaller businesses do not have the same bargaining power and have long complained about the charges and services that they receive from FIs; they have less bargaining power. The threat posed by substitute products is high in the sector as there is an extensive choice of suppliers that meet the needs of financial service customers. The bargaining power of suppliers is not such an issue in this service sector, as most FIs create their own offerings, but the business is affected by the supply of money and credit in the interbank market.

Marketing strategies

competitive strategies: strategies that enable the organization to compete against its rivals

In reviewing FIs' **competitive strategies**, essentially three broad categories of marketing strategies can be seen to be open to them: defensive, offensive and rationalization. These are set out in Figure 12.2.

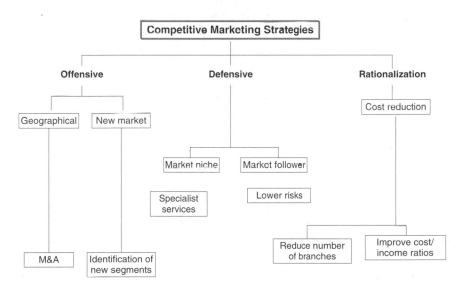

Figure 12.2   An overview of FI competitive marketing strategies

Being offensive

FIs have a choice of offensive marketing strategies that they can pursue as described below. For the last two decades, FIs have been adopting very offensive strategies; however, this is changing in the current difficult conditions.

Geographical expansion strategy: in spite of the highly competitive marketplace, FIs are always looking to enlarge their geographical footprint. In spite of the high costs of branches, FIs, particularly banks and the larger building societies, understand that a physical presence is a means of growing. As part of a global growth strategy, RBS acquired the Dutch bank ABN AMRO, for which they paid far too much, resulting in the bank's huge losses in 2009 and the resignation of the chief executive.

Penetration strategy: this is a straightforward strategy where an FI will try to grow by selling existing products to its existing customers or, as it is known in financial services, cross-selling. Developments in information systems, specifically data mining, have supported this strategy, as FIs have been able to estimate the probabilities of success of targeting individual customers or segments of customers with selected financial offerings. This is an ongoing strategy, which has largely arisen from the saturated state of most financial service marketplaces in Europe, with the strategy of relationship marketing arising from penetration.

New market strategies: although much of the 'old' EU is probably saturated in terms of financial services, there are countries applying to join the EU, such as Turkey, Macedonia and Croatia, which offer potential for new markets for established companies to target. The Volvo Group, for example, has begun to offer finance for leasing and instalment credits, along with insurance and fleet solutions, to the truck and aero companies in Turkey. The identification of new segments is of vital significance to FIs, but the saturated markets offer little chance for this. The discovery of the sub-prime market and the ability of 'securitizing' the risks that this segment presented proved highly attractive to many FIs. The fall-out from the activities of this new market strategy continues to reverberate around the world. Figure 12.3 adapts a familiar model in marketing to show how FIs could develop **growth strategies** that might be appropriate during and after the credit crunch.

growth strategies:
strategies that will enable the organization to grow

The model is developed around existing and new products and customers. From these two core dimensions, four alternatives emerge: penetration, product development, new markets and, finally, diversification. The model has its limitations, which are related to changes in marketing since it was

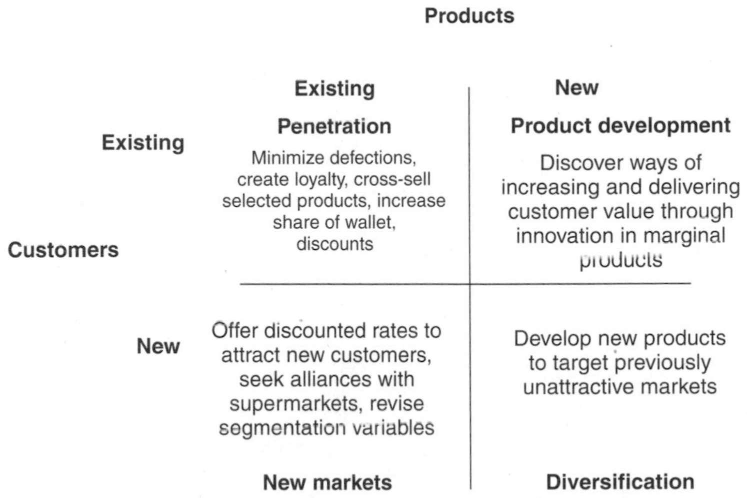

Products

		Existing	New
Existing		**Penetration**	**Product development**
		Minimize defections, create loyalty, cross-sell selected products, increase share of wallet, discounts	Discover ways of increasing and delivering customer value through innovation in marginal products
Customers			
New		Offer discounted rates to attract new customers, seek alliances with supermarkets, revise segmentation variables	Develop new products to target previously unattractive markets
		New markets	**Diversification**

Figure 12.3 Growth strategies for FIs
Source: Adapted from Ansoff (1957).

first developed. There is a real danger that there may be an over-emphasis on product development rather than innovation. Innovation is more likely to be the outcome of a market-driven inspiration rather than the need to just get another product out into the marketplace, although there have been recent suggestions that growth can be achieved through innovation (Datamonitor 2009). Recent contributions to marketing that cite value, and the role of the customer in creating that value (Grönroos 2006, Vargo and Lusch 2004), offer a way forward for FIs in this challenging period. Locating new customers is difficult in mature and even saturated markets; this has led to the practice of encouraging customer switching and, more notoriously, the provision of home loans to customers who really were not credit-worthy. Diversification is considered as the riskiest of strategies but some companies seem to be able to pull it off – for example, Richard Branson with the Virgin brand. Moreover, diversification may be the only way that FIs can grow.

Market leader strategy: this strategy can involve larger FIs acquiring smaller players or, perhaps, FIs that may be in a vulnerable position. Nationwide has been taking over smaller building societies for some time – for example, the Portman and, more recently, as a result of the credit crunch, the Cheshire and Derbyshire building societies. Grupo Santander has also been able to make further acquisitions in the credit crunch, such as part of the Bradford & Bingley and Alliance & Leicester banks. This strategy can have dangerous outcomes; Lloyds

Banking Group was brought nearly to its knees by the takeover of HBOS. Market leaders also tend to advertise heavily.

Market challenge strategies: within Europe, opportunities for growth also exist through alliances with supermarkets – for example, Asda stores offer a credit card in partnership with GE Capital; Marks & Spencer's Money is owned by HSBC. The retailers have developed strong brands, something which the banks that they are allied with have not been able to achieve. Nonetheless, these alliances have allowed the banks access to markets that they might not have reached on their own. Cross-selling has not been the success that FIs might have hoped for, as customers, both personal and commercial, seem happy to be 'multibanked'; indeed, to a certain extent, it has been in their interest to be so. FIs have made the assumption that customers view financial services rather as they do, that is, insurance, current accounts, savings and investment opportunities are all part of one category or, at least, related. Supermarkets are aware, for example, that they need to make sure that they have the largest share of a consumer's spend, but this spend varies from consumer to consumer. However, customers may not see financial services as being like a supermarket trolley and instead be prepared to buy insurance from one provider, save with another and have a current account with another still. If this is the case, then the whole concept (and metric) of share of wallet is highly questionable. If customers view the various financial services as quite unrelated to each other (who talks about 'my financial services provider'?), then the aim of gaining as a large a share of a customer's wallet appears misguided.

protection strategies: strategies that enable organizations to respond to harsh or volatile conditions

Protection strategies

Figure 12.1 also provides some examples of how FIs can protect themselves in a highly volatile situation. Trading conditions have been favourable to FIs in the last decade or so and management teams may be ill prepared for developing strategies for the current climate.

The **market follower** will reduce risks and there is evidence that many banks are just not lending, either to consumers or to businesses. Small businesses in the United Kingdom, for example, are experiencing considerable difficulties, as their banks are not providing them with the finance that they need to continue trading (fsb.org.uk). The housing market in the United Kingdom slowed significantly as buyers struggled to find finance for house purchases.

The **niche strategy** is highly favoured by smaller building societies; it is a strategy where a company or organization identifies a small market or segment of customers whom they believe they can serve exclusively. Smaller building societies have, to some extent, been able to do this over the years, concentrating on their 'heartland' customers – that is, those who live within the geographical environs of the society, which often has a strong link to an area, such as the Kent Reliance Building Society. It is a sad outcome of the credit crunch that several of these small, worthy organizations have had to be taken over by other larger mutuals as described in Exhibit 12.2.

EXHIBIT 12.2

Bailing out the Barnsley

Barnsley Building Society is based in Yorkshire in the United Kingdom; it has only eight branches, 60,000 members and is the 34th-largest society in the United Kingdom. Having built, over many years, a strong presence in the community, the society was obliged to approach its bigger rival, Yorkshire Building Society, seeking a merger. The situation was a result of investments made by the society in Icelandic banks, which had failed with a possible loss to the society of £10 million. The Barnsley is the latest victim of the implosion of the Icelandic banking system, which has seen hundreds of thousands of UK savers losing access, for the time being, to any money they held in accounts with the Icesave Internet bank and other Icelandic banking operations. The society had its money on deposit with Kaupthing Singer & Friedlander (KSF) and with the Heritable bank, owned by Landsbanki, the parent of Icesave. However, the Barnsley has found itself in exactly the same position as dozens of local authorities, charities and other organizations; collectively, they had more than a billion pounds on deposit with Icelandic banks. They were not covered by the United Kingdom's Financial Services Compensation Scheme and will have to wait for the outcome of the current negotiations between the United Kingdom and the Icelandic governments to see how much money, if any, they will get back. Some jobs may go as a result of the takeover. Staff in the branches, which will keep the Barnsley name, will be kept on, but some of the 50 staff in the Barnsley's headquarters may be lost when they are transferred to the Yorkshire's head office. The Building Societies Association (BSA) revealed, in October 2008, that its members had about £200 million in Icelandic banks, but said this amounted to just to 0.05 per cent of total assets.

Compiled by the authors from www.bbc.co.uk, www.bsa.org.uk and www.barnsley-bs.co.uk.

Building societies are part of the history of financial services in the United Kingdom, but their numbers are continually shrinking as they are taken over or have converted to banks, suggesting that what they offer may no longer be valued sufficiently by most financial services customers. Although a niche strategy may be difficult to pursue, Doyle (2002) draws attention to certain niche companies, but, again, in a mature marketplace, it is difficult to maintain such a position. A niche company has to deliver superior value to its target market. This can be achieved through offering superior service quality to these customers (for example, First Direct probably achieves this) and is achieved when the FI knows, understands and meets the requirements of its market. The alternative is to offer lower prices to its market, which has often been the argument of the smaller societies, although the evidence of this has not always been clear. Adopting a niche strategy or being a niche company has some potential for FIs but the maturity of the marketplace makes the strategy more challenging than it may at first appear.

Diversification is a strategy where an FI will take new products into new markets and, as such, is higher risk than the other protective strategies. Looking at the development of new products, involves, according to the latest definition of marketing (see marketingpower.org), understanding how to co-create value with customers. Traditional new product development for financial services has always been problematic, mainly because competitors can easily replicate the developments in new products and enhanced services. The concept of understanding how to improve and deliver value may not yet have been fully absorbed by FIs, but the integration of product and delivery offers potential for some creative thinking; again, however, replication remains a problem. The diversification option has been tried several times in the past, notably in the 1980s where many financial services took over estate agencies in the United Kingdom in order to facilitate the selling of mortgages and house insurance. For many FIs, it was a highly expensive and largely unsuccessful strategy, although Skipton Building Society still owns Connells Estate Agents. The credit crunch may discourage diversification strategies for the time being.

It is far more likely, for the time being, that FIs will be pursuing **rationalization** strategies, which consist of reducing costs through improving cost/income ratios. In terms of marketing, this might include selling more to existing customers, with concentration on particular customer segments, avoiding high-risk loans. As shown in Exhibit 12.3, this is a common response in difficult market conditions.

EXHIBIT 12.3

Job losses

Ulster Bank announced that it was to amalgamate 60 branches of mortgage provider First Active into the rest of the bank. This amalgamation meant cutting up to 550 staff in the Irish Republic and up to 200 in Northern Ireland. A voluntary severance package was available to staff. The merger, completed towards the end of 2008, resulted in an organization with more than 1.8 million customers, 295 branches and an ATM network of more than 1,250 across the island of Ireland. Ulster Bank acquired First Active in 2004 and, between them, the two subsidiaries employed around 8,000 people. The Ulster Bank group, one of Ireland's so-called 'big four' banks, said it was looking to cut costs throughout all areas of its business. The plan included making the business a single brand in the Republic. The bank, founded in Belfast in 1836, said its plans in Northern Ireland included measures to support customers experiencing financial difficulties. The plan also included funding for the provision of debt advice, staff secondment for debt agency work and a six-month postponement on house repossession after a customer first goes into arrears. Ireland's banking sector continues to come under intense pressure as recession squeezes the one-time 'Celtic Tiger' economy and the housing market plummets.

Compiled by the authors from www.telegraph.co.uk, www.skynews.com, www.bbc.co.uk and www.ulsterbank.co.uk.

FIs, as with many companies, may not always fully appreciate the contribution that staff make to the successful running of the business, seeing staff as a cost rather than an asset. Although it is absolutely vital to manage the cost/income balance effectively in good as well as bad times, a knee-jerk reaction to harsh conditions of letting staff go does not always take into account the knowledge, skills and enthusiasm that staff bring to organizational success. These assets can be very hard to replace when the economy starts to grow; other companies will be looking for staff as well at that time. In order to respond to the credit crunch, a rationalization strategy has immediate appeal but there are always options in the way that this strategy can be operationalized which need to be based on scrupulous analysis and the setting of creative objectives.

A critical process in strategy development is to identify key performance indicators (KPIs). Key performance indicators are those metrics that an FI will use to measure its success. The following performance measures have been suggested as appropriate for FIs (Accenture 2008):

- Maximize the return on marketing investment. Use integrated marketing, customer and financial data to develop, implement and monitor marketing resource allocation (MRA) strategies to maximize shareholder value.
- Increase brand value. Ensure that the company and product brands hold the most value for customers and, consequently, generate greater value for the company at large.
- Increase the acquisition and retention of profitable customers. Maximize the profitability of customer relationships.

- Optimize the development and launch of new products. Ensure that the right new products are developed and launched to maximize customer relationship value and market share.
- Win the war for marketing talent. Attract, develop and retain the best people within the marketing function.
- Organize the marketing function for efficiency and effectiveness. Maximize the time during which employees and activities are adding value to the organization.
- Reduce the time to learn required competencies. Reduce the elapsed time from day-one introduction date to the time it takes for a marketing employee to meet the targeted performance level. This reduction may include the time to performance for a new hire or for an existing marketing employee with a new job responsibility, technology to use, or product or service to support.
- Build trust, restore confidence and to act in accordance with statements about **corporate social responsibility**.

Adapted and extended from www.accenture.com/
Global/Research_and_Insights

corporate social responsibility: in marketing terms, this refers to adopting practices that, at least, do no harm or aim to achieve good

This last point is one that has been added by the authors as an objective that could be developed as part of post-credit crunch strategies. Customer confidence in FIs has been weakened further and a proactive response would be to think about how the current situation provides opportunities to really work on this situation.

If diversification has proved problematic for FIs in gaining sustainable growth, it is worthwhile returning to the growth opportunities that may be derived from existing and new customers. It is important to remember that marketing is concerned with both the acquisition and retention of customers (Drucker 1963). The issue of customer retention has not always received due consideration; the attraction of new customers was always regarded as the prime indication of growth. However, this has changed dramatically as companies become aware of the costs of customer turnover (or churn) and information systems have provided the means of tracking customers, calculating their value to the FI and estimating probabilities of further purchases. Financial services have been no different from other industries in this tendency, with strategies directed at penetrating new markets or gaining market share playing the dominant role. Shareholders, who often receive undue consideration in strategic planning, interpret an increase in market share as a 'good thing', with a resultant increase in earnings per share and price/earnings ratio (see Table 12.2). However, an increase in market share in itself is not necessarily the 'good thing' that shareholders and investors may think. The matter of how success is measured is an increasingly contentious topic as marketers argue for metrics that are more appropriate for marketing strategies.

The costs of gaining new customers can be very high – such as research, advertising and other start-up costs, including credit checks. Additionally, the projected revenue of new customers can only be estimated, so an FI cannot always predict how much money a particular customer will bring in. Attractive rates for savings products, credit cards and mortgages, for example, attract customers who are very rate-aware (the industry term is the far from polite: 'rate tart') and who then will move when any discounted rate expires. Although FIs are very aware of the financial costs of these rate-aware customers and price their products accordingly, the 'costs' of customer churn are nonetheless high. These costs have had to be recouped somehow and, in the past, have been recovered from existing customers who have noted with considerable dissatisfaction the attractive rates offered to new customers while they quite literally pay for being loyal to the FI. Developments in information technology enable FIs to look at individual customers and calculate their value to the organization, which has led them to appreciate their existing customers a little better.

Saturated markets and intense competition have demonstrated to strategic planners in FIs the benefits of retaining customers and related marketing concepts such as relationship marketing and customer loyalty. FIs have embraced both of these ideas with enthusiasm, if not with the requisite expertise. Relationship marketing has developed into customer relationship management (CRM), where, in many cases, customers receive poorly directed marketing messages aimed at cross-selling. Customer loyalty is a precious and delicate flower that has also been poorly understood, as mentioned above. Great progress has been made, although the credit crunch has opened up an abyss under the feet of FIs and customers alike. Credit crunch notwithstanding, business must go on and FIs have to try and balance marketing activities that support both the acquisition and retention of customers (Farquhar 2005). This balance, in terms of strategic planning, requires them to encompass the trade-offs between increasing market share and customer lifetime value (Johnson and Selnes 2004).

Social responsibility and stakeholder thinking

Traditional marketing strategies are modelled on a military analogy and much of the terminology, such as 'offensive' and 'defensive', relate directly to that way of thinking. In Table 12.2 there is a set of objectives, which are directed towards social responsibility. A quick check of FI websites indicates that socially responsible behaviour is prominently displayed on the pages – see, for example, the Portuguese Banco Espírito Santo (www.bes.pt/sitebes/cms.aspx?labelid=BESresponsabilidadesocial).

However, in order really to address socially responsible objectives and to move forward from pre-credit crunch practices, a re-evaluation of strategy may be desirable. Most FIs justify their actions on the basis that they have a duty to their shareholders, with customers also being cited. What if, however, there are other groups to whom they have a duty. The term 'stakeholder' has already been mentioned in earlier chapters and has been defined as 'any group or individual who can affect or is affected by the achievement of the organization's objective' (Freeman 1984: p. 25), thus drawing into strategic management a number of players erstwhile overlooked. The value of identifying and working within a stakeholder framework is that it enhances corporate strategy by recognizing the complexity of understanding the roles and interactions of companies and stakeholders and moves management on from the 'reigning orthodoxy of shareholder value' (Freeman 1984: p. 11). This change in approach means that businesses engage with a range of stakeholders whose views of the business may vary greatly (Andriof et al. 2002). The benefits of such a strategy are that former competitors collaborate rather than battle, changing the business landscape. As stakeholder thinking has evolved, engaging with stakeholders is perceived as a proactive partnering, whichthen begins to involve similar dimensions as relationships, such as trust, commitment and reciprocity (Andriof and Waddock 2002), which are the very qualities that FIs should be seeking to strengthen. Within a stakeholder environment, businesses do not respond to stakeholders individually but instead have multiple interactions and experiences (Ambler and Wilson 1995). As a means of managing the multiplicity of interactions, it is essential to identify a company's stakeholders; the basis for this identification is through the three variables of power, legitimacy and urgency (Mitchell et al. 1997). Power is derived from being in control of the resources; legitimacy is concerned with the convergence of organizational practice with the wider social system; and urgency or attention-getting capacity is the ability to impress with one's claims or interests (Mitchell et al. 1997). This analysis allows both the identification and saliency of stakeholders to emerge and identifies amongst them seven ranked categories, from dormant to definitive (Mitchell et al. 1997). In the shorter term, a more straightforward approach is suggested. Through a series of actions, FIs can direct their efforts to stakeholders to try to restore confidence through exhibiting trustworthy behaviours.

Relationships and brands

The target of branding activities is generally considered to be the customer; however, it has been recognized that in services where the brand is often enacted between an employee and the customer, this exclusivity of firm/customer in branding breaks down. If the brand exists in the employee's mind as well as the customer and the firm, there also may be others in the brand environment whose role needs to be explored. An important clue here is the assertion that branding needs to be considered subservient to customer relationships (Rust *et al.* 2004) or that the relationship proposition fits in a consumer-brand context (Fournier 1998). The concept of stakeholder has long been acknowledged in relationship marketing (for example, Buttle 1996, Payne *et al.* 2005, Kumar and Reinartz 2006) and has some representation in branding (Gregory 2007, Maio 2003). Models of stakeholders in relationship marketing have been developed (Christopher *et al.* 2002; Kumar and Reinartz 2006; Yau *et al.* 2007) which consist of a number of different parties in the relationship. There are differing suggestions about the constituents and the number of stakeholders, although customers and employees/internal markets are common to most assessments. The value of the models is a reminder in planning and analysis that a narrow focus on the customer is insufficient for competitive activity and that a wider perspective is desirable.

Brands are only a means to an end, which is the building and sustaining of relationships (Rust *et al.* 2004). In support of this assertion, there are frequent overlaps between branding and relationships – for example, the antecedents and consequences of branding are analogous to those of relationship marketing (De Chernatony and McDonald 1998). Branding is a holistic process that provides focus to the internal relationship between the service company and the employees and which should come alive in the external relationship. Within a business-to-business context, stakeholders in the various models include companies, where the strength of the brand will influence decisions to repurchase or to renew (Roberts and Merrilees 2007). A conceptual study suggests that the brand strength of the focal firm in any network will moderate the relationship between partner firm performance and customer evaluation of the focal firm (including brand image) (Morgan *et al.* 2007). The stakeholder model as part of branding has gained some currency in marketing. Gregory (2007), for example, has recently proposed a model demonstrating different levels of stakeholder power and interest with the organization that guides communication with stakeholders. Brands can evolve not only by intent, but also through the participating stakeholder network/community. Brands evolve: a way to manage the evolution of a brand may be to harness the brand stakeholders so that the values of the brand are maintained.

An important and valuable dimension to stakeholder involvement in branding has been noted by Merrilees *et al.* (2005), who argued that interorganizational linkages can be enhanced through an application of stakeholder theory. The implications for branding are that the favourable messages that branding seeks to send to a wider range of stakeholders, who have a range of 'relationships' with the brand, need to be consistent and appropriate for that stakeholder. Furthermore, there is the important consideration regarding the creation of value, which has usually focused on the company customer (Payne and Frow 2005), but the concept of stakeholder suggests that value has to be created for *all* stakeholders. Rust *et al.* (2004) develop the concept of three forms of equity, based on value equity (quality/price/convenience), brand equity (customer's subjective assessment of a brand's offering) and relationship equity (switching costs), that, overall, make up customer equity. Although this concept has been developed for a statistical calculation about customer lifetime value, the three equity types lend themselves to reworking for understanding stakeholder equity. For example, for suppliers, what is their idea of value *vis à vis* their exchange with the company? How important is the brand to them in deciding on how to respond to a contract? How strong are the bonds of the relationship? What costs are there for the company and its supplier in switching suppliers? Models of stakeholder branding are beginning to emerge in the financial services marketing literature. Jones (2005) has produced a model of stakeholder brand equity that identifies the processes behind brand value creation; however, this model simply defines stakeholders as primary and secondary. Brand managers need to prioritize stakeholder relations according to their possible impact on brand value creation; there is something counter-intuitive about this suggestion, as the acknowledgement of stakeholders implies some notion of egality/equity/fairness.

Brands as relationship builder

The antecedents and consequences of branding are analogous to those of relationship marketing; for example, the rationale for branding for a marketer is as a way of communicating to the consumer relevant values that competitors find difficult to emulate (De Chernatony and McDonald 1998). Branding is a holistic process that provides focus to the internal relationship between the service company and the employees and comes alive in the external relationship. Given the concentration on the communication with the customer, is it legitimate to suggest that there may be a lack of appreciation of other stakeholders in the relationship?

In Table 12.2, social responsibility objectives are shown. It would seem that very nearly all FIs have made statements about social responsibility; indeed the Ecology Building Society and the Co-operative Bank have positioned themselves clearly as FIs with a conscience. There is some slight confusion between ethical marketing and social marketing. For the purposes of this discussion, these two areas are considered together, although ethics is the foundation for developing a socially and environmentally responsible strategy. Definitions of business ethics vary but there is some consensus that ethics is a standard for judging the rightness of an action, either in itself or in relation to other people. The Financial Services Authority (2002) has provided a framework of core values for the industry as follows:

- to be open, honest, responsive and accountable
- to be committed to acting competently, responsibly and reliably
- to relate to colleagues and customers fairly and with respect.

Not only is the encouragement from regulatory authorities to develop ethical practices, but also customers and other stakeholders are seeking evidence of ethical, social or environmental activities as part of their selection criteria. What are the implications of these requirements for FIs? Exhibit 12.4 provides an indication of how the Co-operative Bank acts.

EXHIBIT 12.4

Ethics and profits: the Co-op way

The bank, which is part of the Co-operative Financial Services group, which positions itself as the high-street leader for ethical banking, has rejected loans from companies involved in fossil fuels, arms dealing, tobacco and those linked to human and animal rights violations, as part of its ethical and ecological policy. Ethical banking would appear to be a growing area as the market value of ethical finance grew from £5.2 billion in 1999 to £11.6 billion in 2005. A survey by the Ethical Investment Research Service in 2004 reported that two-thirds of people wanted their investments to be more ethically sound. The Co-operative Bank's profits grew by 11.7 per cent in 2006 and many customers join the bank solely because of its ethical policies. The bank plans a major expansion programme, and recently announced plans for 12 new corporate banking centres over the next five years; it is currently in talks with Britannia Building Society about joint actions. Jonathon Porritt, the founder and director of Forum for the Future, said: 'The Co-operative Bank's Ethical Policy remains at the leading edge of corporate ethics, and has provided a clear challenge to the rest of the sector that there are certain lines that should not be crossed.' To have declined £325 million of loans based on customers' ecological concerns, of which the largest portion concerns saying 'no' to the extraction and processing of fossil fuels, is noteworthy at a time when we all need to consider the enormous adaptations that will be required to challenge climate change.

Compiled by the authors from material from www.financialadvice.co.uk and www.cfs.co.uk.

Other FIs have developed positions and policies in a number of related areas, including corporate social responsibility (CSR), sustainability (Crédit Agricole), social commitment (Grupo Santander), corporate responsibility (Commerzbank) and community outreach (Alfa Bank). One model of CSR presents a company's social obligations as comprising economic, legal, ethical and philanthropic responsibilities (Carroll 1991). As businesses are created as economic entities driven by a motive for profits, economic performance underpins the other three. Legal responsibilities require businesses, in this case FIs, to comply with local, national and international law and regulations. Ethical responsibilities are as suggested above. Philanthropic responsibilities are the expectations that the bank will engage in programmes that promote welfare and goodwill. There has been more guidance on developing policies that meet ethical and socially responsible behaviour; this has centred on a number of dimensions (Bhattacharya and Sen 2004), which have been modified and extended here to suit financial services.

1. Employee diversity that includes gender, race and disability
2. Employee support such as union relations, concern for safety and health, development
3. Product development to include safety, suitability to customer needs, avoiding funding of unethical or environmentally damaging projects
4. Collecting, storing and using information responsibly
5. Overseas operations, in terms of behaving responsibly in new markets, understanding networks
6. Impact on the environment, such as recycling, minimizing pollution, reduction in waste, innovation in work practices
7. Community support, to include financial support for charities, the arts, the disadvantaged.

Researchers into CSR have also observed that there is a degree of self-interest in pursuing ethical and socially responsible strategies, as there is an impact on customer satisfaction (McDonald and Rundle-Thiele, 2007). There is abundant evidence on FI websites that many of them have subscribed to one of the several interpretations of socially responsible behaviour, ranging from sponsorship of the arts to the support of farming in developing countries, consistent with points 6 and 7 above. Of course, there is always information that rather undermines FI messages. In May 2008, Friends of the Earth announced that UK banks are funding rapid expansion of biofuel production in Latin America, leading to large-scale deforestation, human rights abuses and rising food prices (www.foe.co.uk).

The immediate future?

As another merger was announced in November 2008 between the Scarborough and Skipton building societies in the United Kingdom; it is becoming clear that the ramifications of the credit crunch will continue to make themselves felt for some time to come across the world. Even though the mergers, acquisitions and failures of FIs may slow, the effects of the crunch are going to be profound and long lasting. Homes have already been repossessed and banks have withdrawn personal loan and mortgage offerings; rates have been increased on credit card repayments. There has been widespread condemnation of those FIs who lent unwisely and then repossessed the homes of those to whom it had provided finance. The credit crunch affects not only FIs and their consumers; it has made inroads also into a number of sectors, such as retail, manufacturing and the hospitality industry.

From a marketing perspective, it is also likely that, in the aftermath of the credit crunch of the late 'noughties', as a result of making savings, FIs may cut their marketing budgets along with other spending, which may be considered optional. This would, of course, be an unwise if not fatal move, at least for some. One of the problems that will arise and, indeed, there is some evidence that it already has, is the loss of any confidence that consumers and other stakeholders may have had in FIs. Even FIs that have borrowed and lent with prudence are finding themselves exposed owing to the folly of others (see Exhibit 12.2), particularly when they are too small or insignificant to attract government or EU support. There is the maxim that to be in debt for £1,000 means that the banks have power over you, but to owe £100 million means that you have power over the banks. Similarly, the larger the amount that the bank owes, the more likely it is that a third party will provide the funds to prop it up. Any FI, professional association, regulatory body or government will have to focus on how confidence in the financial system, never mind individual FIs, can be rebuilt. Marketing and marketers have the requisite expertise to, first, gain insight into how stakeholders now view FIs and then to begin to develop strategies, not marketing messages alone, to deal with the long, slow haul of rebuilding confidence and, perhaps, a degree of trust into the system.

The rise of the alternatives

The current environment of financial services marketing could be an opportunity for the newer entrants in the marketplace to increase market share. There are also some well-established institutions, such as National Savings and Investments, that could play a part. This particular government-owned investment and savings organization is, rather unsurprisingly, trusted by 25 per cent of respondents, compared to a figure of 16 per cent with high-street banking brands (Mintel 2008). The organization appointed a new head of PR and media relations in November 2008, with the intention of optimizing its trusted position in the marketplace (www.nsandi.com). There may be some constraints on how competitive they can be; it is also possible that commercial FIs would complain if NS&I were too successful.

Nonetheless, there is a real opportunity for alternative providers to gain market share in the aftermath of the credit crunch by offering services that are untainted by the short-termism of some of the FIs. Banks are, however, strongly embedded in the fabric of modern society and, as mentioned throughout the book, customers are very disinclined to switch, especially to non-traditional FIs.

Marketing more than ever

Will the map of financial services change? There have already been threats to major names, such AIG, Fortis Bank and Northern Rock and disappearances such as Lehman Brothers, reducing the number of providers. Concentration among FIs means less choice for consumers of financial services. For example, the takeover of HBOS by Lloyds TSB in the United Kingdom would normally have breached competition rules. Equally, regulation will probably tighten, at least in the short term and offer some protection to the consumer. From a marketing perspective, there may be a temptation, as FIs attempt to repay loans and restore their balance sheets to pre-crunch levels, to cut marketing expenditure. This would not be a prudent move as marketing is needed more than ever to develop strategies for what may be a new and infinitely more cautious marketplace. At the same time, there are a number of competitors that have not been involved in loss-making activities and who are in a position to increase their market share, for example Grupo Santander and Tesco. The large FIs need to ensure that they have strategies in place to compete against these companies.

One of the most critical areas that should be addressed is the rebuilding of trust not only among consumers but also with stakeholders. As discussed in Chapter 6, findings of the FSA reveal that most financial firms will mislead their customers if they can make more profit by doing so. Regulatory bodies, in particular the United Kingdom's FSA, have not been able to demonstrate convincingly that they can control FIs. Good marketing practice, however, should focus on the role of trust in maintaining relationships with stakeholders. Post-credit crunch, FIs need to ask themselves how trust can be re-established and, arguably, be strengthened. So far, there is little evidence to suggest that FIs are going to radically reappraise their short-term approach to strategic development. Figure 12.4 provides an illustration of how FIs can widen the basis for re-establishing trust to their stakeholders.

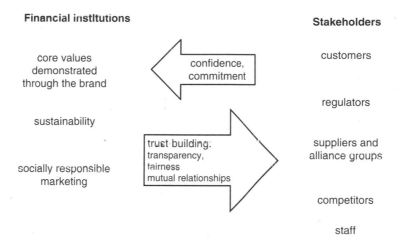

Figure 12.4   A stakeholder model of trustbuilding for FIs

This outline model suggests a way in which FIs might respond to the environment post-credit crunch, building on the data in the TOWS analysis (Table 12.1). For many of the larger FIs, their immediate duty is often to shareholders but, as the credit crunch has shown, this restrictive view is not sustainable. If they widen their audience to include a range of stakeholders, a more sustainable outlook may prevail. However, there are deeply embedded cultures that may take years to unlock.

By focusing on building trust within their stakeholder environment, FIs may begin to rebuild or even strengthen the confidence which their risk-prone behaviour lost. By adopting a long-term perspective, espousing their brand values and embracing wholeheartedly and explicitly socially responsible behaviour, they may begin to re-establish themselves and even develop business practices that are in line with many other companies.

Summary

- The link between objectives and strategy is demonstrated.
- Marketing strategies for financial services have been considered and evaluated in this chapter, especially considering strategies for growth highlighting the difficulties for FIs.
- A discussion of offensive and defensive strategies has shown how FIs need to balance the acquisition and retention of customers.
- Developing niche strategies and following the idea of being a niche company is considered in financial services, pointing out the problems of this strategy in a mature marketplace.

- FI adoption of corporate social responsibility is considered, with gaps identified between the rhetoric on the websites and evidence from green charities.
- Opportunities for companies largely unaffected by the credit crunch are evaluated, and whether they are able to maximize their advantage.

References

Accenture (2008) *Experiencing the Brand; Branding the Experience*, downloaded 15 August 2008.

Ambler, T. (2003) *Marketing and the Bottom Line*, 2nd edn, Harlow, FT Prentice Hall.

Ambler. T. and Wilson, A. (1995), 'Problems of Stakeholder Theory', *Business Ethics: A European Review*, Vol. 4, No. 1, pp. 30–5.

Andriof, J. and Waddock, S. (2002), 'Unfolding Stakeholder Engagement', in J. Andriof, S. Waddock, B. Hustedand S. Rahman (eds), *Unfolding Stakeholder Thinking*, Sheffield, Greenleaf.

Andriof, J., Waddock, S., Husted, B. and Rahman, S. (2002) *Unfolding Stakeholder Thinking*, Sheffield, Greenleaf.

Ansoff, H. (1965), *Corporate Strategy*, Boston MA, Harvard Press.

Bhattacharya, C. and Sen, S. (2004) 'Doing Better at Doing Good: When, Why, and How Consumers Respond to Corporate Social Initiatives', *California Management Review*, Vol. 47, No. 1, pp. 9–24.

Buttle, F. (1996) 'Relationship Marketing', in F. Buttle (ed.), *Relationship Marketing: Theory and Practice*, London, Paul Chapman.

Carroll, A. B. (1991) 'The Pyramid of Corporate Social Responsibility: Toward the Moral Management of Organizational Stakeholders', *Business Horizons*, Vol. 34, pp. 39–49.

Christopher, M., Payne, A. and Ballantyne, D. (2002) *Relationship Marketing: Creating Stakeholder Value*, Oxford, Butterworth Heinemann.

Datamonitor (2009) 'Weathering the Storm', London, Datamonitor.

De Chernatony, L. and McDonald, M. (1998) *Creating Powerful Brands in Consumer, Services and Industrial Markets*, Oxford, Butterworth Heinemann.

Doyle, P. (2002) *Marketing Management and Strategy*, Harlow, FT Prentice Hall.

Drucker, P. (1963) *The Practice of Management*, London, Heinemann.

Farquhar, J. D. (2005) 'Retaining Customers in UK Financial Services: The Retailers' Tale', *Service Industries Journal*, Vol. 25, No. 8, pp. 1029–44.

Financial Services Authority (2002) 'An Ethical Framework for Financial Services', discussion paper, October. London.

Fornell, C. (1992) 'A National Customer Satisfaction Barometer: The Swedish Experience', *Journal of Marketing*, Vol. 56, January, pp. 6–21.

Freeman, R (1984) *Strategic Management: A Stakeholder Approach*, Boston, MA, Pitman.

Fournier, S. (1998), 'Consumers and Their Brands: Developing Relationship Theory in Consumer Research', *Journal of Consumer Research*, Vol. 24 (March), pp. 343–73.

Gregory, A. (2007), 'Involving Stakeholders in Developing Corporate Brands: The Communication Dimension', *Journal of Marketing Management*, Vol. 23, No. 1–2, pp. 59–73.

Gronroos, C. (2006) 'Adapting a Service Logic for Marketing', *Marketing Theory*, Vol. 6, No. 3, pp. 317–33.

Hollensen, S. (2003) *Marketing Management: A Relationship Approach*, Chelmsford, FT Prentice Hall.

Johnson, M. and Selnes, F. (2004) 'Customer Portfolio Management: Towards a Dynamic Theory of Exchange Relationships', *Journal of Marketing*, Vol. 68, April, pp. 1–17.

Jones, R. (2005) 'Finding Sources of Brand Value: Developing a Stakeholder Model of Brand Equity', *Brand Management*, Vol. 13, No. 1, pp. 10–32.

Kumar, V. and Reinartz, W. (2006) *Customer Relationship Management*, Hoboken, NJ, J. Wiley & Son.

McDonald, L. and Rundle-Thiele, S. (2007) 'Corporate Social Responsibility and Bank Customer Satisfaction', *International Journal of Bank Marketing*, Vol. 26, No. 3, pp. 170–82.

Maio, E. (2003) 'Managing Brand in the New Stakeholder Environment', *Journal of Business Ethics*, Vol. 44, pp. 235–46.

Merrilees, B., Getz, D. and O'Brien, D. (2005) 'Marketing Stakeholder Analysis: Branding the Brisbane Goodwill Games', *European Journal of Marketing*, Vol. 39, No. 9/10, pp. 1060–77.

Miles, D. (2004) 'The UK Mortgage Market: Taking a Longer-Term View', HM Treasury, March.

Mintel (2008) *Branch to Broadband: Channel Evolution in Financial Services*, April, London.

Mitchell, R., Agle, B and Wood, D. (1997), 'Towards a Theory of Stakeholder Identification: Defining the Principle of Who and What Really Counts', *Academy of Management Review*, Vol. 22, No. 4, pp. 853–86.

Morgan, F., Deeter-Schmelz, D. and Moberg, C. (2007) 'Branding implications of partner firm-focal firm relationships in business-to-business service networks", *Journal of Business and Industrial Marketing*, 22, 6, 372–382.

Payne, A. (2000) 'Customer Retention', in Cranfield School of Management, *Marketing Management: A Relationship Marketing Perspective*, Basingstoke, Macmillan Business.

Payne, A., Ballantyne, D. and Christopher, M. (2005), "A stakeholder approach to relationship marketing strategy", *European Journal of Marketing*, 39, 7/8, 855–871.

Payne, A. and Frow, P. (2005) 'A Strategic Framework for Customer Relationship Management', *Journal of Marketing*, Vol. 69, October, pp. 167–76.

Porter, M. (1980), *Competitive Strategy: Techniques for Analysing Industries and Competitors*, New York, Free Press.

Porter, M. (1985) *Competitive Advantage: Creating and Sustaining Superior Performance*, New York, Free Press.

Roberts, J. and Merrilees, B. (2007) 'Multiple Roles of Brands in Business-to-business Services', *Journal of Business and Industrial Marketing*, Vol. 22, No. 6, pp. 410–17.

Rust, R., Zeithaml, V. and Lemon, K. (2004) 'Customer-Centered Brand Management', *Harvard Business Review*, September, pp. 110–18.

Vargo, S. and Lusch, R. (2004) 'Evolving to a New Dominant Logic for Marketing', *Journal of Marketing*, Vol. 68, January, pp. 1–17.

Yau, O., Chow, R., Sin, L., Tse, A., Luk, C. and Lee, J. (2007) 'Developing a Scale for Stakeholder Orientation', *European Journal of Marketing*, Vol. 41, No. 11/12, pp. 1306–27.

www.cfs.co.uk

www.financialadvice.co.uk

www.fsa.gov.uk/pubs/discussion/dp18.pdf

Further reading

www.cim.co.uk

www.eiris.org

www.alfabank.com/research

www.allianz.com

www.foe.co.uk

www.plainenglish.co.uk/press_releases/did_jargon_cause_the_credit_crunch

Exercises

1. Go the website of the Building Society Association (www.bsa.org.uk) and choose two of the smaller building societies listed there. Look up their websites, identifying any features, offerings or messages that convey something of distinction to the reader. On what basis could any of these societies build a claim of pursuing a niche strategy?
2. Looking at two media channels (e.g., networking sites, newspapers). Note who is advertising. Are these advertisements those of FIs who could be considered market leaders? What other indications of market leader strategies are these FIs giving?
3. Looking at the list of guidelines for social responsibility and the ethical proposals for the financial services industry, draw up a set of brief suggestions for an Internet-only insurance provider.

CASE STUDY

Tesco – the rise and rise of a food retailer

Tesco, the United Kingdom's largest retailer (with ambitions to be the leading provider of many other products and services to UK households), has put in motion plans to stamp its not inconsiderable dominance on the domestic financial services sector. Having learned about the industry through a joint venture with the Royal Bank of Scotland (RBS), Tesco became the sole owner of Tesco Personal Finance (TPF) after buying out its partner for £950 million in 2008. The timing of this buy-out was impressive, as RBS has since revealed its exposure to the credit crunch. TPF currently offers its customers insurance, credit card, personal loan and savings products; RBS will continue to provide the products sold. The business has over 5 million customers across the United Kingdom, Ireland, Hungary and Poland. Tesco's CEO, Sir Terry Leahy, is convinced that services can potentially provide a larger and faster-growing market than food. Tesco is a cash-rich company: it has 'branches' everywhere, a robust Internet infrastructure and it can afford to be highly selective about the customers to whom it offers financial services. There are over 14 million savers who save with the non-traditional sector of financial services (e.g., Sainsbury's, Virgin), 42 per cent of whom fall into the A and B categories of the classic socio-demographic profiles – that is, they are relatively well-off professionals or retired.

In the case of TPF, Leahy predicts that financial services could boost the group's profits by £1 billion a year at some point in the future, with pre-tax profit for 2008 estimated at £240 million. Staff from RBS have joined TPF to head up the venture, with a further 200 RBS staff transferring to Tesco once the acquisition is completed. Following the takeover, TPF plans to increase its in-store presence and develop a wider range of savings products. The news that Britain's biggest retailer could eventually compete with high-street banks has a ring of inevitability about it and will be seen as a challenge by the United Kingdom's retail banking sector, already reeling from the credit crunch and the threat of having to pay back billions of pounds in unfair bank charges.

Data from 2008 states that Tesco serves 20 million customers a week, with a reported a 10 per cent rise in first-half profits to £1.45 billion, a rise on shares from 17.7p to 387.6p due to the better-than-expected results. Sales from the group's international stores in countries such as Ireland, France, Turkey, Czech Republic, Thailand and China were up 27 per cent, and trading profit rose 28 per cent to £346 million. The venture into the difficult US market is anticipated to show a £60 million loss from the Fresh & Easy chain. In the UK business, which operates 1,673 stores, like-for-like sales (excluding petrol) were up 3.7 per cent; non-food sales rose 4 per cent, compared with 8 per cent in the second half of the previous year; toys, entertainment and electrical goods performed well; but fashion sales were down. Tesco's Reward card scheme already provides the company with unrivalled customer information which will put it in a good position to compile predictor models of customer propensity to make financial services purchases. By opening a current or cheque account, it will gain an even better picture of consumer spending at the level of the individual, which will put it well ahead of other potential rivals such as Virgin Money, Sainsbury's and Marks & Spencer.

Tesco has chosen this challenging time in financial services to commit even more of its precious funds, won in the vastly more competitive and much lower-margin business of supermarket retailing, to a seemingly ailing banking sector. The retailer claims that consumers were seeking a safe haven for their cash and the banking crisis presented it with an opportunity. Other organizations have chosen this time to make some acquisitions, Grupo Santander swooping in to pick up Alliance & Leicester for less than a third of the bid price it offered and had rejected a couple of years ago. Tesco senses that not only are the banks desperate for capital to shore up otherwise distressed balance sheets, but that it too would like to expand into an industry which still generates two to three times the margins available in its existing market. There is an opportunity to forge even greater alliances with customers by developing proactive strategies, which banks only started to wake up to once the chips were down; conditions for some FIs are very promising. Tesco is in a very strong position to create a presence in this marketplace, having been able to grow exponentially by building a brand that reflects service, price, transparency and efficiency under a brand loyalty that banks could only dream about. An example of their understanding is the launch and promotion of their comparison site – Tescocompare.com, with the suffix of –com underlining the international dimension of their offering. Tesco's Finance and Strategy Director, Andrew Higginson, will assume a new Tesco Board position as Chief Executive of Retailing Services. Higginson will lead a strengthened services team, including a new CEO and Finance director for TPF and a new CEO for Tesco Telecoms. He will retain his responsibilities for Tesco Group strategy but will relinquish his role as Finance Director of Tesco once a suitable successor has been put in place. Benny Higgins, a leading figure in the banking industry, has been recruited to run the new wholly owned TPF business. Higgins brings huge experience, having run the retail banking divisions of both RBS and HBOS.

Banking is far more complicated than the retailing of grocery products and is bound with more regulation and demands for compliance than the retailer has ever had to negotiate before, in spite its successes in the face of allegations of anti-competitive practices. Tesco will need to commit a considerable amount funding in order to get a full banking licence to meet the capital adequacy requirements of both national and European regulators. It is thought, however, that with the retailer's track record and the levels of consumer confidence behind it, it will be able to raise the required funding from investors. As the rest of the banking sector share prices still languish in the doldrums, it is likely that it won't be just Tesco and Santander that enter this shark-infested fray to not only win the hearts and minds of banking customers, but their wallets as well.

During a particularly anxious period, Tesco said it had seen the number of applications for savings accounts double as people searched for a safe home for their money. The intention is for the retailer to cash in on its reputation, based on its understanding that customers are looking for somebody they can trust; it is a good opportunity for a challenger brand, like Tesco. The first current accounts took 12 months to become available because the supermarket had to build systems to operate the business. Mortgages will follow 'in due course'; again these offer a source of profit. Terry Leahy said the wider banking crisis was undermining consumer confidence and urged the banks to start lending again to avoid job losses. As a retailer with unrivalled knowledge of its marketplace, he observed that consumers change faster than companies and he accused banks of not being set up for the changing marketplace.

Questions

1. Describe the strategies Tesco is pursuing with its move into banking? How will it attract customers from its competitor banks post credit crunch?
2. How is the Tesco brand going to be positioned to compete against existing FIs?
3. What might be some of the reservations of customers with regard to moving their finances to Tesco? What might persuade them to do so?
4. What are the advantages to Tesco of having a large proportion of relatively well-off customers saving with them?
5. How might Tesco defend its customers from responses from traditional FIs to lure any customers back?

Compiled by the authors from www.guardian.co.uk www.bankingtimes. co.uk, www.tesco.com. and www.financial-insights.com.

Index

Key: **bold** = extended discussion or term highlighted in the text; e = exhibit; f – figure; t – table.